The Enemy Among Us

David Fiedler

To Dr. Michael Loberg —
Hope you enjoy these
tales of WWII
POWs in Missouri.
David Fiedler
June 2004

The Enemy Among Us

POWs in Missouri During World War II

David Fiedler

Missouri Historical Society Press • Saint Louis
Distributed by University of Missouri Press

07 06 05 04   2 3 4 5

Library of Congress Cataloging-in-Publication Data

Fiedler, David, 1971-
    The enemy among us : POWs in Missouri during World War II /
    David Fiedler.
        p. cm.
    Includes bibliographical references and index.
    ISBN 1-883982-49-9 (alk. paper)
    1. World War, 1939-1945--Prisoners and prisons, American.   2. World
War, 1939-1945--Missouri.   3. Prisoners of war--Germany--History--20th
century.   4. Prisoners of war--Italy--History--20th century.   I. Title.
    D805.U5F44 2003
    940.54'7273'09778--dc22
        2003015221

Distributed by University of Missouri Press

Design by Robyn Morgan
Printed and bound by Friesens, Canada

Cover: Italian POW Augusto Bier, on left, with other POWs and GIs at
Camp Weingarten. Courtesy of Edmee Viscardi.

Back cover: Identification card for Giuseppe Zanti, an Italian POW held at
Camp Clark in Nevada, Missouri. Photograph by Pete Puleo, Sr.

Endpapers: POWs at Louisiana, Missouri, November 21, 1943. Courtesy of
Terry Culver.

To my family

and

to the soldiers of every army who came to Missouri,
and the residents who treated those boys as their own.

Contents

Foreword

FROM THE FAMED HILL AREA of south St. Louis to the annual St. Louis Strassenfest, Missouri is rich in Italian and German influences. People of Italian and German descent had firmly cemented their cultural imprint upon the area by the time American GIs set foot upon European soil to rid the world of Nazism and Fascism. During World War II, as David Fiedler informs us in *The Enemy Among Us: POWs in Missouri During World War II*, nearly half a million prisoners of war were sent to the United States, including the approximately fifteen thousand men who were ordered to stay in thirty camps located throughout Missouri.

How must it have been for these men, to suddenly find themselves across the ocean, far from the reign of Mussolini and Hitler and on Missouri farms? *The Enemy Among Us* records the statistics of the POW population in Missouri during World War II and the feelings of the men who were housed in the camps, but more important, it chronicles the remembrances of the Missourians who came face to face with the enemy. With few exceptions, the "foe" label was summarily dismissed as Italian prisoners prepared pasta dishes for their new Missouri neighbors and German prisoners performed plays and concerts for area residents. A remarkable bonding across cultural, political, ethnic, geographic, and national boundaries occurred among these imprisoned men and the communities they served over the very human pursuits of art, music, and cuisine. The Missourians were fiercely patriotic, many of them immigrants or descended from immigrants, and possessed a strong affection and loyalty for this land. Like all Americans, they were proud to sacrifice for the war effort by helping to ration resources and by sending their women to work in the factories while their men were sent across the Atlantic to fight. Yet these citizens could look beyond the Nazi or Fascist designation and see German and Italian people who shared many of their same hopes and fears, joys and sorrows.

The United States administration during World War II determined that practicing the ideals for which we were fighting—liberty and democracy—and applying that American credo to the enemy was the best way to combat Nazi and Fascist ideology. These prisoners of war, upon the end of hostilities, returned to their homelands, eager to share news of their experience in the land of the free. True to America's dual nature, however, during this time the proclaimed enemies of America enjoyed greater freedom and benefits than Japanese Americans who were interned in camps by their own nation. Also, African American soldiers, who risked life and limb half a world away fighting on behalf of their country, returned home to a segregated world of Jim Crow, limited opportunity, and acts of racial terrorism. We must acknowledge that we are heirs to this American legacy, still striving to match deed with creed.

Though there is a barrage of work that romanticizes this period in U.S. history, Fiedler's work is the first piece of scholarship to focus on the relationship between Missourians and German and Italian prisoners as they met not across the battlefield but across the table in, say, a Chesterfield family's kitchen. This cultural symbiosis is sorely needed in our own time. Careful reading of *The Enemy Among Us* offers a valuable perspective instead upon the allies among us. In this increasingly global community, allies must be found in a world where we are more and more dependent upon one another to simply guarantee sustainability.

In the pages of this remarkable addition to the Missouri Historical Society Press catalog, David Fiedler reminds us that the relationships that developed between the foreign POWs and the Missouri residents during this era of tumult and strife were born of a recognition of a shared humanity. Examination of our shared humanity allows us not only to discover and acknowledge difference but also to reveal and expand the common ground. And that common ground is the only basis for actions that will result in a better future for all who will follow, and thus our only assurance that we can meet our obligation to leave this world better than it was when we inherited it.

—ROBERT R. ARCHIBALD, PH.D.
PRESIDENT, MISSOURI HISTORICAL SOCIETY

Preface and Acknowledgments

In October 1993 I was at Fort Sam Houston, Texas, attending the Officer Basic Course for the Army's Medical Service Corps. We took a break one day at the Camp Bullis training area outside San Antonio, and I sat on a concrete cistern cover underneath a shade tree. I happened to look down, and there etched into the concrete in German were the words "Built by the German prisoners of war, 1945." I was floored. Prior to that moment I had absolutely no idea that enemy soldiers were held in the United States during World War II. I ran my finger over those letters in the concrete, put there almost fifty years prior, and the fascination I felt started me on a journey that has led to this point.

After learning about the Missouri chapter of the POW story during a visit to the excellent U.S. Army Engineer Museum at Fort Leonard Wood, I submitted a proposal to *Missouri Life* magazine for a story on the topic, and their acceptance is what really got this whole thing started. I had nearly a year to write the piece, and the research I did for that article, which appeared in the October/November 2002 issue, formed the foundation of this book. Some material from that article was used here, as were passages that may have appeared in similar form in articles for the *St. Louis Post-Dispatch* (May 2002); in the spring 2003 *Gateway Heritage*, a quarterly published by the Missouri Historical Society; in *Route 66* magazine (summer/fall 2003); and in publications by the Sappington-Concord Historical Society and the Jackson County Historical Society.

The information in this book came from a number of sources. First, articles in local newspapers from the towns where the camps were located provided much of the historical framework, while military documents, including camp inspection reports and official government correspondence, added much detail. Next, published works by Dr. Arnold Krammer (*Nazi Prisoners of War in America*) and Louis Keefer (*Italian Prisoners of War in America, 1942–1946*) offered a great deal of information on the POW program on a national level. When this was combined with Missouri-specific information on the POW camps contained in graduate-level theses written by Derek Mallett and Paul Gieringer, it provided a significant amount of material on which to draw. Finally, personal interviews with those involved in the camps offered the most insight. The people with whom I was so fortunate to visit include former POWs, servicemen, civilians who worked with the prisoners, and residents of the towns in which the camps were located.

As with any work of this nature, there are many people to thank. Derek Mallett and Terry Culver generously shared their own research with me, allowing access to work they had gathered through countless hours of their own effort. I am also indebted to the late Stanley Drury, who over the course of a lifetime amassed an amazing collection of information on Camp Weingarten, and to his wife, Teresa, and Dr. Max Okenfuss of Washington University for making it available to me. This book would not have been possible without the material they gathered. Dr. Arnold Krammer was unstinting in his help and encouragement, and I can only hope to be half as gracious as he is in my own dealings with others.

I am grateful to Tricia Mosser, former editor of *Missouri Life* magazine, who read an early version of the manuscript and offered many helpful suggestions that improved its clarity and organization. My brother, Brian Fiedler, helped with cataloging and organizing photographs. Tim Friemel headed up the "East Coast Research Bureau" and earned himself a researcher's badge at the Library of Congress through his trips there on my behalf. Others, including Pete Puleo, Sr., Kevin Wade, and Bill Berry, assisted greatly with their help in interviewing, interpreting, and connecting me with people who appear in this book whom I would have never otherwise had the chance to meet.

You won't find this listed in any tourism guide or state fact book, but in my opinion, Missouri has more nice people as a percentage of its population than any other place. I know because I met them. They are the people who helped me with this book in so many ways and are unfortunately too numerous to name individually. These are people who sent me newspaper clippings and photos. They are also the pros who work behind library counters and reference desks and answered my many questions with patience and good humor, and who often went out of their way to dig up additional material related to my quest. I also met these people in local museums and historical societies, and they devoted much time and energy to this project. They are also the folks who provided names of people for me to call and dug around in their attics and basements for old letters and memorabilia. So, to you who helped, I offer a sincere and hearty thank you. I hope I can repay in some small way the many kindnesses you have shown me.

Additionally, the staff of the Missouri Historical Society Press—Lauren Mitchell, Robyn Morgan, Kathleen Strand, and Josh Stevens—were marvelous to work with throughout this process, and what you hold in your hands is the final result of their hard work. In particular, Lauren deserves great credit for her efforts as lead editor and for her patience with my quirks.

Finally, to my wife, Shelly, thank you for your support and encouragement, as well as your patience with my sometimes obsessive preoccupation with this project.

Camp Locations

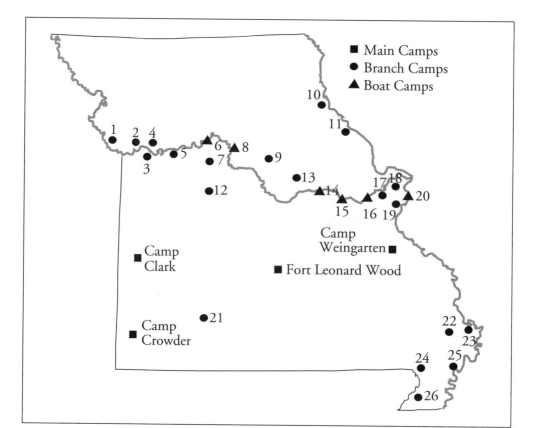

Main Camps

Camp Clark, Nevada
Camp Crowder, Neosho
Camp Weingarten
Fort Leonard Wood

Boat Camps

Chesterfield Riverboat **16**
Gasconade **14**
Glasgow **8**
Grand Pass/Malta Bend **6**
St. Louis **20**
Washington **15**

Branch Camps

Charleston **23**
Chesterfield **17**
Columbia **9**
Fulton **13**
Hannibal **10**
Independence **3**
Jefferson Barracks **19**
Kennett **26**
Lexington **5**
Liberty **2**
Louisiana **11**
Malden **24**

Marshall **7**
Marston/Portageville **25**
Orrick **4**
Riverside/Kansas City **1**
St. Louis/Baden **18**
Sedalia Army Air Field **12**
Sikeston **22**
Springfield **21**

Introduction

Between 1942 and 1945, more than 400,000 Axis prisoners of war were sent to the United States. Of this total, more than 15,000 ended up in Missouri and were held in thirty or so camps located around the state, where they remained until the end of the war.

Despite the number of prisoners, their widespread presence, and the great deal of contact they had with ordinary citizens, few people today realize they were here. Camps surrounded by barbed wire and guarded by watchtowers and patrolling dogs dotted the landscape. Captured labor—Germans and Italians—worked in the fields picking cotton, detasseling corn, and digging potatoes as replacements for the men who had been sent to war. In most cases, it is only those who were there who remember. Maybe they were local civilians employed in the camps or farmers who hired the POWs as field help. Maybe they were just little kids, small enough to remember only the sight of the fences set back from the road or the sounds of a language they didn't understand. Maybe they just remember holding on to a grown-up's hand as the men in uniforms marched by on their way to a work assignment.

This is the story of how 15,000 men came suddenly to Missouri, taken from fighting half a world away. They came as our enemy, but in many cases they left as friends or, at the least, with a more positive view of the United States. They worked here and lived here, and just as quickly they were gone again, in most cases leaving nothing more behind than memories with those who resided nearby or worked in the camps.

Captured German soldiers marching through Aachen, Germany, in October 1944. Courtesy of National Archives.

Chapter One

Coming to the United States: Life in the Camps

M arilyn Grant was only seven years old when the Italian soldiers came to Sikeston, Missouri. It was July 16, 1944. "I don't know if someone told me I was experiencing history, but I realized it was important," she said.

The soldiers—prisoners of war sent to the United States after capture—worked for her father, Elmer Grant, Sr., who managed the C. F. McMullin Estate near Sikeston. They lived first in a collection of tents, then in simple wooden barracks with both heat and running water. The men chopped cotton and detasseled corn grown there to create hybrid seed.

In particular, Grant recalled later being invited with her family into the POW barracks for an authentic Italian meal prepared by the prisoners. "They were grateful for the fatherly treatment they received from my dad while working there," recalled Grant. "It was a wonderful meal, actually given to us out of their food allowance." The POWs sang and played on improvised instruments in a sort of after-dinner serenade, creating memories for a little girl that have lasted a lifetime.[1]

The POW Experience

In Hollywood and in literature, prisoner of war camps with their fences and guard towers are uniformly miserable places. That wasn't the case for those in Missouri and elsewhere in the United States. Life as a POW in the camps scattered across the state was a surprisingly pleasant experience. The men ate well and were quartered under the exact same conditions as the Americans assigned to guard them, and the prisoners were often accorded a great deal of freedom. The internees frequently worked on local farms, often "guarded" only by a bored GI snoozing under a shade tree.

They organized camp theater troupes, sports leagues, and orchestras; read books, newspapers, and magazines at the camp library; and took classes that in many cases counted for academic credit back home.

Karl-Heinz Richter was a German POW sent to Camp Crowder in Neosho, Missouri, in September 1944 after being captured in France, flushed out of a barn by American GIs. He recalled the day he arrived at Crowder and first saw the POW barracks, whose appearance impressed the Germans. "We were pleasantly surprised to see such a clean and comfortable place," he said simply. "It had been a while since we had had such comforts."[2]

Although Missourians ultimately experienced few problems with POWs in the state, those living near these camps were often initially uneasy to learn that the government had decided to put large numbers of "aliens" in their area. One anonymous writer sent a letter to the War Department in July 1942 expressing his concerns about the plan to establish a large camp near Weingarten, Missouri:

TO THE WAR DEPARTMENT:

Of all the ridiculous things done by the U.S.A. before and after December 8, 1941, this takes the prize:

"WEINGARTEN, MO., SELECTED FOR ALIEN INTERNMENT CAMP.

Weingarten, town of 99 inhabitants in Ste. Genevieve County, Mo., 75 miles south of St. Louis, has been selected by the War Department as the site of an internment camp for aliens."

So reads today's *Post Dispatch.*

Doesn't anyone in Washington know that Ste. Genevieve County, Missouri, is as german as Germany, and that putting an alien enemy camp there is about as safe as putting it in Berlin? The people down there, many of whom have been here for several generations, speak English with a german accent that can be cut by a knife or don't speak English at all—German is still their mother-tongue, and Germany is still their Fatherland. By putting an alien enemy camp down there you are simply inviting escapes, which will be winked at by the natives, and the aliens can find refuge with their hun friends in

St. Louis, Cincinnati and Milwaukee. The dutch town is full of germans who are indignant at Japan, but hold nothing against Germany.

Better put your camp near Lidice, Ill., or some other place not adjacent to such german centers at St. Louis, Cincinnati and Milwaukee. Or, if you MUST put it at Weingarten (even the name of the town is german) for political purposes, then for heaven's sake put only Japs in it, or even Italians might be safe there, but keep the huns out or you'll have to keep an army down there to keep the huns from escaping with the aid of their S. E. Missouri friendly enemies.

AMERICA FIRST AND ALWAYS.[3]

The letter—a bit exaggerated in places, of course—was likely written more for effect than out of actual sentiment, but some of the people in the towns designated to have POW camps were understandably concerned about their safety. They were also worried about the influx of Army personnel who accompanied such an operation and about the way their town might be changed.

But by and large this turned out to be a pleasant time for those involved, whether interned soldier, guard, local resident, or civilian employee at the camp. As often happens, life fell into a rhythm of days and nights, work and rest—even if it was done behind a fence. Friendships sometimes developed between POWs and guards or locals. Although none involved sought the circumstances that brought them together, when the experience was over no one could forget how life changed when POWs came to Missouri.

Setting the Stage

The question of how the American government ended up with so many prisoners in the United States—more than 400,000 over the course of the war—is an interesting one. Prior to the onset of World War II, President Franklin D. Roosevelt had appointed Major General Allen Gullion to the role of provost marshal general, responsible for military police and POW operations in the coming fight. However, even with Gullion in office, the United States was nowhere near ready for the number of POWs it would eventually receive once the internees were shipped from North Africa and Europe.[4] America's most recent experience with POWs had been in World War I, and only about 5,000 German sailors captured from ships in U.S.

waters lived in a handful of stateside camps. Few senior military or political leaders had any experience in the matter of prisoners of war, a significant disadvantage to the POW operation in the war's early months.

However, after the Pearl Harbor attack in December 1941, it was suddenly plain that America was hip deep in the war, and the POW matter became just another reality to deal with. POWs were not a priority though, as the U.S. government's main concern during those first months of 1942 was understandably centered on fighting a global, two-front war and not on setting up a back-home bureaucracy to deal with prisoners of war.

The United States' main ally, Great Britain, had been in the war much longer and consequently had already taken large numbers of prisoners. With more than 250,000 German and Italian soldiers held in England, finding a place to put additional prisoners was becoming a near crisis. Because of this, in August 1942 the British proposed that the United States accept an emergency batch of 50,000 enemy prisoners from Britain to relieve some of the pressure on the crowded island and that the Americans should also take an additional 100,000 on three months' notice. The United States agreed and shifted the preparations process into high gear.

Security was the most important consideration in planning for the POWs, and the government spent a disproportionate amount of time worrying about how difficult it would be to keep the first batch of troops, men from Field Marshal Erwin Rommel's tough Afrika Korps, behind the fences. "No one made any provisions for anything other than security, because we assumed the vaunted Afrika Korps was going to be the toughest kind of thing," said Maxwell McKnight of the provost marshal general's office. McKnight said the government feared sabotage more than anything, recalling incidents some twenty-five years prior when German agents blew up the Black Tom munitions plant in New Jersey. "We were very conscious of these things from a security standpoint, so our whole concentration was that you build the damnedest and the cheapest that you can for security purposes."[5]

Early on in 1942, the War Department decided that for several reasons it made sense to transfer prisoners held by the American military back to the continental United States rather than try to hold them in Europe. McKnight explained the rationale: "If we kept prisoners in such large numbers, under the Geneva Convention, we would have had to supply them with all kinds of food and medical needs of one kind or another. This would have cut down our transportation facilities to support our own troop efforts." Moving them stateside eliminated the problems of feeding and housing the prisoners in a war zone and reduced the likelihood of escape and renewed participation in the war.[6]

Prisoner Processing

A prisoner's path from battlefield to stateside POW camp was often a sputtering start-and-stop process. It began with capture, when a soldier was shuttled to a processing station. There, GIs collected basic biographic information for tracking and intelligence purposes and performed only minimal processing. Prisoners received a serial number and were fingerprinted and photographed. The information collected was used to create an ID tag and unique personnel record. In most cases, prisoners also received a cursory interrogation to find out if information useful to the Allied war effort might be uncovered. Both the processing and the interrogation were hit-and-miss propositions because of the chaos of the battlefield and the shortage of personnel clerks who could speak German or Italian. The information gathered at this stage was frequently incorrect, especially when a POW processing station was swamped with large numbers of prisoners captured at once. In those instances, GIs sometimes had the prisoners complete their own personnel forms, creating confusion and error, particularly when prisoners jotted down their own information and added the picture of another man and the fingerprints of a third.[7]

Axis prisoners of war are herded out of the city almost wholly unguarded as Allied armies enter Tunis in May 1943. Library of Congress.

After that basic information was taken from prisoners, they moved by truck or train to collection points near the major ports of embarkation. Here they waited for transportation, reading material donated by the Red Cross or other agencies, writing letters home, or simply passing time as best they could in the usually crowded grounds of the holding areas. The length of their wait depended mostly on the availability of an empty vessel to carry them across the sea.

Harold Drake of Platte City, Missouri, was normally a medic on troop ships, and he made fourteen trips across the Atlantic during the course of the war. However, because of a personnel shortage, on one occasion he was pressed into overnight guard duty at one of these holding camps while his ship waited offshore to pick up the men. "There were two thousand Italians in this camp in Sicily, and all I had was a pistol. I didn't even know how to get the thing out of the holster," said Drake. "The whole night I was scared that the POWs were going to club me, but all they cared about was getting to Brooklyn."[8]

The trip across the Atlantic generally took six weeks and ended at one of three American ports—Boston, Massachusetts; Camp Shanks, New York; or Norfolk, Virginia. Other than the occasional contact with an enemy submarine or fighter plane hunting convoys, the trips were uneventful. No ship carrying POWs was ever sunk, and usually the prisoners' biggest problems were seasickness, overcrowding, and boredom.[9] "The prisoners didn't have much to do on the ship, so they had to entertain themselves. They did a lot of singing," recalled Drake. "Man, they would get out there on the deck and it was really beautiful."[10]

Upon arrival at the ports, POWs filed down a gangplank to the pier, carrying all their personal possessions, and immediately found themselves in the reception area inside an enormous tin-covered warehouse built right on the docks. The scene made quite an impression on Italian POW Aldo Ferraresi, who, though he was unaware of it at the time, was on his way to the POW camp at Weingarten. "Everything smells clean inside, the wooden floor is spotless, the workers and the soldiers are well dressed and immaculate. I see right away the Americans are very, very clean and that their personal hygiene is much higher than ours (we are stinking dirty)," wrote Ferraresi in his diary. "We are divided from the Germans, thank God, and we go through another frisking, while our baggage is inspected. We strip and put all our stuff in a canvas bag, attach a nametag to it, and with only a towel march naked to a disinfestation station."[11]

The newly arrived POWs also got a fresh haircut, and here Drake got pressed into duty once again, this time as a barber. Standing with clippers, he gave each soldier a quick trim. "We'd peel all their hair off," Drake chuckled, "and by the time it was done I had a pile of hair up to my hip."[12]

Next came the quartermaster's office, which was responsible for collecting, storing, and eventually returning the POWs' personal items, and on to another stop where the prisoners showered and their clothing was deloused. "We pass in front of wooden boxes where an American soldier is standing with a sprayer. Front…back…bend over…front again. The liquid burns our skin, but only briefly, then it is finished. We proceed, show our nametag to some colored soldiers (white teeth in chocolate faces) and they return our clothes, which have also been disinfected," wrote Ferraresi. "We get dressed again in the same large room we started from and we are out again in the open air. The whole operation is really magnificently organized with plenty of materials and personnel!"[13]

The POWs had one more stop—a brief appointment with personnel clerks to verify and amplify their personal information on file. To Ferraresi, the actions of the clerks were a bit abrupt. "But the surprises are not ended. We enter a big tent, an American grabs first our left then our right hand and takes our fingerprints," he wrote. "This may seem offensive, but we learn that it is a common practice in America. Farther ahead, more soldiers and some typists take our names, ages, addresses, dog tag numbers and so forth. At last, we're led to our trains."[14]

The reception process complete, the men climbed onto trains to begin the final leg of their journey to the camps, usually still wearing the uniforms they had on at the time of capture. The view out the windows of these troop trains as they rolled across the country offered the Italians their first glimpse of America.

In addition to the great American landscape, Italian POWs riding through the Midwest in August 1943 also might have gotten a look at Gene Waibel. Waibel was an eighteen-year-old American serviceman who had just been inducted into the Army at Camp Grant in Rockford, Illinois. He was piled on a train with the other fresh-faced recruits and headed for the next phase of Army life, basic training at Jefferson Barracks in St. Louis, when they passed through Union Station in downtown St. Louis. Their train was waiting on one of the sidings when the recruits looked over and saw a coachload of Italian POWs sitting on the tracks right next to them. "I thought it was sort of funny, and sort of ironic," said Waibel, who noted no real exchanges between GIs and the POWs, except maybe a couple of them giving one another "the finger." "Here they were, coming from the war and we were just starting off, heading right into it."[15]

Ferraresi could have been one of the POWs at Union Station that day. He rode on a troop train from Newport News, Virginia, all the way to the camp at Weingarten, which would become his home:

We are loaded on railroad cars, beautiful with velvet seats and iced water any time we want it! The railroad cars are not divided into compartments as in Italy, but they form a great room. We are assigned three officers every four seats. We could pretend to be tourists, except that we have only a uniform with short frayed pants, the windows are barred up to a certain point and the escort is always close, with rifles at the ready and loaded.

I have not touched food since last night and I am really hungry. I look at myself in a mirror and see that I lost many pounds, and my face shows it. I tell myself that maybe some day we will be in shape again. Just then some American soldiers come, like waiters, carrying two slices of bread for each of us, cheese and sliced salami. I eat very slowly, because I do not want to get sick.

From the train we see immense depots of every supply imaginable, rolling stock, wire, metal and wooden poles, plus factories and charming little houses hidden among the greenery and cars, cars, cars everywhere. The people look at us without the hostility of the Frenchmen; on the contrary, they wave to the escort and to us. I think I have to change my ideas about the Americans. At 6 pm the American soldier-waiters returned with paper plates, wooden forks and small glasses. For dinner we have cheese, one egg, prosciutto, salad, iced tea and grapefruit. We think we are in heaven!

In the meantime, the train passes endless forests, valleys green, and rivers of clear water. Everything is green, small nice homes, and always, in front of each house, a beautiful car. On a country road we see a farmer towing a wagon of vegetables behind his beautiful car. We reach St. Louis, and tomorrow will go to the POW camp at Weingarten.[16]

On the way to Camp Gruber, Oklahoma, German POW Helmut Hörner's POW troop train stopped for a while in St. Louis on April 27, 1945, and he made note of the experience and of people he saw there, including a number of kids near the tracks:

When they notice that we are watching them, the little ones stick their fingers in their mouths while the bigger ones hop the tracks and come to our wagons, where they stand in shock. Although they do not stop gazing at us, they do seem a little more trustful. Certainly they think we are the damn Nazis who come from legendary old Europe about whom their teachers have told so many horrible things.

Since the train does not appear to be ready to leave, a large group of people gathers around the window.... When one of the railroad workers starts up a conversation with us, even the girls come closer. Not one of our usually adventuresome group moves from his place even though the girls generously make their way to us with blouses filled with risk and desire. It's not that we are not taken with the charm of their hills and valleys, but it is our neglected clothes, long, unkempt hair, three-day beards, and the whole shitty situation that keep us in our places. But even the workers are not in their evening dress and when we are addressed in German by one of them through the crack in the window, everything seems to happen naturally.

"How are you, my countrymen?" an old and quite worn worker asks us in a Schwabish dialect and looks compassionately through the dusty window.... "Here boys, a few cigarettes." The old man appears once again before the window and shoves three packs of Lucky Strikes through the crack, something that is happening at the same time all along the train.

"That's the goddam Germans!" bellows a fat, recently arrived Yankee, shaking his head and nervously chewing his cigar as he sends the men back to work.

A short time later the train moves out again. Accompanied by the friendly good-byes of the girls and children, we fall into the dreams of an endless night.[17]

Locations and Setup of the Camps

As the first batches of prisoners began to arrive in the United States in the fall of 1942, the government scrambled to find places to put them. To handle the initial crowd of fifty thousand sent from the United Kingdom, it first reclaimed any facilities that were ready to use with minimal investment of time and effort. These included unoccupied space on existing military bases (where approximately 60 percent of camps would be located) along with places such as abandoned Civilian Conservation Corps (CCC) camps last used during the Great Depression to house thousands of unemployed young men working on government projects around the country.

Despite these efforts, the space available to hold POWs was still not sufficient, and so at the end of 1942 the government took steps to secure land for additional camps. Several factors were considered when selecting locations, the first of which was security. To limit the possibility of escape and resulting sabotage to U.S. interests, initial regulations directed that the POW camps should be isolated from major population centers and not near coasts, shipyards, munitions plants, or any vital industries. As a result of this policy, more than 80 percent of the 155 total base camps in the United States at the end of the war were located in the South or Midwest. With the need for POW workers and the low number of escapes, the government soon eased the restrictions on camp locations, and eventually POWs lived and worked in nearly every state in the country.

The Army established four major camps in Missouri: at Camp Crowder in Neosho and at Camp Clark in Nevada, both in the southwest corner of the state; at Fort Leonard Wood in central Missouri; and at Weingarten, south of St. Louis between Ste. Genevieve and Farmington. Prisoners from different armies were not mixed in the same camp, according to government policy. The main camps, the ethnicity of the prisoner population, and the dates the camp held those prisoners were as follows:

Clark	Italians	December 1942–June 1944
Clark	Germans	August 1944–October 1945
Crowder	Germans	October 1943–May 1946
Fort Leonard Wood	Italians	December 1942–June 1943
Fort Leonard Wood	Germans	June 1943–April 1946
Weingarten	Italians	May 1943–October 1945

Although the camps in the United States were located in areas quite geographically diverse—from the Arizona desert to the Missouri Ozarks to the Kansas plains and even in the hills and mountains of Colorado and New Hampshire—the basic plan for the large camps was fairly standard. Each camp was set up in large rectangular compounds, each designed to hold a thousand prisoners. Eight-foot-high barbed-wire fences made even more formidable with a two-foot overhang surrounded the compounds. Guard towers along the perimeter of the camp overlooked the fences and were manned twenty-four hours a day by American GIs armed with machine guns. Guard dogs often patrolled the perimeter. Searchlights swept the compound and fence lines. Said POW Fritz Ensslin, "The camp looked like a cage for wild animals. It was illuminated by dozens of spotlights to an extent that it made you think it was daylight at midnight.... It was an unforgettable first impression."

The security measures not only kept the prisoners in but also helped local residents feel better about having a POW compound nearby. Francis and Rita Schwartz lived across the street from Camp Weingarten. Said Rita of a time they saw the camp's security in action:

> There was one time when we all realized how well protected we were. A group of us were sitting in the yard. We had been playing cards, and some of us had been playing croquet. We heard a plane, but we didn't see it. The evening had just come in and things had gotten dark. All of a sudden lights were on everywhere. You could read a newspaper in my backyard. The lights stayed on until they found the plane.[18]

These massive camps were divided into thousand-men compounds, which were then further broken down into POW "companies." In a sense, the compounds often operated as their own communities, maintaining a cluster of barracks, mess halls, latrines, and recreation facilities. Each compound held a POW canteen, where prisoners—using money earned by

This camp canteen drawing appeared in the Fort Leonard Wood POW newspaper. Courtesy of Franz Engelmann.

working or through the standard $3 monthly allowance paid to enlisted men—could buy such items as toiletries, cigarettes, ice cream, and sometimes limited amounts of 3.2 percent beer, generally the same items available to American GIs at the camp's main post exchange (PX). "Stores were established in each 1,000-man camp where we were able to purchase all our necessities and many luxu-

Canteen coupon, Fort Leonard Wood. Courtesy of Terry Culver.

ries like chocolate, mineral water, toilet articles like the finest soaps, aftershave lotions, hair grooming lotions, safety razors, peanuts, etc.," said Ensslin of Fort Leonard Wood. "At the end of each working day we also received a ration for two bottles of beer at ten cents each. The beer was brewed in St. Louis and was called Alpenbraeu."[19]

While items at the camp stores seemed like unusual and unnecessary luxuries, these canteens were in fact guaranteed to the prisoners by the Geneva Convention. Signed by the United States and forty-six other countries in July 1929, the Geneva Convention essentially established the rules for treatment of prisoners in wartime and through ninety-seven different articles governed just about every aspect of POW life, including housing, food, recreation, mail, and internee labor.

Ultimately, the camps constructed to house the prisoners in Missouri and elsewhere were considered quite comfortable and accommodating by those interned within. In many cases, the prisoners found life there to be more luxurious than the conditions they had as experienced anywhere else as soldiers, even in their own armies.[20]

Organizational Structure

The military organization and structure these soldiers had previously followed did not go away upon capture. Communication between the prisoners and the camp administration was generally channeled through POW spokesmen, who were responsible for seeing not only that directives from the camp administration were followed but also that the camp commander and his staff were made aware of any prisoner requests or complaints. Additionally, the spokesmen's influence was heightened by the Geneva Convention, which authorized them to represent the prisoners when the camps were inspected by the various agencies responsible for POW welfare, including the Swiss Legation, the International Red Cross, and the YMCA. Through these agencies, the men had access to direct lines of communication with the German foreign office and military high command. Their accounts of conditions in the United States had the potential to affect Axis treatment of American prisoners in Europe almost at once.[21]

Below the spokesmen in the internal camp hierarchy were the compound leaders, who were the elected heads of each one-thousand-man compound. These men had the POW company leaders in their respective compounds reporting to them, and so through this chain, fairly effective control could be maintained within the largely self-governing POW camps. This system worked well, and the U.S. government found that in most cases it could manage the prisoners best by leaving them alone to handle their own day-to-day affairs within the compound. "The first sentence of English picked up by the Italian sergeant in charge of sick call at the war prisoners' internment camp [at Weingarten] was: 'You are a goldbrick,'" wrote Rufus Jarman of the *St. Louis Post-Dispatch*, who visited several of the Missouri POW installations. "He now uses that time-honored term of the American

Army to scold his fellow prisoners, who he believes are pretending illness to skip a day's work."[22]

Barracks

The barracks buildings that housed the POWs were standard Army design—long, rectangular one- or two-story buildings. The main POW camps were virtually identical to regular troop housing areas, with the major difference, of course, being that these barracks were surrounded with guard towers and a double barbed-wire fence.

The POW quarters were so accommodating that they earned the moniker "The Fritz Ritz" among many GIs. The interior of the barracks held open-bay quarters, and the men typically had a bunk, a footlocker, a wall locker, a small shared table and chair, and an area on the wall for display of personal items. These were the usual family photos, religious objects, or pinup girls. Prisoners frequently displayed nationalistic or patriotic items, so small portraits of Adolf Hitler or stylized swastikas or other symbols of National Socialism sometimes appeared. This was permitted by the Geneva Convention, which allowed POWs to maintain their military courtesies and customs, a practice that included the Nazi salute coupled with the accompanying "Heil Hitler" ringing out over the Missouri hills. These sights became less frequent during the late stages of the war as the provost marshal general's office (PMGO), the War Department agency responsible for POW camp administration, became less permissive of overt displays of Nazism and the POW population became less convinced of the movement's merits. Finally, with the demise of the Third Reich, the War Department no longer allowed the trappings of Nazism to be displayed. On V-E Day, May 8, 1945, German soldiers were stripped of all rank, and by January 4, 1946, most camps had been cleared of all traces of the Nazi Party and its flags, ceremonies, and symbols.[23]

Clothing

Most prisoners arrived at the camps wearing the uniforms in which they had been captured. In addition to often being quite soiled and tattered, the uniforms were frequently unsuited for the camps' climates. For instance, Rommel's Afrika Korps summer uniforms, with their lightweight, short-sleeved shirts and shorts, were appropriate in Tunisia but not in Missouri in the winter.

As a result, the camp supply office issued the men several complete sets of work clothes immediately upon arrival. These work uniforms were often retread threads that, while certainly serviceable, could be considered

painfully old-fashioned. "Clothing is blue denim or old Army or CCC stock dyed blue; 1917 blouses and salvaged cavalry breeches are now POW issue," wrote Lieutenant George Paddock, describing the work uniforms issued to Weingarten prisoners.[24]

Much like the distinctive black and white stripes of the jailhouse suit, POW garments carried a four-inch "PW" stenciled in white on the backs and sleeves of PW shirts and on the pant legs of trousers. POW "comedians" quickly pointed out to their fellow soldiers that these letters probably stood for *pensionierte Wehrmacht*, which translates approximately into "retired soldier." After a time, officers were not required to wear these markings, the implication being that it impugned their military dignity.

An example of POW uniforms. Courtesy of U.S. Signal Corps.

At first, U.S. authorities wanted the prisoners' ID number prominently displayed on the outer layers of their clothing. This idea was abandoned for several reasons. The initial painting of the unique numbers on each set of clothes caused much extra work; prisoners' clothing was always getting mixed up in the laundry and sorting by number took a great deal of time; and the prisoners, intentionally or not, would often obliterate the POW number markings painted on their clothes. Eliminating the requirement that the POW number be maintained on all prisoner clothing and requiring that the internees themselves maintain the brightness and clarity of the "PW" markings on their garments went a long way toward making life easier for supply clerks involved in POW operations.[25]

In terms of a complete wardrobe, prisoners were issued

1 belt	1 wool coat	4 undershirts
2 pair cotton trousers	1 overcoat	4 pair socks
2 pair wool trousers	1 pair shoes	1 raincoat
1 pair gloves	4 pair drawers	1 wool shirt[26]

Although this camp-issued clothing, required to be worn during the workday, was certainly an ample wardrobe, soldier uniforms were still a common sight at the camps and were frequently donned in the prisoners' free time. POW tailors patched any holes in the original military uniforms and could also fashion entirely new ones when material was available.

Food

Internees in Missouri and elsewhere enjoyed the same range and quality of food as did American troops located stateside and were in fact eating better than GIs at the front, who dined on canned rations or from field messes. Many gained weight and strength as a result of the quantity and quality of food available to them in the prison camp mess halls.

A typical camp menu in July 1944 was as follows:

Breakfast: corn flakes, cake or bread, marmalade, coffee, milk, sugar

Lunch: potato salad, roast pork, carrots, ice water

Supper: meatloaf, scrambled or boiled eggs, bread, coffee, milk[27]

At first the prisoners had trouble getting used to the food they were served. It wasn't bad, just different. Italian POW Salvatore Davide had sailed from Casablanca to Boston in mid-1943 on the *Mariposa*, an American ocean liner converted into a troopship. He was first sent to Fort Leonard Wood, then transferred to Weingarten. His widow, Annette Davide, recalled the prisoners' reaction to typical items on an American menu, foods that were wholly foreign to them:

They got things like hotdogs and corn, and then the Americans brought in containers of jello for dessert. The containers were those great big metal cake pans, and they put them right in the middle of the table. These were all young, virile men, and when the jello was placed on the table, naturally it would quiver and shake. So they would nudge one another and touch it with their fingers, and laugh and bump the tables and say, "Well, isn't that just like a woman?"[28]

Eventually, instead of these standard American dishes, the Italians received ingredients better suited to preparing the dishes they had enjoyed back home. Officers of the PMGO believed that significant waste of food was occurring simply because of the difference in dietary preferences between the various prisoner groups and thought that if prisoners were to receive food more to their liking, they would eat more and throw away less. As a result, on July 1, 1944, Washington notified the camp authorities that they could modify the POW menus to better suit the prisoners' tastes.[29]

What this meant for Italian POWs was that they would begin receiving increasingly greater supplies of pasta, onions, paprika, tomato paste, and olive oil and less of the items that they didn't want. Germans, too, were able to obtain more potatoes and dark bread and were soon enjoying meals similar to what they might have had in mother's kitchen back home—pork and pigs' knuckles, wurst and fish soups.[30]

The Italians' gift for creating wonderful dishes was not lost on the Americans. When it came to meal preparation in the POW compounds, the Italian mess sergeants were completely in charge and had the freedom to choose their own help and create custom menus and dishes from scratch, limited only by the availability of ingredients. As the POW cooks improvised, transforming basic Army chow into delicious Italian cuisine, word began to spread among Americans at the camps. "The prisoners received the same issues of food as the American soldiers did," recalled Jarman, who visited the Weingarten camp as a writer for the *St. Louis Post-Dispatch*, "but where the Americans would throw a piece of beef into some water and boil it, the Italians would beat it, roll it, knead and marinate that same cut of beef and produce some delicious *pièce de résistance* instead of plain old boiled beef that the U.S. soldiers were trying to chew."[31]

POWs, including this pair of Italians at Camp Crowder, manned camp bakeries. Courtesy of Missouri State Archives.

U.S. personnel began to ditch their own mess halls in favor of eating in the POW compounds, and the camps' administrators were constantly running hungry GIs out of the POW mess. Even so, the Americans still managed to enjoy the POW-prepared delicacies. Edmee Viscardi worked as a clerk in the supply division of the Weingarten camp and recalled how one POW, Augusto Bier, used to bring them pastries from the camp bakery each morning. "He'd pick up a big basket full of doughnuts the first thing and bring it to us," she recalled. "They were absolutely wonderful. He was able to get it from the bakery because we were the Quartermaster area and supplied the bakery with everything they needed. We figured that if we were giving them all this stuff, we should at least get something back in return!"[32]

Another civilian employee of the camp, Francis Schwartz, sometimes drove a trash truck into the POW compound, and the prisoners would invite him in for coffee and rolls, said his wife, Rita. Not only did Schwartz get to dine with the Italians, but he also got the baked treats "to go," she recalled. "The prisoners would hide baked rolls they had cooked. It was the best stuff," she said. "The Italians would cover the food, wrap it up with heavy wax paper and put it out with the garbage" for Schwartz to take with him back to his family.[33]

Even the Germans' cuisine was prized by the Americans. The German prisoners at Camp Clark complained to a Swiss inspector in December 1944 that some of the American GIs working in the compounds were in the habit of coming through the POW mess and eating their food. The camp's executive officer promised the Swiss representative that he would investigate and that these GIs would be stopped.[34]

When it came to lunch while out on work assignments, prisoners in the field as contract labor on area farms were supposed to be supplied with food for lunch by the government. However, as a matter of both practical-

ity and hospitality, the POWs were frequently fed from the farmers' pantry, just as any other farmhand.

Otto Deutschmann lived in the Kirkwood/Des Peres area of St. Louis and in 1943 started going to a satellite POW camp in Chesterfield in his pickup to ferry prisoners that his uncle, George Deutschmann, had contracted to work in his greenhouses. Typically it was a group of about ten

Crowder POWs worked in the mess halls. Courtesy of Missouri State Archives.

POWs. Otto recalled one day around noon when everyone stopped working to take lunch under a shade tree. Otto's father, also named Otto Deutschmann, asked the prisoners what they had with them to eat. "They had a gallon vinegar jug full of black coffee, two boiled eggs, a little bit of pie and some bread," said Otto. "As soon as he saw that, my dad sent me straight down to the grocery to buy a big pile of lunchmeat and a gallon jug of beer." The Deutschmanns provided lunch for the prisoners every day after that, a common occurrence on farms around Missouri. The POWs did bring food from the camps, but in the opinion of most farmers, not nearly enough to feed people who had been working hard in the fields all day. "After that we killed two hogs and hung them in the cooler in the tavern," said Otto, referring to the Village Bar on Manchester Road in Des Peres, owned at the time by George "Wimpy" Schinzing. "From then on, my mother would feed them in the basement every day."[35]

All in all, the food enjoyed by the prisoners during their time in the United States was so good that some POWs wrote their families and told them not to send them food in gift packages. They said they were getting plenty to eat here and that the people back home should keep the food for themselves, where it was really needed.[36]

Recreation

During their leisure hours, prisoners enjoyed a wide range of ways to pass the time, and sports offered perhaps the most important diversion. POWs held boxing matches; played volleyball, basketball, and tennis; and put on soccer matches that the whole camp frequently followed with intense interest.

Uniforms and equipment were donated by the YMCA, the Red Cross, and the Catholic Aid Society or purchased through the profits made by the POW canteens and allowed the internee teams in many cases to look like "real" teams that might have played in a league back home. "Sports started right after breakfast, and our camp had a whole slate of outstanding teams in soccer, handball, volleyball, etc. Athletic activities were taken very, very seriously," said POW Alfred Klein. "The Camp Championships, especially in soccer and handball, were so exciting that even our guards participated as cheerleaders from their towers and attended the games on weekends with their families shouting from the sidelines."[37]

Arts

Along with sports, music and theater provided much pleasure to the POWs. Prisoners at each camp quickly organized chorus groups, orchestras, and theater troupes, and they put on shows for their fellow prisoners as well as for the American servicemen and civilian employees at the camps. In some cases even people from nearby communities were invited to attend.

Weingarten POW Giuseppe Zazza recalled the number of gifted artists who were part of the shows that were put on for the enjoyment of both prisoners and area residents:

Many of the men at the camp had been somebody important. There were movie stars, musicians, theatre people, songwriters, and so on, a lot of smart people. Everyone joined together and organized a theatre group. I played banjo in the orchestra.

We put on shows for thousands of people in the camp theatre, and had plenty of civilians from the nearby towns who paid to see us perform.

One of Weingarten's POW orchestras. Courtesy of Kent Library, Southeast Missouri State University.

One of the acts was a striptease, and it was impossible to know that the female impersonator was a man!

We had a tailor to make our costumes, but we also got clothes from outside, and somebody gave us a sewing machine.[38]

Education

In their free time, prisoners at Missouri camps had the opportunity to participate in a number of classes through a program initiated by the POWs themselves. The camp "universities" were among the most impressive aspects of POW life. Many camps offered more than two hundred classes in an array of subjects, including basic English, engineering, literature, and business. Because of the broad range of experience and expertise found in the internee population, much of the instruction was given by POW "professors," though in some instances classes were taught by Army personnel or instructors drawn from the civilian population. POWs could also earn college credit via correspondence courses through recognized universities such as the University of Chicago, the University of Minnesota, and the University of Wisconsin.

Internees would select one of their own as a study leader to be responsible for establishing the curriculum, and from this a number of courses would be taught, complete with lectures, study sessions, and final exams. Although there was some disruption in the program, such as when prisoners moved from one camp to another, the quality and competence of the education received was substantial. This was evidenced when the German Reich

Ministry of Education announced in May 1944 that full high-school and college credit would be granted for courses taken by German prisoners in the United States.

These educational credits in many cases allowed the prisoners to return to postwar Europe with significant advantages in career development or in the pursuit of additional schooling. In addition to attaining high-school equivalency diplomas, German POWs could take final exams for professional training schools and certification tests to become teachers.[39]

Because, on average, a lower level of literacy was found among Italian soldiers, the courses offered at the camps housing Italians were generally of a more basic nature. Enlisted Italian POWs interned at Camp Weingarten, for instance, had only an average of a fourth-grade education prior to entering the service; most officers had at best completed only high school.

This POW classroom drawing appeared in the Fort Leonard Wood POW newspaper. Courtesy of Franz Engelmann.

This meant that elementary English and Italian courses focusing on reading comprehension and grammar along with classes on basic mathematics were most utilized by the internees there.

Participation in the program was erratic, and only a minority of prisoners enrolled in the classes. The PMGO estimated that only 40 percent of the officers and 10 percent of the non-commissioned officers and enlisted men at Weingarten took part in any portion of the formal study program, and inspection reports from the other camps frequently addressed the prisoners' lack of interest in educational opportunities.

To complement the classes, a library in each POW compound offered prisoners a broad range of reading material. Newspapers, books, and magazines lined the shelves in each camp, although the quality and quantity of the material varied throughout the course of the war. Many of the items were donated, either by the YMCA or by communities surrounding the camps. In the case of the Italian prisoners in particular, the Roman Catholic Church provided many books to stock the POW library. German prisoners of war benefited from the generosity of Lutherans in the United States, who sent in more than 140,000 books after the church requested donations for the camp libraries. As of November 1943, the Lutheran Commission for Prisoners of War identified the following types of materials that were most needed:

1. Textbooks (high school and university levels), languages, literature, natural sciences, mathematics, geography, history (antedating 1930), art, commercial studies, philosophy and medicine. Books on politics are excluded, as are all books making reference in any way to Fascism, Nazism, and the like.

2. Classics: Goethe, Schiller, etc.

3. Music: Choral music with German text for male chorus or choir; Beethoven, Bach, Schubert, etc., for solo instruments; chamber music, orchestra or voice; also light German music, Strauss, Lehar, etc.

4. Phonograph records: Bach, Beethoven, etc., operas and any German music and songs.[40]

English-language material, although less in demand than items printed in the prisoners' native tongues, was still popular. Through newspapers and magazines as well as radio programs, they were able to keep fairly up to date with events back home and in the world at large.

Mail Service

POWs also maintained contact with their loved ones through the mail. Although postal service in Europe became largely unreliable during the later years of the war, prisoners were permitted to send and receive letters and packages to and from their families throughout their period of confinement. Internees could mail one or two letters and one postcard each week to friends and family abroad or to "blood relatives" in the United States. POW historian Judith Gansberg notes that blood relatives, as defined by the U.S. government, did not include mothers-in-law. "In several cases these neglected women wrote repeatedly to their congressmen about this rule," wrote Gansberg in *Stalag, U.S.A.: The Remarkable Story of German POWs in America.* "The prisoners objected, too, but with less fervor."[41]

Internees sometimes feigned family relationships with American citizens to get around this restriction. One Camp Clark POW routinely addressed his former supervisor William McDonald as "Dear Uncle Bill" when writing to him from other camps after transfer.

Mail was tremendously important to maintaining morale and a feeling of connectedness with events unfolding half a world away. Camp Weingarten internee Aldo Ferraresi wrote in his diary on September 4, 1943:

> Today is the best day since I have been captured. Lieutenant Vianello, from the camp's post office, calls and gives me a letter from home! I have been without any news for four months.... I ran to my room and read the letter quickly, then I read it again, slowly, slowly. I picture the two persons I most love in the world writing this letter from my father's study, with their eyes full of tears [and] I cry like a baby.[42]

Outgoing mail was collected from the internee orderly rooms and checked for contraband or any problematic material and then forwarded to the district postal censor at New York, where censors would process it within twenty-four hours. Even though the mail was processed quickly, letters and postcards sent to Italy often did not reach the intended destination, and the prisoners received little return mail. "Because of disruption of the Italian postal system or, perhaps, deliberate delay," wrote Lieutenant George Paddock, "none of the two-letters-and-post card sent by the internees reached Italy; there is no mail from home."[43]

Hermann Half, a POW at Camp Crowder, experienced the maddening frustration of the mail situation. He recalled:

> I got married when I was twenty, and in fact I was married for just fourteen days when I had to go back [into the service], and that was the last time I saw my wife. She wrote almost every day, and I never received any of the letters at Crowder. I was quite despondent, you know. You'd come back from work and everyone else would have letters and they'd tell you, that's all, that there wasn't any mail for you.

Although Half's wife was receiving his letters, the ones she wrote never went through. She tried everything to reach her husband, even going through the Red Cross and handing the letters to GIs returning to the States, pleading for their delivery, but each avenue was unsuccessful.[44]

Even when mail was received, another significant irritation was the delay of letters to POWs caused by military censorship. Interestingly, most of the hindrance was in mail sent to POWs from inside the United States, particularly from the East Coast. A camp inspection report noted:

> It has been found that letters to prisoners from relatives in this

country, particularly from relatives around New York City, require from 25 to 30 days to arrive at the camp. It is, therefore, the consensus of opinion of the prisoners that the District Postal Censor is responsible for delay of foreign mail as well as domestic mail.[45]

The effect on the prisoners of delayed or undelivered mail was so significant even the chaplains in the camps hoped to find a way to break through the bureaucratic logjam. At a January 1944 meeting held at the Hotel Statler in St. Louis, a number of chaplains working in the area of POW ministry discussed if the Lutheran Commission for Prisoners of War might be able to take steps to expedite the transportation of mail from Germany, since there seemed to be "unusually long delays" in this matter. However, the group conceded that the American Red Cross and the War Prisoners Aid were doing all within their power to improve the situation and that the difficulties were the result of largely unresolvable problems with transportation.[46]

Religious Life

Of course, the chaplains' main interest in the POW camps was not fixing the mail. POWs were permitted by the Geneva Convention to practice their religion, an assurance that included being able to attend services and to have clergy minister to the internees. In line with these guarantees, chapels sprouted in nearly every POW compound in the Missouri camps. Often at first these were simply empty barracks, multipurpose spaces that housed a vaudeville performance by the POW theater troupe on Saturday night and then a High Mass on Sunday morning. Later, structures were built specifically to be used as houses of worship, and in some cases the decor was quite ornate. "Each sector has its own chapel, built by the prisoners and decorated with frescoes, paintings, sculptures, and stained glass windows," wrote an inspector, who noted that Mass was said every day at camp. "The prisoners have received many gifts for the ornamentation of their barracks."[47]

At the Fort Leonard Wood chapel, two services were offered each Sunday, one by a Catholic priest, one by a Lutheran pastor. The men who ministered to the confined were German POWs supervised by an Army chaplain. Weekly attendance averaged just over 10 percent of the 3,000-man camp, with approximately 200 men coming for Catholic mass and 125 Protestants appearing at their own services. This is in contrast to Weingarten prisoners, who were the most faithful attenders of the Missouri POWs, with 75 percent attending Mass each week.[48]

Much of the ministry to the prisoners in Missouri and elsewhere took place outside the structure of the Army's Chaplain Corps, especially during

Interior of one of the POW chapels at Camp Weingarten. Courtesy of St. Louis Archdiocese Archives.

the first months that the POWs were arriving in the United States and the Army was still trying to make sense of the problem. Many times the local pastor, after volunteering or being sought out by the camp commander, simply assumed the responsibility of ministering to prisoners nearby.

The largest Lutheran church body in the United States at the time, the Evangelical Lutheran Synod of Missouri, Ohio, and Other States (now the Lutheran Church–Missouri Synod), was headquartered in St. Louis.[49] Because of the predominantly German background of its members and the strong Germanic current that ran through the church body (which still had a third of its congregations conducting services in German even at the onset of World War II), it was in especially good position to minister to German POWs, of which approximately 40 percent came from a Lutheran background.[50]

Lutherans in the United States responded to a call for German literature, and 140,000 books came in from all over the country. While the Lutheran Church used most of these books to stock POW camp libraries, specific texts forming the foundation of Lutheran doctrine were set aside for the creation of private libraries for theological students and pastors who were among the prisoners. The Nazis had not exempted these men from the draft, and more than two hundred POW pastors benefited from these essential texts. These men were able to take their theological libraries back home with them at the end of the war, along with communion sets and pulpit gowns they had been given by Lutherans in the United States.[51]

Like the Lutherans, members of the Roman Catholic Church moved quickly to minister to POWs. Parishioners donated many books for the libraries, along with musical instruments and sheet music. The local parishes reached out to minister to the prisoners in a number of ways. Members of St. Ambrose Parish from St. Louis's Italian community in the Hill neighborhood chartered a bus so that twenty-four members and their pastor could travel to Weingarten to visit with Italian internees in that camp, and they sponsored visits for the prisoners with Italian families in St. Louis.

Despite these efforts, the continuing Nazi presence in the German camps dampened POW enthusiasm for religious participation. In a September 1943 letter to the national Catholic military vicar, Bishop John O'Hara, Army chaplain Charles J. Meyer wrote of the problems he was having in getting German Catholic POWs to partake of the sacraments:

> In my last report of the Fort Leonard Wood Interment Camp, I stated that there was a cause why the prisoners did not receive the sacraments more often. At the time I thought that it was confidential, but since then I have found out that it is known by many.
>
> The German government forbad their soldiers to confess to anyone except a German army chaplain, and most of the prisoners claim that this holds also for the prisoners of war in this country, and we have not been able to convince them that their obligation of receiving the sacraments supercedes this regulation. Some of them are glad to make use of this excuse for not receiving the sacraments, but some otherwise good Catholics are afraid that they will be reported when they return to Germany, for there are some rabid Nazis among them.
>
> Most of them are convinced that those in power will still be in office when they will return to Germany and it would be difficult to convince them otherwise.[52]

Although the chaplains struggled against the influence of the Nazis in the camps, they were not the only ones to battle this group. One of the biggest challenges that the U.S. government faced was the internal control of the POW camps by hardline Nazis. It is arguable whether the government ever really broke the power of the group, though it tried to thwart the men through a number of different approaches.

Controversy over Conditions in the Camp

The fine treatment of POWs in American camps provoked a rumble of discontent among the U.S. population. The extensive recreation program, a varied and hearty menu served in the POW mess halls, and the availability of items to POWs that were off-limits to civilians provoked many complaints that POWs were being treated too well.

In the administration of the camps, the United States was determined to treat the prisoners decently and strove diligently to follow the guidelines of the Geneva Convention related to prisoner treatment. Ultimately, this treatment led to numerous complaints of "coddling" of the prisoner population. Citizens were angered by POWs enjoying items most people were denied because of rationing. The press picked up on this grumbling and carried stories about POWs held stateside in "country-club conditions" while U.S. soldiers were fighting and dying overseas. It didn't take long for the politicians to chime in, too, and soon the War Department was trapped in a storm of criticism.

The U.S. policy of treating the prisoners well was undergirded by the War Department's belief that several positive and highly desirable results would occur. First, and least tangible, the United States treated the prisoners kept in the States fairly because it was the right thing to do. Certainly the United States had failed from time to time to act consistently with its role as a major proponent of democracy in the world during this period—most notably in the internment of American citizens of Japanese ancestry—but to repress and mistreat these prisoners of war would have been a gross violation of the principles of freedom and decency.

Second, the United States knew that after the fighting was over, the Germans and Italians held in the United States would return to their homes and in many instances play pivotal roles in the re-establishment of government and society in postwar Europe. The government realized it had an incredible opportunity to educate these men on how a true democracy operates, which could in turn have a significant impact on the politics and stability in the countries to which they returned. In the latter years of the war, this attempt to educate prisoners on the positive features of an open and free society moved from a passive effort to an active phase as the United States initiated an immense re-education campaign, designed specifically to immerse the internees in the principles of democracy, to leave them with a favorable inclination toward the United States, and, as much as possible, to prepare them for active and participatory citizenship upon their return home.

Third, the U.S. government felt that providing firm but fair treatment consistent with the guidelines of the Geneva Convention would enhance the smooth operation of the stateside POW camps. Not only would the camp administration have fewer troubles related to internment camp disturbances, behavioral problems, internal sabotage activity, and escape attempts, but maximum use of POW labor would be easier to achieve if prisoners felt well treated and content with camp routine.[53]

Finally, the United States believed pragmatically that how it treated POWs held in American camps positively affected the treatment of American prisoners of war held in Germany and encouraged the surrender of German soldiers who knew that they would not be subject to abuses. "This punctiliousness [about observance of Geneva Convention standards] was due chiefly to a desire to protect American servicemen in the hands of the Germans in Europe," wrote historian Robert Billinger, "though the moral imperatives accepted by ratification of the Geneva Convention were also frequently cited."[54]

Even though the U.S. government learned that the American POWs in Europe were not being treated as well as the prisoners held here, the POW administration refused to change its philosophy toward foreign internees in the United States. Although some believed that there was retaliation behind the 1945 "food shortages" that prompted the government to modify camp menus that spring, it was the only official act that even came close to punishing the POWs. As Archer L. Lerch, provost marshal general beginning in June 1944, said, "Atrocity stories ought not to stampede us into abandoning the American way of doing things."[55]

This high-minded approach concerning the treatment of POWs held on American soil was fine in theory but did cause some problems in practice. On ships returning to the United States carrying German and Italian POWs along with wounded Americans, the POWs were supplied with writing paper, cigarettes, and books and played shuffleboard and staged wrestling and boxing matches, while wounded Americans watched their enemies enjoying these pastimes. "An American soldier, just about recovered from his wounds looked down at the empty swimming pool," reported the *Washington Daily News*, "and said wistfully: 'Gee, I wish the prisoners would ask for some water in the pool, so we can all have a swim.'" Indeed, they traveled in accommodations equal to or sometimes better than the U.S. servicemen.[56] "[Our ship was] one of those 9,000 ton *Santa Rosa*-type cruise ships, with the big swimming pools and all. I've never forgotten that trip," said Weingarten POW Ennio Calabresi. "We were one of a hundred ship convoy. The view was great, because we were a hospital ship in the center of all the other ships. We lived in five-high bunks, but were allowed on deck, where we played cards or slept. We were very happy the war was over for us."[57]

Despite these sound reasons for ensuring good treatment of enemy POWs, back home "most of the American public neither understood these official motivations nor particularly cared," wrote Billinger. "American civilians, who had neither experience with nor understanding of the lot of the prisoners of war, were irritated that 'Nazis'—as all German POWs were indiscriminately called at the time—received food that seemed, and often was, of higher quality and greater quantity than that available to home-front Americans affected by rationing."[58]

The War Department found it difficult to explain why the United States should treat so well those who had until just recently borne arms against the country. The Geneva Convention was clear, however, that prisoners of war must be given the same quality of food and housing as that of the soldiers of the host nation. In some cases that meant that U.S. servicemen went "down" to the level of POWs. If the prisoners at a temporary work camp slept in tents and ate canned rations for most meals, the Americans guarding them did too. It may not have seemed fair that the GIs guarding these POWs were denied comfort for the sake of interned enemy prisoners or that the prisoners in some cases had access to items rarely available to U.S. citizens, but the Army was convinced that it was the best approach, and ultimately politicians were too.

During hearings of the House Military Affairs Committee, in spring of 1945, the Army was largely able to convince the representatives that its treatment of POWs was not overly soft and that it was in fact in the United States' best interest to avoid retaliation against the enemy POWs because of the poor treatment of American POWs held in Europe. In his appearance before the committee, assistant provost marshal general B. M. Bryan testified that this approach was paying off in the United States' efforts in Europe. Bryan cited a recently received report from General Dwight Eisenhower's headquarters testifying that word of good treatment of German POWs had filtered back to Europe. The result, said Bryan, was that this evenhanded treatment made German soldiers increasingly willing to surrender and also favorably affected the condition of American POWs in German captivity.[59]

Ultimately, the committee agreed with the Army, concluding that "for us to treat with undue harshness the Germans in our hands would be to adopt the Nazi principle of hostages." Additionally, the committee felt that the Army's policy had already "paid large dividends," as stated by the Red Cross and U.S. commanders in Europe. "Had promises [of fair treatment] not been true, and believed, victory would have been slower and harder, and a far greater number of Americans killed."[60]

Camp Inspections

POW camps in Missouri and elsewhere were frequently inspected by various independent groups to ensure humane treatment of the internees and that the United States was upholding the principles of the Geneva Convention. "There were frequent inspections of the facilities. These were made by authorities from the outside, designated or agreed upon by the highest military authorities," said Captain Eugene Phillips, head of Camp Weingarten's quartermaster operation. "They were of food, water, sanitation, records of services, finances and compliance with the Geneva Convention regulations for Prisoners of War."[61]

Chief among the groups that sent representatives to tour the Missouri facilities and assess conditions there was the Swiss Legation, which as a group from a neutral country served as the "protecting power," representing the rights of the prisoners under the power of international treaty. The Swiss Legation also served as the official channel for POW communications with their home governments, carrying reports about treatment. Allegations of abuse or neglect toward POWs held in the United States could have almost immediate repercussions in the treatment of American prisoners held overseas. It is for that reason that camp commanders were usually attentive to concerns of the visiting inspectors of the Swiss Legation and also why reports of these visits went almost immediately to the PMGO in Washington, D.C.

After the Italians surrendered to the Allies, the work of the Swiss Legation was largely replaced by visiting representatives of the Italian embassy and Italian department of state, since the two nations were no longer at war. On the humanitarian side, inspectors from the International Red Cross Committee and the International YMCA visited specifically to assess physical needs of the prisoners and to provide materials for the library, theater, and sports programs. Equally important was their role as mediators for resolving problems that arose between the prisoners and the administration, circumventing the morass of official channels, which often provided quick benefit to POW morale and camp efficiency. These agencies provided millions of dollars' worth of items to POWs for recreation, education, and entertainment, greatly enhancing the prisoners' quality of life.

American government agencies also conducted inspections of the installations to make sure that things were running well and that the regulations concerning POW camp operation were observed. In addition to having a State Department representative accompany the officials from the international agencies, officials from the War Department made regular rounds of the camps on their own, documenting problems as well as the positive aspects of the prison camp operations. The concerns these inspectors addressed ranged from minor to significant. A report submitted December 29, 1943, by Captain Robert Heinkel following a visit to Camp Weingarten highlights the types of issues with which the PMGO was concerned. Although the physical plant was satisfactory in Heinkel's report, he noted conditions of the camp that he thought could be improved. "As at the other Italian camp visited, Camp Clark, it was found that in some places the outside policing of the compound was not all that was to be desired," wrote Heinkel, disturbed by trash and debris lying about. "It is apparently difficult to impress the Italian prisoners of war with the importance of maintaining a well-policed camp."[62]

Unfortunately, the problems these inspectors dealt with often landed on the other end of the severity scale. Combating Nazi violence in Missouri's German POW camps was a significant concern, and one that they encountered much more frequently than complaints about camps with rubbish on the ground. To combat the Nazi influence, the Army would eventually adopt a re-education program for German POWs.

Trends in Prisoner Population

The weekly report issued July 1, 1944, by the PMGO showed how the prisoner population mushroomed in the two short years after the first batch of POWs was accepted from Great Britain. On that date there were 353 camps in the United States that had been designated as prisoner compounds. Eighteen more camps were under construction. They were located in thirty-nine states from Maine to California, from Florida to Wyoming. A breakdown of prisoners held in these camps by nationality and military designation on this date looks like this:

	Officers	NCOs	Enlisted	Total
German	4,350	30,106	108,058	142,514
Italian	2,642	1,934	11,034	15,610
Japanese	23	143	403	569
Total	7,015	32,183	119,495	158,693

Interestingly, a number of the men captured and counted as German POWs were not Germans at all but had ended up serving in Hitler's army under a variety of circumstances. Maxwell McKnight, who served as chief of the POW Special Projects Division in charge of the re-education of German prisoners, recalled a phone call he received one day from one of the commanders of the internment camps. "McKnight, you sent me some Germans, but they don't speak any German. I don't know what they speak, but it is not German," said the bemused officer. It turned out that the men were Russian, and they joined an ethnic and national medley of soldiers wearing the German uniform who were actually Dutch, French, Austrian, Czech, Yugoslav, Polish, Arab, Luxembourger, Swiss, Russian, Hungarian, Romanian, and even Jewish (at least three of whom were held in U.S. camps). These men had been pressed into service by the Nazis from conquered areas, and many surrendered as soon as they met a soldier from one of the Allied armies. Although their service may not have been voluntary, the fact remained that these men had been captured as part of the German armed forces and remained interned in the POW camps until the end of the war.[63]

The number of prisoners held in the United States reached its peak in May 1945. More than 370,000 German and 50,000 Italian POWs were interned at 155 main camps and 600 branch camps scattered across American soil. The U.S. government also held a small number of Japanese prisoners during World War II, but their numbers barely reached 5,400 at their peak in August 1945, and no camps for Japanese POWs were ever established in Missouri.[64] The best estimate of the POW population in Missouri puts the total somewhere around 15,000 men. Because of their presence in small towns and big cities throughout Missouri, the work that the prisoners performed, and the lives they touched in the process, the memories of the camps linger on.

Crowder POWs prepared food in many of the post's mess halls. Courtesy of Missouri State Archives.

Facing: POWs served GIs in the post's mess halls. Courtesy of Missouri State Archives.

Chapter Two

Labor and Re-education Programs

Like unwrapping a present, one of the unanticipated yet enormously positive aspects of the POWs' presence in the United States was their role in providing work. Shortly after the American entry into World War II, an immense labor shortage happened, especially in agriculture and other labor-intensive industries. Because of both the numbers of men going into the military and the increased demand for labor in industries producing items for the war effort, the well ran dry for workers in agriculture and other "nonessential" efforts.

The first use of POW labor was on the military installations where the prisoners lived, both in the maintenance and administration of their own POW camps and in support of the activities of the larger installation. This was particularly the case at Fort Leonard Wood and Camp Crowder, which held large numbers of American troops. There, POWs often worked side by side with civilian employees in the laundry, in the motor pool, and in other areas in support of post operations. "The PWs helped us and were very nice, very polite," said Lillian Meyer, who worked as a cashier in the PX at Weingarten. "I was a little afraid at first because I didn't want something to happen." That initial sense of uneasiness eventually gave way to a mutual regard between the prisoners and American workers, comfortable enough even to be punctuated with occasional mischief. "They were always pulling some kind of practical joke," said Meyer of the Italian POWs. "We would have lunch ready, and then they would say that they didn't have enough time to eat. We would remove the lunch only to hear the POW's laugh and say they were only joking. I liked them. They were very down-to-earth."[1]

Because of the severe dearth of labor in the country, the government took what it perceived as a calculated risk and began contracting out small groups of prisoners to local farmers for agricultural work beginning in the fall of 1942. This was a balancing act: the need for workers was so great that despite the government's unrelenting fear of prisoner escapes in those early days, for the first time the prisoners were permitted to work outside their camps, though not without some high-level hesitation. President Roosevelt worried publicly that Germany might arrange for the capture of trained saboteurs who might then escape in the United States to carry out their mission of destruction, and FBI director J. Edgar Hoover warned ominously that every escaped prisoner of war "trained as he is in the technique of destruction, is a danger to our internal security, our war production, and the lives and safety of our citizens."[2]

Despite this ongoing concern about POW escapes, the experiment continued without significant problems, and the government authorized use of prisoners in increasingly larger numbers on farms near the camps. State agricultural interests clamored for as much POW labor as they could get, setting the stage for rapid expansion of the program. Knowing how pressed farmers in the Springfield, Missouri, area were for help, Congressman Marion T. Bennett saw an opportunity to score points with his constituents in August 1943 when, after a visit to Camp Clark, he raised the possibility of using its POW workers on area farms.[3]

Fortunately for the Army, Missouri agriculture, and Congressman Bennett, any initial fears the government had of POWs escaping from work details proved groundless. Almost from the first day that small groups of POW began working on American farms, it was apparent that the prisoners were not going anywhere. Prisoners who sneaked away from the camps were generally motivated only by boredom or homesickness and were never known to have performed any acts of sabotage. In fact, the worst crime ever committed by a POW on the lam was slipping into an unattended automobile and requisitioning it for his own use.[4]

"They had it pretty good," said Vernon Davis of the Italian prisoners who were housed in the former clubhouse of an old horse track in Riverside, Missouri. "You couldn't have driven those boys out of there, even if you wanted to!"[5] Most were content to pass time in the camp until the end of the war; those who weren't usually recognized the futility of trying to get home. They had no money, few options for travel in such a huge country, and little sympathy among Missourians. They also usually lacked a convincing command of the English language. For most prisoners, though, the reason that they chose not to run away came down to the question, Am I better off here than I would be elsewhere? The answer was usually yes. The few escapees were usually captured not far from the camp within a day or two. As this realization about the low risk of escape began to register with military planners, they saw the increased possibilities for use of prisoner labor in areas far beyond the range of the main camps.

Big Moneymaker

POW wages were consistent among countries, established through international agreement to create a common standard based on prevailing wages in Europe. Because these POW pay rates were so much less than the going rates for labor in the United States, the government made a profit. While POWs received $.80 a day for their work—roughly the same rate as the $21 a month American privates received in 1941—the contractors still paid for the labor at the prevailing local rate, which was usually higher. The U.S. Treasury hauled in $100 million in 1944 alone on POW labor in the United States. Much of the money was used to pay for the feeding, housing, and medical care of the prisoners, as well as other expenses, and it was because of this that the POW program was essentially self-supporting.[6]

In addition to monies coming into the treasury from POWs contracted out to private industry, the War Department also saved an estimated $80 million in work the prisoners did on military posts. For instance, a POW work detail assigned to perform lumber salvage at Fort Devens, Massachusetts, saved the government $385,000 in an eight-month period. "Without the POW labor," wrote historian Judith Gansberg, "the Army would have had to spend that amount on new material."[7]

German POWs at work in the Camp Crowder paint shop. Courtesy of Missouri State Archives.

Per the Geneva Convention, only the lower ranks of enlisted men were required to work. Noncommissioned officers (NCOs)—sergeants and above—could not be compelled to perform labor, only to provide supervision over other enlisted POWs. In that light, at first it did not make much sense to the American government to pay these men who did not perform any actual work. It didn't take them long to reconsider this, however, for reasons not so much related to gaining more bodies in the field as to minimizing the problems back at the camp that brewed in the unoccupied hours of idle men. "In order to restore and maintain the morale of the high-ranking German NCOs, and also to increase the efficiency of PWs working for private contractors, it appears desirable to allow the camp commanders to send approximately one of these high-ranking NCOs with each group of prisoners as over-seers or straw bosses and to pay the $.80 per day from government funds," wrote Provost Marshal General Allen Gullion after visiting several midwestern POW camps. "These non-coms would perform only supervisory work. At the present time, the German master sergeants and warrant officers have not agreed to perform common labor with the other enlisted men and, therefore, have much time to promote trouble and foment unrest while in their barracks."[8]

POW Workers

The typical day at POW camps in Missouri and indeed across the United States was remarkably consistent. With few variations, each location followed the same basic schedule. "The work day at Weingarten begins with reveille at 0515; breakfast is at 0630, and roll call and sick call at 0700. At 0730 the work details assemble at the stockade gate," while the MP company assigned to guard the details waited outside to march them away, wrote Lieutenant George Paddock, an officer at the Weingarten camp. "Recall sounds at 1130 and dinner is at 1145; work call comes again at 1300. The prisoners are back in their stockade at 1700, with supper an hour later and the evening free until lights out at 2200."[9]

Farmers and civilian employers who contracted for prisoner labor were generally pleased with the work performed for them. "Most private employers have been satisfied with the work of prisoners, although some have not had satisfactory experiences by being afraid of the prisoners or by trying to drive them too hard," said Gullion. "There have been no claims from contractors for damage done by prisoners."[10]

An inspection report of the branch camps at Atherton and Orrick, Missouri, praised the work of the prisoners on area farms. "Accustomed to smaller farms and very limited acreage in Italy, the prisoners scrupulously remove every weed," wrote an inspector. "Their thoroughness has astonished local farmers. These prisoners have already been credited with saving crops for which local labor could not be found. It is for this reason that this experiment is proving highly successful."[11]

The efficiency of a work detail of German prisoners from Fort Leonard Wood assigned to a haystacking project impressed and surprised a local farmer in similar fashion. A visitor to the camp noted that "a farmer had estimated that three days would be required for ten carefully-selected prisoners to stack the hay on approximately thirty acres. The prisoners completed the job in less than one day."[12]

Although the Geneva Convention prohibited labor under hazardous or dangerous conditions, agricultural work, where most of the POW labor was engaged, did not fall into that category. Fortunately, few injuries to POWs were reported in the course of the labor program, and of those that did occur, most happened while transporting prisoners to and from work assignments. In one case, a Weingarten POW was caught by a telephone line when riding in a truck and jerked out of the back. As a result of the injury, the man received treatment at O'Reilly General Hospital in Springfield until he recovered enough to return to Weingarten. Another more serious accident occurred when two German prisoners were killed and eight were injured when an Army truck transporting them to Camp Algona, Iowa, struck a refrigerator truck near Harrisonville, Missouri.[13] In the case of a such a labor-related accident or injury, a form of workmen's compensation for POWs took effect and a prisoner in the hospital still received half his wages, $.40 a day, while recuperating.[14]

Crowder POWs constructing stone drainage ditches and revetments. Courtesy of Missouri State Archives.

Setting up Branch Camps

Because of the acute labor shortage, it soon became apparent that the prisoners should be located where their work was needed. As a result, the Army established more than twenty small branch camps. The size of these camps was tied directly to the amount of labor needed there, usually between 50 and 250 prisoners. Initially, there was hesitation in setting up branch camps because of the enormous number of men that the provost marshal general believed would be required to effectively guard the POWs. Major General Gullion cited the Weingarten camp commander's calculation that it would take approximately ninety soldiers to guard three hundred POWs at a side camp. However, in the early days of the war, devoting that number of American soldiers to POW operations not crucial to the war was just not possible. The labor needs were certainly there; Gullion noted that if "sufficient guards were available, side camps could be established in southern Missouri to pick cotton during this period and to clear drainage ditches throughout the winter," work that was desperately needed.[15] As it turned out, only minimal numbers of GIs were needed to maintain control over prisoners outside the camp because of the small number of prisoners who tried to escape.

While the barracks situated in the main POW camps were lined up like soldiers in formation, housing for POWs at the branch camps was a different story. Prisoners lived in riverboat camps at Chesterfield, St. Louis, Gasconade, Missouri, and several other sites. These "quarterboats" were equipped with a galley and everything else the soldiers needed for day-to-day living.

In the Missouri River bottoms west of St. Louis, what looked to passing motorists like quaint little tourist cottages was actually housing for POWs working on the Hellwig Brothers Farms in Chesterfield. At Riverside, in the Kansas City area, prisoners bunked down on the former site of a horse track, staying in the old Jockey Club.

Tent camps were a common sight when prisoners worked on agricultural projects in small towns with ample open space nearby. Tents were used at branch camps all around the state and were the most common housing for locations that were established for a relatively short period of time. Both POWs and servicemen alike used the canvas Army field tents for protection from the elements. At the Hannibal, Missouri, ballpark, Clemens Field, tents stretched from home plate to the outfield, housing prisoners working a shoe-sorting project at a factory near the Mississippi River.

Dormitories at former National Youth Administration camps housed prisoners at Fulton and Louisiana, Missouri, and POWs stayed in barracks on the sprawling grounds of O'Reilly General Hospital, the massive federal medical complex at Springfield. "I remember the POWs," recalled Stan Borgstrom, who was at O'Reilly from July 1944 until January 1946. "I always wondered why they had their own barracks, movie hall, mess hall and just had complete freedom of the area. No fences around, no guards that I remember.... I often thought if they would send some of them back to Europe to tell how good they had it, they would all surrender."[16]

An Italian POW named Vincenzo Mancuso remembered POWs bunking down in empty buildings at Stephens College during a 1944 summertime corn-detasseling project in Columbia, Missouri. Legendary Missouri professor Donovan Rhynsburger, who chaired the Department of Speech and Dramatic Art and directed the university theater for forty-three years, occasionally regaled dinner companions with tales of the POWs living in fraternity houses at the University of Missouri that same year.[17]

Effects of the Labor Program

The use of prisoners in U.S. fields and factories was an extraordinarily important component of the homefront war effort. The government calculated that during the war, prisoners in the United States performed a

Crowder POWs on an ash and trash detail. Courtesy of Missouri State Archives.

total of 19,567,719 man-days of work on Army posts and 10,181,275 man-days of work for contract employers, more than half of which was in agriculture. In Missouri the prisoners picked cotton, harvested vegetables, detasseled corn, dug potatoes, tended plants in a nursery, and worked on farms across the state. Other work was found in a limestone quarry, on levees, in a handful of factories and warehouses, and on military bases.

POW labor was invaluable to both the U.S. war effort and the domestic economy. "All in all, the use of prisoners of war in lieu of civilians or American soldiers at military establishments resulted in a government savings of more than 131 million dollars, while the collections from POW contract work netted a total of 39 million dollars," wrote U.S. Army historians George Lewis and John Mewha. "[Although] this amount cannot be considered as a complete reimbursement to the United States for the costs involved (housing, food, guards, transportation, etc.) from the time of their capture to their release,… the labor performed by the POWs made a valuable contribution toward the settlement of the costs involved." Lewis and Mewha expressed the final impact of the POWs in this way: "Both civil and military authorities have stated that they could not have performed their functions except for the use of prisoners of war."[18]

Re-education Program

To combat the Nazi influence and to increase the likelihood of a successful transition to an open German postwar government, during the last years of the war the Army engaged in a special covert re-education program designed to teach German POWs the merits of democracy. This program, which was championed by First Lady Eleanor Roosevelt, came close to violating the Geneva Convention articles that prohibited instruction on political ideologies because of the potential for brainwashing, but the United States went ahead nonetheless, seeing a significant opportunity to affect the leadership of postwar Europe.

Even though the Army project was highly secret, at the time of its development a few civilian groups in the United States were publicly advocating the same type of program to re-educate the Nazi soldiers held in America. Perhaps the most prominent and vocal group was the committee headed by Gerhart Seger, editor of the German American newspaper *Neue Volkszeitung*, formed in the spring of 1944. This group contained a number of prominent Americans including Congressman Howard McMurray of Milwaukee, Wisconsin; nationally syndicated columnist Dorothy Thompson; and Thomas Mann, the widely read German author living in exile in the United States. "About twenty five percent of the German prisoners…are fanatical Nazis, about sixty percent are in between, and about fifteen percent anti-Nazi," declared Seger. "Up until now, the policy of the government has been to separate the anti-Nazis from the others, which only results in the exposure of the major group to the violent Nazi propaganda."

The intent of the committee was to pull the minority group of hard-core Nazis away from that large bunch wavering in the middle so that those less convinced of the values of National Socialism could instead be informed about democracy.[19] Seger's group and others advocating a program of re-education and philosophical reorientation were driven by the increasing coverage in the U.S. press of the activities of Nazi factions in the POW camps, which often occurred right under the noses of camp administrators. The influence wielded by ardent Nazis and Fascists over their comrades turned out to be one of the most significant challenges experienced by the United States in the administration of the POW program during World War II. "Already the Nazis are organized in the prisoner of war camps throughout America. Any German prisoner who shows any interest in democracy or America is punished by his fellow prisoners," wrote Seger. "The Nazis in our prisoner camps have even organized Gestapo units."[20] Those who were anti-Nazi and anti-Fascist were often in danger of physical attacks by their fellow prisoners. Some took to sleeping with a club near their beds and would relieve themselves in a bucket at night rather than venture through the dark to the latrine.[21]

Anton Kuehmoser, an Afrika Korps POW at Fort Leonard Wood, recalled a prisoner there who had been stabbed to death by another prisoner, a hardline Nazi internee who had been a member of the SS.[22] "Even in the camp here, we had Nazi rules. Some of the Nazis forced everyone to gather for an evening every other week for indoctrination," said Kuehmoser. "Anyone who skipped got a warning the first time. The second time, he got a visit from the 'Holy Ghost,'" an SS executioner.[23]

Nazi POWs also held secret kangaroo courts or midnight tribunals in which "disloyal" prisoners could be convicted of treason and executed, usually by beating or forced suicide—in one case a prisoner was locked in a room for an hour with a rope with which to hang himself. Being beaten to death by a Nazi gang was a certainty if he failed to follow through. Sometimes the crime was simply being suspected of complicity with the Americans or even criticizing the Third Reich's policies.[24] Estimates of German POWs killed by their countrymen range from one hundred to three hundred men. The pressure to conform to the Nazi standard extended beyond the fences of the camp as well, as Nazis also threatened the nonconforming prisoners with reprisal against families back in Europe.

An incident that occurred in March 1944 at Camp Chaffee, Arkansas, about one hundred miles south of Camp Crowder, was a typical example of this Nazi violence. Hans Geller, a twenty-one-year-old paratrooper held at the camp, seemed to have no reason to fall into disfavor with Nazis at the camp. Geller was twice wounded in combat and had three brothers who had been killed in action while fighting for Germany. However, Geller spoke English and enjoyed his work at the camp, getting along well with his American supervisor. He stepped over the line with the Nazis when he requested that two new men working with him be transferred, since their political activities were getting in the way of their duties. On March 25, 1944, a POW tribunal found him guilty of disloyalty, and that night he was beaten to death after being lured into the darkness from his barracks under the pretense of meeting a new arrival from his hometown. Fellow prisoner Edgar Menscher was convicted of the murder and sentenced to death. President Harry S Truman later commuted his punishment, and Menscher served twenty years at Fort Leavenworth, Kansas.[25]

Much of this intimidation problem stemmed from a failure by U.S. authorities in the first year of POW operations to accurately assess the political beliefs of individual POWs and to segregate them accordingly. Although they separated prisoners to a minor extent—enlisted men from officers, Navy personnel from the Army, and the like—the government learned the hard way how important it was to separate the extreme Nazis and Fascists from the more ambivalent men. Although the problem was present to an extent among the Italian POWs, the issue was much more severe among German prisoners.

According to Maxwell McKnight, who headed the POW Special Projects Division, which aimed to re-educate Nazis, the influence and control of Nazi elements in the camps was initially seen as a positive feature. "Who could best get a work detail cracking? The Nazi noncoms. And the guys would go out swinging in the morning to work details singing the 'Horst Wessel' song," said McKnight. "They were going to show the Americans on the camps posts! The efficiency in the laundry at every camp, post, and station where we had prisoners increased a hundred and fifty percent. And beautiful work! I mean, shirts came out clean! And at night they'd go back, and of course, they'd go into the camps singing the Nazi songs."[26]

This problem of virulent Nazism infesting the camp populations would be alleviated as the war went on for several reasons. First, many of the prisoners captured during the later years of the war were draftees who had been drawn from society at large and were not as deeply indoctrinated as the first waves of internees, which were almost entirely Afrika Korps troops, some of Hitler's elite and most well trained soldiers. Additionally, these later internees were somewhat more disillusioned with Hitler and National Socialism than the earlier crowd because because of Germany's embarrassing defeats in North Africa and Russia. Eventually the POW administration improved its ability to identify Nazi prisoners and actively separated the most hardened ones from the general prisoner population.

The government's initial lack of response to calls for action led Dorothy Thompson and Dorothy Bromley of the *New York Herald* to take the problem directly to Eleanor Roosevelt. They wanted to bring to her attention the acts of Nazi violence in American camps against neutral or anti-Nazi prisoners. After McKnight of the PMGO met with Roosevelt, "She said, 'I've got to talk to Franklin. Right in our backyard, to have these Nazis moved in and controlling the whole thought process! What do you think this does to us?'"[27]

After this frank discussion of the problems in the POW camps, the first lady took the issue to her husband, who sent the matter to the Secretaries of War and State, Henry Stimson and Edward Stettinus, Jr., respectively. These men passed the issue in turn to the new provost marshal general, Major General Archer L. Lerch.

A number of avenues were used to reach the German POWs with the desired information about the merits of democracy and traditional Western civilization. Films provided for use in the camp entertainment programs carried messages countering the Nazi assertion that the United States was decadent, inefficient, and corrupt. German-language books that presented more accurate depictions of American and German history were placed in camp libraries. Additionally, a national German POW newspaper was created, as well as individual newspapers at each camp location. These publications gave the more democratic prisoners an opportunity to reach their fellow POWs with an anti-Nazi message and provided a platform to discuss the options for democratic governance in postwar Germany.

POWs at the camp in Chesterfield established one such paper, *The Chesterfield-Herold*, and declared their intent in a statement of purpose in the first issue, published April 1, 1945:

> This publication is the forum for the free airing of opinion. It is the platform for frank discussion. For advice and suggestions, we welcome questions and critical feedback.
>
> This paper is a school for the teachers and the learners, the takers and the givers, a humanistic institution and citizenship school in miniature.
>
> BRIDGE TO THE WORLD is the name of our paper, because it will strive for an understanding of the world, because it will bring the goodness and greatness of the world to our place here through personal reporting, because it would like to show the world our love of freedom and our desire for peace.[28]

Interestingly, at the same time that the Special Projects Division—the intentionally bland name given to the program to belie its true purpose—was undertaking this unprecedented (at least in the United States) project to influence the German prisoners, the division also warned its staff in a secret memo that the project was not to be "overdone." The POWs were to be "democratized" but not "Americanized," noted historian Arthur Krammer, for while "the prisoners were to be sent home to live in Germany as favorably inclined to the United States as may be possible, they are not to be so encouraged as to try to remain in the United States, or to return to the United States as immigrants."[29]

The American government worked hard to keep the program a secret to prevent a possible corresponding program of indoctrination of American

POWs held in Germany. The two hundred U.S. officers and enlisted men who had been selected to implement the program trained at a secret location in Fort Slocum, New York, eight hours outside New York City, taking part in a series of lectures and seminars conducted by officer and civilian specialists who had worked with Germans in Europe prior to the war. Instruction included an overview of the program itself, a detailed analysis of German history and psychology, and a look at the mindset of a POW. A large portion of the study aimed to immerse students in German propaganda, provided tools for countering it, and offered ideas for ways to incorporate positive democratic propaganda through every possible avenue.[30]

The project remained a secret until after V-E Day in May 1945. Five months after the start of the program, the American public and the U.S. government at large—still unaware of the existence of the program—were vocal in their criticism of the War Department's failure to address the issue of POW philosophical orientation.

Success of the Project

While difficult to gauge precisely, the Special Projects Division was successful in influencing the thinking of many German POWs to some degree, moving them to view the United States and democracy in a more favorable light. These results were measured in several areas. First was *Der Ruf* (The Call), the nationwide POW newsmagazine that began bimonthly publication beginning in March 1945 and was compiled by a cadre of dedicated anti-Nazi prisoners under the supervision of the Special Projects Division. The paper featured high-quality literature and sophisticated analysis of current events. Distributed through the camp canteen network, *Der Ruf* was selling seventy-three thousand copies of each issue by October 1945.[31]

Additionally, the Special Projects Division assumed control over the prisoners' education programs and libraries, gradually and subtly replacing volumes that had contained pro-Nazi information and sentiment with new texts. The division also commissioned a set of purchasable ($.25 at the canteens) paperback books that eventually comprised twenty-four titles featuring well-known German authors such as Thomas Mann and Heinrich Heine. These books were popular with prisoners, and the PMGO concluded that while "there is no absolute measure of the influence upon the minds of the Prisoners of War of the good books made available to them...surely these books have exerted some influence and perhaps a great one."[32]

The Special Projects Division also influenced the movies shown for POW entertainment. Prior to the implementation of the Intellectual Diversion Program, films had been chosen by the prisoners themselves, and selections frequently presented a damaging or inaccurate view of the United States, such as films depicting gangsters, crime, and violence and portraying American life as decadent and morally corrupt.

In lieu of these motion pictures, the Special Projects Division began supplying the camps with documentaries provided by the Army Signal Corps and the Office of War Information as well as popular Hollywood films that provided entertainment that didn't focus on or glorify the less positive side of life in America. The film program was wildly popular, tallying 8.2 million admissions between June 15, 1945, and January 31, 1946. This worked out to an average of thirty feature films seen by each POW in the United States. Even better was the fact that the program paid for itself, generating more than $1.2 million from ticket purchases.[33]

After the fall of Germany, the PMGO also required the showing of Nazi atrocity films as a tool in the re-education program. Reaction to these films varied widely. Some internees displayed shock and horror, while others completely doubted the validity of the images shown on the screen, believing them to be doctored products of a U.S. propaganda lab. German POW Walter Meier worked at branch camps in Independence and Marshall, Missouri, in 1945. He said he and the other Germans at the camps were astonished to find out about the concentration camps and the treatment of Jews in their home country. "We would hear rumors, but very few would believe them. We thought they couldn't be true," said Meier. "But when we saw the pictures the Americans showed us, we were ashamed."[34]

Setbacks

While the United States undoubtedly had some success influencing the prisoners of war and their opinions about democracy, a change in U.S. policy concerning the treatment of POWs at the end of the war damaged the progress that had been made and gave many internees a degree of bitterness toward the United States.

In stark counterpoint to the treatment the prisoners had received in the first years of the war was the policy implemented by the War Department in the spring of 1945. Whether in response to the continuous charges of coddling that were being raised against the government for the perceived soft treatment of POWs, as retribution for the horrible treatment endured by American POWs that had been increasingly publicized in the American press, as a result of actual food shortages at the end of the war, or as a combination of all three, beginning in March 1945 American authorities greatly curtailed the quality and quantity of food served to the prisoners.

Simultaneous to the government's pleas to the American public for the conservation of food because of the increased demands of the armed forces and rapidly diminishing reserves, officials implemented this change in the POW camps based on a reinterpretation of Article 11 of the Geneva Convention, which required that prisoners receive rations equal only in nutritional value to those furnished to regular base troops; it did not mean that identical items had to be served. Rations were immediately cut, and prisoners received a daily maximum of four ounces of meat per person, and other items in short supply, such as canned fruits and vegetables, butter, and sugar, were substantially reduced. Camp commanders were instructed to implement the following meat substitutions at once:

a. Meat from swine will be limited to feet, hearts, livers, kidneys, tails, and neck bones…and oily pork not acceptable under existing specifications for Army feeding.

b. Meat from veal will be limited to utility grade carcasses….

c. Meat from beef will be limited to shanks, flanks, skirts, livers, hearts, kidneys, ox tails, tripe, brains and green bones….

d. Fish will be limited to the cheaper grades of salted or round dressed fish.[35]

Within weeks after V-E Day, beef was served only twice a month, and eggs became a rarity. More vegetables were added to replace the rationed items, and the camp menus relied heavily on the seasonal changes of local produce.[36]

In addition to these changes to the prisoners' table, other restrictions were issued. The sale of items previously available to prisoners in the canteen, such as cigarettes and beer, was curtailed, and the $3 monthly stipend was ended. The combined effect of these changes was to undo many of the POWs' positive feelings toward their host nation, its people, and its way of life. "They were talking about how wonderful it had been" prior to these cutbacks, said the Reverend William Gabler, who ministered to the POWs at the camps in Chesterfield. "'We really thought we had learned something about the American way of life,' they said, 'and now this happens. We are really disillusioned.'"[37]

Whether or not this policy was intended as retribution specifically against the German POWs, as most people believed, it had to be applied in all camps,

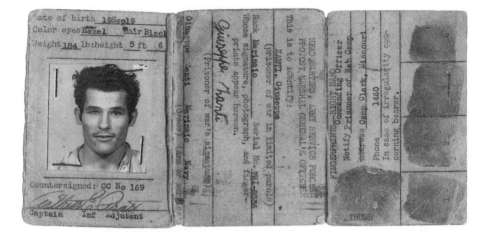

Giuseppe Zanti's POW ID card. Photo by Pete Puleo, Sr.

including those holding Italians. This was particularly troubling, as Italy had been an ally of the United States since October 1943, and for a time this policy applied even to men in the Italian Service Units (ISU). These units, first organized in early 1944, were special military groups composed of Italian volunteers working in the service of the United States who served in a status almost identical to American GIs on military bases around the country.

Ultimately most of these Italian prisoners would be returned to Europe in a matter of just a few months. Although some bitterness lingered, the internees mainly remembered the good treatment they had received during their time in the States. Giuseppe Zanti was an Italian submariner sent to Camp Clark in 1942 and later transferred to Jefferson Barracks in St. Louis. Zanti, who immigrated to the St. Louis Italian community on the Hill in September 1954, took off his hat and clutched it to his chest as he recalled his time in the United States. "The Americans," he said, "they treated us too good. Too good."[38]

Greetings from

_____

_____

PW CAMP, WEINGARTEN, MO.

Hospital Detachment Mess Hall, PW Camp, Weingarten, Mo.

Souvenir Folder of

PW CAMP

POSTAGE
1½¢
WITHOUT
MESSAGE

WEINGARTEN, MO.

*Souvenir folder of PW camp at Weingarten. Curt Teich & Co. Chicago, U.S.A. ©
1945. Courtesy of Edmee Viscardi.*

Chapter Three

Camp Weingarten

ITALIAN PRISONERS HELD AT CAMP WEINGARTEN "were gay, jolly and cheerful," wrote *St. Louis Post-Dispatch* reporter Rufus Jarman. "They were really in about as good humor as could be expected of men being held far away from home against their will. I had the feeling that they were damned glad to be out of that war."

Jarman described the men of the camp, one of the largest POW camps for Italians in the United States:

> The Italian noncommissioned officers especially were tall, handsome, dark-skinned men, heavily sunburned, with liquid brown eyes, many with mustaches and plentiful black hair—the types you expect of upper or middle class good-looking Italians.

> What was most surprising to me was the great abundance of little short men with sort of monkey faces and short haircuts, like scrubbing brushes. They looked entirely different from what we usually think of as "typical Italian types," and I suppose they must have been peasant farmers. They seemed to have little to say, spoke no English apparently and showed mighty little reaction to their surroundings. I got the impression that they were rather vague as to where they were and why, and that their thoughts were back home among their broccoli and tomato patches.[1]

Established at Weingarten, a sleepy little town on State Highway 32 between Ste. Genevieve and Farmington, Missouri, the camp had no pre-war existence, and unlike the other major camps in the state, it never served any military function other than as a pen for Italian POWs. After the last of the prisoners were transferred from the facility in 1945,

it closed completely, and traces of its presence have all but vanished from the landscape.

Weingarten's creation came about as the government realized in early 1942 that the United States would soon have to begin accepting huge numbers of enemy POWs from its European allies. Missouri's central location and mostly rural landscape offered a number of sites suitable for POW camps. The government sent engineers to the state to scout locations in the spring of 1942.

During the government's review of potential sites, the Chicago, Burlington, & Quincy Railroad (CB&Q) offered land for a camp at several possible locations, including Maryville, Missouri, and Centerville, Iowa. Early in the war, President Roosevelt named Ralph Budd, chief of the CB&Q, to serve on the National Defense Advisory Commission. There, Budd reported directly to Roosevelt and frequently advised him on use of the nation's railways for the war effort. Donation of land was no noble act of charity; rather, self-interest drove the offer, as Budd and the other CB&Q officials certainly knew what locating a camp on one of the railroad's lines would mean in terms of increased revenue. Hauling in the building supplies for the camp's initial construction phase, as well as U.S. personnel, POWs, and all the goods to sustain them during the life of the camp, would be essentially the same as adding an entirely new midsize town to the route.

The government ultimately declined the railroad's offer, based on camp location guidelines instructing that facilities for POWs should not be located in areas with a mean annual temperature of less than 56 degrees Fahrenheit, based on the savings in construction and heating costs from placing camps in more moderate climates. This restriction was eventually changed, and camps appeared in Iowa, Minnesota, Wisconsin, New Hampshire, and a number of other northern states.[2]

Weingarten Selected

Additional standards directed that facilities holding enemy soldiers should be located far from major metropolitan areas, ports, and strategic industry sites, and the little town of Weingarten, situated in gently rolling hills some twelve miles west of Ste. Genevieve, fifteen miles northeast of Farmington, and ninety miles south of St. Louis, was a natural choice because of its isolation. After seeing the town and the surrounding area, the engineers surveying potential sites "were not long selecting its picturesque location, a unique but ideal setting."[3]

"When traveling from Farmington to Ste. Genevieve, one passed through this small town—but very quickly. The church on the right, a few houses, a small parochial school, a grocery store, and you were out of town," recalled Pauline Laws McKamey, who began working at the camp in February 1943. "But, undoubtedly, government officials were looking for just such a place for a facility to house prisoners of war."[4]

With the original capacity of the camp planned for 3,000 prisoners, the Army needed to acquire nearly 850 acres to house the POW barracks and assorted buildings required for support of such an operation. Ultimately the camp was enlarged to the point that some 5,800 POWs could be held there, and approximately 380 buildings of all types would be constructed on an expanded 950-acre site. This assortment of buildings included a hospital, a theater, a fire station, kennels, a blacksmith shop, and a bakery, in addition to numerous administration and barracks buildings.[5]

The final stages of the site-selection process in June and July 1942 saw a flurry of activity in Ste. Genevieve and St. Francois Counties, which comprised the area immediately around Weingarten. A swarm of federal surveyors, engineers, and Army personnel descended on the area, and their activity stirred up a storm of nervous speculation among local farmers who feared government seizure of their land. By July 1, 1942, residents knew that the government had authorized a $2 million project in the vicinity, though they were still in the dark about its nature and purpose. Rumors held that Weingarten and Hurryville, another small town in the area about five miles north of Farmington, were being considered as possible locations for placement of the unknown project. Some speculated that the government project was actually a large bombing range with an auxiliary airfield. Most of the people in the area figured the range would be built along the tracks of the Missouri-Illinois Railroad, between Weingarten and the Farmington junction, which was three miles north of Farmington proper. These opinions were solidified by the activities of surveyors, who had shown interest in a sizable tract four miles north of the junction along Highway D. The ground they examined was almost entirely in Ste. Genevieve County, with a small portion lying in St. Francois County.

The excitement grew exponentially when, just over a week later, a large surveying party checked into the Ste. Genevieve Hotel, where they were joined by engineers from Fort Leonard Wood. This band of planners included approximately fifty government surveyors there to multiply the work of a small office already situated in Ste. Genevieve. For several weeks the men in the first group had made numerous trips in the area between Ste. Genevieve and Farmington and were spotted researching land titles at the county seats in both Ste. Genevieve and St. Francois Counties.[6]

Government agents refused to disclose the exact nature and purpose of their activities. Finally, on July 13, 1942, the War Department officially acknowledged Weingarten as the site of a massive POW camp, a project for which approximately $2 million was allocated.[7] Farmers believed the government would seize their land at once, leaving them with standing crops in the fields and only thirty days' notice to vacate their property. Additional murmuring about a governmental tendency toward long delays in making payments for property seized in other areas only added to the uneasiness.[8]

As it turned out, the farmers' fears over swift federal action to remove them from their land were valid. Only three days after the announcement of the selection of the Weingarten site, the government began working to formally seize land for the camp. A condemnation suit to acquire nearly eight hundred acres of land was filed in a U.S. district court on July 16, 1942, and by July 23 the War Department had a real-estate office in the courthouse to move property for the camp from individuals to the government's control. U.S. district attorney Harry C. Blanton, who filed the suit, said that the orders to take legal action giving the government immediate possession of the land came straight from Washington, D.C. The price of the properties was to be announced after the land was already seized and would be determined only through subsequent legal proceedings.[9]

"It was just too fast," said Judy Schwartz Kreitler, whose great-grandmother, Mary Jaeger, was among those evicted by the government. "About a month before they bought up all the land, all these government cars kept showing up. Nobody knew what was going on. They were surveying before they even told [the landowners]."[10]

The Camp—A Welcome Arrival?

It might seem that residents of Weingarten and surrounding areas would be thrilled by all of the activity and the accompanying influx of money that would come into the area through construction contracts and goods and services used during the creation and operation of the camp. If nothing else, one might think simply the sheer number of new people with cash to spend would be a boon to the area economy and would provoke at least minimal enthusiasm in the local population. Not so, according to an account in the July 19, 1942, *St. Louis Globe-Democrat,* which said that most of Weingarten's ninety-nine inhabitants were greeting news of the camp with "dour reservations." Mrs. August Hogenmiller, who with her husband ran a general store held by members of their family since 1880, asked, "If they keep the prisoners fenced in and don't let them out or us in, what difference to business will it make yet?"[11]

Of course, the people most disrupted by Camp Weingarten's creation were those who were displaced by its construction. A dozen families, including the Jaegers, Harters, Sampsons, Donzes, and Stantons, lost part or all of their farms, where much of the land dated back to when it was originally homesteaded.

"I'm going to be raising Japanese instead of pureblood Hereford cattle," joked Henry Harter, who eventually would cede 150 acres to the government. His wife found it funny also that their son, Lieutenant Austin Harter, was in Alaska "keeping a lookout for the Japanese while Japanese are to be moved into our pasture." The Harters' comments reflected the initial belief that Japanese would be housed at Weingarten, but ultimately, the five thousand Italians who ended up there made it one of the largest camps in the country.

Any humor in the situation was lost on elderly people like Mary Jaeger, who was displaced by the camp. A newspaper account identifies her as being "past seventy, frail and bent with hard work." She spent a lifetime on the land, and for her, the forced move would be particularly difficult. "Now where do I go to die?" she asked tearfully. "To empty fields when we were married my husband and I came, and for fifty years through snow and rain I have helped to build our home so it would last."[12]

However abrupt the removal of the landowners, it seems that they were ultimately compensated fairly by the government for the land that was taken from them for the camp, at least according to Wilson Donze, a descendant of one of the displaced families. The Donze family was forced to sell twenty-four acres of good farmland inherited from Donze's maternal grandfather. His father was paid about $100 an acre by the government for the family farm when other comparable land was being sold for $50 an acre, said Donze.[13]

Camp Construction

Work began on the camp almost as soon as the government purchased the land. The *Farmington News* reported July 25 that the major contracts for the camp construction were out for bid. On August 10, 1942, McCarthy Brothers Construction of St. Louis signed a $1.6 million contract to construct the camp, and just three days later six carpenters began readying for the first task—building a one-thousand-foot rail spur to the camp. The Missouri-Illinois Railroad, the "Mike & Ike," served the camp, and on these side tracks into the camp the men built loading platforms, coal bins, and everything else that was necessary for complete rail service. Passenger service was discontinued on the Mike & Ike several years prior to the opening of the camp, "so when the G.I. and P.O.W. specials began rolling by it was a real treat to the folks along the line, especially the Lead Belt residents," wrote *The Lead Belt News.*[14]

Because of the great numbers of men needed for the construction phase, the U.S. Employment Service opened an office in an empty store in Weingarten to handle hiring for the camp. Union labor was a significant presence, with carpenters for the project being hired through the Farmington local and other types of laborers receiving work assignments through the Building and Construction Trades Union at Ste. Genevieve after they paid the $22 membership fee.[15]

In October, the first commanding officer, Lieutenant Colonel Floyd E. Thomas, arrived. Just a couple days later he hosted a visit to the camp by a group of area newspaper editors who were invited by the public affairs officer, Major Frank Reed. The usual government vagueness so popular during wartime applied to this field trip as well, and Reed smothered specific details about the Weingarten operation. At that point, the government was still acknowledging the installation only as an "alien internment camp" and would provide no other reference to the type or nationality of the people who would be interned there. The editors naturally had a lot of questions about the camp's operation, but most went unanswered. Adding to their frustration was the government's directive that any articles written about the camp had to be cleared before publication.

The official activation of Weingarten as a military post on November 4, 1942, nearly went unnoticed among the frenzied building activity at the camp. This was a nonevent, anyway, as the arrival of the prisoners was still more than six months away. As it was, any speeches or marching bands would have been drowned out by the sound of hammers and saws, so not many gave this milestone much notice.

Although the inhabitants of the village of Weingarten were less than enthusiastic about the project because of the way it steamrolled their peaceful burg, the residents of the greater region were happier about the government's plan, for it had created jobs in an area that was substantially underdeveloped. "The economic times were so bad that the people in the area welcomed news of the camp," recalled Stanley Drury, a local historian who also worked at Weingarten during its construction. "The people figured it would mean an economic boom. The expectations turned out to be greater than the reality, but the camp did provide jobs—good paying jobs. In building the camp, laborers at the camp earned $.625 an hour, while carpenters' helpers earned $.75 an hour and carpenters got $1.25," said Drury. "For those times, the wages were extremely high."[16]

Eighteen-year-old Bruce Starnes of nearby Doe Run, Missouri, got a job at the camp in September 1942, after a friend was hired at Weingarten. Starnes drove a truck carrying building material such as lumber and roofing material from the railroad to the construction sites. "There were gangs of carpenters, electricians, and roofers working on all kinds of buildings in various stages of completion, lined up one right after another," recalled Starnes, who stayed on through Christmas 1942, until that phase of the construction was finished. "We worked six days a week, and I remember a definite feeling of 'we've got to get this done.'"[17]

GIs Arrive at Weingarten

Following the activation of Weingarten in November 1942, servicemen assigned to the camp began to arrive, even while the installation was still under construction. Sergeant Quinton Bianco was among the first group of GIs to be stationed at Weingarten and recalled the day he came rolling in on the Mike & Ike:

At 10:30 A.M. the train stopped at a little group of houses. "This is Weingarten, fellows." Wondering just where the Camp was, we found out shortly enough as somebody spotted a guard tower beyond one of the cottages.

American GIs arriving at Weingarten. Courtesy of Edmee Viscardi.

There were quite a group of officers to greet us and they all looked rather pleased to see us for we were the first real troops to reach Weingarten. We embarked in a light drizzling rain, there was the command, "Right Face!" and away we went. Up the road about 100 yards, a turn left and there was the camp....

Yes, we felt pretty good when we broke ranks and discovered that fires were already burning in the barracks' stoves, cots with bedware were already unfolded and in place and an excellent hot meal of roast beef was ready in the mess hall.[18]

When Captain Eugene Phillips arrived on December 19, 1942, the lack of officers' quarters meant he and a buddy bunked in Farmington for a few weeks. "There were no living quarters, primarily for no water," recalled

Phillips, who ran the camp's supply operation. "I lived in Farmington with another lieutenant for a few weeks while all of us were trying to get ready to receive the prisoners."[19]

Mary Lou Correnti and her husband, Nicholas, were stationed at Fort Leonard Wood when their orders came to report to Weingarten. "I thought we were going someplace exotic," said Correnti, whose husband was an Italian-speaking U.S. Army doctor. "We went down after Christmas in 1942 and lived in Farmington with almost all of the other personnel from the camp."[20]

By January 1943, some two hundred GIs were already at the camp, with more showing up each day, dragging dufflebags and suitcases nine hundred yards to camp from the railway spur down the road. This walk afforded them their first good look at the surroundings of their new home, which for many would be quite an adjustment. When Weingarten's isolated location was combined with what was at first a somewhat limited transportation system, the result was a dearth of opportunities for recreation and entertainment. For young soldiers, this situation was virtually guaranteed to run morale at the camp into the ground. "One sore spot was the lack of transportation from camp, either eighteen miles west to Farmington or thirteen miles east to Ste. Genevieve," recalled Bianco. "One lone bus a night left for Ste. Genevieve at 6 pm and if one missed it he could wait many minutes on that lonely road outside the main gate to hitch-hike, so few were the autos on Highway 32."[21]

When Major General Allen Gullion, the provost marshal general in charge of all POW operations, visited Camp Weingarten in 1943, he noted that "the camp commander at Camp Weingarten desires a service club for his enlisted men. The enlisted men are overworked at this time and are located in a rural community, 65 miles from St. Louis, Mo. A service club should reduce the AWOL and desertion cases."[22]

The recognition of this situation by both camp leadership and local authorities as a hardship for the troops prompted quick and impressive cooperation between military and civilian officials. On January 28, Ste. Genevieve mayor Clarence J. Hinne asked for the creation of a recreation facility in his town to provide opportunities for servicemen during their off-duty hours. Additionally, Hinne sought to provide wholesome diversion for both servicemen and local residents. Envisioned was a series of activities such as dances, athletic events with area high schools, and the like, which would both provide entertainment and promote friendship among the military community and those in the surrounding area. In yet another component of this program, Hinne requested the names of individuals who

American GIs at Weingarten
pose in front of the Stockade
Office. Courtesy of Norma
Overall Jacob.

GI barracks at Camp Weingarten.
Courtesy of Kent Library, Southeast
Missouri State University.

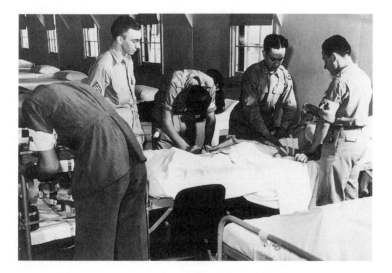

Lieutenant N. A. Correnti of the U.S. Army Medical Corps treats an
Italian prisoner at Camp Weingarten's post hospital. Photograph by
Buel White of the St. Louis Post-Dispatch, © 1943. Courtesy of the
St. Louis Post-Dispatch.

would be willing to entertain military personnel in their homes on national holidays, as a way of fostering interaction with those stationed at the camp as well as boosting morale of the servicemen, who in many cases were a long way from home. This request was favorably received, and on February 6, civic leaders met with a Weingarten representative to put in place a basic program of social events and athletic competitions.[23]

Later that month the first activity was held, a basketball game in which the Ste. Genevieve High School boys' squad defeated the men from Weingarten 36–26. Basketball was a big passion for people in the area, and the contests against area teams drew much interest, from both GIs and local residents. The sports section of *The Weingartener*, a camp newspaper for American personnel, devoted a fair amount of ink to coverage of the team.

The coach of one of the Weingarten squads wrote to the Ironton Jaycees to arrange a contest in December 1943, and one of the players recalled the scene when the GIs traveled there for a Monday night game:

> The Ironton gym wasn't any too big, but it was a nicely built court with a horse-shoe balcony, one end being a stage. The civilians were soaked two-bits to get in and perhaps they should have had their money refunded as the town team soaked [the] 408[th Military Police Company] 42 to 22.

> But if we didn't enjoy that ballgame at least we spent a sociable hour afterwards in the local drug store. Quite a number of the town's lasses were about and fortunately they were not very shy. Don Pfeister spotted two of them sitting alone in a booth and a half-hour later he had their addresses and promises to visit Weingarten soon.[24]

These athletic competitions with Weingarten servicemen squaring off against area teams eventually expanded to include softball—the *Ste. Genevieve Herald* reported that a squad from the 408th Military Police (MP) company lost to the Farmington Jaycees 6–5 in a tight June 1943 contest—as well as bowling and basketball leagues within the camp. The contests continued throughout the life of the camp.

This focus on positive community relations was emphasized at Weingarten. Following the tour of the camp for local newspaper editors in October 1942, in March 1943 a large group of World War I veterans from the American Legion and their wives were the guests of camp officials. A total of 107 people came from Farmington alone, and Legionnaires from the Missouri cities of Perryville, Ste. Genevieve, Bonne Terre, and Flat River were present as well. Each legion post group ate the noon meal ($.50 per person) at a different mess hall, was welcomed by Major William R. Dwyer, commanding officer at Weingarten, and was given a tour of the installation. In May, Missouri governor Forrest C. Donnell visited the camp, where he and other VIPs enjoyed a chicken dinner at the Officers' Club. Also in May 1943, the 407th MP Company participated in a parade at Farmington tied to the district convention of the American Legion being held there; a week later they marched in a Memorial Day parade in Ste. Genevieve.[25]

Weingarten officials held a number of "open house" events at the camp in conjunction with the opening of war-bond drives. Residents attending events at the camp clambered into Army trucks for narrarated tours of the POW facility and were treated to entertainment programs in the camp theater. To push bond sales, camp officials organized parades and guard-dog demonstrations in area towns and gave jeep rides around the countryside to those who purchased bonds.[26]

The Day the Prisoners Arrived

Despite the positive spin put on the Weingarten installation by the camp administration (as well as local officials thrilled by the dollars being pumped into the area's economy), the fact remained that a prisoner of war camp was being built. Throughout the period of camp construction and during the arrival of the first groups of prisoners, Weingarten residents were slightly apprehensive, wondering if perhaps they should be concerned for their own safety. Part of this was the fear of the unknown, but another part was the justified recognition that eventually the camp would be home to several thousand men who until only recently had been active enemies of the Allies, bearing arms against the United States.

That day finally came when the first POWs, Italians all, arrived on May 7, 1943. Edgy, armed MPs met the POWs at the Weingarten depot, which was situated at the end of the branch line from the main railway from Ste. Genevieve. They expected fierce and dangerous men—after all, these were the feared Black Shirts from Mussolini's Security Service, roughly comparable to Hitler's SS battalions.

"The whole post was on the 'alert' and no one allowed on pass. A shipment of prisoners was expected during the night and with 407 [one of the Military Police Escort Guard Companies] on guard practice around the camp, 408 [MPEG Company] had to be ready to go to the train and bring the PWs into camp," wrote Sergeant Bianco. "Everybody, except the cooks and clerks, had to lie on the bunks through the night fully clothed and ready on a moment's notice to put on field jackets and belts and 'fall in' outside the barracks."[27]

Azilee Lohrke McKeone of Cape Girardeau, Missouri, had gone to work at Weingarten in December 1942 and remembered clearly the tension at the camp on the day of the prisoners' arrival as the MPs escorted the Italian POWs from the depot, down a gravel road, and to the internment camp about nine hundred yards away. "It was cold and rainy, and there were guards every two feet from the train to the compound," recalled McKeone, "and here were these *very* young boys in shorts, tee shirts and sandals (I think some went into service at fourteen in Italy) who came here from North Africa, glad to be in America and looking forward to warm food and clean beds."[28]

Prisoners arriving at Weingarten. Courtesy of Edmee Viscardi.

Francis Schwartz lived across the road from the north gate of the camp and talked about the commotion accompanying the arrival of the prisoners. "That was where the prisoners came in," he recalled, gesturing at the entryway. "The depot people wouldn't ever tell us when the prisoners were arriving." Added his wife, Rita: "I heard a CLANG, CLANG, CLANG from the depot. The prisoners were being marched off and walked across to the camp. They were a rough looking group with beards. I later learned that the first group of prisoners were Black Shirts."[29]

Yvonne Donze of Ste. Genevieve was nineteen when she went to work at the camp. She started work on New Year's Day 1943, after applying for work at Weingarten through civil service. She was selected to help with processing the newly arrived prisoners. "They brought them in big cattle cars on the railroad," she said. "I was one of four girls sitting at a table with a typewriter and an interpreter. Some of these men had rags around their feet and hadn't seen a woman in ages. That was the most exciting thing."[30]

For these weary soldiers, coming to Weingarten was often a big relief, and for reasons that went far beyond the chance to look at a pretty girl. It would be the first time they had been in one place for any more than a couple days since the start of the war. The men—mostly veterans of the fighting in North Africa—had endured many months of hardship as combatants, and although conditions in Africa often did improve for them after being captured, the temporary camps in which they were held until they could be sent to the United States were often still quite primitive. Also, they had just taken a trip across the Atlantic lasting anywhere from eighteen days to a month under crowded and occasionally dangerous conditions with the ever-present threat of submarine attack.

Even though things improved substantially upon their arrival in the United States, past lessons taught them to always doubt that a pleasant situation would last. On the train ride from Norfolk, Virginia, to Weingarten, Giuseppe Zazza kept thinking the comfortable conditions were some sort of trick. "It was paradise! We were in first-class, and we thought, could it be propaganda?" recalled Zazza. "In the dining cars, the tables were already set, and we went up ten at a time without guards." After a while, the reality set in that in many ways, the prisoners had left the war far, far behind. "It seemed like we were civilians again," said Zazza. "We carried nothing with us on the trip, except the uniforms we had worn in battle. Everyone aboard the train was impressed by glimpses of Chicago and St. Louis before we got to Weingarten."[31]

After months of experiencing hardship and danger on the battlefield, the prisoners were understandably almost overcome with emotion at the prospect of enjoying comfortable beds and regular nourishment. "In the mess hall we found jugs of milk, both white and chocolate, pork chops, soup, bread, all so good! But I still didn't believe it. After the meal, I slipped four or five slices of bread in my pocket because maybe tomorrow would be different," recalled POW Ennio Calabresi of his arrival at Weingarten. "Gradually we got used to eating regularly, and then we started getting more pasta instead of the things we didn't like so well, like corn. Soon, all the American officers and enlisted men were eating at our mess, because the food was cooked better."[32]

Their first meal did not belie the treatment they would receive during the rest of their stay. In June 1943, editors of a number of Missouri newspapers were invited to tour Camp Weingarten, and the *Farmington Press* provided an account of the visit, testifying to the excellent manner in which the POWs were treated:

From our observations at the camp we can safely say that every term of the Geneva Convention relating to the care of PWs is being carried out at Weingarten....[T]here is no question but that they will have a healthy respect and liking for this country, rather than a burning hatred as would be logical if they were ill-treated while here.[33]

Sergeant Bianco believed that the Italians' internment went so smoothly was because of the way they were treated. "We never did have much trouble with those PWs, for they must have realized what a good spot they were in," wrote Bianco. "No worries until the end of the war, and excellent food and shelter given them."[34]

Though the prisoners' early days in camp were the most stressful for all concerned—the prisoners, the guards, the civilians who worked in the camp, and the people living in the nearest towns—once a routine was established, everyone relaxed markedly. During these first weeks, the comforts of good food, hot showers, and clean beds were still new, and the POWs had not yet had the time to worry about the length of time they would have to wait until they could go home.

Conditions at the Camp

Once arrived, the POWs began to get their bearings. Aldo Ferraresi kept a diary of his time at Camp Weingarten, and those pages describe the wonder he felt as he quickly became familiar with the place.

"We are busy discovering our new 'home,' the PX, the 'club' and so forth. We eat very, very well," wrote Ferraresi. "We are issued lightweight pants (long and short), underwear, a strange-looking jacket and an even stranger hat. These replace our uniforms, which are tattered. I save my insignia of rank and the insignia of my regiment."[35]

The number of prisoners at Weingarten grew rapidly: by September 30, 1943, there were 992 officers and 3,515 enlisted prisoners of war housed at Weingarten. Their new home within the POW camp encompassed some 160 acres within the nearly 1,000 acre military reservation and was ringed by two tall, lighted, barbed-wire fences with a barbed-wire overhang. Twelve standard octagonal watchtowers lined the perimeter, each thirty-five feet high with a line of fire possible in any direction. Guards armed with machine guns manned the towers in rotating eight-hour shifts.

Initially, three companies of Military Police Escort Guard (MPEG) troops guarded the compound. While work was being finalized on the camp during the spring months of 1943, the three MPEG companies that eventually provided security at the Weingarten camp were in the final phases of their training across the state at Camp Clark, with six other MPEG companies that were to be used at other Missouri POW camps. On March 21, 1943, they arrived at Weingarten after being activated as the 407th, 408th, and 410th MPEG Companies.

Thirty-four guard dogs, mostly German shepherds, patrolled the camp perimeter at night and growled out problems in the unattended warehouses after hours. Although Weingarten ultimately did not experience significant problems with escape, the uneven terrain in and around the camp was a source of concern. The illumination on the fence caused many shadows, and there were "many blank spots in the field of fire from the towers because of the many gullies and hills running through and around the camp."[36]

Ultimately, the guards in the towers watching the POWs ended up wholly unarmed, carrying no ammunition, a fact that understandably would be kept secret from the prisoners. After a young American serviceman died from a wound accidentally self-inflicted while on duty in one of the towers, the guards carried no rounds in their weapons. This was probably a good idea for other reasons as well. "Continual guard duty could become mighty boring, and the boys were starting to show it with some foolish actions. [A soldier named] Lutz, one night on guard, pulled the trigger of his gun to see if it was loaded—it was," recalled one Weingarten MP. "Another time, Bob Henderson swore up and down that the tower machine gun 'went off by itself.'"[37]

An American soldier mans one of the Weingarten guard towers. Courtesy of Kent Library, Southeast Missouri State University.

The nice thing about a camp freshly built from the ground up was that everything was new and modern. Weingarten benefited from its water supply pouring forth from its five deep wells, and the post engineers were proud of the installation's sanitary sewage system, noting that it was composed entirely of underground pipes. A visitor from the Swiss Legation, Dr. Benjamin Spiro, observed that the toilets at Weingarten were all of the modern "flush" variety and that hot and cold running water was available throughout the camp.[38]

Roads running through the camp were made from local limestone, and buildings were constructed from wood and Celotex, a composition board used frequently for insulation that looked for all the world like regular old tarpaper. The hospital, administration building, and nurses' quarters were steam heated, and pot-bellied stoves warmed the rest of the buildings.

In each of the POW compounds was a building that served as its administrative hub. These 20-by-100-foot structures were divided into three sections. The front third served as the orderly room for that compound, where the administrative details of the section (things such as duty rosters, permissions for sick call, etc.) were handled. The middle third of the building was for supply storage, and the rear section of the building served as the company day room, where informal recreation and relaxation took place.

Weingarten had a total of four compounds for the internees, and a fifth outside the camp fence housed the U.S. personnel guarding them. Some of the buildings were constructed on concrete foundations, while others sat on wooden posts sheared close to the ground. Nearly all had wood floors; only the ones that would receive the most consistently heavy use had floors made of poured concrete.[39] Each of the barracks in the enlisted men's compound held between thirty-four and thirty-six men, while officers were assigned one or two to an "apartment" of sorts, composed of a living room and bedroom. These arrangements provided 40 square feet of space per enlisted man or 120 square feet per officer.[40] This different treatment was intentional and typical of military protocol concerning the internment of officers at Weingarten and at other camps around the country. "There was little association or even communications between the officer compounds and those of the soldiers," recalled Captain Phillips, who headed the supply division and was at Weingarten during the entirety of its operation. "They just had no reason or occasion to interact."[41]

In addition to maintaining living quarters separate from the enlisted men, officers were also given their own recreation and canteen areas. This disparate treatment even went as far as the monthly allotments made to POWs. Each month of their confinement, enlisted prisoners received a flat

$3 payment in camp script to use in the canteen to purchase toiletries and other necessities such as cigarettes, candy, and beer. Contrasted with that was the payment received by officers: lieutenants and captains, $20 per month; majors and colonels, $30 per month; general officers, $40 per month. Officers did not have to work but could certainly choose to do so, and many augmented their monthly allotment with another $20 or so a month they could earn in the POW labor program.

What little interaction existed among ranks was a result of enlisted men serving as orderlies for the Italian officers. Those officers not of a rank eligible to have an orderly or aide-de-camp could pay enlisted men to do their laundry and perform similar tasks. As such, the work detail for some of the enlisted men involved not laboring as a farm hand or fixing shoes in the shoe repair shop but in hauling baskets of dirty clothing from the POW officers' quarters to the camp laundry.[42]

In recreation, too, the officers had special privileges and were accorded a great deal of freedom. The camp commander permitted these men to leave the camp during the day to take walks in groups of twenty to thirty, accompanied by a lone American officer. "No difficulty has been experienced with prisoners on these conducted tours outside of the camp," noted an inspector to the camp.[43] Even the clothing issued to the prisoners reflected this difference in status. While enlisted POWs had "PW" painted on the back of their shirts and on each pant leg, officers' clothes bore no such markings.

Interaction with Employees at the Camp

Although civilians employed at the camp quickly got used to working closely with the POWs, there was often an initial period of unease. "I was pretty scared when I first went to work. The hospital was inside one of the compounds and we girls had to walk through an area where there were a lot of Italians. But we pretty soon learned that they were all just human beings, and treated us with much respect," said Susie Henderson, who worked as a dental assistant at the camp. "There were about thirty Italian enlisted men working nearby, and one Italian doctor. They were nice men. I still have the group photograph they all signed for me."[44]

There were six people in Henderson's immediate section of the hospital, and one of her counterparts was married to an American GI who was being held as a POW in Germany. "Every day during lunch hour she'd take a special treat to some prisoner-patient in the hospital, hoping someone would be doing the same for her husband."

When working together on a daily basis, it didn't take long for the civilian employees of the camp and the POWs to develop a certain unspoken

The Italian POW staff at the Weingarten hospital. Courtesy of Terry Culver.

camaraderie, even if the language barrier prevented a deeper friendship. "Of course, communication was a bit of a problem," recalled Pauline Laws McKamey, who worked in the camp dental clinic. "But, by learning a few Italian words and making a lot of signs, we could communicate with the prisoners fairly well, especially those working in the clinic. We might have been a little fearful the first week or two, but the friendly, happy-go-lucky attitude of the prisoners soon dispelled that fear."[45]

Although the civilian employees of the camp certainly enjoyed having the POWs around, the camp authorities did not tolerate any violations of the strict rules that governed interactions between the internees and camp staff. For example, it was strictly forbidden for prisoners to touch the employees. "One time when I was working in the dental clinic, one of the prisoners came up to me and stroked my hair," recalled Yvonne Donze, who began working at the camp as a nineteen-year-old. "My boss saw him do it, and the prisoner was taken to the stockade."

Another prisoner who worked in the camp offices figured out a more appropriate and ingenious way to demonstrate his fondness and friendship for Donze, without putting himself at risk of getting into trouble. "He called me on the phone and said he had a present for me, and I said, 'Oh?'" recalled Donze. "He said 'Un momento,' and then he sang Schubert's 'Ave Maria' for me. He had the most magnificent voice. He could have been an operatic tenor."[46]

Guards at Weingarten also operated with a great deal of trust when it came to the POWs. "The first day I saw these five prisoners in the back of the wagon holding pitchforks, with a guard at the front with his back to them," recalled Teresa Drury, who began working at the camp while she was a seventeen-year-old. "I thought, 'Oh no, they are going to kill him!' but I found out that it wasn't that kind of situation at all."[47]

Drury was hired to work as a memorandum receipt clerk for the quartermaster's office and had special memories of one prisoner, Augusto Bier, who ran errands for the office and kept the place clean. "It was fantastic," she recalled of the close bond all in the office formed with the prisoner. "To communicate, I used my high school Latin, he used Italian and we would pantomime to get the meaning."

Bier made the daily requisitioning run at the camp bakery each morning, bringing a basket full of baked goods to the staff of the quartermaster officer. With these warm rolls and his equally warm personality, he became a favorite of the staff in the quartermaster's office, and at the end of the war they held a going-away party of sorts. They weren't allowed to provide alcohol to the prisoners, but Drury recalled a way that they got around the prohibition.

"The interior walls of the buildings were unfinished 2 x 4 studs," she recalled. "We'd pour a drink and set it on one of the boards where the prisoners could reach it and then turn away. When we'd turn back around, the drink would be gone."[48]

Augusto Bier (on left) with Italian POWs at Weingarten. Courtesy of Edmee Viscardi.

Upon closure of the camp, the staff of the quartermaster's office gave Bier several farewell gifts, including a pocketknife, handkerchiefs, some socks, a bottle of whiskey, and some cigars. Joking that he could always sell the gifts if he ran short of funds, Bier said, "This must mean I'm a capitalist now" and stuck the cigar between his teeth.[49]

Phillips also recalled the special fondness he felt for Bier:

Most of us developed some special friendships with prisoners. My favorite was August Beer [*sic*] who was from northern Italy and of

Austrian ancestry. He was my office handy man (I was the camp's director of supply) and was with me almost my entire tour of duty there.

August was a delightful young married fellow with two children. He always carried the children's photograph, and we'd sometimes see him secretly studying it. At our office Christmas parties, he received many small gifts and treats, especially from the women on the staff. I have a photo of the two of us saying goodbye as he boarded the train at the start of his long journey home.[50]

Drury also had contact with Bier after he departed the Weingarten camp to return home. "He wrote and asked for a care package after he'd gone back to Italy," she said. Bier's family had suffered during the war, and he faced challenges upon his return. While at Weingarten he had learned that bombing in his hometown had blinded one of his children. "They were just people like we were—just nice people," said Donze. "They didn't want to be fighting either."[51]

Drury recalled several occasions in which the prisoners were helpful and compassionate. One day the prisoners cooked food for the workers in the quartermaster depot, where she was employed. She went to fetch the goodies but fell on the wooden sidewalk and sprained her ankle while carrying the bowls and platters back to the office. "I was a bloody mess," she remembered, "with splinters in my hands and food strewn everywhere."

Prisoners were prohibited from touching American personnel, but the POWs who saw her fall were the only ones nearby, and so they began yelling to draw attention and to attract assistance for Drury.[52] On another occasion, a woman who worked with Drury was thrown from a horse near the camp stables where some prisoners were working. Fearing that the woman had broken her neck, they climbed the fence to help her.[53]

Many times these relationships continued through correspondence after the war, as in the case of Susie Henderson. She corresponded with "Johnny," as they called him, a prisoner who worked as the interpreter for the dental office, until his death in 1962. While working at Weingarten, the two formed a unique arrangement that allowed Johnny to circumvent the unique difficulties love sometimes imposes. Johnny had a girl back home that his family had arranged for him to marry, but he was in love with someone else. Because Johnny worried that his family would find out he was mailing letters to his true love and not to the one they had selected for him, Henderson addressed and mailed the letters to his girlfriend in Italy for him. Her handwriting on the envelopes was intended to mislead the small-town postmaster who might have otherwise noticed and fed the information straight into the local gossip mill. Henderson also recalled that some of the camp personnel liked Johnny so much that they would sneak him out of the installation hidden in the trunk of their car and take him into town with them on weekends.[54]

Naturally, this wasn't the only bit of mischief that took place between employees and prisoners. Floyd Fadler drove for a local bus line, hauling prisoners back and forth between Weingarten and their work site in a limestone quarry and kiln nearby. "Right at first, the prisoners were a little rough, but they calmed down before long and were really nice," recalled Fadler. Weingarten authorities first sent a guard and interpreter along for the trip, but soon it was just the interpreter. The interpreter carried a rifle, said Fadler, but "he used to do some of the driving while I took a nap, and he'd even let one of the prisoners hold his gun." If the bus got a flat tire, "the prisoners would make me go sit under a tree while they changed it," recalled Fadler.

With the Italians driving through the area every day, the children in houses lining the route from the highway to the quarry began to anticipate their passing. "It got to be so that every day, those kids would line up and wave, and the Italians would throw them candy," said Fadler. "Sometimes I would bring my little daughter with me, and the men would fight over who got to hold her on their lap during the drive."

The men got along well together. The prisoners invited Fadler to dinner frequently and gave him small gifts such as a handcrafted cigarette case, which they engraved with a nail and hammer, and a ring they made from melting and recasting silver dollars. They got to be such good friends that Fadler began stopping the bus each night at a tavern on the way back from the kiln so that the everyone could have a cold beer to crown the day's work. "Every night, they'd all get off and have one beer, then get back on," said Fadler, "all except one guy who never got off the bus."

Pretty soon, Weingarten authorities got wise to what was happening and put an end to this POW happy hour, warning Fadler "never to stop the bus again except for an emergency." The prisoners suspected the lone man who never came in for a drink had tattled on them, and pretty soon he was no longer riding the bus with them. Fadler believed that angry, thirsty POWs had bumped off the teetotaler, but no evidence in the camp records supports this.[55]

Perhaps it was because of the way the camp sprang up from an empty plot of pasture ground to a bustling installation home to thousands of people that civilian workers at Weingarten seemed to have mostly positive experiences during their time at the camp. "Everyone was in the same boat," said Edmee Viscardi, whose husband, Paul, was a GI at the camp. "It was fun getting to know a lot of new people, and really sharing this big adventure that we were together all a part of."[56]

In December 1943, the camp commander, Colonel H. H. Glidden, gave awards to those civilian employees whose performance ratings had been good for at least a six-month period. Among those recognized were nine men working in the engineering section, including John Uding, August Wehner, Hy Eisenbeis, Joseph Trautmen, Richard Klein, and Walter Baum. Judging from these names, the letter to the War Department (printed in chapter 1) asserting that Ste. Genevieve County was as German as Germany, was right on target.

The camp hospital also recognized the performance of its staff with a banquet to celebrate the completion of its first full year of operation. The dinner, held January 3, 1944, included fifty-seven military personnel, fifteen civilians, and seventy-two POWs, three of whom were doctors. The feast celebrated the fact that the hospital experienced no loss of life during the first year of operation. In addition to the fully equipped 265-bed camp hospital, this group operated four smaller clinics, one in each of the four compounds, that were staffed by POW doctors. Sick call averaged eighty men daily, and average patient count in the hospital was about one hundred, including both GIs and prisoners.[57]

"The hospital was equipped with the very best medical equipment, as was the dental clinic within the hospital," recalled dental assistant McKamey. "[We had] chairs for four dentists, a waiting room, office, a supply room, and a laboratory."[58]

One employee who didn't win any awards at the banquet that evening was Edgar J. Brady. Brady, who served as the chief clerk in the quartermaster's office, was arrested at the camp in November 1943, charged with accepting a bribe from a Chicago businessman in connection with the sale of thirty-four thousand pounds of scrap shoes.

Brady conspired with Sam Korelstein, a Chicago junk dealer, on at least one occasion when Korelstein paid Brady to learn competitors' bids on lots of scrap shoes, said Gerald B. Norris, head of the FBI's St. Louis office. Norris asserted that Korelstein, who was arrested in Milwaukee on the same day Brady was taken into custody, approached the clerk with the bribe on November 3, 1943, during a meeting at the camp. Upon learning from Brady that competitors' bids ranged from $.01 to $.02 a pound, Korelstein immediately submitted a winning bid of $.025 a pound for the shoes and assumed the agreement to buy the lot of scrap shoes from the government. The day after the purchase, Korelstein met Brady in a Ste. Genevieve hotel room and paid him $200 for the information.[59]

Relationship between Locals and Servicemen

Like many other communities, Ste. Genevieve and the surrounding areas suddenly found themselves short of eligible young males because of the war effort. Understandably, the local girls were drawn to the GIs—including many who hailed from such "exotic" places as Connecticut and California—and the soldiers naturally returned their interest. They met during formal functions at the camp such as USO dances, as well as during informal, everyday exchanges that took place at Weingarten or in one of the towns nearby, where some personnel found housing or came for entertainment. Local historian Stanley Drury estimated that by his count, at least twenty-five marriages took place between servicemen and local women as a result of this interaction.

American officers at Weingarten relax during off-duty hours. Courtesy of Norma Overall Jacob.

"With warm, summerlike weather, the men were roaming over the countryside with their 'Class A' passes and came back with glowing reports about the hospitality of the nearby towns of Ste. Genevieve, Farmington, Flat River, River Mines, Fredericktown, etc.," recalled one Weingarten GI. "People were very friendly and there were many available girls—civilian competition being nil as the draft boards had plucked out most of the males."[60]

Especially during the period of initial construction on the camp, when there wasn't much to be found within the Weingarten perimeter but mud and sawdust, most servicemen found housing in towns nearby. Later, once GI housing was available on the Camp Weingarten grounds for single and enlisted men, it would be mostly officers and their families who resided in the surrounding communities, and they proved to be positive, active participants in their surroundings. As a local newspaper wrote, "Surely there was never a better group of army officers and their families than those stationed at Camp Weingarten. Many of them resided in Farmington and Ste. Genevieve, being active workers in various local organizations. They were greatly missed when they had to leave."[61]

Recreation for Servicemen at the Camp

Life at Weingarten could veer to the boring and lonely side of the road for a young GI stationed there. Most of the men were far from home, and the camp sat seventy miles from the action of the big city in St. Louis. However, a vigorous athletic and social schedule filled with tennis matches, basketball games, movies, and dances helped to ease the isolation, and the American soldiers enjoyed a recreational menu that surpassed that offered to the POWs, if only because the GIs had the chance to go on dates.

Intramural contests held among the individual American GIs and their units were an immensely popular way to pass the time and generated a lot of interest and sometimes good-natured controversy. For instance, following a table-tennis tournament in the spring of 1945, the newly crowned champ, Private First Class Stuart Eutsler, was transferred from Weingarten. Naturally, the first runner-up, Private First Class William F. "Red" McCormick, wanted to know if he automatically assumed the title, and the hubbub centered on whether he could accept it by default or if he would "have to fight all-comers for the vacated Eutsler throne."[62]

McCormick was not only famous for his skills at table tennis but also for his deftness at sketching likenesses of fellow servicemen and others at the camp. The *Ste. Genevieve Herald* carried an account of his activities in its regular gossip column:

> Long recognized as Weingarten's Mount Parnassus, garden of the arts, Barracks 214 has taken an even tighter grip on its claim to being the camp's home of the muses. Music and literature have long flourished there, but now the graphic arts have moved in and taken over with Pfc. William (Red) McCormick setting up shop for the professional production of portrait sketches.
>
> Rates are two dollars for a handsome likeness in color and business is booming with sittings scheduled for every empty interval in the arduous guard routine. The list of satisfied McCormick clients promises to duplicate the camp's full strength report since to date there has been unanimous agreement on the artistic excellence of the McCormick product and on the unfailing verisimilitude of the sketches.

An arts and crafts shop, which was "somewhat smaller than a barracks but considerably larger than a sentry booth," was situated in a building near the post's theater and was overseen by Corporal Wilbert Irvine. The shop was available to American servicemen during off-duty hours, and patrons could produce wallets, key cases, footlockers, lighters, and ashtrays, as well as putter with plastics, jewelry, painting, and sculpture.

Irvine, who taught arts and crafts as a civilian in Buffalo, New York, was there to give advice and to assist as needed, as well as "to instruct neophytes in such important matters as just where on a lathe the materials go and fingers don't."[63]

A *Herald* reporter wanted to ask questions while visiting the shop one afternoon in April 1945 but thought the better of it. "There was also a sergeant busy with a piece of wood and a jig saw. We don't know what he was making," wrote the newspaperman. "We didn't ask. The information we might gain didn't seem quite worth the finger he might lose."[64]

To add to the list of social opportunities at the camp, in mid-August 1943 a club was established for off-duty noncommissioned officers and others to relax and socialize. Master Sergeant George A. Baumeister was elected as president of the organization, and First Sergeant Warner H. Waller served as chairman. Initial membership was 105 thirsty

American servicemen at Weingarten enjoyed recreation and fellowship. Souvenir folder of PW camp at Weingarten. Courtesy of Edmee Viscardi.

GIs. It didn't take long for GIs to warm up the club, which stayed open two hours later than the PX, another popular hangout.

"At first, not many of the non-coms would drop in but soon we found it was nice to walk up there for a beer or coke after the PX had closed. However, the most popular feature of the club was the table on which red-hot poker games were played. And the stakes were not small either—

Murphy won 60 dollars one night," recalled one of the MPs stationed at Weingarten. "Dues were a dollar a month, fair enough to be able to sit down on a wicker davenport and take it easy while sipping a coke, listening to the jukebox and reading the paper. One of the non-coms at Headquarters must have had a little 'pull' as a telephone booth was installed in the club and, with no charge to call Ste. Gen, that phone got a workout."[65]

"What would an N. C. O. Club be without music other than the juke box?" asked *The Lead Belt News* in its recap of the camp's history in 1946. "They were not long in discovering several talented musicians, so a jive and hill-billy band was organized. To those of you who were privileged to hear them, you will admit they were plenty good.... They certainly played a major role in the life of the club. The N. C.'s are due much credit on forming such a good club and the splendid operation of it for indeed it was an added credit to the camp."[66]

This "hillbilly ensemble" must have made quite an impression, as their talents were also referenced in *The Weingartener*, the official newspaper of the camp for American servicemen and civilian employees of the camp. "The club's hillbilly ensemble—once heard never forgotten," said the paper, "has distinguished itself by rolling mountain music down a steeper grade than has ever before been attempted."[67]

Naturally, parties and dances were popular pastimes for the American servicemen, and during the period of Weingarten's operation, a number of events were held that brought orchestras and other live music outfits to play at the camp, along with truckloads of girls from the surrounding communities. Typical of these types of events was the "All Post Party" of April 15, 1945. Sponsored by the headquarters detachment, the fest featured a crooner-turned-GI, identified by the *Ste. Genevieve Herald* as Private Hentz, "formerly of Abe Lyman's orchestra," with music provided for the dancers by Kassel's Cape Girardeau Swing Timers. The party was a hit, enough so that a repeat was planned for June 16, when the Jefferson Barracks orchestra would be on hand to "give out with the rhythm," with the party starting when "cymbals begin clanging at 8 P.M."[68]

The encore event was kicked off by a picnic supper at the Officers' Club, which ended up being moved indoors by rain. Hosted by the medical detachment, guests that night danced to a thirteen-piece band from Jefferson Barracks. "The dance was scheduled to close at midnight, and at midnight the band left the stand. Since no official poll was taken on the question, it is impossible to report whether it was the inclement weather or the charm of the Headquarters and Medical Detachments that kept the guests circling the dance floor to canned music after midnight."[69]

Of course, not every dance was a hit. One Weingarten GI recalled a dance in December 1943 that just didn't seem to go well:

A dance at Weingarten on a Friday night…was a royal flop. First, the camp orchestra got peeved because they weren't allowed the use of the Camp's drums at an outside night club (the "Red Rooster") and refused to play, the "refreshments" were nothing but cake and sour punch, and the bright lights were on the seating area instead of the dance floor. (Guess the chaperone who brought the batch of Ste. Genevieve girls was playing it safe.)

The records for dancing were played over the movie sound system and it just didn't lend much atmosphere to a dance when one couldn't see where the music came from. But if that wasn't all bad enough, the lights were suddenly turned off at 11—the dance was over, just like that!![70]

A dance held the following month was a much more successful affair. The live band, composed of eight GIs and four POWs, kept things moving on the dance floor, but the real action came after the music ended. "Everybody claimed to have a darn good time at the dance," said Quinton Bianco, "but there was one sour note afterwards." It seems that a few of the prisoners were lingering around the theater, having helped with the decorations. Some of the girls who were there, feeling sorry for the prisoners, asked them to dance. About the same time, GIs who had just come down from an eight-hour shift on the guard towers found out that the prisoners were dancing with American girls and headed for the theater. "We couldn't blame those fellows for getting sore," wrote Bianco in his diary. "Here they were missing a dance because they were supposed to be guarding the PWs and the same prisoners were at the dance. Quite a fuss about it at HQ the next day and it wasn't to happen again."[71]

Werner Waller was one of those who came from a world that was far outside of Ste. Genevieve and St. Francois Counties. The native of Waynesboro, Mississippi, was stationed at Weingarten from November 1942 through early 1944. He passed his free time "just bumming around, going to shows or whatever," in Farmington and Ste. Genevieve.

A bus route circulated between Farmington, Weingarten, and Ste. Genevieve, hauling soldiers, locals, and civilian employees at the camp, whoever needed a lift from one spot to the next. Waller and other soldiers rode the bus to the clubs in Ste. Genevieve and the area's "honky-tonks," as he called them, finding entertainment when and where they could.

In the end, however, the yoke of domesticity fell heavily on Waller after he was snared by the charms of a Ste. Genevieve beauty, and his days of "just bumming around" came to an end. They married and what he thought would be just a temporary stop in Missouri became permanent.[72]

"There was a lot of intermingling of cultures because people from Ste. Genevieve would not normally meet people from so many different parts of the country," said local historian Drury.[73]

Weingarten GIs, like servicemen everywhere, could be endlessly creative in their quest to meet the local girls. On one trip to Fort Leonard Wood for training, soldiers riding in the back of a truck scribbled their names and addresses on slips of paper torn from a note pad and tossed handfuls out as they passed through little towns on the way. Nobody seemed to notice the papers fluttering down from the back of the truck until the men rolled through Steelville, Missouri. There, three teenage girls, hearing the calls from the soldiers, spotted the pieces of paper and dashed after them. "When we rounded the corner, it seemed the whole female population was chasing the slips," recalled one GI on the back of the truck that day. "And, by golly, some of the fellows did, later, receive letters from Steelville lasses."[74]

Reportedly, the first wedding bells rang at Weingarten only a month after the arrival of the prisoners. Lieutenant Louis F. Cartier and Margaret F. Sands tied the knot on June 5, 1943, at the Weingarten church with an honor guard standing in ceremony. The groom was so overtaken by nervous anticipation of the event that he forgot to pay for the marriage license. Fortunately other American officers collected enough to secure the important document and provide official sanction to the union. At the end of the ceremony, the bride and groom were "romantically enthroned in a GI chariot" and transported in a convoy around the camp area. Yvonne Donze recalled that all the prisoners who were walking in the compound cheered for the newly married couple riding in the jeep. Another American officer held his wedding at the camp itself with one of the prisoners playing the bridal march on the piano.[75]

Visiting the Camp

Growing up, Cleva Laws lived near the Weingarten camp, and she remembered visiting it as a teen with some friends who knew soldiers there. Although she came from the small town of Millerswitch, Missouri, she went to high school at Ste. Genevieve and recalled the attraction the American soldiers at the camp held for the local girls. "There were eight of us girls who graduated in 1944, and that spring a couple of times we all went to visit," said Laws. "We walked from Ste. Genevieve High School over to Weingarten or sometimes would ride the bus they had that went between Weingarten, Ste. Genevieve, and Farmington. The fare was $.10 for us, which I think was less than the regular rate."

Security wasn't so tight in the camp that getting in was any problem. "We never needed a pass to get into the camp," said Laws. "We knew the soldiers and went as a group, so we were always able to walk right in." One might think that it would be intimidating for a teenage girl to waltz into a POW camp, but this thought never crossed the minds of Laws or her friends. "We really went there on a lark, and it turned out to be a lot of fun," she said. "We went there to see some of our older friends who worked in the camp and of course wanted to have a chance to talk to the [American] soldiers there."

The GIs were also glad for the diversion. Most were there because they had been injured or had some other minor medical problem that precluded them from being sent to the front. Though many longed to be where the action was, they surely didn't mind the opportunity for a little flirting, and several even ended up married to Laws's friends who were there that day.

Though they went to visit the American men at Weingarten, Laws remembered how the girls were presented with a closer look at the Italian POWs as well as they strolled through the camp. "As we walked around, we could see the prisoners in their barracks. They were kept back from us a little bit, but we were able to talk with them through these screened-in porch areas where they were," she recalled. "Many actually spoke quite good English."

One of the prisoners used his ingenuity to augment the camp diet, remembers Laws. "He had created a sort of 'sticker' or hook that he was using to catch small animals," she said. "While we were there, he showed us a possum that he had caught with it and that he was cooking." Laws said that she and her friends just accepted the quarry at face value. "We didn't think too much about it," she said. "It was just another way to get by when everything was rationed. Probably more than anything we were impressed by his ingenuity at getting more meat."[76]

Norma Overall Jacob lived in Farmington during the years of the camp's operation and remembers the prisoners being trucked through town on their way to work at Butterfield's Greenhouse. She was almost twenty years old when the camp opened.

"Us girls would be walking along the road when the trucks with the Italians would come rolling through town," remembered Jacob. "They'd be going crazy, waving and whistling to us. It was like they had never seen a girl before. Of course, we'd smile real big and wave right back to them."[77]

Though Laws and Jacob enjoyed these brief encounters with the Italian POWs, there were a couple of incidents that had area inhabitants a bit more on edge.

POW Escape

On September 10, 1944, two prisoners managed to escape from Weingarten after digging their way under the fence surrounding the camp. The men got as far as Ste. Genevieve, twelve miles to the east, before being apprehended. The MPs fetched the Italians from Ste. Genevieve without incident after citizens notified them that the men were seeking help at houses on South Fifth Street.[78]

One of the residents who reported the escapees was Catherine Papin. Her husband had left at 2:30 P.M. that day to work the evening shift at the Mississippi Lime Plant, and so she was alone with her small children when the two men came to her house and knocked on the door. "I saw these two fellows walking across the fields as if they were avoiding the road," Papin said. "They came down the hill, knocked at my door, and asked if I had a room they could rent for the night."

The prisoners' dress and thick accents gave Papin an immediate clue that something was up. The men were wearing brown uniforms and each carried a heavy winter coat on what was a very hot day. "I told them, no, I had a family and no empty room, so then they tried my neighbor, and she told them to go to the hotel."

As soon as the prisoners left her doorstep, Papin called a tavern nearby— Toad's Saloon—and asked for help. The barkeep wouldn't leave his place untended. "I was pretty alarmed, because I had several small children at home at the time," said Papin. "I called the bartender again, and told him to watch for the military police and to stop them when they went by."

By now, the escapees had climbed into an empty boxcar at the feed store nearby. They were hiding inside when the MPs arrived, though the MPs checked the boxcar and didn't see anything. The American soldiers checked the boxcar a second time at Papin's insistence and then collared the two men, who were each carrying a block of cheese and a long butcher knife.

"You see, the boxcar was lined with brown paper, and the men's uniforms were brown. They blended right in. They almost didn't get caught," said Papin. "If they hadn't looked a second time, those policemen would have thought I was full of baloney."

The MPs asked the two Italian POWs what they were trying to do, said Papin. "They said they just wanted to go home. They were just homesick boys," she recounted. "Evidently they didn't realize how far from home they were."

Even though this incident may have spooked area residents, most Italian POWs had no desire to try to make a run for it. "We could roll back the fencing at 10 o'clock in the morning, at 11 o'clock all the prisoners of war would be gone," said Colonel Glidden, camp commander, remarking on the contentment of the Italian internees, "and at 12 o'clock they would be back—waiting for their noon meal."[79]

Riot at the Camp

On September 1, 1943, some prisoners—a surly handful of men, all members of Mussolini's Black Shirts—decided to fly the Italian flag over their barracks. Orders from the War Department prohibited such activities, and the POWs were told to take down the flag. After they refused, a company of MPs armed with billy clubs was formed to take over the compound by force. The Italians responded by throwing rocks, sticks, and other objects at the GIs, and several were cut when hit by the projectiles. After the first group of Americans was unable to regain control of the compound, a second group was sent in. This group, too, was forced to retreat, with one officer and several enlisted men suffering the indignity of being "roughly manhandled during the excitement, suffering considerable cuts and abrasions."[80]

On a third attempt, the Americans entered the compound, now having traded their billy clubs for bayonets. This time they were successful in quelling the fracas. "Colonel Glidden went into the compound a day later and apparently fixed things up," wrote Bianco in his diary. "The ringleaders were placed in the PW guardhouse and kept seven days on a diet of bread and water in solitary confinement. But, by golly, the first night in, with 408 [Bianco's unit] on guard, somebody smuggled in, somehow, a carton full of eats—salami, jam, etc."

The thrill of the incident lasted for a while, remembered Teresa Drury. "One of the officers got hit in the head with a rock. There were one or two drops of blood," she said. "A couple of them were laughing about it later because he got a Purple Heart out of it, getting wounded for his country, you know."[81]

The men involved in organizing the riot eventually were moved to one of the Weingarten branch camps so as to minimize their disruptive influence on the other prisoners, said Stanley Drury. "They were later sent to a St. Louis plant [the camp in Baden], to get them out of the guards' hair at Weingarten."[82]

Death of a POW

The first POW death at Weingarten took place on February 9, 1944, when prisoners found a fellow Italian dead near his barracks. Camp authorities investigating the circumstances of his death said the twenty-six-year-old Italian private had no enemies, and no evidence of foul play was discovered. The prisoner, who had been in the camp since August 1943, was buried with full honors in accordance with Italian military tradition, according to Captain Burton W. Marston, Weingarten public relations officer. The man was buried in a special cemetery built by prisoners specifically for their fellow Italian POWs, situated on a hill overlooking the camp, with a central cross elevated on a mound. Each grave was marked with a concrete slab and headstone, and the entire plot was enclosed with a fence and hand-wrought chains.[83] Though the soldier had died of hemorrhage resulting from a knife wound to the neck, the death was ruled a suicide. This was often the easiest explanation for a POW fatality that occurred

Italian POWs had their own well-tended cemetery at Camp Weingarten. Courtesy of Kent Library, Southeast Missouri State University.

under murky circumstances and that might never be explained, said Captain Eugene Phillips. "In the [enlisted soldiers' compounds], some strife developed in small Mafia-like organizations, sometimes resulting in deaths and injuries thought to be triggered by stealing or homosexual jealousy," recalled Phillips. "Our investigations did not reveal much, as they were quite secretive about what happened among themselves. Decisions had to be made, however, and most deaths were deemed suicides."[84]

In total, five POWs died during the duration of the camp's operation. After Weingarten's deactivation, their remains were moved in November 1945 to be permanently interred in the military cemetery at Jefferson Barracks in St. Louis.[85]

Weingarten Prisoner Labor

Once the government began the program in March 1943 to utilize

POW workers to ease the labor shortage in the United States, the demand for their help was nearly insatiable in agriculture and industry. By June 1943, prisoners from Weingarten were being used as farm labor in the area, and as the summer went on, the number of POWs working both inside and outside the camp only increased.

Although it would be months before the formal labor program was in full swing, less than a week after the POWs' arrival the prisoners were at work. Heavier-than-normal rainfall caused the Mississippi River to climb over its banks, threatening homes and farmland. The POWs fought the flooding as a sandbag brigade to reinforce levees, an effort that was the subject of a *Life* magazine photo essay in May 1943. The prisoners worked around the clock to plug fifteen gaps in levees ranging from fifteen to one hundred feet wide, left from flooding the year before.

POWs line up to battle flooding in downtown Ste. Genevieve. Courtesy of Norma Overall Jacob.

An article in the *St. Louis Star-Times* reported the prisoners' work on May 17, 1943, stating, "The men worked with a will and many times broke into a dogtrot as they carried sandbags to points threatened by flood waters rising along the levee."[86]

Because the existence of the POW camps in the United States was still considered a "secret" operation by the government at that point in the war, the accounts hesitated to acknowledge the actual number of prisoners, their location, or their activities. These news accounts, especially the publication of the *Life* photos, were somewhat electrifying, among the first public acknowledgments that Axis prisoners were indeed in the United States. Although the government allowed the photos to be printed, it still required that the faces of the men in the photographs be blurred out and did not allow the prisoners to be identified specifically as Italians.

Prisoners would be used again in flood control the following spring. In April 1944, around 150 men were sent from Weingarten to Elsberry, in Lincoln County, Missouri, to battle high water. That same month, 800 additional Weingarten POWs went with 200 guards to Perry County, Missouri, immediately south of Ste. Genevieve County, to repair and reinforce levees in an attempt to keep the river back. A tent city popped up to house them at Perryville High School and in the Seminary Grove on the grounds of St. Mary's of the Barrens Seminary as they fought flooding in nearby St. Marys and Claryville, Missouri, and across the river in Kaskaskia, Illinois. After an eighteen-day battle, the river receded and the POWs returned to Weingarten. Although some crop damage occurred from "seep water," no levees in the areas were broached, and the efforts of those who fought the flooding protected about thirty thousand acres of crop land from inundation and saved the county an estimated $1 million.

Local organizations honored all those who helped, including the eight hundred POWs, their guards, and one thousand combat engineers from Fort Leonard Wood. Public ceremonies took place at the high school football field and at Seminary Grove, where resolutions of appreciation were read before the assembled soldiers.[87]

For more regular occupation of Weingarten POWs, the government established a shoe-repair operation on the camp grounds. About forty Italians were employed there at the start, repairing three hundred to four hundred pairs of Army shoes each day in a space that took up some forty-five hundred square feet. These were not trained cobblers but rather ordinary prisoners who learned to fix shoes on the job. Their training "started on the original backlog of 150,000 pairs pitchforked from boxcars by the swamped second lieutenant in charge."[88] Their direct supervisor turned out to be an Army private whose civilian background as an expert shoemaker was put by the military to good use—something that usually doesn't happen, as any veteran will tell you.

"The Army just picked up some draftee who knew how to manufacture shoes," said Stanley Drury. "They hustled him out to Weingarten as an instructor in shoe repair."[89] The young soldier didn't even go to basic training—he was shipped directly from his induction center to Weingarten, where he taught shoe repair through demonstrations and sign language.

Later, an American sergeant of Italian descent, fluent in Italian, was added to help run the effort. When this was coupled with an English-speaking Italian navy warrant officer, who worked voluntarily as a supply clerk in the operation, the shoe repair shop really began to hum along with maximum effectiveness. At its peak, seventy POWs worked on the line, and production topped out at five hundred pairs of shoes each day.

"Internees work on the long line, sorting, stripping, repairing and refinishing the stream of shoes," wrote Lieutenant George Paddock. "Composition heel wedges and reclaimed rubber soles save the use of leather or rubber stock. Sixty percent of the shoes sent to Weingarten are repaired and reissued; the rest are cut up into leather and rubber scrap and shipped out as salvage."[90]

Of all the prisoners who worked outside the camp, the largest number—generally one thousand each day—were engaged in agriculture. Because of the pressing need for labor, area farmers were ready to arrange for help as soon as possible. Contracts for POW labor were written in St. Francois County as early as June 5, 1943, and POWs were engaged in Ste. Genevieve County immediately thereafter.

Among the local farmers who hired POWs was Cleva Laws's father, who farmed in nearby Millerswitch. She recalled the Italians working on their farm: "My dad used them to haul hay and to shock wheat. Also a guard or two came along with them as part of the arrangement." To Laws it appeared as if the prisoners enjoyed being out in the field. "It seemed as though they liked having the chance to work outside," she remembered. "They were happy to have the fresh air and change in routine."[91]

In addition to working in agriculture outside the camp, prisoners were used in a variety of tasks related to the operation of the camp itself. POW Ennio Calabresi volunteered to help with the building of an obstacle course to be used for physical training of American GIs.

It was in a little pine forest, and it took us about two months to build. We got eighty cents a day. We worked for two U.S. officers, a captain and a lieutenant, both engineers. It was beautiful. The best part was the end of the day, when we returned our tools—there was a desk near the shed and I would steal the newspaper left there. I couldn't speak English or understand when it was spoken to me, but I could read it.

Every night that newspaper gave me all the news I needed. I even knew when they were fighting in my home town. After the obstacle course was completed, I didn't do anything besides work at odd jobs around the camp, like lots of "police call," picking up the paper trash, cigarette butts, and such.[92]

Eventually the POWs requested to use the obstacle course in order to keep in shape. The course record was 1 minute and 50 seconds, jointly held by two Americans from the 410th and 555th MPEG Companies, though an Italian POW was able to cover it in 2 minutes even, as reported in the March 24, 1944, *Farmington Herald*. The water hazard—the most challenging aspect of the whole course—apparently sunk many who would aspire to break the 2-minute mark.

Because the labor shortage was so extreme virtually everywhere in the United States, the prisoners' much-needed service would be applied far beyond the area immediately around Weingarten. Already just a month or two after the reception of prisoners at the main camp, the branch camps affiliated with Weingarten were being readied to accept the transfer of the Italian POWs. On July 31, 1943, some seven hundred prisoners were sent by train to Iowa to help detassel corn for the Pioneer Seed Corn Company and the DeKalb Agricultural Association.

"This is a stalk-by-stalk operation which must be completed almost at once throughout an entire field, and is particularly suited to internee labor," observed Lieutenant Paddock. "Two trainloads of prisoners have been shipped to Iowa destinations where 'side camps' will be maintained in the corn areas, under guard of Weingarten detachments."[93]

They worked at camps at West Liberty, Marengo, and Shenandoah through mid-August and, operating in groups of forty to fifty, processed some forty-four thousand acres of Iowa corn. Though their time there was relatively short, the prisoners and the guards who escorted them had a big impact in the towns in which they lived and worked, both in the results of their efforts—an additional ten to fifteen bushels per acre of hybrid seed corn—and on the people they met.

"The members of the guard companies that escorted the PWs to Iowa reported a fine time was had by all," recalled historian Drury. "The Iowa folks couldn't have been nicer. Many touching scenes at the rail stations as the townsfolk bid the boys of the guard companies goodbye."[94]

"The draft board had stripped that town of 1,500 completely clean of young men and when 90 beautiful soldiers dropped out of the blue, people couldn't do enough for the boys," recalled one GI who made the Iowa trip. "Just walk into town and someone would invite you up for supper...golf, skating rink, swimming, dances.... The people of the town even did our washing."

Word spread around the countryside about these wonderful GIs at West Liberty, and girls were driving right up to the quarters at the fairgrounds grandstand to pick up "dates" for a night out on the town. When it was time to go, the Iowans were saddened to see their new friends leave. "The whole town turned out to trainside the day of departure from West Liberty with more than a few tears flowing from female eyes at the thought of separation," said one soldier who was part of the Iowa detachment.[95]

Weingarten POW Detail

Even though it couldn't match the excitement of being able to travel somewhere as exotic as Marengo, Iowa, to work, prisoners at the base camp kept busy with an amazing array of details in and around the installation. Eighty men worked in the shoe shop, and 75 more in the hospital, while another 40 worked in the stables, tending to the "horsepower" that was used for many types of hauling around the camp. The post engineers claimed 220 more for work such as fixing roads, painting, and carpentry. The quartermaster's office used 100 POWs for work in post warehouses, cold storage, and the motor pool, while an additional 230 Italians worked in the camp's many mess halls.[96]

Bill Barnes recalled the Italians working at the quarry and lime plant at Glen Park, Missouri, located at the north end of Ste. Genevieve County. "They were happy to be here," said Barnes, who worked at the quarry. "They'd laugh and laugh at the guys still fighting in the war while they were here eating good and sleeping in comfortable beds."

Barnes said the group of about 15 prisoners worked hard but managed to have fun, too. "There was one real comical fellow that they all got a kick out of, and I did too," remembered Barnes. "He dropped a rock on his foot one day and was laughing and hopping all around, holding his foot."[97]

The unions weren't laughing at the presence of the POWs in the quarry, however. When the American Federation of Labor (AFL) got wind of the prisoners working at the Glencoe Lime and Cement Company in Pevely, Missouri, they protested publically, saying that they were "opposed to use of any war prisoners in general" in competition with American labor.

Weingarten motor pool. Souvenir folder of PW camp at Weingarten. Courtesy of Edmee Viscardi.

Colonel Glidden told the *St. Louis Post-Dispatch* that the union's claims were nonsense. Glidden pointed out that the War Manpower Commission had certified use of the prisoners because of a bona fide shortage of workers and that the AFL quarry workers' union, which represented employees at the Pevely plant, had also given approval to the certification. Prisoners continued to work at the plant, but this incident showed how organized labor continually opposed use of POWs in many industries despite the widespread and ongoing labor shortage.[98]

Despite the occasional flare-ups with the unions such as what occurred at Pevely and with German POWs in a gypsum plant in north Kansas City in 1945, using prisoners for work outside the camps went well, and prisoners generally liked being able to work elsewhere. It offered them the chance to enjoy new scenery beyond the fences of the camp, additional opportunities to interact with civilians, and a change in routine. And whether working on post or outside the camp, the prisoners valued the chance to work for another reason—the pay. On top of the flat $3 a month each enlisted POW received to cover basic expenses whether they worked or not, each man could earn $.80 for a day's work, funds that could be used in a number of ways. Some gambled with the canteen money, a fairly common form of entertainment among the captured soldiers. "You could always tell when it was payday," said Teresa Drury. "You'd walk by and hear the dice rolling down the floor."[99]

A good deal more was spent at the canteens that operated in each compound. Weingarten POWs operated these little shops that sold the same items available to American GIs in their PX. Typically, four POWs from each compound worked in the canteen, which purchased stock and resold it for a profit. The canteen also paid a rental charge to the camp for use of the equipment needed to operate the facility.

During the first month of operation, the initial two canteens located in the POW compounds posted $3,300 in sales. Profits from the canteens remained with the POWs and could be put back into the canteen operations or could be designated for the prisoner recreation fund and used to purchase library materials or equipment for music or sport. Additionally, Weingarten prisoners designated a considerable portion of the canteens' profits to both stateside charities and agencies providing aid and assistance in Europe. An effort in February 1944 to benefit the Infantile Paralysis Fund raised more than $700. Of this total, POW enlisted men contributed $200, all earned by long days of working at $.10 an hour. POW officers also contributed $200, and an additional $300 was donated from profits earned by canteens operated by the POWs in their compounds. The POWs contributed $3,500 during a later drive to help the American Red Cross distribute clothes to their countrymen in Ally-occupied Italy.

POWs also benefited from an arrangement in which half their money was automatically deposited into special individual accounts designed to be paid out upon repatriation at the end of the war. The Italian soldiers could also use their wages to purchase items to ship home to war-ravaged Italy. "The prisoners were allowed to spend up to $15 at the canteen at a time for stuff to send to their families," said Drury. "They sent care packages to their families."[100]

Educational Programs at the Camp

For prisoners at Camp Weingarten, their stay offered an opportunity for educational advancement that often benefited them greatly upon their return to Italy. "The average prisoner of war interned in the U.S. had only four years of schooling," noted Drury, and even in the Italian officer corps only six hundred of the nine hundred had completed high school. Initially, the most popular courses were basic Italian and English language classes, with the instructors being drawn from the student body as well as a pair of Catholic priests from St. Louis, Father Anthony Palumbo and Father Carl C. Poelker. This duo organized and oversaw the program and also conducted religious services at the camp during the first months of Weingarten's operation.

Officers could select from the following courses offered in their compound: Italian literature, Latin, philosophy, French, Spanish, German, English (ten levels), music (piano and composition), singing, drawing, painting, and sculpture. In addition to receiving an education, officers who had been educators in civilian life often served as instructors for the classes offered to the enlisted men. Because of the lack of formal schooling among the enlisted men, these classes were primarily remedial elementary-level instruction, though English, mathematics, and drawing also were offered. "The attendance, while never very high, was fairly good," wrote a Swiss inspector. "The greatest accomplishment [the prisoners] have to their credit is elimination of illiteracy."[101]

By 1945, prisoners could enroll in classes in calculus, electricity, shorthand (beginning or advanced), physics, financial mathematics, analytic geometry, algebra, hydraulic construction, mechanic construction, and English I, II, and III. Despite the wide range of instruction offered, 60 percent of the Italian prisoners did not enroll in any course, perhaps preferring the soccer field to the classroom or else simply seeing no benefit in participation.[102]

One result of the changing political scene in Italy was that as the government was reshuffled after the fall of Mussolini's regime, so too was the curriculum at Weingarten. A three-part series of courses that examined different areas of Italian civil and criminal law was dropped after the focus of the course, the Fascist code, was no longer in effect in Italy. A course on American law was substituted in its place.

POWs at Weingarten also took a broad range of correspondence courses for college credit. Topics included business courses such as accounting and insurance; classical studies of the Roman comedies and Greek tragedies; general liberal-arts courses such as history, sociology, and international relations; and instruction in practical matters, including beekeeping and air conditioning.[103]

To augment and enhance these opportunities for education in the prison camp academy, internees organized for themselves a number of conferences and lectures featuring POW "experts." Subjects included the operas of Giuseppe Verdi; bases of the social thought of the modern era; profiles of contemporary artists; and an introduction to *The Divine Comedy*, with particular emphasis on purgatory.

Camp libraries at Weingarten served as a resource for the POW classes as well as an opportunity for recreation and education. The officers' library was the best stocked, with several thousand volumes in circulation, along with several daily and weekly newspapers available, including the *St. Louis Globe-Democrat* and *The New York Times*. Along with these English-language publications, the officers' library received several American Italian-language papers, including *Il Progresso Italo Americano*, which the prisoners did not see as being of any "special value" in terms of its literary or news content. Quite a number of periodicals on a broad range of subjects was received as well. The selection ranged from the standards—*Newsweek, Time, Life*—to *Movie Stars, Better Homes and Gardens*, H. L. Mencken's *American Mercury*, and for animal lovers at the camp, *Dog World*.

The surrounding communities donated many books, and a number of Catholic parishes stepped up as well, such as St. Charles Borromeo, which donated the entire library from the church rectory. The Archdiocese of St. Louis also provided many books, along with an assortment of musical instruments.[104]

A letter from Monsignor John Cody to Colonel Glidden in May 1943 details well the types of assistance the St. Louis Archdiocese afforded the Italian prisoners. The camp had only been open a week when Cody went to take firsthand stock of the prisoners and what they needed. Within a day of his return, Cody had rounded up an amazing collection of musical instruments, comfort items, and other supplies to benefit the prisoners.

"I am happy to inform you that one thousand packages of cigarettes were sent this morning from Saint Louis and should be delivered to you sometime tomorrow morning," wrote Cody. "Again I wish to renew to you my offer to assist you in any way possible. Already about six pianos are lined up for you and by the first of next week, I shall have a considerable number of musical instruments, playing cards, etc."[105]

Religious Life at the Camp

The St. Louis Archdiocese teamed up with area Catholics to play a significant role in the religious activity at Camp Weingarten. Initially, there was no full-time military chaplain at the camp, and so for the first few months the Reverend Joseph Gassner, pastor of the local parish and the same man who saw only "nuisance value" in the camp when it was announced, provided spiritual guidance to the Weingarten soldiers. The New York–based military ordinariate, John O'Hara, who oversaw the war-related work of the Catholic Church and provided extraordinarily detailed guidelines to priests in the field, authorized Gassner to celebrate as many as three masses every Sunday within the camp itself should the number of servicemen warrant it. However, the priest found it unnecessary to conduct services there as the sanctuary was within easy walking distance of the camp, and soldiers enjoyed worshiping with the parishioners at Our Lady Help of Christians, as well as attending church in Ste. Genevieve.

The arrival of the prisoners in May 1943, however, required a whole new level of pastoral resources to adequately care for the religious needs of the POWs. During his visit that month, Cody brought along a young priest from St. Louis named Gerold Kaiser who, having recently returned from Rome, was able to speak fluent Italian. Kaiser was well received by both the prisoners and the American servicemen, and after the visit began making weekly trips to the camp, arriving every Friday and staying through Monday to celebrate Mass, hear confessions, and provide religious instruction to all interested persons.

"Despite his youthful age, [Kaiser] has a great deal of tact and prudence and his work at the Prison Camp has been blessed with extraordinary success," wrote Cody to the Army chief of chaplains. "At the beginning of the month of July, the Commanding Officer on one of my weekly visits to the Camp asked me if arrangements could be made to permit Father Kaiser to reside at the Post and he as Commanding Officer would be most happy to have Father Kaiser take up quarters with him."[106]

The Army appointed Kaiser a military auxiliary chaplain, and he began celebrating three masses each Sunday, two in the prisoner compounds and one at the station hospital for both the Italian and American patients housed therein. Kaiser's work among the prisoners—which would last the duration of the camp's existence—was soon augmented by the arrival of the Italian-speaking Reverend Joseph Parent and a POW priest, the Reverend Mario Palestro. Prior to his arrival at Weingarten in September 1943, Parent had ministered to Italian POWs at Camp Clark before that facility had changed over to holding all German prisoners. Palestro, whom Cody called a "very kind little man," had been a priest in the Italian diocese of Vercelli and at Weingarten was permitted to travel freely among the compounds, ministering to prisoners without the usual supervision of the guard. With three Catholic chaplains on the camp duty roster, ministry to Catholics— both American and Italian—kicked into high gear.[107]

Of all the Missouri camps, Weingarten had the most consistent long-term POW participation and interest in religious activities, with two-thirds of the prisoners attending Mass regularly. "Religion plays a very important part in this camp," wrote a visitor from the Red Cross. "An Italian chaplain says mass every day. There are three beautifully decorated chapels adorned with magnificent sculptures."[108]

Even though all the POWs and a considerable portion of the American GIs were Catholic, Protestant servicemen would soon receive their own shepherd beginning in October 1943 with the arrival of Captain John F. Mitchell. Chaplain Mitchell had been pastor for a fourteen-hundred-member congregation in Atlanta, Georgia, before he entered the service, volunteering to perform his ministry among the men and women of the armed forces instead. In addition to his preaching at Weingarten, the July 14, 1944, *Farmington News* noted that Mitchell was the speaker at a week-long revival at Chestnut Ridge Baptist Church.

"Much tribute is due the Chaplains, both Catholic and Protestant, who labored so faithfully in the spiritual program," said *The Lead Belt News*. "Services were conducted in the library and theater until the chapel was completed. The help of many fine Christian men, both officers and enlisted, talented singers and musicians made it possible to render some wonderful programs."[109]

Indeed, the efforts to provide religious ministrations to the Italian prisoners of war was a significant part of the attempt to make their time as captives in a foreign land a bearable experience. And this was not lost on the prisoners, as expressed by the camp spokesman in a letter to Cody just days before the return to Italy:

On the eve of the repatriation of all Italian Officers of this Camp, may I take this occasion to express to you, on their behalf and mine, our deepfelt gratitude for the constant and benevolent assistance and innumerable kindnesses you have so unstintingly extended to us during the period of our internment at this Camp.

All of us will carry back to our homeland an everlasting remembrance of the highly humanitarian work which you have done in our behalf, and which has greatly contributed to lessen the hardships of our internment, the worries over the condition and fate of our loved ones, and the moral anguish occasioned by the great distance separating us from our land.

Very Respectfully yours,
Colonel Michele Ruta
Camp Spokesman[110]

Sport as a Diversion

Though Italian soldiers may not have done well in the war, they would have conquered the world if their enthusiasm for soccer and other sports could have decided the matter. A variety of sources, including the YMCA, the PMGO, the Red Cross, Italian aid societies, and the like, all outfitted the prisoners with sporting equipment and games, and they put the gear to use. Before the men could play soccer, however, they had to play at being construction engineers. The camp's uneven terrain initially prevented the designated recreation area outside the POW compounds from being used, but the men labored in their free time to level the field and remove all the rocks. Because of the size of the project and the erosive nature of the soil at the Weingarten prison camp, it took several months of work before the field was ready. To alleviate the erosion problem, the Italians created drainage ditches lined with cemented stone, and their work demonstrated the excellent masonry skills they had brought with them from home.

Until the soccer field was ready, the POWs made do with volleyball and bocce courts, which did not require nearly as much space, as well as a couple small soccer yards squeezed into the compounds between the barracks. The small size could not limit the fervor with which the POWs played, however, and because of the noise generated by their intensity, the men imposed a rule of silence upon themselves during volleyball matches, punishing any violator with a foul.[111]

By 1945 the prisoners' athletic program was a veritable wide world of sports. Although only 45 percent of the POWs participated in any type of organized athletics, the Italians who were involved enjoyed the chance to compete in soccer, volleyball, basketball, tennis, bocce, boxing, table tennis, shuffleboard, and discus. "Big crowds were turning out each night for the volleyball contests in the compounds," remembered one Weingarten GI, "and you could hear the roars of the crowds anywhere on the Post."[112]

As one might imagine, such a broad array of athletic pursuits required equipment to match, and Weingarten was certainly well stocked. A March

1945 survey of sporting stock at Weingarten showed eight pool and snooker tables, eighteen table-tennis tables, and one hundred basketball uniforms on hand at the camp. An assessment of the athletic facilities available to the internees counted twenty-two bocce fields, two gymnasiums, four tennis fields, three soccer fields, nine outdoor volleyball courts, and five outdoor basketball courts.

Another form of entertainment was the movies shown three times a week in the theater operated by the War Department. POWs packed the seats of the post theater to catch the latest offerings from Hollywood, and despite their lack of knowledge of the English language, the men thoroughly enjoyed the movies, clapping, hooting, or weeping at all the appropriate times. Seating capacity for the films was 750, and with the addition of bleachers, some 1,200 prisoners could watch at once. Admission for the afternoon showings was $.15, the same rate as for the U.S. GIs who attended in the evenings. Dodging that admission charge seemed like a good idea to a dozen POWs who tried to sneak into the back of the theater one afternoon in January 1944, but the thirty days they received in the guardhouse after they were caught surely made them wish they had paid the fee instead.[113]

The feature film on February 15, 1945, was *Having Wonderful Crime*. Shorts, including newsreels, cartoons, or brief educational films, preceded the films. *Having Wonderful Crime* followed three: *This is America, Bikes and Skis*, and *Sliphorn King of Polaroo*, an animated short à la Walter Lantz featuring a quirky little trombone player who fell off a ship while crossing the ocean and washed up on the island of Polaroo.[114]

POWs could also be involved in creating one of the camp's Italian-language newspapers, distributed free of charge and funded by profits from the canteen. With a different paper being published by each compound, the production was irregular and depended in large part on the availability of materials and the interest and energy of prisoners to put them together. That they were produced in a POW camp by no degree lessened the quality of their contents. *La Luce* (The Light) appeared in December 1945 by Weingarten prisoners transferred to Fort Crook, Nebraska, held there as a temporary stop on the way home to Italy. *La Luce* ran forty-five pages and included poetry, short stories, camp news, theatrical reviews of camp performances (written in the voice of a snooty theater critic), and a dozen pages of crossword puzzles and other word games.

Much of the writing in *La Luce* and the other papers was very good. One article, written by POW Antonio De Vecchi, was called "Closing the Parenthesis" and referred to the period of imprisonment that he and the other prisoners were experiencing as a difficult "parenthesis" in life. With repatriation so near for the prisoners, De Vecchi longed all that much more for the "closing of the parenthesis," a return home and a better, happier future:

> Some day, when we speak to our children about the events of war we will certainly not forget, among our grimmest memories, the spiritual battles of our imprisonment, the awful phases of the last, hard-fought struggle which led us back to life, to our dear ones, to the matchless horizons of our country....

> But, with faith in god, with confidence in ourselves, and with the generosity of spirit which characterizes us as Italians, we will be able to stand straight again and to go forward again in life.[115]

The papers were widely read and highly anticipated. For example, beginning in February 1945, a paper called *L'Ortica* (The Wait) was published by Compound 2 prisoners. The two hundred copies they printed and distributed throughout Weingarten and the branch camps ultimately touched fifteen hundred POWs or more as estimated by the commanding officer, with copies read and reread as they were passed from prisoner to prisoner.

Arts and Culture

Like internees at other POW camps, prisoners at Weingarten were adept at devising forms of entertainment, including a variety of cultural activities such as music and theater. In a place the size of Weingarten, many men of considerable talent could be found, and the performers were sometimes veterans of professional troupes such as what one might have seen on the stage at La Scala.

In October 1943, the Italians put on their first performance, with talent raised solely from their own ranks. Seven hundred prisoners enjoyed the vaudeville-style show, complete with settings, scenery, and dialogue for the three-hour production. Prisoners also provided music at the show, with a number of native melodies mixed with popular American jazz tunes.[116]

A December 1943 War Department inspection report noted there were "three orchestras organized in the camp and an active little theatre group organized." The prisoners went so far as to construct an outdoor theater where shows were given during the summer, and they used the camp theater for performances during the winter. These orchestras were amazingly well supplied. For instance, the one in the officers' compound was equipped

Camp Theater Building and Gymnasium, PW Camp, Weingarten, Mo.

POWs enjoyed the theater at the camp. Souvenir folder of PW camp at Weingarten. Courtesy of Edmee Viscardi.

with two pianos, a drum set, five violins, three saxophones, five guitars and banjos, an accordion, two flutes, and a cornet.[117]

Even when not performing the music themselves or hearing it played by a top-notch orchestra, the Italian prisoners still enjoyed music. A regular practice each Sunday for the officers was to gather in the music hall and listen by radio to the opera from the Metropolitan Opera House as well as the symphony concerts from New York, Philadelphia, Boston, and Chicago. Prior to the performance, a competent officer would give a short talk, and afterward a review of the concert or opera was published in the prisoners' camp newspaper. All this nearly succeeded in creating the impression that the men had actually attended the performance. Approximately two hundred officers attended these "concerts" each week.[118]

In addition to music and theater, the Weingarten POWs excelled in a number of other areas of the arts, displaying skills in painting, creating furniture, and making jewelry and other handicrafts. Items made by the prisoners included lockets, picture frames, and models of submarines, battleships, and tanks. Although the primary reason for their creation was simply to fill the hours, the items created by the prisoners often were given to military personnel and the American civilians working in the camp as gifts or else were traded for cigarettes or other desirable items. "The PW's must have made a fortune off us GIs by selling their hand-made rings and cigarette cases, wonderfully made from silver coins or mess kits," remembered Sergeant Quinton Bianco. "Amazingly well done also were the pencil and paint drawings made from our snapshots or enlargements of beloved ones."[119]

Francis Schwartz recalled the Italians' skill in creating elaborate and decorative furniture pieces, usually fashioned out of scrap wood scrounged from the camp, cast-off crates, and packing boxes. "The prisoners made items like a table without nails," he recalled. "The braces look like pieces of vine wrapped on each side to secure the legs to the table top."[120]

Even the chapels located in each compound benefited from a coupling of the artistic abilities of the prisoners with a natural rivalry among each set of barracks. The Italians went wild with creativity and effort at Christmas and were especially elaborate in constructing miniature scenes from Bethlehem, fashioning statues from clay as well as creating other lifelike figures by draping burlap bags over roughly human-shaped wooden frames and then covering the material with a thin layer of paint or cement. One of the scenes included a complete cityscape, with hotel,

Italian prisoners sketching and painting during their leisure time at Camp Weingarten. Photograph by Buel White of the St. Louis Post-Dispatch, *© 1943. Courtesy of the* St. Louis Post-Dispatch.

village, and manger, complemented by a sky made of backlit cardboard with holes cut out for stars.

Gardening was also a popular pastime, as much greenery—flowers, plants, and small trees—was used to beautify the compound areas. Bianco described the passion for plants some of the Italians displayed: "Many of the

PWs are marvelous gardeners, and they have started numerous flower beds in the space between barracks buildings. The flower gardens are in all designs, one being a map of Italy."[121]

This sentiment was echoed by Colonel Glidden, who mentioned the beauty of their work in an October 1943 letter to Archbishop John Glennon of the St. Louis Archdiocese. "The invitation extended through Monsignor Cody to visit us is always open," wrote the colonel. "Let me suggest that now is a beautiful time of the year and that a visit prior to a destructive frost would permit you to see what the Italian soldiers interned here accomplished in the matter of their many flower gardens."[122]

This painting was given to Ward H. Overall, who supervised the carpenter shop at Weingarten, by one of the POWs there. Courtesy of Wilson Overall.

Colonel H. H. Glidden was popular with the camp staff as well as with the POWs. Here he cools off with Lieutenant George Jacob (right) and another officer in August 1944 in a fishpond at Weingarten. Courtesy of Norma Overall Jacob.

The camp's beauty was greatly enhanced with the Stark Bro's Nursery's donation of twelve hundred shrubs in April 1944. The nursery, in Louisiana, Missouri, was one of Weingarten's side camps where POW labor was utilized. In addition to the shrubs, POWs sprinkled grass seed on any bare patch of soil around the camp and trimmed and cleared several wooded areas of undergrowth and debris.

Mrs. Ernest Anderson of Cedar Rapids, Iowa, wasn't so sure that spending money to beautify the POW camp was a good idea. She wrote a letter to Eleanor Roosevelt, protesting the allocation of $40,000 for landscaping at the Weingarten camp. Brigadier General B. M. Bryan, director of the aliens division and later assistant provost marshal general, was tasked with drafting a reply. In his response, he assured Anderson that no waste of money or labor was involved in the project, noting that the project was one of erosion control and revegetation and, moreover, that only $9,868 of the requested allotment was actually used.[123]

Along with the landscaping and flower gardening, prisoners grew a great portion of the vegetables feeding the camp beginning in 1943, when seventeen acres were devoted to a truck garden. The next year, under the supervision of a Captain Buckley, the station veterinarian, this plot was expanded to sixty acres, with the early plants being started in hotbeds. From these efforts, $12,000 worth of produce would be produced for the camp commissary to supply both POW and American mess halls.

In 1945, the garden was enlarged again to seventy-five acres, with twenty acres planted in cabbage and another twenty acres in tomatoes, the remainder being sown in other varieties of vegetables, including lettuce, peas, beans, onions, peppers, potatoes, sweet corn, sweet potatoes, carrots, beets, turnips, and spinach. In mid-September 1945, the value of these crops already harvested would be estimated at $17,000 with several weeks still to go in the season.[124]

The eventual aim of these gardens was to make the camp self-sufficient in its need for vegetables, both by being consumed as fresh table fare in the summer months and by canning gallons for consumption in the winter. More important to some, as reported in a regular gossip column in the *Ste. Genevieve Herald*, was that in 1945, the gardens produced enough rhubarb to make ten tasty pies for the headquarters detachment mess.[125]

Feeding the Five Thousand

The Italian cooks at Weingarten and other camps were renowned for their ability to take regular Army mess hall chow and, with a little tinkering with the ingredients and tailoring of the spices and method of preparation, turn it into something completely different, a culinary delight that lifted one straight from the POW camp to a sunny Sicilian hillside. This made the POW mess always in demand with American GIs, when they could slip in unnoticed.

"Some American soldiers complained that the prisoners were eating better than they were," recalled Pauline Laws McKamey. "If so, it was because the Italians had better cooks. Their food was highly seasoned and very flavorful."

This difference in the mess hall was more than GI opinion, though. Official reports documented the quality and skill demonstrated by the Italians in food preparation. "The food is prepared in the Italian way under the care of Italian prisoner cooks. The rations are ample and excellent," noted one inspector. "We were invited to eat at the table of the higher Italian officers together with the American commander. The meal consisted of spaghetti, grilled steak with potatoes, salad and little white onions, followed by cake, fruit and coffee. The food for the privates is also very good."[126]

Captain Eugene Phillips was in charge of requisitioning the necessary foodstuffs for several thousand Italian prisoners as well as the GIs at the camp. It was a difficult task on occasion, he recalled. "I had to secure contracts to purchase some of the items from the local population. The dairy farmers in the area weren't real happy about having to sell milk and other products to us for use with the prisoners while these items were rationed for normal Americans," said Phillips. "I eventually had to give them the impression that these Italian prisoners, who were normally as fun-loving and unthreatening as could be, were really dangerous men who might riot and cause serious problems if they were not properly supplied with the necessary items. Through much talking, the farmers were convinced that by providing the camp with these items, they were helping to keep it a calm and peaceful place. That was how the contracts were secured."[127]

In addition to one POW who caught and cooked a possum, another incident demonstrates, however, that the culture gap was never completely closed in the kitchen. "Cats weren't safe around them," said Francis Schwartz, getting ready to tell the nearest thing Ste. Genevieve County has to an urban legend. "They'd butcher every one they could get a hold of."[128]

As the story goes in one version, an American GI was eating in the PW mess when he tried a dish he didn't recognize but found absolutely delicious. The soldier complimented the cook on the delightful flavor of the food and asked the prisoners what it was, recalled Teresa Drury, for he had never tasted anything like it. The Italian description of the dish didn't quite convey the main ingredient, so the cook found the simplest way to make himself clear.

"The prisoner just smiled and said 'meow,'" said Drury.[129]

Stanley Drury, Teresa's husband, continued the story on another occasion. "That guy just heaved and heaved. Then, while they were driving him out to take him to the doctor, he saw a cat run out in front of the truck. That's when he really got sick."[130]

Another version of the story told by Susie Henderson identifies a civilian employee named Robert Baum as the person who ate a cat sandwich. "You like cat?" asked the prisoners, after Baum finished the sandwich. "He didn't come to work for days after that."[131]

Schwartz's version of the tale has a similarly "explosive" ending. This time it was an American GI who was tricked into eating a "catburger." He liked it, even while the chef was describing its ingredients in Italian. When the translation came, and he learned that he had supposedly been served cat meat, that's when things erupted, as it were. "He ran up and ate all the herring Joe Berling had to get the taste out of his mouth," said Schwartz.[132]

Interaction between POWs and Locals

In between moments of excitement such as the riot or the escape were days of unremarkable routine, where life went on in a mundane cycle of work-eat-sleep. Rita Schwartz recalled how she and her daughter would watch the prisoners at the depot across the street from her house. Her daughter, who was quite young at the time, would talk to the men through the fence.

"The Italians used their own stamps to buy her candy," recalled Schwartz, describing how they would use camp coupons received in lieu of wages as currency in the canteen. "When my daughter heard the truck—and those Army trucks were very loud—she would run outside for her candy."[133]

At that same time, Schwartz was pregnant with another child. After she delivered the baby, an interpreter who worked with the prisoners at the depot told Schwartz that one of the Italians had asked to see her newborn. Schwartz carried her baby across the road and let the man look at her child through the fence.

"The PW stood there and cried. The interpreter explained to me the prisoner was saying that he had never heard from his six kids and that he had heard the area where they were living had been bombed. He didn't know if they were alive," said Schwartz, remembering the man's longing to see his own children. "He would look at my baby in my arms and say, 'oh, bambino, bambino.'"

Mary Lou Correnti had a similar experience. Correnti had a little girl whom the POWs fawned over continually, and one of them who worked as a tailor in the camp made the girl a pair of tiny corduroy overalls.[134]

One Italian POW, Armando Boscolo, described the feelings that led to the prisoners' fascination with kids and why they reacted the way they did on the rare occasions they got to see them. For the prisoners, it was a way to feel human again, to connect with the world beyond the fences. They missed female companionship during their confinement, of course, but:

Worse, in a way, was the impossibility of seeing children, which for me represent the continuity of life and give life meaning, the reason for being.

Only once, in three years of captivity, did I see women—two of them—and a child. They were outside of the enclosure in the American zone. I was enchanted, watching the three of them as though in a dream. While the women talked steadily, the child, dressed in a little red overcoat, sat on the grass playing with some stones.

All at once, he got up and took some steps. I was startled, and had there been no barbed wire I would have run to help him, for I feared that one so tiny shouldn't be allowed to walk alone. In that second I realized that I'd lost all sense of the dimensions of normal life. I was truly buried alive. This was for me, as it was for other prisoners, the lack of liberty hardest to bear.[135]

Marge Best Schramm was another who encountered at first hand the POWs' fondness for kids. She lived on the family farm outside of Farmington and was just eight or nine years old when her father, Edwin Best, hired twenty-five POWs to help around the place at harvest time.

"When I first saw the men, they really scared me," said Schramm. "I never heard them speak anything but Italian and I couldn't understand it, of course. Mother said that I had to be nice to them though, because they probably had family at home, little girls like me, and missed them a lot."

Despite the girl's fear of the men, the exchange was good for all concerned: Farmer Best was pleased enough with the work that he hired the prisoners on several other occasions, the POWs got to enjoy a hearty lunch under a shade tree in the Bests' yard, and little Marge got over her initial hesitation. She still has two coins given to her by one of the prisoners, small coins that came from half a world away.[136]

Italians on the Hill and Weingarten

Having such a large population of Italian soldiers just seventy-five miles from St. Louis was a great source of interest for those living in St. Louis's Italian American neighborhood, a place called the Hill. Many of the residents of this tightly knit community had been born in Italy and so naturally had an affinity toward the POWs. In some cases, they sought out the interned soldiers for friendship, visiting them at the camp and taking them to St. Louis for weekend visits.

Weingarten had a straightforward policy on visitors coming to the camp to see POWs. Internees could have visitors if both they and the visitor made a written request approved by the camp commander. During the visit an interpreter had to be present, and after the visit was complete, prisoners were patted down to prevent concealment of contraband.[137]

In September 1943, Father Fiorenzo Lupo, pastor of St. Ambrose Catholic Church, the largest Italian parish in St. Louis, chartered a bus for twenty-four residents of the Hill. They drove the seventy-five miles of winding roads just to visit the POW camp and to talk to the Italians in person. Another group of Italian Americans from "the big colony in St. Louis," as one out-of-state GI called it, came later that month to put on a stage show in the camp theater for the POWs.[138]

Italians living on the Hill also sent the bus to Weingarten on a number of Sundays to pick up the prisoners and bring them to St. Louis. The men were dropped off at St. Ambrose, where they attended Mass and dined with Hill residents at some of the area's many Italian restaurants. After an afternoon of visiting, they returned to the camp in the evening. Another man from the Hill who had immigrated to the United States after serving in the Italian army during World War I visited Weingarten at least every other week. He helped the POW officers get around the delays caused by American censors by sending and receiving their mail.[139]

Corporal Frank La Piana, an American GI, saw the hospitality of those who lived on the Hill in person. La Piana, who was with the 110th Medium Automotive Maintenance Company, was assigned to accompany an Italian officer from Camp Carson, Colorado, back to Camp Weingarten, and while changing trains in St. Louis he experienced some of that enthusiasm and fondness the Italian Americans in St. Louis felt toward those from the old country:

In St. Louis, we had a seven- or eight-hours layover before taking a train to Ste. Genevieve, so I decided to tour the town by streetcar. A young woman in the seat behind us noticed we were speaking Italian, and we ended up going to her father's bar and grill, and then to their home for dinner. I placed my automatic [service revolver] in a drawer and everyone was very relaxed.

Afterwards, a long line of friends and neighbors came just to meet a real Italian officer. I felt as though I was exhibiting some big movie star! But it was a great way to pass some time.[140]

Josephine Signorino's father, Joseph DeGregorio, an Italian-born U.S. citizen and resident of the Hill, was completely taken by the notion that there was a big crowd of Italian soldiers at Camp Weingarten. As soon as DeGregorio got word of the camp's opening, he took his wife, Sally, and seventeen-year-old Josephine and roared down to Weingarten in the family's 1939 Packard on the first available weekend. He would be a fixture at Weingarten as often as possible in those days of rationed tires and gasoline. Both the family and the prisoners looked forward to the visits, and Signorino especially enjoyed the trips to the camp. Naturally the young beauty drew a lot of attention. "It was great being there," she smiled, remembering those hot, sunny days in the summer of 1943. "I was the only girl at the camp."

In the course of these visits with the Italian soldiers, the DeGregorios struck up a surprisingly strong friendship with one particular man, Virgilio Priore, and began to see him regularly. "He and my father had a lot in common," said Signorino. "They both shared a sense of respect, of fidelity, of honor. Their word meant everything, and I think they saw that in one another."

The bonds they formed in those early visits would continue through letters and phone calls after the war. "He was a fine gentleman, an artist," recalled Signorino. "He painted a beautiful picture of me from a black and white photo my father gave him." Priore was a musician, and Signorino's mother would send him sheet music for popular American tunes. They became so close that Sally DeGregorio was a godmother to one of Priore's sons. Ultimately, their friendship would last nearly forty years, until Sally's passing in 1979.

Even though Priore developed a great friendship with the whole DeGregorio family, he was particularly fond of Josephine, who found herself drawn to him in return. "He finally proposed to me, but I was too young to handle it," said Signorino. "I told him that we could see what would happen if he wanted to wait until after the war. I was really unsure about leaving the country."

Even though a more cynical or skeptical mind might view this marriage proposal as simply one way for a bored POW to find a little diversion, or to perhaps increase his chances of being able to come back to the United States after the war, Signorino never saw it that way. She was convinced that Priore's intentions were noble and genuine and that his affection for her went beyond a barbed-wire barricade. "He was a man of great honor, very educated and intelligent," she said of Priore, who was her senior by several years. "I could tell by his words and actions that he was sincere and quite serious about his proposal."

After the war, Priore returned to Italy, and Josephine DeGregorio became Josephine Signorino when she married a local. The family lost touch with Priore after Signorino's mother died, but even sixty years later Signorino still thought from time to time about the man who was so very close to her family, the man who once proposed to her. "I miss that friendship, those letters he used to send," she said.[141]

Having these opportunities to visit with the great crowd of friends and relatives in the Italian American community in St. Louis and the greater United States would eventually mean that the prisoners would have to say good-bye to them as well. There was so much contact between POWs and Italian Americans that before their impending departure, the Italian POWs asked if would be possible for them to give their farewells to relatives in the States by telegram or telephone or even to visit with them at the port of departure before they shipped out, a request ultimately denied by the government.[142]

Worries about Home

Like men of any nationality separated from their families by war, the Italian prisoners at Weingarten were understandably concerned about the fate of loved ones who remained back home.

In an August 26, 1944, letter to Ernest Wagner, general manager of the Missouri Hybrid Corn Company in Fulton, Giuseppe Grondona thanked

Wagner for sending a picture of his son. Grondona had met Wagner and his family while working on a corn-detasseling detail in Columbia.

"When I saw the picture of your good boy, I was thinking of my two, same age. They still live on the battlefront," Grondona wrote. "Three days ago I received a postal-card from one of my friends in Zurich. He told me that in April [some five months prior] my family was well."[143]

This lack of knowledge and absence of specific information coming from the areas of Italy that had been greatly affected by the conflict contributed "very much to the demoralization of the prisoners" at Weingarten toward the end of the war. "Lack of news from home, misinterpreted news read in the papers, and false reports coming from friends creates a state of individual disquiety, which has its effects on the mass of the prisoners," wrote Guy Metraux, an inspector with the International Red Cross."[144]

Colonel Glidden was sensitive to these issues among the men at Weingarten, and his ongoing warmhearted treatment of the prisoners as well as his specific actions and reactions to POW concerns during times of mounting uncertainty were noted in several inspection reports. Even though most of these problems were just as far beyond his control as they were beyond the POWs' control, the awareness he and his staff displayed certainly alleviated the prisoners' anxiety at least to some small degree.

Mail call at Weingarten. Courtesy of Norma Overall Jacob.

One historian described a "barbed-wire syndrome" that frequently sets in among POWs, a state of mind that can have very real, very detrimental effects on the prisoners:

> Mentally, prisoners of war tend to turn retrospective, and "exist in a sort of mental coma" which makes them totally unaware of their surroundings. It is this penchant for escape from reality and the tendency to idealize and romanticize the past while taking a dark view of the future that has to be combated in prison camps....

POW Paul Markl's sketch of life in Camp Clark captures the feeling of loneliness and loss of hope that affected all prisoners to an extent. Courtesy of Dagmar Ford.

A prisoner retains the ability to think but not to act upon those thoughts. Thinking for the sake of thinking, however, often leads to brooding, embitterment, pessimism, for the prisoner can only perceive the future theoretically, he "cannot influence or form it."[145]

It was exactly this situation that Colonel Glidden and his staff tried to alleviate. "The American authorities, and especially the Colonel, understand the state of mind of the prisoners," wrote Metraux. As noted by another visitor:

Colonel Glidden has always shown the greatest interest in the camp in general and the prisoners in particular.… How pleasant and human it is to visit with the Commanding Officer and usually a group of prisoners in the different POW canteens and have refreshments with all of them, and even more to go with him to dinner to some of the prisoner of war mess halls.

No one can overestimate how much these things mean to the men behind the fence. These might look like ordinary small things but they are not. They are of great importance to people who are cut off from ordinary life and the rest of the world. It helps them feel that they still are human beings.[146]

Given the problems with the mail service to Italy and the delays caused by the censorship process, the Catholic Church provided assistance to prisoners by facilitating communications with their families through other channels. "In several of my visits at the Compound, I was beseeched with requests to locate people, and I would ask that you immediately prepare a form which we may have printed to make such a search," wrote Monsignor John Cody to Father Gerold Kaiser, who ministered to prisoners at Weingarten. "We could distribute these forms though the compounds and perhaps locate missing relatives, friends, etc."[147]

Using these forms, church officials worked to connect Italian POWs with relatives in the United States. "I thought perhaps that periodically you might forward to us a list of relatives who live in this vicinity together with the name of the prisoner who is making the inquiry," wrote Edward Gaffney, an official with the chancery office in New York. "We might then search the city directory as well as the telephone directory to establish the residence of these people in New York.… The local newspapers as well as the Catholic press and Italian press would also cooperate, and in that way I am quite sure many of the relatives can be located."[148]

Naturally, the prisoners were grateful to receive such assistance, and the Church took merited satisfaction at connecting these men with their families. "The Chancery Office of St. Louis, with the hearty approval of the Commanding Officer at Weingarten, has been assisting the prisoners to locate relatives, friends and acquaintances here in the United States," wrote Cody in a report of the Catholic Church's work at Weingarten. "Already we have succeeded in finding relatives for many of the men, even in cases where only a name was given us as a clue."[149]

Church officials also used the Vatican Information Service to route messages through Rome to families of the prisoners back in Italy. Cody noted in August 1943 that Italian prisoners transferred to Weingarten from Fort Leonard Wood who had used the service in April were beginning to receive return messages from their families.

"In this morning's mail I received two replies from families who were sent messages from Fort Leonard Wood by their prisoner of war sons and from this it would appear that the Vatican Information Service has succeeded in transmitting the messages sent from Fort Leonard Wood," wrote Cody to the Reverend Amleto Cicognani, the apostolic delegate to the United States from the Roman Catholic Church.[150]

Prisoners desperate for word from home were thrilled by this possibility. Major Alessandro Tarasca, the Italian officer over Compound 2, wrote the St. Louis Archdiocese with a request for help and note of the Italians' appreciation for this service:

> I am writing to you a list of P.O.W. who haven't heard from their families for a period of six months or over. At the same time, I would be very grateful if you could send me about one thousand blank telegram slips so that I can distribute them to my soliders so that they might wire home.
>
> It would be a great act of humanity for which you have my deepest devotion and gratitude and also that of my men.[151]

Cody's response was to send not just a single batch of one thousand slips as requested but to ask if a thousand more message forms might be sent each week from the apostolic delegation's office in Washington, D.C., to the camp at Weingarten. "The prisoners of war are more confident in forwarding their messages through the Vatican and many of the superior officers have informed me that they would rather communicate a brief message than write a letter which they knew would never be delivered."[152]

Ultimately, this effort by both the Catholic Church and the camp administration to connect prisoners with missing relatives was a great success in terms of easing the anxiety of both prisoners and the lost family members in Europe. Because of the positive impact he knew it would have on the men under his watch, Colonel Glidden even relaxed the rules in these attempts to find loved ones of the prisoners.

"Despite regulations to the contrary, Colonel Glidden has never interferred with our work in searching for the missing relatives of the prisoners of war at Camp Weingarten," wrote Cody. "We have had some fifteen hundred requests and we have been able to [find] some nine hundred persons for the prisoners of war from this number."[153]

Prisoners Return Home

As the war in Europe wound down in the spring of 1945 and an eventual return to Italy transformed from a distant possibility to an impending reality, both the Americans and the Italian POWs knew that the prisoners faced a difficult time when they arrived home.

"It did seem a shame that those PWs should have ever had to fight— they should have remained in the homeland, working on the farm, in the post office, the factory, drinking the beloved 'Vino,' etc.," wrote Sergeant Quinton Bianco in his diary. But if wishes were horses, then beggars would ride, and there was no question that going back to reestablish life in war-ravaged Italy would be a challenge. Prisoners spent a lot of time discussing what it would be like and often argued their strong opinions as to how the postwar government should be organized.

"The 408th was now having the same five PWs continually working in the kitchen and one of them was the likeable, big, muscular and jolly Primo," wrote Bianco. "One of the other Italians was quite the Fascist and a lively discussion, through an interpreter, could be had…but as Primo once said, 'when war over, Russia no win, England no win, Germany no win—nobody no win.'"[154]

By late summer 1945, the single issue that occupied the prisoners' minds was the question of repatriation and when exactly it might take place. By that time, it had been almost exactly two years since Italy had surrendered to the Allies, and nearly six months since the end of the war in Europe. A delegate from the Italian embassy came to visit the prisoners at Weingarten and witnessed the intensity of their desire to return home, as well as their anger at the perceived unfairness of the process used to select those who were being shipped back:

The main concern of the prisoners, both officers and enlisted men, [is] related to their repatriation and how quickly this could be accomplished. The officer group was particularly outspoken in this regard. They seemed to feel that they had been detained in this country too long and without justifiable reason. They contended that some prisoners less deserving than they had already been returned to Italy and that in such cases it appeared to them that preference had been given to individuals who were members of prominent families in Italy.

They stated also, that some of those who had been returned were known to have strong fascist leanings. It is significant to note that their criticism of the way in which repatriation arrangements have been handed was directed to the officials of the present Italian government, as well as to the American authorities.[155]

The Weingarten prisoners were also interested to know how they would receive payment of the funds that had been credited to their accounts for participation in the POW labor program. They wanted to have an arrangement created whereby they could get their money in hand immediately upon arrival in Italy.

"They pointed out that in the light of existing economic conditions in Italy they would have urgent need for this money, and that delays would impose undue hardships on their families," wrote a State Department's representative who accompanied the delegate from the Italian embassy.

The process in place for cashing out the prisoners' accounts was basically in line with that request. Upon departure from the United States, the prisoner received a nonnegotiable certificate for the amount owed him in U.S. dollars. Upon arrival in Italy, the funds could be converted to lira through the U.S. Army disbursing officer.

Along with that certificate for the money accumulated during their time at the camp, prisoners were allowed to keep all items of clothing that came in the standard POW issue, with the exception of overcoats. Additionally, each POW could take two woolen blankets and a mess kit.[156]

The End of the Camp

Beginning with the first groups sent home in August, the process of shipping the Italian prisoners home moved quickly. By mid-September 1945, half the prisoner population had departed, and only 2,000 internees remained of the 4,500 held there just a couple of months before.

"A contingent of 657 Italian prisoners of war held at Weingarten, Mo., sailed for home yesterday aboard a Liberty ship from Jersey City, N.J.," reported the *St. Louis Globe-Democrat* on September 13, 1945. A total of 452 officers and 205 enlisted men composed this group, and although Major Frank Kingsland, who had replaced Colonel Glidden as camp commander in July 1945, told the newspaper's reporter that he could not provide any further details, information out of Jersey City indicated that the men were going directly back to Italy, where they would be liberated upon their return.

Even at a POW camp, the closing of the facility is a somewhat bittersweet experience. At one point during the camp's operation, Susie Henderson received some goldfish from a friend and kept them in the dental clinic where she worked. She in turn passed them on to a prisoner after he had asked about how he too could get some. The man had created a flower garden with a small pond in the center and thought the fish would make a nice addition. "It was sad, because when the time came for the camp to close and the men to go home, here comes this same prisoner with two pails of water filled with his goldfish for me to return to my friend," said Henderson.[157]

"I remember when we closed everything," said Teresa Drury. "We were open seven days a week. My typewriter, on the last day, was already in a crate. When I typed my last report, they nailed the top on the crate."[158]

Meanwhile, in the midst of this effort to shut down the camp and send the prisoners home, the last Weingarten wedding was being planned. Farmington native Norma Overall was getting ready to marry First Lieutenant George "Jake" Jacob, who had served at the camp throughout its existence. Jacob was so heavily involved in activities necessary to shutter the installation, he barely had time to think about his impending nuptials. "He was the last officer to leave the camp. Always said he 'locked the camp up' on November 1, 1945," said Norma Overall Jacob. "He and I were the last to be married at

George and Norma Jacob on their wedding day, October 13, 1945. Courtesy of Norma Overall Jacob.

Camp Weingarten. Our wedding reception was held in the Officers' Club on October 13, 1945, and three weeks later the camp was closed tight."[159]

Captain Joseph Waxer, with the POW Special Projects Division (the component responsible for the prisoner re-education program), visited the camp about the same time to assess the status of the reorientation activities among Weingarten POWs. In a fine example of bureaucratic thoroughness, as a follow-up to his September 26, 1945, inspection concerning the intellectual diversion program, Waxer filed a report saying that he had nothing to report.

The final labor report issued from the camp, dated October 15, 1945, listed just 604 NCO prisoners in the camp population, with no officers and no enlisted troops remaining. On it, Major Kingsland noted, "Prisoners of war reported hereon transferred to custody of Commanding Officer, Prisoner of War Camp, Fort Crook, Nebraska, per Par 1, Special Orders 235." No mention of the camp's closing was made in the local press, though the event was marked by a small piece in the *St. Louis Globe-Democrat*: "The 790-acre Prisoner of War Camp at Weingarten, Mo.,... has been declared surplus and its prisoners will be moved to camps outside the Seventh Service Command, it was announced yesterday."[160]

In a July 1946 retrospective, *The Lead Belt News* wrote of the local residents' fondness for the servicemen stationed at Weingarten, a piece that marked the way the soldiers and the camp had affected their lives: "In general, they were a swell group of fellows who will not soon be forgotten.... The latch string is always out with a hearty welcome and a standing invitation extended to them at all times."[161]

Options for Postwar Use of the Camp

After Weingarten officially was declared surplus property in September 1945 and closed completely by the government in October, a number of proposals were floated for its use. In January 1946, Thomas Inkley, operator of the Ste. Genevieve County Marble Quarry, suggested to the American War Dads organization that they sponsor an effort to have the Weingarten site turned over to the Veterans Administration as a permanent hospitalization center for veterans with tuberculosis.

Copies of Inkley's letter recommending adoption of the plan were sent to St. Louis mayor Aloys Kaufmann and the Ste. Genevieve Chamber of Commerce to garner their support, and after several local VFW and American Legion posts joined in endorsing the plan, it was forwarded to General Omar Bradley, whom Truman had appointed in August 1945 to head the Department of Veterans Affairs. Several other Farmington patriotic and civic organizations made similar requests.[162]

In the meantime, the government started the process of removing buildings from the site of the former installation and reusing the structures in other places whenever possible. On February 26, 1946, the War Assets Administration declared seven hundred frame buildings at Weingarten surplus housing and offered them to the city of St. Louis, saying that they could be removed as soon as the city could furnish a site for them. Though not originally intended or used as housing, these structures could "be converted into three- and four-room apartments, with one or two bedrooms, according to the size of the family."[163]

The Citizens Emergency Housing Committee coordinated the transfer of the buildings to the St. Louis area. The committee had originally sought twenty-four hundred units from Weingarten but ended up with less than a third of what they requested.

"We'll take the 700 gladly, and we have sites available for them," said J. Wesley McAfee, chairman of the committee, and indicated that a representative of the committee was in Chicago to collect specific details of the buildings' construction and exact requirements for transporting and reconfiguring the buildings for residential use. Sale of the structures was limited to veterans who lived in the St. Louis area at the time of their induction into military service, and priority for purchase was established on the basis of need by the Veterans Service Center in downtown St. Louis.[164]

Other buildings were removed and re-erected at various colleges around the state as makeshift living quarters for former GIs who enrolled as students after the war. Some of the structures even were transported outside Missouri. A number of Quonset huts, those ubiquitous World War II metal shelters, ended up in South Bend, Indiana, and were used as housing for returning veterans enrolled at Notre Dame University in an area on campus known as "Vetville."[165] The guardhouse, purchased by Paul and Gilbert Ray for $513.13, was used to build the first six units of the Twin City Motel in Crystal City, Missouri.[166]

By the spring of 1947, the government was looking to unload surplus property from the camp any way it could. On March 22, 1947, Orvil R. Olmsted, regional director of Federal Public Housing, announced the sale of eighty-eight miscellaneous buildings for removal from the site and reuse elsewhere. Priority holders, including war veterans and the like, had just over a week to exercise their status; after that, bids would be open until April 10. People from all over came to purchase the structures, and soon a small army of hammer- and crowbar-wielding men and women swarmed the former campgrounds.

Among the local crews tearing down buildings at the camp for use of the lumber elsewhere was the littlest workman of all, ten-year-old Wayman Starnes. Starnes, whose brother Bruce had been involved in the camp's construction in 1942, was hired by a man from nearby Doe Run, a schoolteacher by the name of George Burch who used his free time in the summer and the wood from the camp to build several homes in and around Doe Run. Burch would tear boards off the building he had purchased and pile them up while Starnes and Burch's two sons, Calvin and Bill, would pull the old nails out of the wood. "We each had a set of saw horses, a hammer, and a crowbar," recalled Starnes. "By the time we were finished, we must have had a pile of nails about two foot high."

Starnes's wages were just a bit better than what had been paid to the camp's former residents, the POWs, who had received $.80 a day for their labor. Burch paid him $1 a day for his nail-pulling prowess, and Starnes still remembers when it came time to settle up. "He gave me six one-dollar bills," said Starnes, who watched the man count the money and lay it into his hand. "Six dollars for six days of work. That was a lot of money for a kid back then, and I was as proud as could be of the money I had earned."[167]

In early 1947, William Downes was looking to build a house and cut costs at the same time. To help with the house he was putting up in Shrewsbury, Missouri, Downes went to Weingarten and bought himself one of the retired barracks from the camp. "When we found out that we had been high bidder in the government auction of the property at Weingarten, we had sixty days to get the building off of the premises," said his son, John Downes, who as a fifteen-year-old boy helped dismantle the structure. "We went down on the weekends and worked to tear it down and then hauled the lumber off to St. Louis."

It was cold that February, and the work was slow and difficult. Trying to dismantle a building so that the lumber could be reused meant removing boards carefully, one at a time. However, discovering a treasure trove of items the Italian POWs had hidden in the eaves and behind the wall panels of their home was a sure way to take a boy's mind off his frozen hands.

"As we dismantled the building where they slept, I found individual serving boxes of cereal they had hidden in the eaves of the building along with candy wrappers," recalled Downes. "I also remember some little scraps of paper with a few words of handwritten Italian. One item I remember was a scrap of aluminum smaller than my hand. It was about one-eighth of an inch thick and had been torn out of something (possibly a plane?) and was badly bent.... What made it interesting to me was that someone had written a few words on it in Italian by making indents with a sharp, fine-point tool, maybe a nail. It was like writing with dots. None of us could read Italian, and now I am sorry I didn't keep it."

Those items for Downes suddenly represented a direct link to the very real people who had until only recently walked the same floor of the building where the boy was working. He realized the human connection, the kind of quirkiness that lies in all people that makes them do things like stash away little boxes of cereal or etch words in a piece of scrap metal.

"I was fifteen years old at the time. The idea that Italians were kept as prisoners of war in Missouri captured my imagination. I looked around at the fences with the guard towers and tried to imagine what it was like to be captured by the Americans in Africa, Sicily, or Italy and sent to a prison camp in the middle of America," recalled Downes. "The impossibility of escaping and find[ing] a way back to Italy must have weighed hard on them. I knew they had been our enemy, but at the same time, I could not help but feel sorry for them."[168]

Even though the War Dads' plan for a VA hospital did not materialize on the Weingarten site as proposed, others were interested in the former camp, seeing much potential in its remaining buildings and the existing infrastructure, with electric, water, and sewage lines already in place.

In August 1947, the War Assets Administration regional office acknowledged that a bid had been made by the Missouri State Division of Mental Diseases on 840 acres of the former campsite for use as an

Two Italian prisoners hang washed clothing out to dry on the back porch of the enlisted men's compound at Camp Weingarten. Photograph by Buel White of the St. Louis Post-Dispatch, *© 1943. Courtesy of the* St. Louis Post-Dispatch.

annex to the overcrowded State Hospital No. 4 in nearby Farmington. The portion of the camp they sought included remaining sections of the 256-bed Weingarten camp hospital. That plan too came to naught, and the land slowly reverted back to farmland and pasture. The original landowners were given first chance to buy back their property, but most declined the opportunity. Even though the wooden structures of the camp were gone, the concrete foundations and old roadbeds that remained on the grounds rendered substantial swaths of the once-productive acreage largely untillable.

Judy Schwartz Kreitler, daughter of Francis and Rita Schwartz, who lived across the street from the camp, and granddaughter of Mary Jaeger, who woefully wondered where she "would go to die" after being displaced by the camp, remembered the treasure hunt she experienced as a girl growing up on the land that had been the Weingarten camp. Her father bought land that had been part of Henry Harter's farm and built a house on what had been the foundation of the commanding officer's quarters.[169]

"We used to find old toothbrushes and shoes, but we didn't know the significance of what we were finding," she recalled. "My brother found an old dog tag of one of the prisoners and we found spent shells. But you know, when you're kids, you find things and put them in a clubhouse and then you forget them."

Even former POWs sometimes returned to the site of their internment. Vincenzo Mancuso was one who had been housed at Camp Weingarten as a POW and later came back to visit while on a business trip to St. Louis, recalled Rita Schwartz. "Mancuso did tell me that he had wanted to come back…that he had plenty of good times here," she said. "He referred to it as 'Hotel Weingarten,'" added daughter Judy. "He said he did not want to go back to Italy because he knew what he was going back to."[170]

Even though the prisoners are long gone from the camp at Weingarten, traces remain. Every spring, flowers originally planted by the Italian prisoners of war burst through the Missouri soil to unveil their showy buds. In 1982, a *Jefferson County (Missouri) Democrat-Rocket* writer described a walk through the grounds of the former camp:

> What remains is merely pasture ground, overgrown with brambles and scrub pine. The only signs of that long-ago habitation are well hidden by the early spring foliage. One comes upon them unexpectedly.

> Here among the trees is a concrete foundation, weeds spreading through the cracks. There, up the hill, is what looks like an overgrown path. A closer look reveals the bare outlines of a once well-traveled road. A line of neat suburban homes lines the outer edge of the forgotten camp. Behind one stands the only startling reminder of Camp Weingarten. A magnificent rock fireplace rises above a slab of concrete, all that is left of the officers' quarters and, luxury of luxuries, the tennis courts.

The fireplace is a sentinel for those who live here and those who visit. It represents a period of time when lives were in an upheaval. Families who had lived a generation or more were evicted. Strangers who had never seen the wilds of Missouri before were transported here to live out several years of their lives.[171]

Camp Clark barracks under construction. Courtesy of Bushwhacker Museum, Vernon County Historical Society.

Facing: Dental laboratory at Camp Crowder. Courtesy of Missouri State Archives.

Chapter Four

Camp Clark

O N DECEMBER 12, 1942, THREE MP COMPANIES under the command of Captain Fred T. Mealy stood in battle gear, ready to receive the first group of 350 Italian POWs at Camp Clark, just outside of Nevada, Missouri. The men had been training at Clark for three weeks in anticipation of the arrival of these POWs, most of whom were captured by the British in North Africa before being sent to the United States. Mealy's men were keyed up that day as they awaited the arrival of the prisoners aboard a special Missouri Pacific train pulling nine coaches and a kitchen car. The MPs assembled near the depot and were making final preparations for the prisoners when word came that the speeding train had gone off the tracks.[1]

After making a brief stop at Rich Hill, Missouri, some thirty miles north of Nevada to pick up bread, the train was just seven miles from the camp, on schedule to arrive at Camp Clark before noon. As the locomotive and its cars sped around a curve, a faulty rail broke under the weight of the train. Five coaches plunged down an embankment, killing two American guards aboard the train and injuring sixty-seven POWs. It was 10:32 A.M.

The scene was utter chaos. Fearing mass escape, military and state police armed with machine guns tore to the derailment site, and ambulances and Army trucks chased them to the scene of the wreck. All roads within ten miles of the overturned train were closed to keep back the crowds of rubberneckers and the curious. But the prisoners did not try to escape. Docile and passive, they milled about, waiting for instructions. The Italians, almost none of whom could speak or understand English, offered no resistance as they were loaded into the trucks for the last seven miles of their six-thousand-mile journey.[2]

"A bunch of people were hurt when the train went off

the tracks, but the people on my car, we were okay. Just a few with some bumps. We just climbed out of the wreck and stood around, waiting for them to tell us what to do," said Giuseppe Zanti, an Italian POW on that train. "They put us on the trucks and took us the rest of the way to the camp."[3]

George Breen, a twenty-four-year-old GI, was on guard duty at the camp, waiting for the POWs to arrive. "It was amazing," Breen said. "The prisoners helped gather up the guns from the guards who had been wounded and killed, and then they just handed them right over to the GIs after they had been collected."[4]

The first group of arrivals was not an impressive lot. Tired and dirty, the soldiers cast an image that stayed with Mrs. Lloyd Davis, who with her husband managed the post exchange at Camp Clark during World War II. "I never saw such tired, filthy, bedraggled men," Davis recalled. "They were still wearing the same uniforms they had on when they were captured in the deserts of North Africa."[5]

Betty Sterett described the scene in a later history of the camp. "No one who was at Camp Clark that cloudy winter day will ever forget the sight of the first contingent of Italian prisoners as they climbed down from the big army trucks and walked, or were carried, into the compound," wrote Sterett, a longtime columnist at the *Nevada (Missouri) Daily Mail and Evening Post*. "Filthy, exhausted and frightened, many clutched small bundles containing everything they owned. Clothed in rags, some were even barefoot. One dark-eyed boy cradled a whimpering mongrel dog in his arms."[6]

History of Camp Clark

Though unexpected, this calamitous start to Camp Clark's service as a POW camp was in line with its swashbuckling existence, one that predated the POW camp by many years. Camp Clark was created April 28, 1908, when the government received title for 320 acres of land just three miles southwest of Nevada, Missouri, establishing a military reservation in an area previously best known for its bloody Civil War history. One hundred well-armed Union troops aiming to clean out the nest of "bushwhackers," or Confederate guerrillas infesting the area, burned Nevada to the ground only forty-five years earlier, on May 26, 1863, and the residents of greater Vernon County suffered incredible abuse from pro-Union militia out of nearby Cedar and St. Clair Counties as well as the border-crossing Kansas Jayhawkers.[7]

All this was still relatively recent history when Missouri governor Joseph W. Folk appointed General Harvey C. Clark, Adjutant General James

DeArmond, and Major W. L. Chambers to select a location for a new training area and headquarters for the Missouri National Guard. The trio visited Clinton, Sedalia, Columbia, Boonville, and Sweet Springs but finally settled on a site near Nevada, in the upper part of the state's southwest corner, about fifty miles north of Joplin and just fifteen miles east of the Kansas line. When Nevada residents heard the news of the site's selection, they were so thrilled by this addition to their community that they immediately raised $6,000 to defray the cost of the rifle range planned for the facility.[8]

At first, the installation was known as Camp Hadley, named for Missouri governor Herbert Spencer Hadley (1908–13), but after a time, Camp Clark became the recognized tag in honor of General Harvey Clark, who had helped pick the location. Clark was a giant in the history of the Missouri National Guard, serving as the architect of its complete reorganization in 1900 and coordinating the relocation of the Guard headquarters from Butler to Nevada when Camp Clark was established.

The camp first saw rather routine use as a target range and training area for the 70th Infantry Brigade and the 110th Engineer Battalion of the Missouri Guard but quickly experienced other, more wildly divergent uses than General Clark probably ever envisioned for his namesake. In 1916, less than a decade after its establishment, Camp Clark was transformed into the mobilization point for six thousand troops going to put down the Mexican border insurrection and to hunt for Pancho Villa in the southwestern United States and Mexico. Within two years, another flood of soldiers, this time some ten thousand strong, arrived at Camp Clark. Instead of going to Mexico, these troops shipped out to Europe to join the final fighting of World War I.[9] Beginning in the 1920s, a grass airstrip stretched across the northwest corner of the post, and Camp Clark was home to an aviation unit whose members flew a Curtiss OX JN-4 "Jenny," purchased by the unit's officers. Perhaps the most famous member of this group was Captain Charles Lindbergh, who in 1927 made the first solo flight across the Atlantic.

Over the next twenty years, the government purchased an additional 1,060 acres to triple the size of the camp, and much-needed improvements were made, including augmenting the camp's sole water source, one meager well dug in the first years of its existence. In 1934 the Works Project Administration, part of President Franklin Roosevelt's New Deal, allocated $27,000 to the War Department for improvements at Camp Clark. This project aimed to provide work for the hundreds of unemployed local men in Vernon County and created the permanent structures built from the distinctive stone and red clay tile that served for decades as barracks and other administrative buildings at Camp Clark.

World War II came, and the camp saw a dramatic reversal in its use. Suddenly, instead of sending American boys off to war in Europe, Camp Clark began receiving soldiers from the other side of the Atlantic. The men in uniform marching around the post weren't greenhorn GIs, they were from enemy armies—captured Italians and Germans shipped to the United States to stay until the fighting was done.

That Camp Clark was used as a prison for POWs was no accident, as residents worked hard to make sure that their camp was not overlooked in the total war effort. They knew from the camp's use during past conflicts that the imminent U.S. involvement in the war meant that the pace would pick up at Camp Clark. For years it had served mainly as the site of the Missouri Guard's summer encampments, and Nevada was abuzz over the possibility that activity at Camp Clark would rev up once again.

Regardless of the ultimate nature of its use, transformation of the sleepy, wooded acreage into an epicenter of military activity, bustling with men and equipment, meant one thing: cash, and lots of it, for area businesses. So the Nevada Chamber of Commerce set about an ambitious lobbying campaign via a special committee headed by E. H. Busiek, encouraging the War Department to look to Camp Clark as wartime pressure swelled the demand for expansion of military facilities.

Use as an aviation training center or an internment camp for aliens topped the list of possibilities. Busiek and his chamber of commerce committee worked with the U.S. senators from Missouri, Bennett C. Clark and Harry S Truman, along with the U.S. representative from the area, Phil Bennett, to influence the War Department to settle on one of these two choices.

The group wanted either option, but Busiek said in the instance of an internment camp for enemy POWs, Nevada was uniquely equipped psychologically to handle the influx of these "dangerous" men, promising that the War Department would experience no backlash from the community. This public outcry had occurred in other towns where POW camps were to be located, including Sedalia, Missouri, where residents protested to Governor Forrest C. Donnell after learning it was being considered for a POW camp.

"We have had a state hospital here for a number of years caring for the insane," said Busiek, "and having found its location near Nevada to be an asset instead of a menace, we do not fear the results of such a camp as much as people might in other communities."[10]

Busiek led the charge from Nevada, writing letters to Colonel John O'Brien and Colonel Walter J. Reed, who were involved in property acquisition for the Army and the Army Air Corps, respectively. Busiek touted the transportation to the site and the availability of both land and housing. "Additional contiguous land, if necessary, can be readily acquired at prices from $25 to $60 an acre," wrote Busiek. "Our Chamber of Commerce would cooperate in the acquisition of such land and help to hold the price down, instead of running it up."[11]

When officials in charge of National Guard properties expressed initial reluctance to release Camp Clark for use of the regular army, Busiek called on Congressman Phil Bennett to "blast these entrenched bureaucrats out of their smug position."

"It all amounts to the reluctance of a few National Guard officials to give up their feather beds, even in these times of stress," wrote Busiek. "We have something [in Camp Clark] that we know the government wants and needs but just a few hogs lying in the trough are still able to obstruct us."[12]

Even though the Nevada committee presented a unified front, the effort was still marked by backroom conversations and political jockeying as the area's elected officials tried to position themselves to take credit for the anticipated new projects at the camp.

Busiek sent a note to Congressman Bennett, complaining about the way the *Nevada Daily Mail and Evening Post* was underplaying Bennett's role in the efforts because of partisan leanings:

> I couldn't talk freely when I called you. Newspaper reporter was sitting in the office. You know how rotten partisan they are. Last week they ran an article saying the Chamber of Commerce through me had written Clark and Truman. They didn't mention you. I raised hell, told them you were the only one working. Today they will run story covering your letter with [Provost Marshal General Allen] Gullion.[13]

Busiek then offered a suggestion about how Bennett, a Republican, might get the credit for the camp and keep the limelight from Truman and Clark, both Democrats.

"Point I want to make is this. If you do get news before news agencies, wire me. I'll get you exclusive on that even if I get wires from Clark and Truman," wrote Busiek. "Two can play that game as well as one. When a project comes through we are going to hold a mass meeting and that will be run by *me* [Busiek's emphasis]. That is when you get your inning."[14]

Despite the distraction of this political game, the effort paid off. After months of campaigning by the area's business interests and politicians, the War Department announced in May 1942 that it was allocating $2.5 million to build an "alien internment camp" at Clark. Construction would begin at once. Nevada was electrified by the news. While citizens had known that new activity was possible at the camp, the chamber of commerce's intensive lobbying campaign had been something of a loosely held secret. Out of fear of jeopardizing the town's chances, the *Nevada Daily Mail and Evening Post* had not publicized the community's effort to land a major government project. And, to Busiek's satisfaction, when the government's decision was finally covered in the paper, equal credit was given to Bennett, Truman, and Clark for landing the camp.

Getting an "alien internment camp" meant that Clark was as likely to hold enemy POWs as Americans internees of Japanese, German, or Italian descent of questionable loyalty. Officials attempted to assuage citizens apprehensive about having large numbers of "aliens" in their midst:

> The building of the internment camp means a large construction project, to house and care for from 3,000 to 9,000 persons. Alien enemies means Japanese, Germans and Italians and any other nationals who may be guilty of subversive activities....

> No one need fear the presence of the aliens who may be interned in the camp for they will be under guard both day and night, guarded from both the inside and the outside and with army officers in charge....

> Any question as to whether you welcome the alien internment camp or prefer some other kind of camp is now out, completely out. The establishment of the alien camp at Camp Clark is part of the nation's war effort, and we, all of us, should, and no doubt do, accept the war department's decision 100 per cent. We are all out for our country in its efforts to win the war.[15]

This effort to reassure the people of Vernon County wasn't just window dressing. The announcement that Camp Clark would be used as an internment center prompted an "undercurrent of apprehension" to ripple through the area. Wild rumors circulated, and some even talked about putting together a petition drive to halt construction.[16]

Despite the efforts of the government and local leaders to calm these fears, the best salve turned out to be plain old-fashioned cash. Once the adding machines started tallying the government funds dedicated to the camp's construction, all the money calculated to come in as a result of the project was enough to soothe the nerves of even the most worrisome of worriers. The chamber of commerce's effort to secure the camp was indeed a windfall for Nevada and Vernon County. The benefits of having the camp meant lots of jobs and cash for local businesses and no unpleasant economic hangover at the end of the war, claimed the newspaper:

> Large barracks, administration and other buildings will be built and vast other improvements made at the camp. This means a large body of workmen will have to be employed, and probably 400 or 500 guards will be employed and some 400 or 500 army officers and men will have to be stationed at the camp to operate it. All of this means a large amount of money will be thrown into Nevada's business channels, through purchases and rentals and everyone will be either directly or indirectly benefited....

> The one greatest advantage of an internment camp over some other war projects is that when the war is over, there will be no disastrous slump due to its establishment.[17]

A good barometer of the general increase in business the camp meant for Nevada and the larger area came through the jump in business on the railroad, both in passenger and freight traffic. With the start of World War II and the creation of the internment facility at Camp Clark, both the Katy (Missouri, Kansas, and Texas) and the Missouri Pacific Railroads were hauling unprecedented quantities of soldiers, civilians, and freight. Passenger ticket sales at the Nevada station jumped from a pre-war average of $3,000 a month to more than $100,000 a month.[18]

The same housing shortage that manifested itself near other POW camps also appeared in Nevada. Thanks to the new facility going up at Camp Clark as well as to operations at the Pioneer Coal Company, a large enterprise located nine miles from town, the National Housing Commission began efforts to renew the housing stock in Nevada to ease the shortage there.

"Speaking from personal experience, my mother-in-law and father-in-law, who have recently come here, are living with us because they cannot find a place. Another relative who recently moved here cannot find a place," wrote Busiek to Congressman Phil Bennett. "It has not been unusual to have utter strangers ring our door bell and ask if we could provide facilities for them."[19]

One Nevada resident opposed the idea to fix up the town's housing stock. He complained that his family had a number of houses that they could not rent and sent newspaper clippings to Bennett and Senators Clark and Truman showing available housing being advertised. Busiek, who said that if materials were made available the town would have at least twenty-five new homes under construction, revealed the true motivation behind the letters to the Missouri congressmen, at least as he saw it. "We have perhaps four or five people in this town who have made a comfortable living for years buying every piece of junk that has gone on the market and now have very comfortable rental incomes from properties that would not rent at all if we did not have an acute housing shortage," wrote Busiek to Bennett. "Naturally they are interested in preserving this type of monopoly."[20]

The housing restoration project continued as planned, and in time the available housing stock in Nevada finally caught up with the need brought on by the servicemen and their families stationed at Camp Clark and the employees at Pioneer Coal.

Construction Phase

With the announcement of Camp Clark's selection to house an alien internment camp, there was no time to lose in getting the site ready. Even as Nevadans were reading about the imminent camp in the newspaper, engineers and surveyors were already at Camp Clark, preparing for the construction that soon would begin. McCarthy Brothers Construction out of St. Louis won approximately $1.6 million in contracts to create frame barracks, mess halls, guard towers, and wire fencing, and work started only a week later, on June 5, 1942. Thirty-two barracks were planned in the initial stage of construction, and with each of the buildings holding ninety-two people, the camp had a planned capacity of nearly three thousand people. At that time, common belief was that the facility at Camp Clark was being built to hold Japanese Americans relocated from the Pacific coast.

A contingent of architects, civilian and Army engineers, officer staff, craftsmen, and laborers converged on the camp to create the facilities needed to hold the prisoners plus a sizable number of Americans who would operate the internment camp. Four prison compounds and a two-hundred-bed station hospital were raised, all surrounded by a double-wire stockade fence, dotted with eight guard towers equipped with electric signals and powerful searchlights. The inside fence was constructed of barbed wire, while the outer fence, set 12 feet farther out, was constructed of hog wire. Both fences were attached to 6-by-6-inch fence posts and had overhanging, break-down "arms" on top that were laced with barbed wire. A road ran around the outside of the 2,100-by-2,700-foot compound, which was patroled by military police on horseback.[21]

At that time, Camp Clark had three entrance gates along its west side.

The southernmost entrance was the entry point for the railroad spur into the camp. The middle gate serves as Clark's main entrance today, while the third gate, no longer in existence, was about 950 feet north. It intersected with Washington Street, which was used as a patrol road around the compound.[22]

U.S. representative Marion T. Bennett paid a visit to Camp Clark to inspect the POW facility there. The congressman, son of Busiek's ally Phil Bennett, took over after his father died in office in December 1942 and was impressed with the camp, particularly with its security measures.

"Surrounding [the camp] is a double fence of barbed wire. Inside the fence is a row of stakes, and prisoners who get closer to the fence than the stakes are regarded as trying to escape and so understand," said an account of the trip carried in the *Springfield News-Leader*. "One of the things that impressed him [Bennett] most is the guarding of the prisoners with dogs. These are vicious and mostly Great Danes, he said. Sentries patrol the fence leading the dogs, which are trained killers."[23]

Victor Jacobs was an American GI assigned to the camp beginning in 1944. He worked with the dogs, both training the animals for use in delivering messages on the battlefield and using them to patrol the perimeter fence at night. "We made two rounds each night, with the dog on the leash," recalled Jacobs. "If

Camp Clark barracks ca. 1960. Courtesy of Missouri Military History Museum.

we saw a prisoner escaping, we were supposed to order them to stop. They got one chance. If they didn't stop, we were supposed to lower the boom on them, which meant either turning the dog loose or using our weapon."

Jacobs never encountered an escaping prisoner, which he was glad about. "I'd hate to see what those dogs could do to somebody," he said. "They'd go for anything they could get."[24]

Especially during the early days of the camp, the government tried to keep a tight lid on the goings-on at Camp Clark. Photographing the camp was forbidden, and the camp commander did his best to restrict the news coming out of the POW facility, something that the local newspaperman found maddening and did his best to overcome.

"The late Ben Weir's efforts when he was publisher of *The Daily Mail* to penetrate the censorship surrounding Camp Clark are a part of local legend," recalled Ken Postlethwaite, an editorial writer at the paper. "He was tossed into the lake at the camp on orders from the camp commander whose voice, the story goes, had been permanently impaired years earlier when his throat was struck by an errant polo ball. 'Throw that man in the lake!' the colonel reportedly croaked to a burly guard."[25]

"I do remember the incident being told to me," said Weir's son, Ben Weir, Jr., publisher of the *Independence (Missouri) Examiner*, who was about two or three years old at the time. "There was some sort of fight that took place after a dinner event where drinks were involved and tempers got out of hand."[26]

Relations between the camp administration and the newspaper improved not long after Ted Schafers arrived at Camp Clark. Schafers, who later retired as senior editor from the *St. Louis Globe-Democrat* after many years at the paper, was working there as a young reporter when World War II started and he was drafted. Because he could write, the Army assigned him to Jefferson Barracks in the public affairs office, where he interviewed returning servicemen and wrote profile stories for their hometown newspapers.

"I could speak German, and so I volunteered for another assignment," recalled Schafers. "They sent me to Camp Clark and I was put in charge of the mail, opening mail for the German POWs."

Schafers's role fell under the public relations office, and his work eventually put him in contact with Ben Weir, publisher of the *Nevada Daily Mail and Evening Post*. Because of Schafers's background as a newspaperman, the two men developed a comfortable working relationship, and Weir finally got the access to the camp that he so badly wanted. "I'd call him and let him know whenever a shipment of prisoners was going to come in on the train, so that he could send someone out to cover it if he wanted," said Schafers.

Though he enjoyed the duty, life wasn't much fun at Camp Clark for Schafers, who was married, with his wife and two small children left behind in St. Louis. "There was a group of us from St. Louis, and we got home perhaps once a month," recalled Schafers. "We'd all pile into an old car and head back. There weren't any interstates then, so it was probably a seven-hour drive. We'd leave at three or four in the afternoon on a Friday, and it would be close to midnight by the time we got home. Then on Sunday after 3 PM, we'd head back again. Those trips were the only thing we looked forward to."[27]

GIs and the Community

As activity at the post increased because of the construction, and with growing numbers of GIs arriving at Camp Clark, Nevadans braced for changes in their community. They knew that having such an influx of soldiers into a small town could cause some stress. "It wasn't so much the presence of the prisoners that caused some disruption in Nevada," said Paul Dygard, a teenager in the town at the time, "it was having all these GIs there with nothing really to do."[28]

The town square was a popular hangout, and of course the students at all-female Cottey College in Nevada were a source of attraction and curiosity for GIs. Several dances were held at the school, and the *Camp Clark Sentinel*, the post's semimonthly newspaper, printed an announcement for one of these events and even played matchmaker in pairing soldiers with suitable girls. "Cottey College will play host to fifty soldiers from Camp Clark at a dance held at the college. Due to the fact that many soldiers will be invited personally, we can arrange for only 50 dates. Anyone desiring to attend, please turn in his name and height to his first sergeant," read this invitation. "Judging from the other dances at Cottey, a good time will be had by all who attend!"[29]

Dygard recalled the first attempt the school made to host a mixer to bring together American servicemen and girls at the school. "It didn't go too well. Here you had all of these proper young ladies and a bunch of GIs, and they tried to put them together," Dygard said with a chuckle. "I don't think they wanted to try that again. They probably warned them to stay away from the GIs after that."[30]

Once away from the watchful eyes of Cottey faculty, however, the natural attraction between young men and women took place in Nevada, as in other towns in Missouri with military bases nearby. Nevada eventually saw a string of weddings between servicemen and local girls brought together through a variety of social activities.

Recalled Joanne Thomas Saathoff, a Nevada teen who visited the camp on a number of occasions:

> Three of my girlfriends and I frequented a favorite dance spot, Hardins. There were many townspeople working at Camp Clark, and the Army personnel dated and married many local girls. As for me, I dated a most perfect southern gentleman from New Orleans, and we spent quite a bit of time at camp when the German prisoners were there. We were allowed to eat there and we spent time at the lake with other personnel and friends from town. There were USO

dances, baseball games, the theatre and picnics.... My southern gentleman went back home after the war and became a lawyer, and is now a retired judge in New Orleans.

During free time, Clark GIs mingled with townspeople at Radio Springs Park, said Saathoff:

On a lazy Sunday afternoon you could find the local teenagers and the Camp Clark personnel swimming or sunbathing in the pool or spending time dancing in the pavilion to the nickelodeon. The length of the pavilion had booths on both sides and lots of time was spent playing cards in the booths or eating snacks from the snack bar. There was a raised area for the band stand and a dance floor of hardwood the length of the building. It was a fun place to spend time.[31]

Joanne Thomas Saathoff with her "southern gentleman," Frankie Zaccaria. Courtesy of Joanne Thomas Saathoff.

Nevada teen Richard Niles recalled the Camp Clark GIs putting on a special revue for residents of the town. The performance, featuring vocal and instrumental performers, short sketches, and other acts, took place in the high-school auditorium. It was a rousing success, said Niles, well received by Nevadans who appreciated the efforts of those who put it on for their benefit. "There were really talented guys from the camp who got involved in this production," said Niles, "and I'm telling you, it was a big thing in town. We didn't see a whole lot of live entertainment in Nevada in those days."[32]

These diversions helped ease the monotony of the duty, but a big part of the reason soldiers from Clark stayed mostly out of trouble, according to Schafers, was the strong emphasis the camp leadership put on proper behavior when off post. "In many towns, the soldiers could be a problem. They'd get off duty and go get drunk and cause trouble. We didn't have too much

Camp Clark soldiers enjoying off duty hours. Courtesy of Joanne Thomas Saathoff.

of that at Camp Clark. We never got any complaints—at least officially—from the community that I was aware of," said Schafers. "Colonel Frakes [the third camp commander] and Captain Hutchins told the men that they'd better behave, and they believed it. They knew they'd better not cross the line."[33]

Most of the American troops at Camp Clark were good soldiers, but operations at the post—as at other POW camps in the state—were still hampered to a significant extent by a lack of quality, well-trained personnel because of the low-priority nature of the operation. Plus, the work itself didn't offer much more than drudgery and boredom. Indeed, "morale among American personnel in 1944 was reported at a 'low ebb.' Studies showed that the camps' administrative personnel felt that they were not active participants in the war, or if they were returned from overseas, believed that they had done their share," wrote historian Edward Pluth. "They became easily disgruntled and 'unmilitary' in their conduct."[34]

The problems continued as the war went on and increasing numbers of able-bodied soldiers were pulled from the camp's guard roster and sent to assignments more directly involved in the war effort. Their replacements were frequently those with maladies, physical or otherwise, that kept them from being useful in other areas. "Most of the guys at Camp Clark were limited service," said Schafers. "They were there either because of some minor disability or because they had been in service in Europe or the Pacific but didn't have enough points yet to get out."

Schafers, who was twenty-seven when he was drafted, noted too that some of the men were at Clark because of their age. "I had one guy who slept next to me in the barracks who was forty-three," recalled Schafers. "He had been a motorman on the streetcars in Milwaukee. They weren't supposed to take somebody that old, but he was single, so they did anyway."[35]

As an illustration of the provost marshal general's problems with staffing POW camps, take the example of five American guards who were assigned to Camp Clark. All were held as POWs in Germany. During that time, the men were mistreated horribly and nearly starved to death, losing in several cases fifty-five or sixty pounds as a result of a diet consisting of a cup of weak coffee in the morning, a thin slice of bread for lunch, and a cup of watery turnip soup in the evening. One remarked soon after his arrival at Clark, "No matter how strict we are in our treatment [of the prisoners here], after you have been a prisoner in their country, it just isn't tough enough."[36]

The War Department suggested these ex-POWs in Europe be used as guards along with other returning servicemen, probably in equal parts to ease the shortage of guards and to fight the charges of coddling of POWs raised by the press and politicians. By employing former POWs, the thinking went at the War Department, the public's perception of the camps as a no-nonsense environment would be enhanced. Though the Army warned that these veterans should be "thoroughly indoctrinated in the provisions of the Geneva Convention and the need for firm but fair treatment," it is no small wonder that mistreatment of the Germans did not occur at the hands of these men.[37]

Don Stukesbary grew up in Nevada and spent a lot of time hanging around Camp Clark as a teen. "The guards were generally a nice bunch of men," recalled Stukesbary. "A good number of them seemed to be from the northeast. Most of them had a minor disability of one sort or another. That's how they ended up with duty at the POW camp."[38]

The *Camp Clark Sentinel* published a piece addressing the guards' roles and the camp, and encouraged them to be vigilant, despite whatever feelings the GIs might have had about the lack of importance of their jobs:

When we read with interest the life or death battles in the Philippines and the Western Front, sometimes our job of guarding these German war prisoners may not seem important. Many of us are here because of injuries suffered fighting these very same men; others, because of physical reasons incapacitating us from combat.

Whatever the reason, it should be kept in mind that behind that barbed wire are hundreds of men trained, some from infancy, to hate us and all for which we stand. Remember also, that many Americans, some our own friends and relatives, died to put these same Germans behind that wire. It is our job to keep them there.

These Nazis won't hesitate to try to escape at the right moment, and we must be particularly watchful at this time when the Germans are fighting the last desperate battle.

In considering our job, another thought might be borne in mind. We have an opportunity to help win the peace by sending back to Germany, once the final battle has been fought, these prisoners with a healthy respect for American strength, authority and fairness. That respect can be gained by all of us remaining soldierly in appearance and action in all our contacts with the prisoners. The American doughboy over there gave them their first lesson. Let's continue that lesson over here![39]

Italians Arrive First

It didn't take long to erect the POW facility at Camp Clark, and the camp was ready by August 1942, well ahead of the initial target date of October 1. The POW camp, some 163 buildings, was officially opened on November 6, 1942.[40] Two weeks later, nine military police companies arrived for intensive training in POW operations. Drilling nonstop, they practiced the proper procedures in transporting prisoners, defending themselves, and quelling POW disturbances. Six of these new MP companies soon transferred to provide security at other Missouri POW camps, including Weingarten and Fort Leonard Wood, and Captain Fred Mealy's three companies remained behind to receive the Italians scheduled to arrive the first week of December.

After the initial mayhem caused by the train wreck was sorted out, Mealy and his men began to take stock of the prisoners. They found that the Italians sent to Camp Clark showed the same diversity in prisoner population as at other camps. Ph.D.'s bunked next to privates who hadn't finished the third grade. The camp's first commanding officer, Lieutenant Colonel R. R. Morrison, commented on those differences:

> When you take a group of men, dress them all alike, put them in rows of bunks in the same kind of barracks and mark them all as prisoner of war, it is easy to forget they are not all alike. One of our prisoners was a college professor who taught sociology and economics, while another was in a famous ballet group and had traveled all over the world.[41]

Another Italian prisoner made beautiful violins during his internment, and several Nevada residents prominently displayed POW artwork in their homes, including beautiful paintings that the POWs created in their free time.

After the initial shipment of 350 POWs, the camp's population grew slowly at first, then began to mushroom as the United States began receiving increasingly larger numbers of prisoners. Within four months this group totaled nearly 500 men, and in April 1943 the group encompassed 284 army troops, 182 sailors, 24 members of the air force, 8 men from Mussolini's Black Shirts, and one merchant marine who asserted to anyone who would listen that he was no POW and that he was being wrongfully held. His protests had no effect, and he stayed at Clark like all the rest. In June 1943, an additional 700 POWs arrived at Clark for a total of about 1,200 men. By September 1943, that number had climbed to over 4,000, and an additional compound was added to hold Italian officers.[42]

During summers in high school, Richard Niles worked at the Double Cola Bottling Company, painting advertising signs on barns and stores. Niles recalled the initial hostility held by many of the townspeople toward the prisoners and the fairly rare occasion where residents went out of their way to directly demonstrate their dislike of the enemy soldiers:

> I don't know how, but word of the arrival of a trainload of prisoners would sweep the town, and many of the citizens would jump into their cars and drive to the Missouri Pacific depot on the east edge of Nevada where the train would be sitting on a siding, until it could be switched onto the branch line out to Camp Clark, about four to five miles to the southeast. I clearly recall seeing townspeople, both adults and young men, engaged in shouting insults and gesturing to the Italians who were hanging out of the windows of the passenger cars returning the favor in their language. The trains were under guard, but the exchange would continue until the cars were pulled out of the train yard.

Niles said he did not recall that happening with any German prisoners. "It was great sport for the young hotbloods of Nevada to go out and mock the Italians. They'd shout insults at them, and of course, the Italians would lean out of the windows and give it right back to them," said Niles. "They were guarded and couldn't get off the train, so it wasn't going to go any further than that."

Niles remembered his conflicting feelings after his mother expressed her reservations about the activity. "My mother had a galloping indifference toward this situation. My dad would take me down to see the train, but she always said that those boys [the Italians] were also some mothers' sons, and that if the situation were reversed, she hoped that our men wouldn't be treated that way."[43]

The newly transferred prisoners to Camp Clark were in a desperate state to hear news from their families. The prisoners had been incommunicado from the time of their capture in North Africa to their transfer to the United States, and the five hundred pieces of mail that arrived in January 1943 were the first correspondence the men had received in many months. Because the letters were so long delayed, and because many prisoners still received no mail, a representative of the International Red Cross who visited the camp in February 1943 declared that the Italians were entitled to use the express message service established by the Red Cross. The representative, A. Cardinaux, noted during his visit that the prisoners had just received a great stock of message forms, and "the use of this new means of correspondence gave them the hope that they would receive news of their relatives in the not too distant future."[44]

The postal censors in New York, who also confounded the Italians at Camp Weingarten, mightily irritated the prisoners at Camp Clark. During an April 1943 visit by the Swiss Legation, the prisoners cited numerous instances where the postal censors held pieces of outgoing mail for two months or more and then returned the item to the sender with directions that certain corrections or amendments be made. The Swiss representative who heard these complaints, Rolf Roth, took with him five examples for submission to the postal authorities and suggested camp authorities obtain a set of rules about materials and information that may be included in prisoner letters and post this information so that all internees might be clear on the guidelines.[45] Unfortunately, any attempt by the United States to improve the mail system was also hampered by the nonexistent Italian postal service from disruption wrought by the war.

"The mail does not function well. The majority of prisoners have not received letters for almost a year. The postal service, in the part of Italy occupied by the Allies, does not yet function for prisoners of war, and the Northern part, which is occupied, is no longer accessible," noted Paul Schnyder of the International Red Cross. "This lack of news discourages the prisoners, who are cut off from the only possible tie with their native land."[46] Schnyder took down some names and addresses of the prisoners most desperate for word from home and promised to send them to Geneva and to the Vatican in hope that they might be able to help the interned men and their families.

The conditions back in Europe caused great morale problems for the men at Camp Clark. Schnyder spoke with a large number of officers and men who were transferred to Clark from the camp at Weingarten. The men languished because of their inability to get any news from loved ones at home coupled with a lack of work, which produced stultifying boredom in the camp. "The condition of their country and the forced inaction to which they are condemned causes them to suffer," wrote Schnyder. However, things would soon change for these Italian POWs, and the men at Camp Clark would be adjusting to new homes in different camps and later, for many of the prisoners, to life in the Italian Service Units, a pseudo-Italian army working on behalf of the United States.

Life at Camp Clark

In February 1943, two months after their arrival in Nevada, the majority of the Italian POWs were still wearing the warm brown wool uniforms the British had given them. Though the prisoners liked the uniform, in most cases it was the only set of clothes they had. The camp administration issued all internees additional sets of clothing as well as retread shoes, previously worn boots that had been repaired and disinfected.

Some of these items came from a store of old clothing used by members of the Civilian Conservation Corps (CCC), one of President Roosevelt's Depression-era work programs. Prisoners weren't thrilled about this ragtag collection of clothing and complained especially about the old CCC overcoats, of which the bottom two inches of the coat looked like they had been hacked off with a steak knife. Some refused outright to wear them. A big part of the problem was caused by the supply officer, who had "a tendency…to issue the poorest articles first." This practice also led to the prisoners being issued underwear that was not satisfactory and three hundred pairs of shoes needing repair being issued to a company where no cobbling equipment was available. Swiss representative Roth called for these problems to be rectified and noted the clothing situation had actually improved somewhat from previous visits.[47]

These occasional problems in POW clothing were a result of an over-taxed military supply system, which naturally encountered a bump here and there in providing clothing stock to four thousand prisoners, especially given the POW camps' relatively low priority in the whole scheme of war-fighting operations. Problems observed by visiting inspectors were frequent but usually minor and included comments such as:

> The stocks of clothing on hand are in small sizes [only] but it appears that sufficient clothing has been obtained of the larger sizes so that no one complained for lack of adequate clothing.

> The prisoners' winter clothing, as received from the Quartermaster Dept, was too small in size due to shrinkage after drying.[48]

Fortunately, such shortfalls were usually temporary, and prisoners were never in a position of not having adequate clothing—unless they elected not to, as in the case of the fashion-conscious POWs who refused the ragged overcoats. In fact, the Army went to great lengths to ensure that prisoners were properly dressed, going so far as to have an American officer accompany the senior Italian officer, a colonel, to Kansas City so he could purchase material to make uniforms for the other POW officers.[49]

The prisoners looking around their new home at Camp Clark saw newly built barracks to match their new clothes. These were standard Army buildings and the same as at other camps—"temporary" housing with thin, tarpaper-covered walls, raised about twelve inches off the ground by concrete pilings.[50]

The first inspection of the camp made by the International Red Cross in February 1943, approximately two months after its opening, provided a detailed description of the barracks:

> The barracks used as living quarters contain approximately 40 beds each. The bedding is good, but there are no sheets. Each barracks is heated by two coal burning stoves and the temperature is comfortable. The climate is mild and it is seldom very cold. In summer it is very hot. The prisoners have arranged well the barracks used as living quarters and have decorated them with paintings and drawings. In each barracks, the prisoners have set up additional shelves and place small chests of drawers which they made in the carpenter shop.

> The barracks containing the showers, the washstands and the toilets is

clean and well-heated. There is running water, both hot and cold, and the prisoners can take showers whenever they desire. A man is charged with the upkeep of the boiler and two stoves. Two men clean the barracks every day, taking turns.[51]

Equally nice, noted the inspector, were the brand-new kitchen facilities, offering the latest in equipment, food preparation accessories, and sanitary consideration. Six cooks and ten assistants worked in each of the two kitchens. The report went on:

The dining halls are clean and bright. There are two rows of tables; each table seating eight. The top of the tables is covered with linoleum, their care being thus rendered very easy. The plates and dishes are of white crockery and when the table is set, make an excellent impression.

All the cooks are prisoners who have had experience. Everybody agrees that the quality as well as the quantity of the food is satisfactory. The prisoners make their spaghetti, macaroni, et cetera, themselves. Pastry-cooks make cakes several times a week. The menus are prepared once a week for the whole week, and the head cook of Company No. 2 has stated to the Delegate of the International Red Cross Committee that the menus in question are not modified as a general rule. The Delegate called for the menus for one day at random.

The menus for February 6, 1943, were:

Breakfast	Lunch	Dinner
Oranges	Beef goulash	Pea soup
Cereals	Lettuce salad w/ mayo	Sauerkraut
Condensed milk	Bread and butter	Beef hash
Bacon	Pudding w/ sweet sauce	Rice
Sautéed potatoes		Bread and butter
Bread, butter, coffee		Cakes, hot chocolate[52]

Along with the barracks and mess facilities, work crews hammered together a hospital at Camp Clark. This medical treatment facility was able to provide care for nearly all injuries and illnesses that occurred in the POW and American populations. A January 1943 inspection report shortly after the camp's opening called the station hospital "particularly well established."

Wrote the Swiss inspector, "There are six doctors and two dentists and attendants. The facilities are adequate, not only for prisoners of war but members of the guard companies are treated in this hospital as well. There are specialists in surgery, in diseases of the eyes, ears, nose and throat. Glasses are furnished those prisoners whose vision is less than 20/40."[53]

In April 1943 there were five patients in the hospital, and while none was seriously ill, their conditions ran the gamut of medical maladies. One patient was suffering from chronic gall bladder trouble for which he was probably going to need surgery, another was recovering from an appendectomy, a third had an umbilical hernia, a fourth was recovering from circumcision, and the last had a minor skin infection.[54]

POW Recreation

Within six months of their arrival at Camp Clark, Italian POWs had facilities and equipment for soccer, basketball, badminton, bocce (an Italian pastime similar to lawn bowling), boxing, softball, and quoits, a horseshoe-like game in which rings were thrown toward a small post.[55]

The initial stock of athletic equipment came from the PMGO in Washington, D.C. While the equipment selection was well intended, Lieutenant Colonel Morrison wrote the PMGO and suggested "that future shipments eliminate baseball (hardball) equipment because of the internees' unfamiliarity with same and possible use of equipment as weapons" and suggested more soccer balls and volleyballs be sent as a substitution.[56]

A week later, Captain Arthur Pratt, adjutant at Camp Clark, sent the PMGO a comprehensive list of suggested items for POW entertainment. This list, which was worked up jointly with the Italian internee camp leader, Warrant Officer Felice Di Giovanni, was presumably intended to be helpful to the PMGO in stocking other camps with athletic equipment, indicating what was useful and what was not. The duo suggested items such as volleyballs, boxing gloves, and card games, and in particular recommended that "baseball, horseshoe, horseracing, mahjong, and cribbage equipment and games be eliminated due to unfamiliarity and lack of interest on the part of internees."[57]

Camp Clark POWs enjoyed access to several tennis courts and playing fields, and the sports program there was well developed, featuring numerous tournaments and competitions among compounds.

Classes at the Camp

Not long after their arrival at the Nevada camp, Italian prisoners organized classes in a variety of subjects, including English. Illiterate prisoners attended "elementary schools." Classes were offered in English, drawing, carving, and painting. Additionally, a bit of cultural exchange took place, as the POWs made Italian lessons available to any GIs and workers at the camp with the time and inclination to study their language. "A school was set up and they not only learned to speak our language, but taught their guards and some of the civilian employees as well to speak theirs," wrote *Nevada Daily Mail and Evening Post* columnist Betty Sterett.[58]

An Italian POW with a Ph.D. in economics served as the camp director of education and set up classes from the primary level through seventh grade. Because of the importance of this work, the second camp commander, Lieutenant Colonel Jack Gage, put the POW on the payroll and funded his daily 80-cent wages out of the POW canteen profits. At the outset of this effort to create a POW academy, the program was somewhat hampered by a lack of books, mainly basic textbooks and other rudimentary equipment. When a representative of the YMCA, Howard Hong, visited Camp Clark and saw the shortages, he went on a buying binge in Nevada, grabbing up nearly all the supplies he could find that might be useful in the camp classes.

"I bought 25 reams of paper, some stencils, and a celluloid drawing sheet to aid them in this enterprise," wrote Hong, who noted that the YMCA earlier provided the POW school with a mimeograph machine and supplies. "A pressing need is for a typewriter. The baby Hermes [pre-war-era typewriter model] procured by us needs a new carriage return spring and is really too light for cutting stencils. Our greatest assistance would be in sending more books for the men and in helping find new books for the canteen, which has sold 35-cent dictionaries and a few texts and books of fiction. More can readily be sold."[59]

Camp Religious Life

It took several months for any sort of ordered religious program to get underway at Camp Clark after the prisoners' arrival. The local priest in Nevada, Father Jolin, did what he could to help the Catholic POWs, but as he could not speak Italian, the language barrier prevented enthusiastic participation. The bishop of Kansas could speak the language but came only an average of every third Sunday. Attendance was still quite strong, however; when Mass was said in Italian, 95 percent of the prisoners attended, and half came even when celebrated in English.

The POW installation at Camp Clark, like other internment sites, lacked a dedicated chapel in the original design, so the prisoners utilized an unoccupied barracks building, adorning the interior with paintings and decorations to create a suitable atmosphere for worship, aided by liturgical articles, candles, and candlesticks provided by the Nevada priest.[60]

In October 1943, an inspector called religious life "perhaps the best developed aspect of the camp." The POWs, having been served by Jolin, now benefited from the service of Father Tosti, a civilian who as a Franciscan mission priest was permitted to live and work in the camp. September 1943 saw the arrival of Father CiaFollet, an Italian-born U.S. Army chaplain, and the POWs anticipated the arrival of one of their own, a POW who was an Italian naval chaplain. Between them, the men celebrated two Masses each Sunday in every compound, as well as vespers in each compound each evening. A highlight, noted a visitor, was the confirmation of twenty men at Camp Clark by military ordinariate John O'Hara, who was president of Notre Dame University prior to World War II. O'Hara, who in his role served as the New York City–based chief of chaplains for the Roman Catholic Church, also presided over the consecration of the chapel in Compound 2 during his visit.[61]

POW Labor Program

Camp Clark lacked opportunities to utilize POW labor in the areas around the camp. Thus, most Clark-based POW labor was limited to the installation itself. "It was very menial work," said Giuseppe Zanti, who was with the first group of Italian POWs to arrive at Clark from Great Britain. "We mostly just walked around the post, picking up trash, stuff like that."[62]

Prisoners usually rotated through several assignments within the POW compound itself, such as cleaning the barracks, performing KP duty, and the like, with the hospital attendants and the cooks being the only personnel assigned to one specific task because of the specialized training and knowledge required for those assignments. The camp administrators were pleased with the results of the work program, as was noted in a February 1943 inspection report that stated that the "work done in connection with the upkeep of the camp does not cause any problems and the prisoners cooperate with the authorities without any difficulty."[63]

Even these jobs within the POW camp were hard to come by; with five hundred men in camp, only around thirty at a time were used in the compound during February 1943, and twenty of these were the personnel permanently assigned to the kitchen or infirmary. The other ten worked in the company offices, in the POW canteen, or as stewards in the dining hall.[64] An additional sixty-four workers were employed in tasks on the Camp Clark military reservation outside the POW installation—thirty sorting wood, ten in the camp warehouse, and twenty preparing a plot of land for a vegetable garden, including construction of a greenhouse and a small hut in which rabbits were to be raised. Four other prisoners worked decorating the mess of American officers. These men painted four murals and several garlands and flags on the walls of the dining facility.[65]

Initially, most prisoners who worked in operations related to their own compound, such as mess-hall cooks, barbers, and latrine orderlies, received no wages. The Swiss representative who visited in April 1943 noted that the POW canteens were earning a 5 percent profit on such items as 3.2 percent beer, soft drinks, chocolate, cigarettes, and toilet articles. By March 1944, the canteens' combined monthly business was more than $25,000, providing considerable funds for POW activities and services.[66] While at first the money was used mainly for buying sports equipment, Swiss representative Roth suggested these funds also be used to pay the men working within the POW compound who received no wages. The camp commander agreed it was a good idea and submitted the proposal to the council of prisoners for their approval.[67] The wonderful irony of the camp commander submitting an idea to prisoners for their approval is an example of how these camps were indeed run in many cases under the premise of willful participation by the prisoners in day-to-day operations.

The Italian prisoners at Camp Clark were an unwitting party to one of the great disputes of the POW labor program. Farmers and many businessmen were elated at the prospect of having this new source of labor to work in their fields and factories as the shortage of workers threatened to put a sharp dent in U.S. productivity. However, one group—organized labor—consistently opposed the use of prisoners in just about every aspect of the American economy. Unions feared that the POW laborers would take jobs away from American workers and that the POWs would be available as a cheaper source of labor than the unionized work force, driving down wages.

The issue came to a head when the Chicago, Burlington, & Quincy Railroad requested 250 Italian POWs from Camp Clark to build a switching yard in Lincoln, Nebraska, and the railroad unions protested. "My God, does he not know that Railroading is a most delicate operation?" asked railroad union chief George Harrison about Secretary of War Henry Stimson. "We carry on night and day in split second schedules. I have not been able to get a reason for turning loose [enemy] soldiers, skilled in demolition practices, so that they may run amok on the railroads."[68]

Despite the government's continued assurances that "the safety of railroad movements would not be impaired and the safety of railroad workers would not be endangered by the use of prisoner labor," the railroad unions, led by the powerful Brotherhood of Railway Clerks and the Association of Railway Labor Executives, threatened a nationwide shutdown if POWs were used for work on the railroads, and they filed suit to block the use of the Clark POWs in a test case to challenge the government's policy. Though the court dismissed the case, concluding the fear of sabotage was unfounded, the unions' opposition, combined with the prospect of more legal challenges and the threatened railway workers' walkout, prompted the government to decide it would be better served by avoiding POW labor assignments in the most heavily unionized components of American industry.[69]

Turmoil at Clark

Even among the normally peaceable Italians, political conflict welled up at Camp Clark on a few occasions. An inspection report from January 1943 noted that camp administrators removed eleven anti-Fascist prisoners from the general POW population because of the unpopular nature of their views. "The commanding officer, seeing that such a state of affairs could only become worse, has separated the prisoners into two groups," noted one observer. The men worked in a separate group in a merchandise warehouse and were not permitted to associate with other prisoners. Curiously, for living arrangements, the men were moved in with American troops temporarily housed in a different compound.[70]

Even this segregation from the main body of Italian POWs was not sufficient. Problems continued with this group, and an examination into the situation three months later revealed the issue wasn't as simple as it originally appeared. Although only four of the men truly claimed to be anti-Fascist, the camp spokesman said all received death threats because of their beliefs. The four anti-Fascists demanded that they be transferred to another camp and threatened to burn down the barracks if this demand was not met.

In response, the camp commander locked up the men in the psychopathic ward of the hospital, where they wouldn't pose a danger, then tried to figure out what to do. One possibility was to have them transferred to another camp; one document mentions the possibility of an exchange of these men for "some of the sanitary personnel at Fort Leonard Wood." Ultimately the men transferred from Camp Clark before setting anything alight, though their ultimate destination was not specified.[71]

The other seven, whom a visiting representative described as being "of dubious nationality who were inducted into the military service in Tunisia and whose loyalty to Italy is open to question," presented less of a problem. The men were still housed in a separate compound and worked unloading supplies for the quartermaster from railcars on the siding near the warehouses. These men told the Swiss representative that "they were perfectly content and had no complaints to offer."[72]

A March 1944 visitor from the Swiss Legation noted the presence of some minor political friction in the camp. "There was found, as in other Italian camps, some friction between the King's Army and Fascist factions," noted Ben Spiro. "In so far as it could be observed it was not thought to be serious."

Though Spiro discounted the severity of the political disagreement, he specifically identified another group of troublemaking POWs who were isolated in a subsection of Compound 1 as being a problem for the camp. He recommended that they be sent to another camp rather than stir up discontent among other prisoners. These prisoners, said Spiro, claimed to have no idea why they were being singled out for punishment, but the Swiss inspector dismissed outright both their complaints toward the Americans and their professed ignorance as to why they were in the isolation compound.

"These prisoners try to maintain that they are deprived of their rights and privileges of the camp in contravention of the specific provisions of the Geneva Convention," wrote Spiro. "The prisoners in the isolation compound, which will accommodate about 200 prisoners, complained that they have committed no offense, that they have not been tried, and that they are without any knowledge of why they are isolated. Their position in this regard is not well founded, since they must be well aware of their unwillingness to work and disposition to stir up trouble among other prisoners who are willing to work." With the Italians' eventual transfer to Camp Weingarten to make room for the incoming German POWs, this band of troublemaking prisoners was dissolved.[73]

Gunned Down at the Fence Line

Captain Mealy remembered well perhaps the most unfortunate incident that took place during his two years as commander of the MP companies at Camp Clark. There was conflict between groups of Italian prisoners in adjoining compounds, and the men began to quarrel through the fences that separated them. At times the discussion grew so heated that men tried to climb the fence between the compounds to get more personal in their confrontation.

"Guns were never allowed inside the prisoner compound, but three armed guards were on duty at all times in each tower," Mealy said. "There were a few trouble makers and we tried to isolate them from the rest of the prisoners. After they continued to ignore my orders that no one was allowed to climb the fences separating the compounds, I stationed a military guard behind a .30 caliber machine gun aimed straight down the fence row."

Mealy and his men then put on a demonstration to show that their order to stay back from the fences was no mere bluff. "We called one of their own sergeants from each compound to watch," recalled Mealy. "We fired tracer bullets so there would be no misunderstanding that any prisoner attempting to climb over the wire would be shot."[74]

The POWs pressed the issue though, edging closer to the fence every day to see how near they could get, remembered Mrs. Lloyd Davis, who worked at the camp. "Finally, one afternoon, an Italian POW got too near the fence while retrieving a ball and he was killed by a machine gun blast."[75]

Colonel I. B. Summers from the provost marshal general's office provided the Department of State with an official account of the incident in response to concerns raised by the Italian government by the shooting at the camp. "About 8:50 PM, 25 July 1943…one of the belligerent group, deliberately walked into the restricted zone looking and moving toward the gun…[and an American MP] duly posted as a guard and having been ordered to fire if any prisoner of war approached in the restricted zone, fired a burst of three shots at the prisoner of war," wrote Summers. "He was hit and immediately taken to the hospital where he was given competent medical attention but nevertheless died at 6:20 AM, 26 July 1943."[76]

Antonis DeFalco, a sergeant major, was the prisoner who was shot down at the fence line. DeFalco's body, along with other POWs who died at Camp Clark, was buried in a small cemetery at the western edge of the camp. After the war, the bodies were removed and returned to families of the POWs back in Europe. Only unmarked white crosses, peeling from years of exposure to sun and rain, mark where the POWs were once buried. In total, nine POWs died at Camp Clark, and other than the one shot at the wire, all indications are that the others died from natural causes or as a result of battlefield wounds.[77]

The first prisoner to die at Camp Clark passed away in January 1943, just a month after the Italians' arrival. The man apparently succumbed to wounds suffered before coming to Camp Clark. Interestingly, Italian POWs were not permitted to attend the funeral, though no reason was given by the Red Cross inspector present at the time. "A death of a prisoner of war has occurred at this camp. After autopsy, the body was interred in the presence of an American Army escort made up of officers, nurses and enlisted men," wrote the inspector. "The camp commander stated that if an occasion of this kind should arise in the future, he would also permit representatives of the Italian interns to be present at the burial if the interned men continue their good behavior."[78]

Riot at the Italian Compound

Of all the incidents that occurred during the time of the Italians' internment at Camp Clark, only the train wreck and the shooting at the fence line were in the same league as a riot that took place June 28, 1943. Just two days before the disturbance, the camp received 719 new Italian POWs from Camp Phillips, Kansas. Five hundred of these men were placed in Compound 3 with the 500 original prisoners from December 1942, while the remaining 219 new prisoners moved into Compound 2.

Within a day of the Camp Phillips group's move to his facility, the camp commander, Lieutenant Colonel Morrison, was receiving reports that the original Clark POWs were "having a bad influence" on the new arrivals, telling them they did not have to work for the Americans. The leader of the third compound, an Italian named Alfredo Albini, had gone so far as to direct the head POW of Compound 2, Sergeant Mario Carradi, not to send out work details.

Morrison's answer was to segregate the Camp Phillips prisoners from the original Camp Clark crew. He directed that all the new arrivals from Camp Phillips be moved into Compound 1. This meant a vacant Compound 2 would separate the new POWs entirely from the Clark prisoners, a necessity given that there was no way to prevent the men from talking to one another through the fence between adjoining compounds. Morrison gave Major L. D. Williams, second in command, the order to move the prisoners on the morning of Monday, June 28, 1943.

When the prisoners in Compound 3—already belligerent—received the order from Major Williams that the two Camp Phillips companies were to be moved, they angrily refused, and the showdown was on. Williams returned to Morrison's office at 2:30 that afternoon and told the commander that the prisoners were refusing to move. The Italians, Williams said, "were in a very threatening attitude, refusing to obey orders and were then in a riotous attitude and were preventing the movement from being carried out as ordered."

In response to this news of the prisoners' insubordination, Morrison ordered out the riot squad and directed them to be at the ready, and he immediately went to the compound and found the situation close to the boiling point. "There I found the Prisoners of War confined in Compound No. 3 in a riot, angrily milling about, talking loudly and angrily waving their hands and fists in a threatening attitude," Morrison recalled in an official statement to the Swiss Legation shortly after the event. "I immediately sent for the leaders of the compound," and four POWs and a POW interpreter reported to Morrison at the main gate. "All five of these men were in an angry, ugly attitude."

THE ENEMY AMONG US

146

Morrison told the Italians that he had given the order for the men to be moved, and that they should return to their companies and control their men. The POW leaders got even more agitated, saying angrily that they had not been given twenty-four hours notification of the transfer. The interpreter told Morrison that the companies would not move unless the Americans used force and demanded that he wire the Swiss Legation.

Morrison then went outside the compound and ordered the MP company that was standing by to prepare to move into the compound in riot formation. The leaders went back down the street from the main gate into the POW compound. The POWs gathered around them shouting, and in Morrison's view, the leaders were clearly encouraging the prisoners to resist the order to move and inciting them to riot if the U.S. troops moved in. Morrison then called up another whole MP company, the 359th, and ordered the men to report fully armed at the third compound to join the one already present.

After the second company arrived, Morrison ordered the first group to enter the compound, to form a skirmish line along both sides of the street, and to arrest the leaders and lock them up. The MPs would then separate the Camp Phillips POWs from the first group of prisoners and move the Phillips POWs from Compound 3 to Compound 1. According to Morrison:

> I took command of the situation personally and my orders were carried out. The 332d formed a skirmish line between companies 1 and 3 and 2 and 4 and started the flying squads to separate the Camp Phillips men from the old men. In some cases where a large group of old men [the first group of Clark POWs] were, we had to use force but as soon as the Camp Phillips men were separated from the influence of the old men they were easily handled.

> When all the Camp Phillips Prisoners of War were checked and moved out and all the old Prisoners of War checked I ordered the 332d MPEG Co. to move out and return to their barracks, also the 359th was ordered to their barracks.[79]

Naturally, the POWs involved in the incident had another account of the story. On behalf of himself and the others, Pietro Zaniboni, one of the men later put under court-martial for his role in the riot, said:

> We did not refuse to carry out orders. We conveyed the orders of the Camp Commander to the men concerned. That was all that we could do. The fact that they refused to obey these orders is not our fault.

When we saw that the situation was becoming tense and dangerous we prepared a telegram to the Swiss Legation urging that a representative of the Legation be sent here at once to investigate the situation. Our telegram was withheld by the Camp Commander.

During the melee, one of the Italians struck an American MP. This soldier, named Donnarumma, was also charged in connection with the riot. In his testimony, Zaniboni attempted to defend the man's actions:

We understand that Donnarumma has been charged with striking Lieutenant Biagi. Donnarumma has a mental history; he is high strung and very tense. At the peril of his life while he was fighting in Africa he crawled through barbed wire under fire to rescue an Australian officer who had fallen seriously wounded in no man's land. He saved the life of this enemy officer. He is a fine type of soldier but his nerves are shattered.

When he saw one of the guards give a bayonet thrust to one of the prisoners during the disturbance and when it looked as if the guards who had been called out were about to fire upon us, he lost his head and struck the officer in the general confusion, panic, and turmoil.[80]

Said GI George Breen of the bayonet thrust, "One of our guards poked an Italian guy in the rear end. It didn't hurt him at all, but he sure hollered when it happened."[81]

Zaniboni asserted that the leaders should not be held responsible for the men refusing to obey orders:

After the men had refused to obey the orders which we conveyed to them on behalf of the Camp Commander, we resigned as camp leaders as, of course, we had no means of enforcing the orders as we have no jurisdiction in such cases.

Had men under our command refused to obey orders while we were still in the Italian Army, of course, the matter would have been taken up by our superior officers, but in our present position all we could do was to convey the orders of the Commanding Officer.[82]

The Italians weren't the only ones in trouble as a result of the riot. In a review of the incident, Morrison also received criticism for his own handling of the situation. The Swiss representative said he was "at a loss to understand the reason" why the prisoners were prohibited from telegramming the Swiss Legation in the earliest stages of the dispute over being moved to the new compound.

"The channel of communication between the prisoner and the Legation is sacred," said Roth. "It ought to be kept open under all circumstances and should never be blocked." Roth further pointed out that he earlier called the attention of the Camp Clark authorities to this fact when previous POW communication to the Swiss Legation was restricted.[83]

Nonsense, said Morrison, who saw the four men detained for their role in the riot as trying to undermine discipline in the camp. In that circumstance, said Morrison, he felt he had "no alternative but to enforce his authority to the fullest possible extent." Moving groups of prisoners from one compound to another was not a situation that warranted the intervention of the Swiss Legation, asserted Morrison, and if he were "to allow the prisoners to communicate with the Legation whenever they felt inclined to do so, they would be writing or telegraphing to the Legation almost daily for no proper cause."[84]

As a result of this disturbance, two leaders of the Italian POWs, Alfredo Albini, leader of Compound 3, and Giovanni Mariani, a member of Company 2, were subject to a general court-martial that took place in September 1943. The two men were charged with violation of the 96th Article of War, refusal to obey lawful orders. The two POWs were represented by attorney J. Miniace, assistant defense counsel, and John Capriotti, an Italian POW who at the request of the accused had been specially detailed to Camp Clark from the Italian POW camp at Weingarten.

The prosecution alleged that there was a clear failure to obey lawful orders, while the defense held that the directives were not lawfully imparted, that they had not been communicated through the prescribed channels, and that the defendants were in no position to carry out the orders as they had previously relinquished their duties as spokesmen for the POWs.

The fate of the four prisoners is unknown. Albini and Mariani's general court-martial was postponed because of the need for further investigation, and no further mention of these prisoners or the riot was made in the Camp Clark records.[85] However, likely as a result of this event, Lieutenant Colonel Morrison was transferred from Camp Clark, and a new commanding officer, Lieutenant Colonel Jack Gage, took over the installation. Gage's arrival marked a new era of good feeling at the camp, said Swiss inspectors who visited Camp Clark shortly after Gage took over.

"It was apparent that Lieutenant Colonel Gage, who entered upon his duties only four weeks prior to the present visit, had already won the confidence and good will of the prisoners who were unanimous in their appreciation of his personal and direct interest in all matters pertaining to their welfare," wrote the inspectors. "The spontaneous expressions with which the prisoners voiced their thanks for his efforts to create and maintain an atmosphere of good will, understanding, and collaboration between the camp authorities and the prisoners were an outstanding feature of this visit."[86]

Trust between Italians and Authorities

With the exception of two escapes and the riot, which arguably could have been averted if handled differently by the camp commander, prisoners at Camp Clark proved themselves trustworthy and able to be left almost entirely unguarded. "Sometimes, we'd go out on a work detail, and there'd be only one guard for a hundred POWs," remembered guard Breen. "If we were in a factory or somewhere, the guard would sit in an office off away from the prisoners. He wouldn't even have to watch the men working."[87]

In fact, this level of trust between the prisoners and the camp administration grew to be so strong that camp commander Jack Gage gave certain reliable Italian prisoners complete run of the twelve-hundred-acre military post in January 1944 without any supervision at all. "A new attitude has just been adopted towards the Italian prisoners," said a January 1944 inspection report detailing this strange situation. "They go to work without guards, on parole, under the supervision of an Italian officer."[88]

"More than a hundred prisoners are now held at Camp Clark by only their word," Gage told the Associated Press. "I place extreme confidence in these men whom I have paroled."[89] Gage conducted a simple ceremony in his quarters in which each prisoner gave his word of honor not to escape, and they did not let him down.[90]

Even with this amount of freedom, or perhaps as a result of it, POW escape attempts from Camp Clark were fairly limited. Five Italians escaped from the camp one day in May 1943 by cutting a hole in the compound fence. From there, they jumped into two unattended cars and sped off before the guards realized what they had done. They got as far as Diamond, Missouri, about seventy miles south of camp on U.S. 71, where they were hauled in the next day when one of the vehicles ran out of gas.[91]

"[The] five prisoners who recently escaped from this camp and stole two private automobiles before being recaptured have been tried by court martial," wrote Swiss representative Roth in a report after the escape. "They are still in detention cells awaiting sentence."[92]

In another incident not long after the shooting of the POW at the fence line, three Italians managed to escape from the POW compound. The men crawled under a fence and jumped into an idle Army car, prompting the largest manhunt Vernon County had ever seen.

The men were on the run for the next two days, making their way from the camp area after hiding out on a back road overnight. Growling stomachs were their undoing, as they were apprehended when they stopped for a meal at a small café in Lamar, Missouri, about twenty-five miles south of the camp.[93] Because the Geneva Convention limited punishment for escapes to thirty days, the government tacked on an additional penalty for the theft of the government vehicle to lengthen the time of their confinement and discourage future escapes.

A unique spirit of cooperation seemed to exist at Camp Clark between the Italian POWs and the personnel. That was partly because two officers and twelve enlisted men assigned to the camp were Italian speakers, a highly unusual and fortunate feature at a Missouri POW camp. An inspection report credited the two Italian-speaking officers with creating a bond of friendship between the prisoners and the camp staff, noting that "both of these young men have been sympathetic to the needs of the internees and their efforts have contributed greatly to the good spirit that appears to exist."

In fact, U.S. soldiers manning the camp attempted to teach the Italians how to play baseball, and officers donated numerous magazines to the prisoner library. These favors were reciprocated by a play the prisoners put on, in English, for the Americans in the post theater.[94]

The good treatment of the prisoners was also responsible for their positive response to American authorities. To the raggedy bunch that arrived dirty and hungry from North Africa, Camp Clark seemed like a paradise. Congressman Marion T. Bennett visited the camp, and an account of his visit in the *Springfield News-Leader* described the conditions the prisoners enjoyed.

The prisoners are well treated and have every modern convenience, including electric dishwashers. They are served their native food prepared by their own cooks and given a bottle of beer a day. They

George Breen, a Camp Clark guard. Courtesy of George Breen.

spend most of their money for cigarettes and extra beer.... They have newspapers with timetables and want-ads clipped out, have radios and listen to them. They seem contented and healthy and strong.[95]

Of the radios mentioned by Bennett in use in the compounds, several were purchased by the POWs themselves, and at least one was provided by the parishioners of Holy Rosary Parish in Kansas City. The parish, situated in a neighborhood of Italian immigrants, made an active and substantial effort to connect with the Italian POWs, including busing them on occasion to the church for Mass.[96]

Departure of the Italians

With the focus of the war shifting, the Italians housed at Camp Clark would soon be moved to other camps around the United States. A great number of Italian POWs signed up to participate in the Italian Service Units (ISU), groups of Italian POWs organized like U.S. Army units that served in support roles on Army posts throughout the United States. Other Italians not signed up for the ISU were consolidated into larger camps, such as Weingarten, to make room for the increasing numbers of Germans being captured. Regardless of the men's next destination, the *Nevada Daily Mail and Evening Post* noted that of the Italian POWs at Camp Clark, "many left with regret, promising to return to America some day."[97]

With the departure of the Italians from Camp Clark in May 1944, Vernon County residents quietly worried about the fate of the camp. In retrospect, the sheer number of prisoners the United States was receiving from the continued fighting in Europe—more than ten thousand German prisoners in June 1944, and nearly thirty thousand more the next month—meant that there was no way the space could go unutilized, but residents anticipated a major loss of revenue.

Fearing the closure of Camp Clark, the president of the Nevada Chamber of Commerce, F. W. Renwick, offered the War Department additional land and utility services. "This community welcomed instead of opposing this project," wrote Renwick, noting that Nevada wanted to do everything possible to assist the War Department in making continued use of the camp.[98]

For several months, the camp was oddly quiet, and residents waited and wondered what was next. There was no thunder of feet on the wooden floors of the barracks, a light layer of dust collected on the tables and benches of the mess halls, and grass started to grow on the soccer field once again. It would be a short respite, though, as the next arrivals were slated to occupy the barracks in August 1944—a group that would be far different from the easygoing Italians.

By late summer 1944, the United States finally realized it had a significant problem within its POW camps. Ardent Nazis—even though they were usually a minority in each camp—tightly controlled the internal operations of the prison camp and generally made life difficult for those who didn't go along. These men maintained their influence over the other internees with threats against them as well as against their families back home—with beatings, blackmail, and, not infrequently, murder or forced suicide. To rein in this problem, the government decided to separate the hard-core Nazis from the majority of the prisoner population, who were less committed to the Nazi philosophy. The provost marshal general designated several camps especially for these agitators, and Camp Clark was marked to hold these Nazis for the Fifth, Sixth, Seventh, and Ninth Service Commands, along with other prisoners from the region who simply refused to work.

Discipline at the Camp

Camp administrators knew what was coming when the first troop trains carrying the Germans rolled into town on August 3, 1944, and they quickly heightened the discipline at the camp to keep them in line. These men were from the Afrika Korps, a highly feared, highly respected fighting force, noted for its discipline and allegiance to National Socialism. In response to the challenge they anticipated from this crew, the camp authorities tried to make an impression on the prisoners from the moment they arrived that there would be no foolishness at Camp Clark.

"Every prisoner was greeted with the admonition, 'Das ist ein strenge militarisches Lager' (this is a strict military camp). Violation of any regulation brought instant recommendation for a diet of bread and water. All vestiges of Nazism were eliminated," wrote Betty Sterett of the *Nevada Daily Mail and Evening Post*. "The swastika was outlawed and any soldier giving the Nazi salute or saying the forbidden words, 'Heil Hitler,' received time in the guardhouse. Everything was done to convince these men the U.S. army had little respect for those who refused to work."[99]

Mrs. Lloyd Davis, who through her work running the camp PX saw literally thousands of prisoners come and go during the war years, described the Germans as "cold and defiant," in contrast with the "lovable" Italians whom she remembered as "easy to get to know." She recalled, "One time, the Germans got very belligerent. They didn't like their food, so they ran outside en masse and turned their plates upside down in the mud."[100]

Grace Davis, like other civilian employees at Camp Clark, had to carry a number of ID cards and permits. Courtesy of Bushwhacker Museum, Vernon County Historical Society.

"In every imaginable way, these men were the exact opposites of their predecessors. Arrogant and defiant, they had been trained from childhood to believe in their superiority," wrote Sterett in the *Nevada Daily Mail and Evening Post*. In an ominous reference to the rigid Nazi control within the prisoner population, the newspaper also described how the discipline within the Afrika Korps made the camp much easier to administer. Sterett continued, "However, because they had been taught to respect discipline, in many ways they were much easier to guard than the Italians."[101]

In addition to the troublemaking Nazis housed at Clark and the non-commissioned officers who by virtue of their rank could not be required to work, the camp received great numbers of POWs directly from the European battlefields. "The prisoner stockpile got everything. Among those from other camps who refused to sign [work agreements], were some of the worst political agitators, prisoners who had been shifted from camp to camp. They arrived with hundreds fresh from the battlefields of Europe whose eyes still bore the shock of battle and defeat. This mixture posed a difficult problem of separation and security control," wrote Ted Schafers in an article in the *Camp Clark Sentinel* that marked the one-year anniversary of the arrival of the Germans. "Those with sketchy records, noncooperatives and suspected political agitators were confined in one compound while those fresh from Europe were placed in two other compounds."[102]

"The prisoners would arrive in trainloads which came directly to Camp Clark from Norfolk, Virginia, where they had come into port. These trains, which were shipped from camps all over the central United States, had fifteen, twenty, sometimes twenty-five coaches, and would arrive at the camp at 2 or 3 A.M.," recalled Schafers. "The PW trains had to be interspersed with regular rail traffic. These other trains had priority, so sometimes the PW trains would have to wait on a siding, for sometimes hours at a time."[103]

Residents of Nevada were aware of the change in the prisoner population at Clark, said Richard Niles, a high schooler at the time. "We didn't consider the Italians to be a great threat to the peace and safety of Nevada," said Niles. "But when the Germans came the whole atmosphere changed."[104] Because of the number of civilian employees from the Nevada area who worked at Clark, the goings-on at the camp were regular gossip.

"Security became much tighter when the Germans arrived, we heard. One rumor making the rounds in town was to the effect that after an escape, the remaining soldiers in that barracks were routed out at night in freezing weather and made to stand at attention barefoot and without coats until the missing prisoner was located, still within the compound," recalled Niles. "I cannot vouch for the truth of the story except to say that it made the rounds in town and there was considerable difference of opinion as to whether that was appropriate discipline or not."[105]

Once the prisoners arrived, processing began at once, said Schafers. Camp authorities knew that they were dealing with a rough bunch of characters and learned early on to scrutinize each batch of new POWs. "We looked for prisoners who were members of the SS, the SA, or Gestapo as well as men who had a history of being political agitators, tough, or just plain unscrupulous. We would check their records and also examine the prisoners for tattoos, which marked them as part of these groups. We were trying to identify the ones who were known to be troublemaking Nazis, so we could keep an eye on them."[106]

Prisoners were thoroughly shaken down for contraband, and all possessions were taken away except for basic toiletries. Camp authorities confiscated all canteen supplies such as cigarettes and candy and issued canteen checks for the value of these articles. Uniforms for prisoners were required at all times. Prisoners at Camp Clark were not allowed to sit or lie down on their beds between the hours of 8 A.M. and 5 P.M. The rule was later modified to allow them to sit on the bunks, but lying down was still forbidden.[107]

If that wasn't enough, all POWs went through a jarring orientation to let them know what they could expect. "All PW's arriving are allowed to cool off for 30 days and get a taste of life in what they call a 'sleep' camp with its unrelaxed discipline and spartan life," noted Major Frank Brown of the PMGO. If they made it through that first step, "then they are considered 'eligible' for employment privilege providing their 201 [personnel] file does not disclose any adverse intelligence information on them and they have no record of previous escape or attempts," said Brown.[108]

Because of the attitudes of the men interned at Clark, and their propensity to cause trouble at the first opportunity, camp commander Frakes and his crew implemented unprecedented measures to control and discipline the POWs. After Brown's March 1945 visit, he called Clark the "strictest camp, from a discipline standpoint, that I have ever seen.... Infractions are dealt with immediately and not by half-way measures." He noted in the inspection report the procedures the Americans had to take to keep them in line. "They [the prisoners] must stand at attention at all times in the presence of an American officer and 'at ease' is never given them," wrote Brown. "A few days prior to the visit of this officer, about 1,500 of them were kept out in the open (in a bull pen) for 15 hours during the night for refusing to cooperate for the 'count.' They were also on bread and water."[109]

The American camp administration had a number of unpleasant options for those prisoners who chose to press the question of how much they could get away with. Some of them visited the so-called blue room of the guardhouse, a "rather dark cell with no bed, a bible to read, a quart bottle of water, and some very stale bread. It has proved very effective for reducing the activities of the 'pressure' leaders," noted Brown. "They are kept in this cell only so long as they refuse to calm down, when they accede they are transferred to a lighter cell and get a little fresher bread. Everything in this camp is earned by good conduct if it is good [sic], withdrawn from them when the rules are not complied with."[110]

Though the lack of work opportunities in the area around the Nevada post was a negative feature of the camp when the Italians POWs lived at Clark, it was not nearly as significant of a problem while the Germans were housed there. Because of its designation as a camp for troublemakers, many of the forty-seven hundred German POWs who were detained there by December 1944 were considered noncooperative and refused to work.

Indeed, these POWs were a nasty bunch, intent on causing problems any place they could. When inspectors visited Camp Clark, the prisoners would flood these representatives with complaints, in almost every case wholly unfounded. As just one example, prisoners complained heartily to

Emil Greuter, the Swiss Legation emissary responsible for German interests, that they had not received shoes. When Greuter asked the camp about these allegations during his December 1944 visit, the administration produced records showing that these prisoners were issued shoes and had in fact signed for them personally.[111]

Prisoners in Compound 3, where "morale was particularly not good" and "at a point where violence might occur at any time," also complained to Greuter that every toilet seat had been removed from one of the latrine buildings. Lieutenant Colonel Frakes explained that the Germans had smashed up eight toilet seats in one day, and so he had American GIs take out the rest of them before they were destroyed as well. "As soon as these prisoners of war in compound 3 behaved," he said, "these toilet seats would be restored."[112]

Compound 3 prisoners also claimed that they were stripped of their clothing when placed in confinement. The camp administration acknowledged the charge, saying when it was hot, some prisoners were put in the guardhouse and only allowed to wear shorts and shoes. However, said the commander, the order was quickly changed and was in effect for only two days.

All these allegations disturbed Greuter, according to the report, particularly because "there were so many complaints to him on the part of the prisoners of war about being kicked around and called swine." When Greuter learned that the "dark room" in the guardhouse, a cell with no windows and no bed, was used on one occasion, he pointed out that its implementation as a punishment was possibly a violation of the Geneva Convention, and Major L. D. Williams, executive officer for Camp Clark, agreed it would not be used again. "The discipline in this camp appeared to be quite rigid," said Greuter, who "concluded this was a punishment camp," as opposed to a mere internment facility designed to hold men until the end of the war.[113]

The handful of German officers at Camp Clark had complaints to offer the inspectors as well, but their gripes were slightly more refined. The officers, who were housed in a different section of the camp than the problem NCOs, were allowed to visit the canteen for a half-hour each day to make purchases. These men were unhappy that they had to be there at the same time as the non-officers and, furthermore, that they were not allowed to take beer back to their quarters. The officers also were dissatisfied with having to do their own laundry and complained that the orderly assigned to them was not required to do this. Greuter pointed out that the American officers at Camp Clark had to pay to have their laundry washed, and if the Germans wished to have their laundry done in the same fashion, it was possible for them as well, provided they were willing to pay for it.

The German officers also complained to Eldon Nelson, the representative from the Department of State who accompanied Greuter, that they were not being furnished bed sheets, tables, and chairs for use in their quarters. "When I asked them if they had ever requested these articles, they replied in the negative," wrote Nelson in his account of the visit, and noted that the stockade commander, Captain Robert L. Hutchins, said he would see to it that they would have these items.[114]

The Germans who were housed at Camp Clark were creative in finding ways to exhibit their surly disposition, as evidenced by a number of incidents recounted in an inspection report made in May 1945. "There were a total of 93 disciplinary cases during the month of April, the average sentence having been ten days (never more than 14) on restricted diet," wrote Dr. Rudolph Fischer of the Swiss Legation. "Fifty-three of these sentences were for failure to obey orders of German compound leaders; 19 were for such minor offenses as sleeping on bunks during the inspection hour, or reporting late for morning count; five were for leaving work detail without permission; fourteen were for insubordination to American officers, and more frequently to noncommissioned German officers; and two were for thefts of food and other articles."[115]

Even the fun wasn't fun with this bunch. "Sixty-three patients were being treated [at the hospital] on the day of our visit," noted the Department of State's Charles Eberhardt, who accompanied Fischer on a trip to the camp in May 1945, "a large percentage of whom were suffering from broken bones received in football [soccer] and fistball [volleyball] games."[116]

Response to Prisoner Behavior

Lieutenant Colonel Frakes knew what was going on. He was low-key but no-nonsense in his approach to dealing with the malicious behavior. For instance, the stockade commander, Captain Hutchins, lifted a manhole cover from one of the sewers in the camp. Squinting into the darkness, he found a giant rotten mess. "Great quantities of bread in loaf size had been thrown into the sewer as were carrots, spinach, corn, dish rags, etc., in a very apparent attempt at sabotage." Frakes's response simply was to order less bread be baked, reducing the allotment for each POW.[117]

"Frakes was a retread officer who had served back in World War I," said Ted Schafers. "He was a fair man who did the best he could in the job he was assigned. He and Hutchins ran a tough camp, and they were tough on prisoners. If any man disobeyed, he was punished at once."[118]

Frakes and Hutchins worked well together, recalled Schafers, and the camp's operation was enhanced by that harmony. "Hutchins had been a sergeant during World War I and stayed in the Army as part of the occupation forces," said Schafers. "I don't know if he had served with Frakes before, but those two were really close. They ran that place."[119]

In a unique reversal of the typical arrangement at other camps, where a small crowd of noncooperative POWs was separated from the larger group, Frakes ordered the creation of a cozy little compound especially for those few Germans who were willing to work. This area, known as Compound 13, was set back from the main prisoner compounds by a distance of several hundred yards. Prisoners here were housed in comfortable stone barracks—with concrete floors, good lighting, and good ventilation—previously used by American personnel. The gates of the compound were left open, and the men went to and from work without guards. The men made good use of the canteen located in their compound, smoking cigarettes, drinking beer, and enjoying favored pastimes forbidden to their more surly counterparts who made up the majority of the POW population.[120]

Frakes would have fed these men better as a result of their cooperation, were he allowed to. At the least, he was able to see they had their own bakery where unpaid POWs could prepare bread. This was a good idea, wrote Eberhardt from the Department of State, as was the practice of keeping the men separate from the other prisoners who did not have such good relationships with the camp's administration. "The writer concurs in the Camp Commander's idea that the group which signs

Camp Clark, Mo. May. 30. 45.

The P.o.W. employees of the

Sewage Disposal Plant, Camp Clark, Mo.

congratulate their principal operator

Mr. W. W. Mc DONALD

to his birthday, today.

We wish you good luck for the future.

Yours most respectfully

Karl
Fritz
Wolfgang
Kurt.

Despite the surly nature of some of the Clark prisoners, others enjoyed good relationships with their American civilian coworkers, as evidenced by this birthday greeting. Courtesy of Bushwhacker Museum, Vernon County Historical Society.

159

up for work, which they are performing in a highly satisfactory manner, should be fed better than the noncommissioned officers who refuse to work and obstruct at every possible opportunity, but regulations do not permit such differentiation," wrote Eberhardt. "The group of workers are kept in a separate compound for their own protection, since the non-working prisoners, strongly Nazi, would certainly abuse them were they kept in the same stockade."[121]

The Compound 13 prisoners who were working at the time of Eberhardt's visit in May 1945 comprised 225 POWs out of the total population of more than 5,000. Eighty of these men were assigned inside the POW stockade, primarily in the hospital, and another 145 worked outside, in other areas of Camp Clark. About 30 were used for "general labor," and the rest were employed as clerks, janitors, shoe cobblers, tailors, and warehouse workers.[122]

As part of their work assignments, the cooperative POWs in Compound 13 engaged in a variety of efforts to improve the camp, but one in particular was a favorite of U.S. officers and NCOs in terms of improving morale: constructing a golf course. "That was Colonel Frakes' big project. He had the POWs build a nine-hole golf course," said Ted Schafers. "The thing had sand greens; there was no grass. You'd hit the ball up close to the pin and it would just stop."

The officers would take to the links about 1 P.M. on most days when the weather was nice, said Schafers, and the NCOs would be not far behind. "We non-coms would sit and wait until we couldn't see their heads anymore, and then we'd grab our bags and play," said Schafers. "This would be about 1:30 in the afternoon, and then I'd come back to the office about 3 P.M., and return all my phone calls and answer any messages that had come in."[123]

Motivating the Men to Work

With the establishment of Camp Clark as a punishment and holding camp for the most difficult noncommissioned German POWs as well as a place to send newly captured Germans, the government created for itself a bit of a dilemma: what to do with the sizable population there—some 5,000 POWs—and how to make them work, as labor was still much needed. While the NCOs technically could not be required to work, Frakes and his men employed a variety of methods to encourage participation in the labor program. These included providing rewards such as increased use of the sports areas and equipment, more movies, and the like to those who cooperated. To punish prisoners for noncooperation, beer and cigarettes were banned from their canteens, and, later, candy and soda were removed from the counters as well. At Camp Clark, though, these motivations worked in only a few cases, as these men seemed to be very resistant.

A March 1945 visitor, Major Brown from the PMGO's labor and liaison branch, described the difficulties for prisoners who wanted to work, caused first by the lack of labor opportunities in the area and then by the Nazis infesting the camp who were intent on punishing "collaborators":

> Since there are no facilities for large segregations an informal list is kept of those PW's who have rather secretly let it be known that they will sign [up to work]. Then when a shipment is called for, a work agreement is sent to the companies involved and left there for 12 hours only. Those who sign are then shipped as soon as possible because trouble results if they remain near the non-signers.
>
> It was definitely stated that a PW can't sign and then remain in the compound with the others. The difficulty is that it takes four days to arrange for a train or several cars on the railroad. Word of when the actual signing will take place is passed around the appropriate compounds several days beforehand. They said that if they leave the list at the compound more than 24 hours too many procrastinate and also change their minds under pressure.[124]

Schafers found the assignment of trying to motivate these non-coms to sign up for work at other camps to be an interesting task. "Our job was to take these fellows and convince them to work. We'd get them to sign up and then ship them out to other camps that needed men so they could be used," recalled Schafers, whose ability to speak German was a big asset. "Some of them wanted to work just because they got so…bored sitting around. I would go around and talk to the others and say, 'Listen, you're going to be here for the duration of the war. If you want to live a little, and earn some money, you should think about signing up. Why not?'"[125]

Although a December 1944 camp census described the population as consisting of 4,679 "non-working non-coms," with no officers other than a couple doctors and one chaplain, the camp's administration decided it should take a closer look at the group there at Clark. Among the many fanatical Nazi NCOs were some soldiers, "quite a few" in the words of the Swiss inspector, who were shipped to Clark directly from the port of arrival at the United States—not sent there because of previous misbehavior at another camp.

Herman Graefe was one of those young soldiers brought to Clark by chance and not misbehavior or political bent. After being captured in France shortly after the Allied landing at Normandy in June 1944, Graefe arrived in New York, then went by train with other POWs to Camp Clark, his home for the next two years. His first feelings about his new home were mixed. Graefe knew he could be at the camp for a long time but had some indication that it might nevertheless be a tolerable experience.

"I knew things couldn't be too bad when I saw several prisoners carrying tennis rackets," recalled Graefe, who described his time at the camp as not unpleasant. "The treatment here was excellent and the food was good," he said, but noted the cold wind seemed to blow right through the thin walls of the barracks.

Graefe had an uncle in St. Louis who would visit occasionally and bring him cartons of cigarettes, making him "the richest man in the compound." The first time he came to the Clark POW installation, he tried to get the camp authorities to release his nephew on bail. The request was flatly refused.

Talk of escaping from the camp remained mostly that—just talk, said Graefe. "There was always talk of it, but very few tried," he said. "When anyone did escape or tried to, the whole camp was made to suffer, if you could call it that. Punishment would be no recreation or a cutback in food for a day or two."[126]

While taking stock of the great numbers of new soldiers such as Graefe, whom the administration counted among the pool of potential workers, camp leadership took another look at the soldiers already there. In particular, they reexamined the documentation presented by the noncooperative internees who claimed to be NCOs. The Americans suspected a number of the men were not actually noncommissioned officers, but rather ordinary enlisted men who tried to pass themselves off as holding the higher rank for the benefits it brought. This misrepresentation was not uncommon, for often a soldier's own word or a single scattered document or ID card—both vulnerable to forgery or alteration—was the only thing U.S. authorities had to go by. The internees were well aware that under the Geneva Convention, NCOs and sergeants could not be forced into labor, as opposed to enlisted men, privates who ranked below the noncommissioned officers and officers.[127]

Given this newfound skepticism of the proffered credentials, the census report from May 1945 now listed 1,568 POWs recognized as NCOs; an equal number who claimed to be NCOs but were not recognized because they could not prove it; 1,729 who were clearly enlisted men; and five officers and five protected personnel—the medical staff and POW clergyman. Those who could not prove their rank were assumed not to hold it, no matter how loud their protests to the contrary.

"Complaint was made by noncommissioned officers that their insignia had been removed," said Swiss inspector Rudolph Fisher. "When this subject was brought up, the Camp Commander stated that his orders were that until they could prove their status as noncommissioned officers they would not be entitled or permitted to wear such insignia and that insignia would be removed."[128]

More significant than the mere wearing of insignia, however, was that those who were unable to verify the rank they claimed—who were now assumed to be enlisted men and available for work—were subject to being shipped out to other camps where labor was needed. "Since this camp has been established principally for detaining non-working, noncommissioned officers," wrote Fischer, "it is being proposed to send at an early date a total of more than 3,000 who cannot prove their status as noncommissioned officers, to such camps as Douglas, Wyoming, and Indianola, Nebraska."[129]

Providing additional motivation to the noncooperative prisoners was the PMGO's statement in July 1945 that nonworkers would receive the least consideration in matters of repatriation. "[It] had a tremendous effect in producing work volunteers," wrote Schafers in the *Camp Clark Sentinel*. "They want to go home, even if they have to work for it."[130]

Eventually, those new arrivals who could be required to work were shipped out from Clark to POW camps across the central United States, including branch camps at Atherton and Orrick, Missouri, where their labor could be effectively utilized. The Nazis housed at Clark for misbehavior remained behind.

Religion

Because of the high percentage of Nazis and other generally unpleasant characters at Camp Clark, the effort to provide religious care and services to the prisoners met with little success. A German army chaplain did his best to reach the few Catholics in the group who would acknowledge any sort of faith, and two POW enlisted men trained as clergy joined him in the effort. "Religious interest of the prisoners of war in this camp is said to be very slight," wrote one visitor to the camp in December 1944, so when the POWs complained about lack of space for classrooms, somebody suggested they partition the nearly unused chapel and subdivide its space for classrooms. Because of the pressure from Nazis in the camp, less than 2 percent of the camp's population—eighty out of five thousand—attended Mass, and the Lutheran services, conducted by two Protestant POW clergy, were "somewhat less well attended" than that.[131]

Classes for German POWs

Ironically, the Nazis' zeal for troublemaking at the camp was matched only by their enthusiasm for learning. The prisoners at Camp Clark were active participants in classes, and a March 1945 report showed the wide variety of instruction they were offered:

Courses in Progress

Name of Class	Number of Course Instructors	Number of Students	Number of Hours per Month
German Literature	3	143	27
History	3	102	21
Geography	2	117	15
Mathematics	2	98	27
Calculate [sic]	1	24	9
English	2	123	33
Shorthand	2	78	21
Physics	1	46	3
French	1	28	12
Bookkeeping	3	68	18
Biology	1	52	3
Technical Science	1	18	9
Latin	1	26	9
Chemistry	1	48	3
		971	210[132]

"There are about 1,500 men attending classes under about eighty teachers," wrote Howard Hong of the International YMCA in a report of his visit to Camp Clark that month. Still, Hong noted that more could be done. "There is need for further development of the school and other constructive activities."[133]

German POWs were enthusiastic about the sports and recreation program and, despite their ongoing battles with camp administration, still managed to enjoy sports and entertainment. Rudolph Fischer of the Swiss Legation commented on the athletic and cultural diversions available to prisoners:

The camp boasts three very good orchestras and an excellent band. The library carries a total of 5,000 books. Probably 50 radios are in use in all the stockades. No less than 20 have been purchased from the prisoner of war fund.

Twenty-six daily *New York Times* reach the camp and the German *Staats-Zeitung*, looked upon very unfavorably by the strong non-working Nazi, is nevertheless subscribed to and read by practically all workers in the camp.

Der Ruf [*The Call*, the nationwide camp newspaper put out by POWs working under the Special Projects Division's reeducation program] is being purchased and read by a large percentage of the prisoners at this camp and, so far as is known, there has never been the wholesale purchase and destruction of this paper that has been reported from some other camps.[134]

Prisoners in the spring of 1945 had an art exhibit featuring more than one hundred entries sponsored by the YMCA, and Hong noted the role the YMCA's donated material played in making arts and crafts possible. "From food boxes, etc., many beautiful pieces have been carved and many hours have been beguiled on less successful work. In the YMCA sponsored arts and craft exhibition recently there were over 100 entries after a certain natural selection had taken place," wrote Hong. "Many men are learning to carve and paint by themselves. A YMCA literary (short story and poetry) contest was also held and considerable interest resulted and a number of good manuscripts."[135]

The "Loving Cup" Incident

In April 1945, Camp Clark was thrust into the maelstrom of national fury about coddling of POWs in American camps. On April 29, radio broadcaster Walter Winchell, long one of the chief critics of the cushy treatment POWs were receiving from American authorities, delivered a scathing description of a soccer tournament at the camp at which the winning team was awarded a trophy, or a "loving cup," as he derisively called it. Winchell, "a man most deskbound generals feared more than Hitler," had a problem with the POW facility at Camp Clark—one supposedly housing the most hardened and incorrigible Nazis in the United States—hosting soccer tournaments for its residents and then awarding trophies to the winners.[136]

Lambasting the POW camp administration as well as the YMCA for providing the trophy, and in the process using this "loving cup" to represent the whole contentious issue of coddling of POWs, Winchell turned the attention of an angry nation on Lieutenant Colonel Frakes and Camp Clark. The response was immediate, and citizens from across the nation demanded Frakes's head and reform of the whole POW internment program. Critical letters poured into Nevada with such volume that Frakes, disgusted with the publicity, eventually sent the trophy back to the YMCA, wanting the whole incident to go away.

The YMCA tried to respond to these charges, as did as a number of prominent citizens in the United States familiar with its work, but the damage was done. Eugene E. Barnett, general secretary of the International Committee of the YMCA, wrote an opinion piece that was carried in the *St. Louis Globe-Democrat* and a number of other newspapers:

> The "loving cup" in question is, in fact, a small trophy about five inches high and described by the commanding officer at Camp Clark as being worth about $2.50. German prisoners in the United States during the past few months have voluntarily contributed more than $20,000 to the YMCA to pay for such items and to help defray the general expenses of the YMCA's service to all war prisoners. In addition, German prisoners in the United States pay for more than two-thirds of all supplies provided for them by the YMCA....

> Under terms of the Geneva Convention, war prisoners' aid of the YMCA provides educational, recreational and religious materials for military prisoners of war.

The most important thing for Americans to understand, said Barnett, was the reciprocal nature of the YMCA's work. While it may seem silly, almost outrageous, for the YMCA to be providing items such as this "loving cup" to Nazis housed in the United States, these steps made it possible for American POWs in German camps to enjoy the same perks. Barnett described the items provided by the YMCA to Americans and the effect it had on morale:

> During the past two years, War Prisoners Aid of the YMCA has sent to American prisoners of war in Germany 1,745,254 sports articles, 244,232 musical articles and 1,280,146 books, together with large quantities of hobby, handicraft and dramatic supplies.

That these have played a major part in making prison camp life more bearable for captured Americans is attested by thousands of cards, receipts and letters from Protestant, Catholic and Jewish prisoners, and by the personal testimony of hundreds of repatriated or liberated prisoners who have returned to the United States in recent months. All supplies sent to American prisoners are free of charge.

This service to American prisoners of war in Germany would not be possible except for the fact that War Prisoner Aid of the YMCA has been providing a similar service for German prisoners in the United States. There is not the slightest doubt that the aid given American prisoners in Germany would have been impossible except for this service to Germans conducted on a reciprocal basis by YMCA workers from neutral countries.[137]

Howard Swain, managing editor of the *Brooklyn Eagle*, was more direct in his criticism of the Winchell broadcast. "It is too bad that the term 'loving cup' should have been applied to a cheap trophy of the kind well known to anyone who has ever conducted a small bridge tournament," wrote Swain. "The neutral nationals who administer prisoner of war work in this country certainly never thought there could be anything about such a gimcrack to warrant any excitement."

Swain discussed the work of the YMCA in Europe as well and described specifically how the YMCA's work among German POWs in the United States directly translated into improved conditions for American GIs being held in Germany. "We are certainly against any effort to coddle German war prisoners here, particularly after the ghastly treatment accorded to some American prisoners in Germany," continued Swain. "But as a price for getting books and games, sporting goods and musical instruments to make life more pleasant for Americans held for months and years in various Stalags, the presentation of an inexpensive cup in this country was cheap indeed."[138]

Reorientation Program at Camp Clark

With the secret re-education program for German POWs in full swing by spring 1945, selected American officers and NCOs from camps across the United States attended the Special Projects Division's school on the reorientation of the prisoners so they could implement more effectively the components of the program in their own camps. Ted Schafers was among those who were sent.

"One day the orders came in, and I was off to New York," recalled Schafers. "It was labeled top-secret and I wasn't supposed to breathe a word of it to anyone. Of course, at that time the war was almost over, and so that sort of thing—not that I ever told anybody—it was a lot less serious than it had been."

Schafers spent three weeks at Fort Slocum, attending classes, lectures, and seminars. There were presentations on the history of totalitarianism in Germany and the philosophies undergirding National Socialism and how these combined in the German body politic to create and to allow the rise of the Nazi state. Soldier-students who, like Schafers, had specific assignments in carrying out the re-education program discussed the merits of democracy and the American way of life. The men absorbed instruction on how those concepts might be combined and presented to internees so that German POWs might be inclined to hold a more favorable view of democracy and American society. The belief held by many in the upper levels of the Department of State and the PMGO was that this would hasten the transition to a peaceful postwar Europe and facilitate the establishment of governments founded on the basis of free elections and free speech.

One of the first things Schafers did when he got back from the course was to organize English classes for interested POWs. He told the prisoners that they should consider signing up for the instruction because it would put them that much farther ahead when they got back home. "I told them, 'There'll be a lot of people speaking English in Europe after this war is over,'" Schafers said with a chuckle. "The classes were really popular, but we always had trouble finding enough teachers."

The key to the program, said Schafers, was finding prisoners who were open to the idea of learning about democracy and focusing on them. "You had guys down there [at the camp] who were disgusted with the Nazis and just wanted a better life," said Schafers. "You'd find a couple of them to work with, and pretty soon you'd have a program going and some sense of the prisoners' temperament and political opinion."

Certain soldiers were more natural and logical candidates than others, Schafers recalled. "There was a guy who worked for me in the mailroom. He was fifty-four years old when they drafted him and had been a professor of history at Heidelberg," said Schafers. "He hated the Nazis, and if they were up to something, he'd tell us about it at once."

The political sentiments of others, of course, ran to the other extreme. "Another fellow, probably eighteen or nineteen years old, who used to drive me to town, he was a dyed-in-the-wool Nazi. He said up until the very last day that the Germans were coming to liberate the camp and that he'd be getting his freedom that way very soon."

Though Schafers's English classes were popular, and he thought he was making some progress in his work, Colonel Frakes wasn't so convinced of the value of the reorientation program. He knew the nature of the prisoners interned at Camp Clark and how that made implementation of any re-education effort difficult. "Colonel Frakes told me one time that any re-education program was bound to fail," said Schafers. "He said, 'I've seen all these men before—back in 1918. They are the same now as they were then. These Germans are warlike by nature and there is nothing you can do to change them.'"[139]

In May 1945, two officers from the PMGO, Major Paul A. Neuland, chief of the field service branch, and Captain Walter Rapp of the Special Projects Division, visited Clark to give the Special Projects Division a report on how things were going with the reorientation program at the camp. Captain Rapp had had an earlier run-in with Major Francis Judkins, commander of the POW camp at Camp Crowder, accusing him of running a country club for prisoners instead of an interment camp. At Clark, Rapp and Frakes also butted heads.

In their account of the visit, Neuland and Rapp noted that camp commander Frakes was well satisfied with the abilities of Lieutenant Howard Vedell, the assistant executive officer assigned to Clark especially to oversee the reorientation program. They said, however, because of the "exceptional circumstances" at Camp Clark, Vedell had not had a fair chance to implement the various components of the re-education effort. Neuland pointed out that of the five thousand German NCO prisoners interned at Camp Clark, only around two hundred were considered "cooperative"—those willing to work and housed by themselves in Compound 13.

"Although some benefits may result from the books, magazines, newspapers, and musical facilities which the assistant executive officer has carefully selected and filtered into the other compounds," wrote Neuland, "because of the rigid rules governing the activities of the noncooperative prisoner of war, Lieutenant Vedell has been unable to establish a well-coordinated reorientation program in any compound other than Compound 13. The assistant executive officer has done an excellent job in the cooperative compound and that is the extent of reorientation at this camp."[140]

During the visit, Neuland and Rapp told Frakes that despite the disruptive nature of the POWs interned in the camp, the commander could not arbitrarily decide to opt out of the command-directed reorientation program for the 96 percent of the POW population deemed noncooperative simply because it seemed like a challenge to administer. In other words, it wasn't enough that Vedell was only working with the two hundred cooperative prisoners in Compound 13.

Frakes gave Rapp many reasons why it was practically impossible to implement the re-education program at the camp. He noted that non-cooperative POWs were not permitted inside any building during the "restricted period," which lasted from 7 A.M. to 6 P.M., and that because of past problems caused by the prisoners and the difficulties in monitoring them, prisoners were not permitted to engage in any recreational or organized educational activities during this time. Also, POWs were not permitted to leave their compound, increasing the difficulty of organizing any program. Instead of having one educational program for the entire camp, it would be necessary to have a separate program for each compound, requiring duplication of effort and large numbers of teaching personnel.

Because Clark was filled to capacity, Frakes continued, there was "no space available for use as reading rooms, day rooms or study halls. Every building has been utilized to house prisoners of war or to serve as a mess hall or supply room." In addition to the lack of space, a shortage of financial resources precluded much activity in the re-education program, which was largely funded by the POWs themselves. Frakes pointed out that the POW camp fund was nearly dried up because the forty-eight hundred nonworkers in the camp had only their $3 monthly allotment to spend in the canteens, and with the beer, cigarettes, candy, and soda pulled from the shelves, there were few items left that the Germans wanted to purchase.

Finally, Frakes noted he had had to "continuously resort to stern disciplinary action" to control the recalcitrant POWs at Clark and "were he to suspend any of the present disciplinary regulations to permit the establishment of a reorientation program for noncooperative prisoners of war, that would be interpreted by those same prisoners as evidence of the laxity and weakness of America."

The men from the PMGO ultimately backed off of their demands that Frakes implement the reorientation program at Clark. "This report is not intended to convey the impression that Lieutenant Colonel Frakes is unwilling to have prisoners of war exposed to the reorientation program, but under the present situation he has neither the facilities nor the type of prisoners of war necessary to successfully promote the program," noted Neuland meekly in the conclusion of their report. "In view of the unusual circumstances prevailing at this camp and other noncooperative prisoner of war camps, pertinent recommendations will be submitted for consideration in a separate memorandum."[141]

Censorship at Camp Clark

In addition to his work organizing what limited components of the re-education program were possible at Clark, Schafers oversaw the mailroom, including censoring what was sent to the prisoners. "I was amazed at the amount of material that came through," he recalled. "One day, a package came through, and it had a big book in it on Otto von Bismarck. I said, 'We need to pull that out,' and somebody objected. 'There's nothing wrong with that,' they said. 'Nothing wrong?!' I replied. 'Why the hell should we send this through for them to read? All the German military is based on von Bismarck and his philosophies. This will just get them going all over again."

Because of his German language ability, Schafers screened other material, too, which was otherwise bound for the prisoners. A German-language newspaper printed in St. Louis that looked fine at first glance gradually grew suspect as Schafers read the publication over a few weeks.

"The paper carried news of the war in Europe," recalled Schafers, who had worked as a reporter prior to entering the service. "They'd carry the accounts of the war in Europe, like normal. They'd talk about the U.S. victories, but then when the Germans won something, they'd publish that, too, but the size of the headline would be two or three times bigger. Because of that I started studying it more, and reading the other articles a lot more closely. I realized that the editor really wanted Germany to win. After that, those newspapers started going into the trash."

The prisoners particularly enjoyed *Life* magazine, with its photo spreads showing a panorama of American life. Even when the magazine printed its famous collection of photographs taken at concentration camps in Europe, the prisoners didn't shy away or change their opinion of the magazine.

"'Those photos are all propaganda, Herr Schafers, just propaganda.' That's what they said."[142]

The Jewish Lieutenant and the Swiss Legation

The noncooperative German NCOs housed at Camp Clark were undeniably a bad lot of characters, bent on disrupting camp life. This posed a considerable challenge for Colonel Frakes and the two men who reported to him and who were directly responsible for the camp's daily administration, Captain Robert Hutchins and Lieutenant Benjamin Lowenberg. Unfortunately, on one visit in December 1944, the representative of the Swiss Legation, Emil Greuter, choose to give far more credence to the complaints and allegations made by the prisoners than they deserved, especially in light of their history as troublemakers. In particular, Greuter believed the accusations of mistreatment the Nazi internees made against

Lowenberg, who was Jewish. Greuter raised the issue of Lowenberg's alleged shortcomings and supposedly poor attitude to the attention of Camp Clark's executive officer, Major Williams, and then "unfortunately in rather blunt language called this to the attention of Lieutenant Lowenberg in the presence of subordinates," including both Lowenberg's fellow American officers and German POWs working in a next-door office.[143]

This incident touched off a firestorm of angry exchanges between the State Department, the Swiss Legation, and the PMGO. Some six months later things still hadn't settled down. In response to the Greuter episode, Charles Eberhardt of the State Department wrote his own scathing account of the situation and included it as part of his report from a May 1945 visit to Camp Clark with Rudolph Fischer, who replaced Greuter as the Swiss Legation representative. Eberhardt essentially accused Greuter of being one-sided in favor of the Germans, of accepting their complaints without question, and of ignoring the difficult job Frakes and his assistants had in trying to operate a camp filled with several thousand malcontents:

> The Swiss Representative [Greuter] who visited the camp last December, appears to have taken at face value most, if not all, criticisms, complaints and charges of the prisoners directed principally against Stockade Commander Captain Hutchins and his assistant, Lieutenant Lowenberg, and to have reported them in considerable detail to the Swiss Legation when all (as recounted to and read by the writer) seemed grossly exaggerated, some of them trumped-up, and others pure fabrication and down-right lies....

> The prisoners who have come to this camp for non-workers have almost, without exception, been the worst element at the camps from which they have been sent. In many cases, they are alleged to have been utterly undisciplined, and on arrival at the camp site...many of them have been unruly, insolent and defiant.[144]

It was indeed a tough job trying to control these men, and fortunately Frakes had the support of both the Department of State and the provost marshal general in beating back both the complaints of the POWs and the allegations of the Swiss representative during his December 1944 visit. Frakes in turn supported his assistants; for that, the men respected him and admired him. Eberhardt described his administration of the camp as one marked by fairness and firmness in a blistering rebuttal of the charges of mistreatment made by the Swiss Legation:

This is the third visit paid by the writer to camps administered by Colonel Frakes. In each camp, the writer has been favorably impressed by Colonel Frakes' (1) military bearing; (2) his strict interpretation and enforcement, from the military point of view, of all orders, directives, and regulations; (3) his unflinching firmness and absolute fairness; (4) the respect and loyalty he evidently exacts and certainly receives from his cooperative subordinates; (5) his ability and willingness to penalize slackness or failure among members of his staff, and to reward them for duty well done.[145]

In perhaps the best irony of all, on the last day of his visit to the camp in May 1945, Eberhardt received word in a telegram from the Department of State that Germany had surrendered unconditionally. As a result, the Swiss Legation was advised it was no longer needed to represent German interests and its inspectors should return to Washington. However, before they left, the prisoners were called out to the parade ground for what would be an unforgettable moment, the reading of the proclamation of Germany's surrender. The proclamation was read to them in good German by the Jewish lieutenant Lowenberg, whom so many of the prisoners detested.

End of the Camp

After the war ended in Europe, life at Camp Clark continued much as usual until August 1945, when Japan surrendered. With fighting completely ended, the United States could turn its attention to the process of returning the POWs to their homes in Europe.

On September 17, 669 prisoners packed up their belongings, swept out the barracks one last time, and loaded onto trains bound for other POW camps. Colonel Frakes left at the same time, having received orders to go to another duty station, and the quartermaster, Major F. Mainz, was left in charge.

The 398 prisoners who remained at Clark after the first group shipped out would not wait long for their own turn. Just three days later they too boarded trains headed out of town, in their case all pointed toward Camp Carson, Colorado, where they would work until the spring. After that final group left, the POW compound was closed. Work continued at the camp for the next several months for a clutch of GIs, while equipment left at Clark was stowed, sent elsewhere, or thrown away. Following the departure of the last GI on December 10, 1945, the Army began the process of transferring the camp from its wartime function as a POW installation and training facility to its postwar phase. Buildings and equipment the Army couldn't use elsewhere were sold as surplus, and residents recalled that whole barracks buildings were available for purchase at $300 each, delivered, and they popped up at various places around town. Fred Rooney bought one and used it to operate a beer joint called Pat's Place for a number of years, and Tom and Lena Mae Harpold used another one to house a restaurant called Harpy's Chicken House. One of the guard towers was used for many years as a concession stand in the southeast corner at Nevada High School's Logan Field.[146]

For two years after the camp was shuttered, literally nothing happened at the military installation, and the land was leased to local farmers for cattle grazing. On June 22, 1947, the Army turned the northern half of Camp Clark over to the War Assets Administration for disposal. The southern half, containing "the state's only full-sized rifle range," was signed over to the Missouri National Guard. The camp sat mostly idle until 1963, when Guard engineers began the process of reviving the camp. Camp Clark has been in almost continuous use ever since by National Guardsmen performing their two-week annual training exercises during the summer months and is home to a couple small Guard detachments that maintain a year-round presence there.

POWs at Fort Leonard Wood etched inscriptions on their stonework. Courtesy of Terry Culver.

Facing: A POW painting doors on post. Courtesy of Missouri State Archives.

Chapter Five

Fort Leonard Wood

Lots of people have gotten their kicks on Route 66 over the years, but prior to 1940 it generally wasn't on the stretch of road that twisted through the Mark Twain National Forest in central Missouri. In fact, the biggest burg in the two hundred miles between St. Louis and Springfield, Missouri, was Rolla, population just 5,141 in 1940. Rolla was laid out in 1858, and Edmund Ward Bishop, founder of the new city, wanted to call it Phelps Center, because his house was right in the center of Phelps County. George Coppedge, another settler, and formerly of North Carolina, favored "Raleigh" after his hometown. As the story goes, the other residents agreed with Coppedge, but only if he didn't insist on that "silly" spelling and used the variant "Rolla" instead.[1]

The area was rugged and mountainous, with many trees and relatively few people trying to pull their living from the meager Missouri soil. However, in 1940 the once far-off drums of war started to reverberate in central Missouri's Ozarks. Three counties in particular—Laclede, Pulaski, and Phelps—would be most affected by an Army post project as people and money flowed into the area on a scale previously unimaginable. The government announcement to establish a gigantic new military base came on October 1, 1940, and was followed immediately by efforts to secure land in the middle of the Mark Twain National Forest in Pulaski County. The main gate to the post would be located between the towns of Waynesville and St. Robert, approximately thirty miles southwest of Rolla.

That this huge Army post ended up in Missouri was something of a surprise. The plan originally authorized by Congress had the Army's new Seventh Corps Divisional Training Center and Engineer Replacement Training Center at Leon, Iowa, a small town in south-central Iowa about fifty miles south of Des Moines and just ten miles north of the Missouri state line. However, the Army's contractor-architect firm, Alvord, Burdick, & Howson of Chicago, learned in their preliminary site surveys that the water table had dropped dramatically at the Iowa location. Having a sufficient water supply would be so expensive there that the Army opted to move the new post to Missouri.

"The training center...will occupy some 68,000 acres of tableland and wooded hills in the Big Piney River country," reported the *St. Louis Post-Dispatch* in a November 24, 1940, account. "The center is expected to accommodate 32,000 enlisted men and 1,200 officers. The first military buildings, in a construction program expected to cost $8,400,000, will be ready for use, army officers hope, by February 1. Buildings planned include 434 barracks, 1,411 mess halls, 14 post exchanges and two theaters."[2]

The land, scantly populated throughout its history, had only around eight hundred people in the sixty-eight thousand acres being purchased by the government who were displaced by the post's creation. Except for a few old ramshackle Civilian Conservation Corps and tourist camps, the terrain was open and undeveloped. Locals expected this project, which swirled up quickly into a hubbub of men and machinery, would provide a great deal of economic benefit to the area. "Owners of office space in Rolla, 30 miles away, have been leasing it for the use of War Department officers and agents until buildings for them are erected at the cantonment," the *Post-Dispatch* continued. "Merchants of nearby towns are preparing for a substantial increase in business, and many men of the region are expecting to get jobs on the construction project."[3]

Four contractors—W. A. Klinger and Sons, Arthur H. Neumann Brothers, Western Contracting Corporation, and C. F. Lytle Company—banded together to form one conglomeration called the K.N.W.L. Company to share the construction responsibilities for this massive project and to pool their resources to overcome the problems associated with bringing the necessary materials and equipment to the isolated site. Already by January 1941, some twenty-three hundred civilian and military personnel were at work; by February that number swelled to eight thousand men hustling to meet the April 15 deadline for completion. Traffic along Route 66 between Rolla and Waynesville expanded at the same rate, with the Highway Patrol reporting a tenfold increase in traffic and a 400 percent jump in accidents in July 1941 along that stretch compared to just a year earlier.[4]

In about seven months, the four firms planned and completed an entire cantonment area of 1,600 buildings, 62 miles of water and sewer lines, and 58 miles of roads. They used 75 million board feet of lumber, 80,000 cubic yards of concrete, 52 miles of tile, 2,500 utility poles, and 2 million feet of wire in this amazing effort. Nearly forty-six thousand people were employed as part of the construction effort. The cantonment area was about 6 square miles, 3 miles north-south by 2 miles east-west, with a 7,000-by-3,000-foot open parade ground in the center around which the buildings were arranged.[5]

With thousands of workers swarming over the new base, along with another sizable crew at work on a new thirteen-mile rail spur from Newburg to the post, housing was suddenly at a premium, and there was an immediate shortage for fifty miles on each side of the base. To fill the need, Barrett & Hilp of San Francisco took a government contract in August 1941 to provide six hundred prefabricated, "demountable" homes in a factory next to the Newburg rail yards. The factory employed 250 men and manufactured ten houses a day. These measures were still not sufficient to keep up with the tremendous growth accompanying the creation of the camp. Almost two years later, still trying to find a way to deal with the housing shortage, military authorities issued a notice to friends and relatives of soldiers that there was absolutely no housing available in the Fort Leonard Wood area. Rooming houses, hotels, and private dwellings were taxed beyond normal capacity as far as Rolla, some thirty miles away, forcing late arrivals, including many women and children, to take up quarters in substandard tourist cabins.

Despite the great number of people arriving in the area, the isolation of the post and the lack of infrastructure put a strain on family life. Presbyterians canvassing the area for potential members noted the challenges facing new residents. "The center of our problem is still in a Government Housing Area on the military reservation," wrote the evangelists. "Over 2,000 people, including over 700 children and 700 women live here. There is only one telephone, no store or drug store, no school or church, no physician, no social life or recreation."[6]

The frenzied rush to get the fort ready to accept and train troops as soon as possible sometimes prompted poor decisions that might have been averted had planners been given more time for review. For instance, the railroad line, which was finally complete in April 1941, was built too close to a target range, and trains carrying men and supplies caused frequent stoppages in training on the range so that rail cars would not be hit by errant munitions. Additionally, the rugged terrain forced the railroad line from Newburg to Fort Leonard Wood to go considerably out of its way to avoid Devil's Elbow, a huge rock outcropping, as well as other natural features unfavorable to railroad track, which added several miles to the trip.

Along with the creation of new housing stock, area cities planned infrastructure improvements. At Rolla, the municipal airport doubled in size, and two new USO buildings—one for white soldiers and the other for "colored troops" in the still-segregated armed forces—were erected to handle the needs of the soldiers passing through. Officials at the post met with superintendents of area school districts to discuss the best way to handle the inundation of children of workers and soldiers from Fort Leonard Wood, and engineers unveiled plans for a new cloverleaf exit at the military base to handle the traffic load on Route 66 that had climbed to nearly four thousand vehicles per hour.[7]

The installation was named for former Army chief of staff Major General Leonard Wood, a medical officer and commander of the First Volunteer Cavalry in the Spanish-American War. There he and his second in command, an officer by the name of Theodore Roosevelt, would lead the Rough Riders at San Juan Hill and elsewhere.[8] The installation was designated Fort Leonard Wood on January 10, 1941, and units began arriving in February. Some of these units stepped in to put the finishing touches on the nearly finished base until the contractors officially turned the property over to the government on June 26, 1941.[9] Though many thousands of trainees would cycle through the post during the war years, it would be home to a substantial POW population as well. McCarthy Brothers Construction Company won the contract to construct the POW facility in October 1942, and prisoners began arriving at Fort Leonard Wood just two months later.

On December 18, 1942, the POW camp was officially activated as the Enemy Alien Internment Camp under the command of Vernon H. Vrooman, Lieutenant Colonel, Infantry. That same day, three Military Police Escort Guard Companies, each with a strength of 3 officers and 135 enlisted men, arrived from Camp Clark, Missouri, where they had been activated and trained. It was also on that day that the first POWs arrived: 662 Italians were processed, confined in Compound 1, and organized into companies under the command of an American officer.

These Italian POWs were held without incident at Fort Leonard Wood, working in the POW compound and to a lesser extent on projects around the post until the entire group was transferred June 22, 1943, to the camp at Weingarten, Missouri, which had become operational as an internment camp for POWs just a month earlier. There was barely a week's worth of quiet at the camp, however, as the first contingent of German POWs arrived on June 29, 1943. By the end of July, more than two thousand Germans were held at the Fort Leonard Wood internment camp. The peak POW population would come in June 1945, when nearly fifty-two hundred Germans would call it home.[10]

Layout of the POW Compound

The POW compound within Fort Leonard Wood comprised eighty-seven acres and was situated well away from the main part of the post. The camp was located adjacent to a small landing strip used by aircraft attached to an artillery training division, and about four miles separated the camp from the post headquarters and the chief cluster of buildings on the installation. Three compounds, each holding one thousand men, made up the major part of the camp, with a fourth section serving as a common recreation area.

In addition to twenty barracks and four latrines, each compound in the camp contained four POW mess halls; a canteen offering various drinks, tobacco, toilet articles, notepaper, and the like; a recreation room; a workshop; a theater; an infirmary; and an administration barracks.[11]

Arlie Carter, a preteen from nearby Dixon, Missouri, worked in the summers at the canteens at Fort Leonard Wood, filling in as needed in the various PX facilities around the post. He spent about a month at the canteen in the POW compound as the replacement for a departed employee before returning to school in the fall of 1943.

"When you saw those boys line up in the morning to go out to work, and then come back in the evening and get cleaned up and come into the PX, their actions weren't really different than our own soldiers'," recalled Carter. "In some ways it was better, because in the other PXs some of our fellows there would drink enough beer to get pretty soused. They'd get to thinking that they could whip the whole world and then some of them would turn around and try to do it. That sort of thing wasn't allowed at the POW canteen."

Carter said that he enjoyed his work in the POW camp and recalled many pleasant interactions with the prisoners. "It may be hard to believe that they would have a twelve-year-old doing this, but I was big for my age so I fudged a little on how old I was," said Carter. "Those prisoners were just as nice to me as our own military. Though we couldn't speak the same language, they were just as congenial as gentlemen could be."[12]

Carter's job was to keep items on the shelves of the POW canteen. An inspector noted in May 1944 that the canteen at Fort Leonard Wood seemed to be particularly well stocked. "The canteen at this camp is unusually well supplied with all articles for which the prisoners might ordinarily be expected to inquire," wrote the Swiss inspector. "Beer, soft drinks and cosmetics are probably the most popular articles. The sales in April [1944] amounted to over $22,000 with a net profit of over $3,000 or more than ten percent."[13]

Barracks were of the standard 20-by-100-foot construction, each sleeping between forty and fifty men, and were covered with black cellotex board sealed with tar between the joints. Shortly after the camp's construction, an inspection report noted that "although the camp is well arranged and is in very orderly condition, the color of the barracks prevents the most attractive appearance. There are very few shade trees."[14]

Although the Italians did attempt during their brief stay to better the initial appearance of their camp, it was the German prisoners—who would end up spending three years there—who put a great deal of effort into improving the looks of their new home, beginning the first day of their arrival. "The prisoners have been industrious in improving the surroundings within the compounds," noted one inspection report. "In addition to drainage ditches, they have constructed rock gardens and extremely elaborate mosaics of rocks which depict in minute detail their regimental insignia and other designs."[15]

POW Fritz Ensslin recalled their efforts to beautify the camp. "We had the opportunity to set up general housekeeping within the barracks during the following few days [after our arrival]. However during the day our camp looked somewhat depressing. It looked almost like the Sahara Desert since there were no trees, grass, bushes or flowers within our camp," remembered Ensslin. "We did our best to improve the appearance of our camp with the help of our camp commander who brought us grass and flower seeds. Our camp looked like a virtual paradise within a few weeks. To our major's great satisfaction, the occupants of the barracks competed against each other in which barracks had the nicest garden."[16]

"Their camp was neat as a pin, with swastikas all over the place, carefully made of small stones adorning the grounds and pathways, as well as on the walls, made of various pick-up materials such as bits of wood, straw and cloth," wrote Rufus Jarman, who visited the camp for the *St. Louis Post-Dispatch*. "As I recall, some photographs of you-know-who were prominent on some walls. These men wore proudly their worn *Afrika Korps* uniforms with long billed cloth caps and a grayish khaki colored uniform, many with shorts."[17]

POW fare at Fort Leonard Wood was the usual Army chow, with improvements made where possible via informal mess hall barter, where POWs would swap ingredients with GI cooks to get more of the items they favored. "The prisoners seem well satisfied with their meals although they require more potatoes and flour and will not eat corn," wrote one inspector of the practice. "There is no demand for special rations."[18] Another visitor from the International Red Cross wrote that he "shared the meals of the prisoners and was able to note that the food is perfect in quality as well as in quantity."[19]

Average cost per day at Fort Leonard Wood in May 1944 to feed the prisoners three square meals was precisely $.5896, as noted by a visitor from the Swiss Legation.[20] Unfortunately, the lack of a prepared garden plot and the poor Pulaski County soil prevented Fort Leonard Wood POWs from enjoying fresh table fare for the first year of their stay. By the next spring (May 1945), however, fifteen POWs were working on a new eight-acre garden, and they hoped to provide produce from that plot to augment the mess hall selection. The vegetables grown in the POW gardens were turned over to the quartermaster and used in both POW and GI messes at Fort Leonard Wood. Tomatoes were the chief item grown, with 22,000 pounds grown in 1944, and more than 37,000 pounds harvested the next year. Prisoners also brought in over 12,500 pounds of cabbage, 7,600 pounds of cucumbers, and 2,800 pounds of other vegetables. These efforts garnered a profit of $1,299.87 for that first year's work in 1944, and in 1945 the gardens netted $1,693.65.[21]

Security at the Camp

Security at Fort Leonard Wood was detailed and systematic. Guard towers equipped with machine guns and searchlights dotted the double row of fencing that surrounded the prisoner compounds. Twenty guard dogs provided additional security, with four dogs patrolling the perimeter at night.[22]

Arlie Carter was usually at the POW PX until 9:30 P.M., when he'd lock the building and walk back to another PX about a half mile down the road to turn in the day's receipts. "They told me during my orientation that if I heard the siren go off in the POW compound, that meant that they thought a prisoner was trying to escape and that they would turn the guard dogs loose to go and get him," said Carter. "I was locking up one night and I heard the siren go off, but I had to get back to the other PX for turn-in, so I just went about my business and headed out of the compound."

Carter was suddenly confronted by a large police dog that appeared from the darkness. The animal didn't bark but came right up to him and sniffed him while Carter froze. "They said that if one of these dogs came up to you, you should just stand still. They would smell you, trying to get the scent of the prisoner," said Carter. "If you took off running though, that animal would set on you and there was no telling what would happen."

After a moment, the animal left the boy, satisfied Carter was not the prisoner he sought. Just as the boy set out again, a guard stepped from the shadows of a nearby building. "Halt!" came the command. Carter stopped again. "Advance and be recognized," said the guard, but Carter misheard the instruction. "I thought he said, 'Go on' or 'it's okay' or something like that," remembered Carter. "I started to take another step when all of a sudden I heard the click of him turning off the safety of that Springfield rifle he was carrying."

Instantly Carter froze again, trying to stand motionless despite his trembling. The guard shone a flashlight in the face of the terrified boy and suddenly recognized him from the camp. "He was as scared as I was," said Carter. "He was afraid that he might have shot me if I had taken one more step."[23]

That guard and the others at the camp came from the three Military Police Escort Guard Companies. Thirty officers and five hundred enlisted men provided the main POW security at the camp.[24] However, once the atmosphere became more relaxed, even brand new recruits were used to supervise POW work details.

Jack Vineyard of Ava, Missouri, was just eighteen years old when he was drafted and sent to basic training at Fort Leonard Wood. Weapons were in such short supply that the recruits used broomsticks to simulate rifles during drills. After just three weeks, these new soldiers were pulling sentry duty at various posts around the installation, and though they had traded their broomsticks for rifles, it didn't do them much good, as they never received bullets, both because of a severe shortage of munitions and the fact they hadn't been fully trained on how to fire the guns.

"Shortly after that we were given another responsibility," recalled Vineyard. "We were to guard the prisoners of war." It was a whole new ballgame for the young soldiers, and they just didn't know what to expect. The recruits never received any training on the handling of POWs, and though this assignment seemed more dangerous than their previous sentry duties, the GIs were still not issued bullets for their weapons.

"Each morning we went to the stockade, picked up a certain number of POWs and marched them out to the woods to clear brush, burn wood, pick up rocks, or whatever needed to be done," recalled Vineyard. "Other days we would take them to the parade ground to place rocks along the banks of the washes that ran through the parade ground."

The soldiers guarding the prisoners would often lie down for a snooze, their rifles unattended by their sides, said Vineyard. "Many a time I saw a POW go over to the young soldier and place his own coat on the sleeping soldier to help keep him warm," remembered Vineyard. "Other times the prisoners would share their lunches with certain soldiers. It seemed like they had better sandwiches than we did. We usually had hog's head cheese sandwiches."

Being around these POWs every day, Vineyard soon began to see the prisoners as people, instead of as an impersonal enemy. "We soon lost all fear of the prisoners and spent many happy days standing there watching them at their work," said Vineyard. "It wasn't a good thing to let us lose a certain amount of fear of these men, but it did happen. I got a different opinion of these men we were guarding, realizing that they were following orders just like we had to do. I could not hate them like I wanted to."[25]

Italian Prisoners

The 662 Italians who arrived on December 18, 1942, as the first residents of the Fort Leonard Wood POW camp probably didn't know their stay would be relatively brief, with their transfer to the brand-new POW camp at Weingarten, Missouri, coming within six months. They probably also did not suspect that during their short stop at Fort Leonard Wood, they would be involved in incidents that helped define U.S. policy and practice for POWs in other camps across the nation. The first incident, a controversy involving a perceived requirement that the Italian POWs salute the American flag, would happen within weeks of their arrival and ultimately require the intervention of the Swiss representatives.

Commander Vrooman ordered the Italian POWs to stand at attention in formation and salute the American flag when retreat was sounded at 5:30 P.M. each day, following the same practice as U.S. personnel. The order came on January 28, 1943, and was effective at once. The Italians naturally protested, and Francesco Brasile, spokesman for the Italian POWs, wrote the Swiss for clarification. Brasile said the Italians' objections were not simply the internal conflict over being forced to salute the flag of another country but were of a practical nature as well.

"There is no American Flag in our camp and we don't hear the music for the ceremony. On January 28 was the first time we had order to do so to stay in attention when American Soldiers saluted the American Flag," wrote Brasile. "We would like to know why this order wasn't put out the first day we came out here to this Camp and why and if we have to do so now."[26]

Three weeks later, assistant provost marshal general Bryan responded to the complaint. The Swiss had sent it to the State Department, which passed it on to Bryan to craft an official government response. In Bryan's letter to the State Department, he cited the same issue having been raised at the POW camp at Crossville, Tennessee, by a German officer just a couple weeks prior to the Italian complaint at Fort Leonard Wood. The letter stated, "prisoners of war should not be forced to pay homage to the American flag on unnecessary occasions, but…prisoners of war who find themselves outside of barracks, huts, and tents during the retreat period of American soldiers will govern themselves in the same manner as our own troops in such circumstances."[27]

An account of the POW operation at Fort Leonard Wood acknowledged without hesitation the lack of guidance the camp administration had in carrying out its work. "Throughout practically the entire first year of its existence, administration and the policies applied toward the Prisoners of War interned at this Camp were necessarily based in large measure upon a common sense interpretation of existing Army Regulations and such War Department Directives as then were available," according to the camp history. "Initially, not a single copy of the Geneva Convention of July 29, 1929, Relative to the Treatment of Prisoners of War was available to the Camp personnel. This lack was remedied by securing a copy and obtaining a translation into English."[28]

Even though the PMGO began publishing a series of regulations and guidelines in an attempt to standardize practices among camps, the Fort Leonard Wood camp had been operational for almost a year when the first one came out in September 1943. These publications, called "Prisoner of War Circulars," were intended to clarify and update the existing jumble of directives, which were often vague and in conflict with themselves and the Geneva Convention.[29]

Evidenced by the flag-saluting incident, the administration was flexible in addressing prisoners' concerns about how they were treated as well as in making occasional exceptions to policy so as to improve the lot of the POWs. This flexibility was demonstrated again in Bryan's response to a somewhat unusual request about two brothers that crossed his desk one day in early 1943. One brother was a POW at Fort Leonard Wood; one was a soldier in active service stationed at Camp Chaffee, Arkansas.

The post chaplain at the Arkansas station wrote the commander at Fort Leonard Wood. "Dear Sir," he began:

We have a Soldier here by the name of Corporal Umbra who is serving our Army and I understand he has a brother who visited Italy and was forced to take up arms against his wishes. He was a Citizen of the United States and now is held as a Prisoner of War in your Camp.

Would it be possible for Corporal Umbra to come and visit him, he has not seen him since 1936.

Please do all in your power to have these brothers meet again.

First Lieutenant Daniel G. Deale
Post Chaplain
Camp Chaffee, Arkansas[30]

Bryan was brief in his response granting approval to this request. "Visits to internees by members of the United States Armed Forces are subject to the same procedure and regulations applicable to other visits," wrote Bryan, a West Pointer from the class of 1922, meaning that the two need only get permission of the POW camp commander. "In addition," barked Bryan, "as a precautionary measure, it is requested that Military Intelligence Division be informed of each visit to an internee by a member of the United States Armed Forces."[31]

German Prisoners

Once the five-thousand-man-capacity all-Italian POW camp at Weingarten opened in May 1943, the first group of POWs at Fort Leonard Wood quickly shipped out for their new home in Ste. Genevieve County. The government anticipated receiving many more German prisoners in the coming months, prompting the consolidation of the Italian POWs in several larger camps. Prisoners from different nations were not held in the same camp, and moving the Italians provided more room for the Germans. The process of organizing a camp on the scale of that at Fort Leonard Wood was no small effort, and so the departure of the Italians after only a six-month stay and the subsequent arrival of German POWs meant that a new internal framework had to be created.

The MPs were edgy, expecting a much greater challenge from the Germans than from the easygoing Italians. POW Fritz Ensslin remembered how keyed up the GIs were when the POWs arrived at the camp at midnight following a two-day train ride from the East Coast. "We were received by a large force of security guards, armed with submachine guns, with their fingers on the triggers ready to fire at us at all times," recalled Ensslin. "Someone called out in broken German, 'Hurry up, Germans, you will get something to eat!' About one o'clock in the morning we were served a dream meal that a reputable hotel could not have cooked better. Some of us were kidding and made such remarks as, 'If we had only known, we would have sneaked across earlier instead of fighting until we ran out of ammunition.' They let us sleep until noon, since we were exhausted by our journey."[32]

POW soccer team at Fort Leonard Wood. Courtesy of Paul Schanze.

Sports

The camp lost its internal POW leadership structure with the transfer of the Italians. It also lost a good bit of the recreational equipment it possessed. When the Italians were transferred to Weingarten, under the approval of both the YMCA and the camp authorities, they took with them nearly everything they were given, such as books and musical instruments. Having those many items leave the camp meant the process of equipping the camp had to begin anew after the Germans arrived.[33]

In addition to restoring the camp's stock of sports equipment in the early days after their arrival, the Germans put quite a bit of work into getting additional fields ready for use in the POW sports program. "The athletic program is active but hindered by the need for more work on the camp field and the need for additional guards to open the field for longer and more frequent periods," observed an inspector from the YMCA.[34] By November 1943 these fields were finished, and the German POWs organized soccer and basketball tournaments between the prisoner companies within the three compounds. When the following summer rolled around, things were running smoothly for the POWs in the athletic program. "Well-arranged sports fields and sufficient equipment permit the prisoners to engage in sports every day during their free time," commented one visitor to the camp.[35] Industrious prisoners put down a layer of crushed lime rock to improve the surface of the playing field, and arrangements were made so that the three POW compounds divvied up the available time, sharing equally the use of the field.[36]

POWs constructed bowling alleys for use of the German officers, and enlisted POWs showed up each day to set pins for them. In May 1944 an inspector noted that "there has been an improvement in practically every form of recreation offered the prisoners.... Nearly $2,000 had been spent in May for the prisoners from canteen funds for athletic supplies, musical instruments, etc." Colonel William S. Hannan dug up some table-tennis tables for the prisoners, and the YMCA sent balls to go with them, as well as checkers and chess sets.[37]

For prisoners with interests beyond the playing field or card table, each compound had a workroom, with a prisoner-installed cement floor used for various purposes. Carpentry and woodworking were practiced along with sculpture and painting.[55] Additionally, enterprising prisoners scrounged enough scrap lumber to build a separate carpenter shop in the area adjacent to the camp entrance. Other intrepid prisoners found a way to use their free time and a little ingenuity to earn a few dollars:

> We also had some [prisoners] who were making ladies' purses out of snake hides. The snakes were caught locally and the purses were sold to American officers to have them as presents for their wives. Some POWs were melting empty toothpaste tubes to make copies of German medals and decorations out of the lead. The medals looked genuine and no American could resist buying a few for souvenirs.[38]

Library

With the departure of the Italians from Fort Leonard Wood, the shelves of the POW camp library were left bare. This was a source of disgruntlement for the German prisoners who longed for reading material of any type. YMCA representative Hong commented that "books are the number one need of the camp" and with the permission of the camp commander bought almost 650 new and used German books and received about 200 more from the librarian of the Eden Theological Seminary in

Webster Groves, Missouri. Hong hauled them to the POW camp just so the men could see that books were on the way, then dropped them off at a warehouse on post for sorting and censoring before they were shipped back to the eager POWs. The reading stock at the camp was thoroughly replenished by May 1944, with approximately 4,000 books on hand, most of them in German.

Newspapers were popular too, though how they were viewed by the prisoners depended on their political views. Each day sixty-four copies of the *St. Louis Globe-Democrat* arrived, and translators compiled a single sheet of selected articles for circulation. The prisoners devoured *The New York Times* because it carried the official communication releases from the German government.

The censors pored over the newspapers and magazines that came into the library, trying to eliminate anything that might be of intelligence value to the prisoners or useful for escape, such as train schedules. One POW noted that much of the prisoners' reading material came from an unanticipated route, however, beyond the control of the censors: "The men who were assigned to the incinerator and garbage removal brought us large quantities of other magazines and newspapers so that we had a good inside view of the American press."[39]

The only German-language newspapers permitted were those sent by religious organizations. There was one in particular, the *New Yorker Staats-Zeitung*, that was disliked by virtually the entire camp because of its strong anti-Nazi orientation. One prisoner went out of his way to gripe directly at the Swiss representative about the presence of the newspaper in the camp. The Swiss inspector told the complainer that according to the camp commander, newspapers, whether English or German, were not forced on anybody, and that prisoners could read any, all, or none as they chose. Another prisoner, an Austrian who had been drafted into the German army, made a point of reading the *Staats-Zeitung*, making himself unpopular with the Nazis in the camp. He even sent off a subscription form so that he would receive it personally and insisted on reading it openly. This public display of disdain for Nazism probably put the man in some danger of physical attack from the ardent National Socialists in the camp.[40]

Theater

For recreation and entertainment, the usual array of sports, games, and performing arts occupied the energy and attention of the prisoners. "Artistic groups were formed within the camp such as cabaret theater and even a dance group consisting of 12 'girls' trained by a ballet master. Among the

POWs in a theater production. Courtesy of Paul Schanze.

spectators of this dance were many American officers who attended the performance on a regular basis," recalled Fritz Ensslin. "They were awed by the dancing girls who were actually boys, by their genuine looks and performance. Girlish-looking boys were picked for that role. They were well-drilled and with the perfect makeup, they looked almost real."[41]

Dramatics were called the "favorite pastime" of the prisoners by one camp visitor.[42] The YMCA provided equipment as well as instruments for prisoner orchestras and props for theatrical performances. In October 1943, four months after the arrival of the Germans, preparations for several camp theaters were well under way, noted a visitor:

> Each compound will have a theater with stage as soon as Compound III completes its work, which is well advanced. Colonel Vrooman gave instructions for the stage wiring, and I sent some curtain material. The theatrical materials in our basic unit will fill a real need here, too. Old clothes to be used "as is" or remade will also be welcome. On the evening of my last day at the camps I saw a variety show staged early for my benefit. The men have done well with so little. One play or entertainment a week is planned for the hospital....[43]

Education

Especially at first, German prisoners at Fort Leonard Wood didn't seem to put much effort into the educational program organized by their fellow POWs, as judged strictly on a count of filled seats. Franz Engelmann was an exception though, preferring the classroom to the soccer field. "In camp, our free time was rounded out with sports, but my interest was in learning English," said Engelmann, who eventually put his language skills to good use at the branch camp at Louisiana, Missouri, where he was given a job waiting on customers at the Stark Bro's Nursery. "Two or three times a week, from 7 to 8:30 P.M. was instruction given by a German teacher. Now and then the sergeant would come by from the office to make sure everything was ok. Through that instruction, those of us in the camp were able to put our knowledge to good use in our work."[44]

Franz Engelmann. Courtesy of Franz Engelmann.

By November 1943, just three months after arrival, basic classes in language, drawing, and mathematics had been organized, but the instruction was dogged by a lack of textbooks and other necessary materials. The curriculum expanded rapidly, however, and by January 1944 prisoners had added classes in English, physics, chemistry, history, geography, and painting.[45] Although the list of class offerings was expanding, the enrollment roster did not experience the same growth. Verner Tobler, a representative of the Swiss Legation who inspected the camp in May 1944, noted "more or less the same disinterest in the schools of the camp is displayed" as observed in a visit the previous fall.[46]

"Among the thousand POWs in our camp, there were many intelligent men with many capabilities such as professors, high school teachers, and foreign language instructors who offered tutoring in almost every language," said Ensslin, who couldn't understand the lack of interest in the classes. "Unfortunately, very few people took advantage of this golden opportunity and I am sure that they were sorry afterwards."[47]

Despite this relative lack of interest on the part of the larger Fort Leonard Wood prisoner population, those who did participate seemed to relish the opportunity for education. In August 1944, a visitor noted that the camp had ten to twelve professors, and the course list had increased to include instruction on metalwork, construction, commerce, medicine, art, and various languages. Also offered were lectures, professional development programs for noncommissioned officers, and preparatory courses for the *Abitur*, the final exam for graduating students in Germany that certified them for additional study at the university level.[48]

Those "professors" and other instructors of classes in the camp took their work seriously, spending much time preparing the lectures and materials. They went so far as to make a request to the camp commander that they be exempt from work so that they could have more time to thoroughly prepare their courses. The request was granted, and the "full-time" POW instructors were paid out of the canteen profits at the same $.80 a day rate as other POW laborers. Additionally, to minimize disruption in the educational program at Fort Leonard Wood, these instructors requested that they not be transferred to one of the branch camps, either, which would remove them from the main body of prisoners.[49]

Given this level of commitment from the instructors, POW interest and participation in the educational program continued to grow. By March 1945 there were twenty instructors who taught seventy day and evening classes in thirty-five subjects. Particularly noteworthy, asserted one inspector, was the "art school," which offered POW-led instruction in oil painting and sculpture. Calling it a "prize development" and "unusually well-developed for an enlisted-NCO camp," the inspector in a March 1945 report noted that the students held an art exhibition for which prizes were awarded.

"The instruction is thorough—to the point of the teacher writing an *Anatomy for Painters* book for use by the classes. The emphasis is on oil painting and sculpture," wrote Hong of the YMCA. "The art and crafts competition and exhibition suggested during my previous visit was a success. Plans are now under way for such an event for the branch camps. The YMCA will again provide awards."[50]

The instructor for the painting classes had been a professional artist in Germany and had a unique gift for reaching the prisoners through his direction. In addition to this instruction, the artist, whose name is unfortunately not known, devoted himself to painting religious artwork. "The master himself was working on a large altar picture which showed good religious, creative force," noted the Reverend Karl Almquist, a visitor to his studio. "He wanted to give this altar picture to some parish here in America. If we could arrange for him to work for a special parish, he would be very happy, he told me."[51]

Religion at Fort Leonard Wood

After the Italians were sent to Weingarten in June 1943, their chaplain, Joseph Parent, felt abandoned. "This camp has been turned into a German camp for German Prisoners of War," Parent lamented to the Reverend John O'Hara, who oversaw the military chaplaincy operations for the Catholic Church from New York. "Due to this fact I shall ask to be transferred.... I feel that a German speaking chaplain would be better. I neither speak nor understand German and I cannot help the men." Parent's request to be transferred to Weingarten was eventually granted.[52] This left the camp without a chaplain during the first months of the Germans' residence there, so a series of temporary civilian pastors ministered to the POWs. Additional help came from three men with theological training from within the prisoner population. They held three Protestant services each Sunday, one in each compound. A civilian Catholic priest came to celebrate Mass, but "after some slight incidents" in October 1943, a German prisoner chaplain was sent from another camp to take his place.[53]

It is not clear what "incidents" prompted the removal of the parish priest who had been ministering to the Germans, but he may have experienced some hostility from the Nazi NCOs, who were strongly anti-Catholic. A letter written only seven months later, in May 1944, by Monsignor John P. Cody, chancellor of the Archdiocese of St. Louis, contained information that might refer to this situation. Cody sent a note to the Reverend John Godfrey of Ascension Parish in Chesterfield, Missouri, in response to a dispatch from Godfrey, who had been experiencing great difficulty in ministering to prisoners at the branch camp in Chesterfield. "The experience which you have had, of course, is not new to me, as we have had considerable trouble at Fort Leonard Wood from whence these prisoners came," wrote Cody. "It became so bad at Fort Leonard Wood that we had to remove a Chaplain lest he might suffer fatal consequences from these barbarians."[54]

Writer Rufus Jarman of the *St. Louis Post-Dispatch* later recalled his impressions of these POWs. "I remember the Germans as raw-boned, hardened men in top physical condition, with sharp, lean, bitter faces," said Jarman. "They seemed arrogant, angry and resentful toward the camp guards, toward me and toward Central Missouri in summer time."[55]

Because of this distrust and hostility toward men of the cloth, from that point through the remainder of the camp's operation, spiritual ministrations to POWs at Fort Leonard Wood came from POW pastors found in the internee population and not from any American civilian or military chaplains. These POW clergymen were approved by the camp commander, and their sermons were subject to review before delivery. In recognition of the value of their services, these preachers were exempted from work but still received the same $.80 a day as POWs on other labor details.[56]

While ministers to the POWs were the beneficiaries of donations of religious books and materials from a number of sources, the Catholic POW priest at Fort Leonard Wood received a most interesting and useful gift. The parents of the former Army chaplain at Fort Leonard Wood, Joachim Daleiden, owned a large firm supplying vestments and other religious garb. Their Chicago-based company, Paramentengeschäft Daleiden, arranged for the POW priest to receive five or six gowns for use in his work at the camp.[57]

Originally, the Fort Leonard Wood POW camp, like other camps, lacked a chapel in the original design of the installation. Services were held in barracks, in workrooms, or in any space available. "This camp, like other camps visited, is badly in need of a chapel for which no provisions were made in the original set-up of the camp," wrote an inspector in January 1944. By February, however, construction began on a house of worship for the POWs and was completed a short time later. "The interior is attractively decorated," noted a visitor in December 1944. "In preparation for the Christmas services, the Catholic chaplain was building a replica of the Manger scene."[58]

"The more approximately church-like surroundings are much appreciated by the worshipers," wrote another visitor to the camp in the spring of 1945, who noted that special services were planned for Good Friday and Easter. "The pastors are rather pleased with the response of the men in terms of attendance and participation at Sunday services and week-day meetings."[59]

By May 1945, attendance at worship was estimated to be about 15 percent of the camp population at the Lutheran service and more than 20 percent at the Catholic mass. The pastors, whose work was described by a visitor as "serene yet energetic," conducted other activities, including a Thursday Bible study where the approximately twenty-five POWs would "speak about problems in their lives as Christians."[60]

The image of heartless Nazis seems inconsistent with the generous financial contributions the Fort Leonard Wood prisoners made to those in need, donating much of the proceeds of their prisoner canteens as well as funds from their own pockets to support a variety of efforts. Internees at the camp contributed $72,682.47 to the American Red Cross, the International Red Cross, and the War Prisoners Aid of the YMCA. During the summer of 1945, prisoners contributed $65,609.91 to the International Red Cross to be used in alleviating human misery "regardless of race or creed." This amount represented an average of a month's pay contributed by every prisoner interned at Fort Leonard Wood.[61]

POW Employment at Fort Leonard Wood

The POWs' money was earned from the many work projects in which they were engaged. On a national basis, by June 1944, the PMGO really had the POW labor program rolling. In that month, some 66 percent of all POWs, excluding those in the Italian Service Units already engaged for the benefit of the U.S. government, were considered available for paid work. The remaining third, those not available, included officers, for whom labor was optional; noncooperative noncommissioned officers (sergeants and the like) such as those who were housed at Camp Clark; hospitalized, disabled, and sick prisoners; and those performing essential unpaid work, such as key jobs in the operation of their own POW compounds.

During that month, of those available for work, almost 90 percent were assigned projects totaling approximately 2.5 million days of labor nation-wide in June 1944, with approximately 70 percent of that work performed on military reservations. The post engineers, quartermaster, and ordnance officers employed most POWs on military bases in construction, supply, maintenance, and upkeep duties. During October 1943, Major Guy C. Thatcher, coordinator of the POW labor details and contracts at Fort Leonard Wood, declared the camp had the largest percentage of men working of all the U.S. camps that were filled to capacity.[62]

Because of the size of Fort Leonard Wood and the complexity of its operations, a great many prisoners were put to work on the post itself, per-forming a host of tasks such as roadwork, construction, and carpentry. Fritz Ensslin described the wide variety of jobs POWs performed at the camp: "Except military duties we were assigned to all imaginable work details like pin boys in the bowling alleys, firing the furnaces in the officers' quarters, garbage removal, incinerator work, cleaning crews for office buildings and clubs, painting carpentry, cabinet making and the like."[63]

POW labor on post reached its peak in July–September 1945 when more than twenty-five hundred prisoners replaced military and civilian workers in a variety of tasks, freeing them up for roles more directly tied to pushing the United States through those last few months of fighting, as well as replacing those who were being released from active duty.[64]

One of the main sources of employment for prisoners held at Fort Leonard Wood was the massive camp laundry. There the men worked as sewing-machine operators, pressers, hangers, tailors, and clerks in the dry-cleaning plant. The tailor and clerk slots were frequently filled with limited-duty prisoners, whose physical condition kept them from more active labor. The value of the work they provided in the laundry was underscored by the government's recommendation to visiting officers that "every consideration should be given to using POWs on such work during the coming winter season which is the peak load period for dry cleaning."[65]

Fritz Ensslin recalled his experience working in the camp laundry:

The voluntary work began approximately ten days after our arrival. Thirty men were needed for the laundry but only ten volunteered of the thousand POWs. We were all curious to find out from the volunteers at the end of the day about their experiences in the laundry. The magic words from the volunteers was that there were "at least 100 girls there in all shades and colors"; the same day another 60 men volunteered. From then on, the laundry was operational 24 hours a day, with 30 POWs on all shifts....

The regulations prohibited conversation during work. Only matters pertaining to work were allowed to be discussed. Love matters, particularly, were strictly forbidden, and if someone was caught, both would be severely punished....

The boss of the laundry, who was as strong as a bear, was impartial and fair. He detested discipline and often closed his eyes to matters that otherwise could have harmed us POWs. My co-worker, Laura, was very shy and reserved at first. She sang almost the whole day.... Despite the strict regulations, she managed to smuggle me a 20-pack of Chesterfield cigarettes every day.[66]

Because the cleaning solvents posed a danger of flash fires, POWs were initially prohibited from work in laundries. However, safeguards were instituted that mitigated these hazardous conditions and allowed use of POW labor. These protections included the dry cleaning being done only in sealed rooms with physical barriers that prevented POW entry.[67]

Jim Rahmy was just a boy when he lived at Fort Leonard Wood with his mother, Eunice Slone Rahmy. She was from nearby Dixon, Missouri, and got a job at the laundry, where she worked in close proximity to the POWs. "I remember one day we went to see her at work," said Rahmy, who at age five was the youngest of three brothers living at Fort Leonard Wood. "I was scared when I first saw the prisoners working with my mother," he recalled. "I thought that they were going to be really bad people."

The reaction of the prisoners to Rahmy and his brothers was anything but scary, as it turned out. The prisoners, many having families of their own back home, were glad to see the boys and gave them a warm reception.

"The ones we saw spoke little English but were still really nice to us," said Rahmy. "They were all really friendly. One guy in particular I remember, a real short fellow with dark hair, tried to talk to me. He even gave me a small coin."[68]

Despite recollections by both Jim Rahmy and Fritz Ensslin of direct and frequent interaction between POWs and civilian workers, the government proudly touted the security measures put in place to protect the female civilians working there. "Women are employed in the same building" as the German prisoners, tour guides pointed out to camp visitors getting a look at the POW operations. "Note two sentries and segregation of POWs by machinery and screen of wire netting."[69]

In addition to the post laundry, POWs also worked in a paper salvage operation at Fort Leonard Wood, an effort that fell under the purview of the post quartermaster. During the war years, many materials were in short supply, and internee labor was critical in facilitating the recycling of these items. Prisoners working in paper salvage operated under the supervision of an American supervisor with no sentries present, feeding machines that bundled scrap paper tightly and then loading railroad cars on a nearby siding with the pressed paper bales. Another group worked to pack salvaged tank tracks for shipment to an Army maintenance depot so the tracks could be repaired and reused.

Prisoner labor was also useful in the administration of the POW installation itself. A history of the internment camp detailed the roles the prisoners assumed in camp operation:

[From July through September 1945] prisoners were trained to perform an increasing proportion of the administrative details at the Prisoner of War Camp. This applied not only to administration within the individual companies and branch camps, but under supervision, to the routine clerical and bookkeeping problems of maintaining the personnel, labor, and pay records for over 3000 prisoners.

Availability of these trained personnel relieved a very critical situation late in 1945 and during 1946 when large numbers, particularly of key personnel, were being lost through demobilization.[70]

For POW Franz Engelmann, there was no question that the best place to work was in one of the many mess halls. From the time of his capture by the British in North Africa until he came to Fort Leonard Wood, Engelmann said hunger and thirst were his "constant companions."

Recalled Engelmann, "Here for the first time we could quiet our hunger.... A special pleasure was working in one of the big mess halls. There were five of us and we had a good job—you could eat whatever you wanted."[71]

German stonemasons in the prisoner population at Fort Leonard Wood created a number of structures around the camp, including ditches, culverts, stone walks, steps, and retaining walls, many of which survive. Two of the prisoners, former engineers, led the project. They planned and laid out elaborate drainage ditches throughout the camp, and using rocks quarried by POW labor they built a number of retaining walls around bridges and culverts, usually six feet high. Work continued on a number of projects, including sidewalks, roadways, and stairs, throughout the duration of the Germans' stay at Fort Leonard Wood. Eventually at least ten master stonemasons worked full-time on these efforts, plus a number of other prisoners they supervised. As recorded in a history of the Fort Leonard Wood POW camp, "The workmanship is excellent." A December 1944 report noted that when "this work is completed, this camp will present a very orderly appearance."[72]

POWs left an inscription on this stonework chimney, a reminder of their presence and handiwork. Courtesy of Terry Culver.

Other prisoners were employed in a shoe-repair shop on the post, where they made up the entire evening shift. The internees worked under the supervision of a POW foreman, who had worked in a shoe factory in Germany. An inspection report noted that the machines were "complicated" but were "handled expertly by workmen this foreman has trained for the jobs." Later, other specialized POW shops opened to take advantage of unique skills a handful of POWs brought from civilian life to the camp. POWs at Fort Leonard Wood worked in a watch-repair shop, a book bindery, and a photo lab.[73]

POW Labor on Local Farms

Most of the POW work at Fort Leonard Wood took place on the base, and few prisoners worked for area farmers. There wasn't a great deal of agriculture in the area because of the rugged terrain and poor soil, and all the training and support activities for the thousands of GIs on post provided ready opportunities for work right there.

In a report on the internment camp, one visitor described the situation:

> The situation of this camp is such that there is no industry near by or large agricultural undertakings in which the prisoners can be employed. The employment of prisoners at this camp is dependent upon the needs of the Fort Leonard Wood post. About 50 percent of the prisoners are regularly employed in the prisoner of war camp maintenance and upon work details at Fort Leonard Wood.
>
> These details are for the most part post maintenance such as quarter-master, automobile repair, road maintenance, laundry, clearing of brush, cutting of timber, shoe repairing, ditching, soil conservation, and a few have been engaged from time to time depending on the season in the harvesting of local crops.[74]

Interestingly, another inspector wrote that the farmers' initial interest in POW labor tapered off sharply when they learned that they would have to pay the going rate for area labor to engage the prisoners' services. "Very few work details have been employed off the Post since there is more than sufficient work to be performed there by all the prisoners," noted Major Earl Edwards, inspecting the camp for the PMGO. "It has been noted that there is no great demand for prisoner of war labor in agriculture as long as the prisoners are not cheaper labor. Apparently free American labor has become available when the farmers have learned that they must pay the going wage for work by prisoners of war."[75]

Edwards's comment seems misinformed, however, in light of both hard statistics on the U.S. labor shortage and anecdotal evidence on the demand for POW workers from Fort Leonard Wood. In reality, a number of POWs worked in agriculture in the area around the post, at first informally on at least one occasion and then through formal labor contracts with area farmers.

Bill Wulff and his three brothers grew up in Dixon, only ten miles from Fort Leonard Wood. During that time, Wulff's father, Louis J. "Louie" Wulff, worked in the construction business as well as on the family's dairy farm. Those two activities meant that the family was eventually quite involved at the post. "My dad spent a lot of time at Fort Leonard Wood," recalls Wulff. "He was the superintendent of three companies from Columbia, and so he was always there because of one project or another they had going."

At the time, the post was still growing and changing, evolving from a small hole in the Ozark forest into a sprawling and active military base. Because of the many construction projects taking place at the post, Louis Wulff often worked directly with the post's commanding officer. When the officer realized Louis could speak German, he was quick to take advantage of the translation skills. Interpreters and other German-speaking personnel were hard to come by, as the Army had placed everyone with those skills in intelligence and other units more critical to the war effort. "Whenever something came up, and the CO needed to talk with the prisoners, he'd ask dad to help him," recalled Bill Wulff. "It was always something he was glad to do."

With her husband so busy with construction at the base, Margaret Wulff took on most of the responsibility of running the dairy operation. Though she was busy with responsibilities at home, Margaret would also take on work at the post's Officers' Club to help make ends meet. Margaret also could speak German, a fact that was not missed by camp leadership. Her language skills also were pressed into service from time to time as the need arose for interpretation between the camp staff and German POWs. These occasional translating favors Louis and Margaret Wulff did for the camp administration during the course of their other duties were eventually repaid, recalled Bill Wulff.

The family struggled at times to balance the demands of the dairy operation, Louis Wulff's construction jobs around the rapidly growing post, Margaret Wulff's work at the Officers' Club, and the other tasks that needed to be done on a Missouri farm. On one occasion, the schedule got too tight to fit in all that needed to be done. "Dad had a bunch of hay out in the field that needed to be put up," recalled Bill Wulff. "He was so busy at the post and with everything else we were doing he just didn't know how we were going to get it done before it rained."

The commanding officer sensed Louis Wulff's concern. When asked, Louis told him about the work that needed to be done on his farm and his fear they wouldn't be able to get the hay in in time. "'Louie, you been so good to us, I'll tell you what,' that man said to my father. 'You take six of them German boys out there with you to get your hay up before it rains,'" recalled Wulff. "We put up that hay in nothing flat."

Through Bill Wulff's recollection, it appears that this exchange, which seems to have occurred relatively soon after the German POWs arrived at Fort Leonard Wood, took place outside of the normal contract labor program and on a strictly informal basis. Wulff believed that although the prisoners were not paid for their work to the best of his knowledge, they seemed to relish the opportunity to be out of the POW camp and in the countryside. These sorts of informal arrangements apparently happened frequently enough that the provost marshal general finally issued guidance gently reminding commanders that they were not authorized to make arrangements outside the parameters provided by the written contracts used in the POW labor program.[76]

Another area resident, John "Toot" Smith of Richland, Missouri, remembered working with the POWs when his uncle Lloyd Thornberry contracted for them to work on his farm. Smith was just eleven or twelve when the German prisoners came to Thornberry's place to help make silage. "His farm was on the Gasconade River, between Richland, Waynesville, and Crocker," said Smith. "We were putting up silage—it was almost all done by hand in those days—using the corn knives to cut the cornstalks, then stacking it and hauling it to the silos with teams of mules and horses."

Smith remembered fifteen to twenty POWs coming out to work, accompanied by a couple of guards who sat in the shade and watched them at their labor. It took two or three days to fill the silos, Smith recalled. "We were glad for the help," Smith said. "They didn't cause us a bit of trouble and we treated them like any other farm hand. Most seemed happy just to be out working." For Smith, what stood out most was the prisoners' reaction to the field mice that came skittering out of the sheaves of cornstalks. "You'd think that they didn't have them in Germany the way they laughed and stomped around at those mice," said Smith. "I can still hear them calling what sounded like 'moose! moose!' every time one would run out."[77]

Relations between POWs and GIs

Gladys Hritsko, a sergeant in the Women's Army Corps, saw prisoners by the truckload—literally—during her time stationed at Fort Leonard Wood. "I got attached to them," said Hritsko, who drove the ubiquitous "deuce-and-a-half," the Army's workhorse 2.5-ton truck, shuttling POWs on work details. "We felt at ease with each other. After all, they were 18- and 19-year-old boys, same age as me."[78]

William Hahn was another GI who worked with the POWs. "I became a guard at Fort Leonard Wood, Missouri, after I had been wounded in the South Pacific," recalled Hahn. "I would have preferred to go to Germany with the 71st Infantry Division, but my malaria kept me from leaving. Still, it wasn't all bad. I had chums among the PWs, and several who worked in the kitchen often slipped me a fryer [chicken] to take home. I also got hot loaves of bread from the prisoners in the camp bakery."[79]

As in other camps, guards and prisoners settled fairly quickly into an easy and comfortable arrangement where the prisoners knew the guards wouldn't hassle them too much if they didn't get out of line, an unspoken agreement their captors reciprocated. Pretty soon, guards and prisoners were helping one another out in almost unimaginable ways. For instance, when climbing in the back of the work trucks to ride out to guard a POW labor team, the guard would often hand his rifle to the prisoners already in the back to hold it as he clambered aboard. Once the GI was comfortably situated on the truck, the POW would hand the weapon back.[80]

St. Louisan Earline Kuthe lived with an aunt and uncle at Fort Leonard Wood in the summer of 1943 and recalled the close relationship between her uncle, O. J. "Andy" Anderson, a civilian employee at the post, and two German POWs he supervised, Paul Schanze and Edmund Koga. "The prisoners really had a lot of freedom," she said, recalling that the Germans were allowed to drive around unsupervised in a jeep with her along as an eight-year-old passenger. "They'd drive fast enough that we'd bounce over railroad tracks because they knew it would make me laugh."[81]

Anderson had a great relationship with the POWs who worked for him, said Kuthe, and they were grateful for the good treatment he gave them. Schanze, who worked in the warehouse, remembered one time Anderson took him along to see the circus, an event he called an "exceptional experience."

The friendship between Kuthe's uncle and the prisoners continued after the war. Following his return to Europe, Schanze wrote Anderson letters, giving him details of his return to Germany and sharing news about his life and family back at home. "Mr. Anderson, you can well imagine the joy and

O. J. "Andy" Anderson in front of his house at Fort Leonard Wood. Courtesy of Earline Kuthe.

happiness felt by me and my family when I returned home. We have already talked a lot about America," wrote Schanze, who fondly recalled his time with Anderson. "I have thought often as well about the work we did together, whether it was in the warehouse or somewhere else."[82]

Mischief

Naturally, prisoners out on work details engaged in a bit of mischief from time to time. Rudolf Krause, an internee at Leonard Wood, talked about how he and his fellow prisoners along with the guards took an Army jeep out for a little "farming" through a Missouri crop field when they were out of range of the farmer. "They learned us to drive a car," he said, recalling the day they bumped and scraped over the ruts, with wheels spinning madly.

On another occasion, he and some buddies stole tomatoes from a nearby garden. "The old woman observed us and called [the guards]. Then they searched me and I had to take my clothes off." Krause was never punished though, as all proof of the crime had disappeared. "We already eat [*sic*] the tomatoes!" he said, chuckling.[83]

In the first months of the Germans' stay at the camp, when security was still tight, Franz Engelmann recalled that the POWs were counted frequently. The process sometimes took hours. "In camp we were counted three times a day, at 8 A.M., noon, and at 4 P.M. An old sergeant, past retirement age, was the counter. It always took a long time, because he frequently miscounted," recalled Engelmann. "200 men were in each company, and whenever he got close to 200, somebody would holler out "199," and he'd think that he had missed one, and would have to start over. And that with 5 companies with 200 men a piece."[84]

Prisoners at Fort Leonard Wood, like other camps, found great fascination with Hollywood movie stars and devoted a considerable amount of time and effort to that interest. Thanks to the newspapers and magazines— including *Life*, *Variety*, and a host of other publications devoted to pop culture—delivered to the camp libraries, coupled with the weekly movie series featuring the latest Hollywood hits, POWs often knew as much as the average American about their favorite stars.

Several found a way to take this fascination a step further and began writing to the actors and actresses, asking if publicity photos might be sent to them. Lauren Bacall, Deanna Durbin, and Vivien Leigh were all favorites of the prisoners and targets of their adoration. The requests were sometimes successful, and in several instances, photos of these stars were sent to prisoners at Fort Leonard Wood. This raised the hackles of camp commander Vrooman, who, given the nationwide clamor over "coddling" of the prisoners, was sensitive to the potential for criticism if word got out of POWs with nothing better to do than write adoring letters to Hollywood starlets.

Because of his concerns, Vrooman asked the assistant provost marshal general if such correspondence was "objectionable." Vrooman got a reply quickly on the matter. "It is the opinion of this office that photographs referred to are harmless. The fact that the photograph has passed the Office of Censorship is evidence thereof," responded Brigadier General B. M. Bryan, though Bryan reminded Vrooman that he could prohibit the photo requests at his camp if he thought it best. "Considerable discretion and extensive responsibility, however, rests with the internment camp commander to act in individual cases."[85]

In another episode that must have made the camp commander roll his eyes, he received a request from a prisoner named Werner Hose to be freed from the camp. Hose had been reading the paper and found what he thought was a way to make better use of his time. "According to an appeal of the Dutch Government in a Milwaukee newspaper, volunteers are sought to join the Dutch Legion," wrote Hose. "The reason: my wife and my daughters are Dutch nationalities. As I consider the Netherlands my second homeland, I wish to offer my services to this legion."

This prospective legionnaire made his appeal in September 1945, six months after the end of the war. Accordingly, the request was denied.[86]

Guard Force Reduced

Because of the low numbers of POW escapes and the critical need for men in other areas of the war effort, the War Department cut in half the number of guards used to monitor POWs at the stateside camps, taking what B. M. Bryan called a "calculated risk." Effective July 1, 1944, the ratio of guards to internees was reduced from one guard for every five POWs to one guard for every ten prisoners. This cutback was put into effect at all camps in the country.[87]

At Fort Leonard Wood, this directive to use fewer guards without any lessening of the control of prisoners meant that guards staffed only two of the six towers, those at opposite corners of the perimeter fence. Two more men were posted at the main entrance to the POW camp, performing guard duty in addition to checking out work details. That meant only four men provided security for the whole camp during the day. At night, two of the corner towers were manned as during the day, one man watched the gate, and two sentries and a guard dog walked the perimeter. Off-duty guards slept in the unattended towers so that they could be ready with spotlights and machine guns in case of escape.

Guards were also removed from fixed sentry positions guarding POW work details on post, with the exception of the post laundry and dry-cleaning facilities because female civilians were employed there. Instead, civilian foremen checked on the POWs while supervising work parties, and guard personnel made counts at irregular intervals, driving around the post from one POW labor detail to another on motorcycles and jeeps.

"There have been no escapes from details under this recently authorized system, American guard personnel are saved and the output of the POW has greatly increased under this reduced surveillance," VIP visitors to Fort Leonard Wood were told while on a bus tour of the camp. "It works!"[88]

With the relatively low rate of escape or sabotage, most work done by POWs at Fort Leonard Wood, as at other military installations, eventually took place without guards, only civilian supervisors. However, post authorities felt that the presence of so many women in the laundry warranted keeping guard personnel there at the rate of one guard for every hundred prisoners.

POW Fritz Ensslin, who worked in the laundry, recalled how the guards' presence at times made the atmosphere unpleasant:

> They tried to make themselves look important in the eyes of the girls. To show off, the guards would sometimes use the stocks of their weapons on us. It was also a laughing matter to us that the guards habitually had their fingers on the triggers of their weapons, ready for use on us if needed.
>
> The American women and the engineers respected and treated us as their co-workers and there were never any problems between us. The guards, however, were always looking for trouble. They were ridiculed even by their fellow Americans on occasion when they used their power to subdue a helpless POW.[89]

Ensslin's observation reflects one of the unfortunate aspects of the POW camps. Though certainly not the situation in all cases, American servicemen assigned to guard prisoners frequently ended up there because of physical problems or a lack of skills that kept them from direct participation in more critical parts of the war. Historian Edward Pluth noted that "the War Department faced a serious shortage of qualified personnel who were experienced in prisoner of war administration. As a partial consequence, numerous camp administrative and guard personnel proved to be incompetent or completely unsuited for such work. Lack of adequate training further hampered efficient administration." This was especially true in the latter days of the war.[90]

Al Griego, a guard at the Fort Leonard Wood branch camp at the Stark Bro's Nurseries in Louisiana, Missouri, remembered American GIs on passing troop trains scornfully calling the the guards "4-Fs," the military classification for men unsatisfactory for normal duty.[91]

"Those soldiers with few qualifications of value to the war effort were assigned to low-priority areas in the backwater of the war, one such area being the POW program. And most of them knew it," wrote Arnold Krammer in *Nazi Prisoners of War in America*. "Consequently the American soldier in the POW program generally viewed his role as that of custodian, far from the 'guts and glory' of the front lines."[92]

Additionally, as the war progressed, able-bodied camp guards were transferred to the front, being replaced by recently returned combat veterans, including those who had been held as prisoners of war, a situation not conducive to positive relations with Axis POWs. James Choate, a former American POW, was freed from a German camp in the spring of 1945 and returned to the United States. Despite his term as a prisoner, Choate had only a year and eight months total service, which wasn't enough time to qualify for separation. The Army sent him to Fort Leonard Wood, where Choate was put to work in the mess hall supervising German prisoners:

They had a shortage of cooks, and I had worked in a bakery before I went in the service for quite a while. So they come in one day and grabbed me and took me down to the mess hall and said, "You're a cook," and left me to feed two hundred men. Can you imagine?

I was lucky they had a bunch of German prisoners of war that were working permanently in this kitchen. 'Course I was kind of glad to get to oversee these buzzards for a while. At first they didn't want to do too much. In fact, whenever I tried to tell one of them to do something, they'd say, "*Nichts verstehe*," didn't understand.

Well, of course they did. They spoke perfect English. I, as I said, had no sympathy. One of them told me he didn't understand when I told him to peel some potatoes, so I grabbed a meat cleaver and I rapped him upside the head with the flat side of the meat cleaver and told him in German. From then on I had real good cooperation from him. I told him I'd been a prisoner of war in Germany, about starved to death, and that they didn't need to expect any more from me than what I got. We were pretty good friends after that.[93]

To the credit of commanding officer Vrooman, he recognized these issues at his installation and took a number of steps to correct them. In addition to increasing the amount of training provided to the men guarding the prisoners, Vrooman made sure his officers and senior enlisted personnel received the required instruction on the provisions of the Geneva Convention, and these men in turn provided that instruction to the GI guards they supervised. He also greatly enhanced the recreational and social activities available, creatively identifying opportunities for fun and diversion for the American GIs, thereby increasing the morale of his troops.

"[The MP companies] have been efficient but turnover in personnel, resulting from the assignment of unsatisfactory men to the companies, has required additional training," noted an inspector in a May 1944 report, who also pointed out the value of Vrooman's actions in building morale:

> To relieve the monotony of their required duties, the Commanding Officer has constructed a beverage garden for the enlisted men, a boxing ring, volleyball courts, and a baseball diamond. He has moved a chapel from a ghost town, located on the reservation, to the camp....
>
> The enlisted men now are building a recreation building from the scrap lumber available on the Post. It appears to be well constructed and should be an attractive addition to the other buildings. The morale of the American personnel was demonstrated by a baseball game witnessed by this officer played against the 291st Infantry. There was much rooting on both sides but particularly by the personnel of the prisoner of war camp. Excellent spirit was displayed. Incidentally, the team has won five out of six games.[94]

A visitor to Fort Leonard Wood in May 1945, who dined with the American officers in their mess hall for lunch, commented on their earnest intent as expressed over the lunchtime conversation, even after Germany's collapse and the subsequent unveiling of the horrors of captivity under the Nazis. "I was glad to hear how they tried to do their best for the prisoners of war in order to show them how men are to be treated in a camp," said the YMCA inspector. "The good will toward the prisoners of war is something to appreciate and be thankful for."[95]

Prisoner Escapes

As the frequency of work assignments outside the camp increased and the number of guards dropped at Fort Leonard Wood, the temptation and opportunity for escape rose proportionally. Though most prisoners saw the futility in an escape attempt, there were several who tried. And though these men were indeed enemy soldiers, their time on the lam was in most cases akin to teenagers cutting class—a chance to get away for a time, to see things, and to live the "good" life before that inevitable return to life behind the wire. The bumbling antics of several of the prisoners reveal their amateurishness and lack of serious intent.

John Morgan, who grew up outside of Waynesville, just past the outer boundary of the post, recalled seeing the prisoners out unattended. "There'd be a group of five or six or so who had walked away from their work detail, and you'd see them coming down the road," recalled Morgan. "They'd be just out looking over the countryside, wanting to see what was out there. And then about twenty minutes after that, you'd see the MPs come tearing along, all excited, trying to track them down."[96]

This sort of event was the occasional result of the Army's adoption of the "calculated risk" policy endorsed in 1944. As one official remarked, "They were entirely inadequately guarded and yet there were no incidents worth reporting." Occasionally, because of fears for the safety of their families, residents would complain about the perceived lack of control that allowed prisoners "to wander up and down the highway…without guard." Investigations of these complaints showed that there was usually a misunderstanding of the guard policy by the civilians who saw these groups of prisoners roaming about and assumed that they were trying to escape.[97]

An example of the administration's relative lack of concern about prisoner escapes is the case of two German POWs who escaped from a brush-clearing work detail. The pair, Ernst Schmitz and Günther Holz, escaped on the afternoon of March 29, 1944, and surrendered themselves April 4 to farmers M. Moorhouse and Oren Hamphill at Falcon, Missouri, in nearby Laclede County. The farmers figured out the men's identities after they sought food at a farmhouse. The escapees were taken into custody by the county sheriff and the highway patrol, which returned the duo to Fort Leonard Wood, where they were confined at the camp guardhouse. Their sentence was for thirty days but was commuted by the camp commander after twenty-one days on account of the good behavior of the prisoners. Though the administration seemed to have a "boys will be boys" attitude, in actuality, their initial penalty was the maximum allowed by the Geneva Convention for escape attempts.[98]

Perhaps inspired by these two, another pair of prisoners working in the post quarry decided to take off one day a month later, April 24, 1944. They hid around the base camp for three days until setting out for Rolla, where they were caught on May 5. They were apprehended after they sought a meal at a local diner. Having no passable English skills, they hatched a plan to pretend they were deaf mutes and then to pantomime their way into a hearty dinner. People in the restaurant grew suspicious after witnessing their antics and then doubly so when they watched the pair try to hop a freight train out of town. Two local woman, Mrs. L. H. Breuer and Mrs. Richardson, followed the men to the train depot and then hurried uptown to notify the city marshal. After being tipped off about the escapees, Rolla lawmen Rowe Fort and Robert Thornhill arrested the escapees without incident at the Frisco Railway Yard and returned them to the custody of American authorities at Fort Leonard Wood. Once back at the camp, they got the same thirty-day confinement in the guardhouse as their predecessors.[99]

These men lasted nearly two weeks out of camp, surprisingly longer than most, but most POWs found life on the run to be considerably less comfortable than their usual accommodations at the internment camp. The Missouri triumvirate of outdoor irritation—mosquitoes, ticks, and chiggers—was usually enough to make even the heartiest prisoner long for the comforts of camp. When cockleburs, poison ivy, and the discomfort of sleeping outdoors were added to the mix, only pride kept most from going back to the camp after the first night.

The most successful escape from not only Fort Leonard Wood but also any Missouri POW camp was that of Rudolf Krause. Krause took off from his work as part of a trash detail on September 10, 1945, nearly five months after Germany's surrender. The FBI finally caught up with him three months later in Orlando, Florida. Krause's goal was to reach a port on the East Coast, then sign on as a seaman on a neutral merchant ship. It seems he almost made it.[100]

Nazis at Fort Leonard Wood

Like nearly every other major German POW camp in the United States, the installation at Fort Leonard Wood had a Nazi minority that influenced the atmosphere to a large degree. "The Gestapo is quite well at work in these German Prison Camps," wrote Monsignor Cody of the St. Louis Archdiocese, lamenting the secret police's influence on the Catholic POWs in a letter to a fellow priest.[101] Although the Nazis' political orientation was distasteful, the Army perceived their regimentation as a positive thing and often wrongly interpreted a smooth-running camp as a sign that all was well. An inspection report credited the lack of visible disturbance to the skill and tactful handling of the prisoners on the part of the camp commander:

The Commanding Officer has stressed the fact that he considers all of the prisoners soldiers and expects them to act accordingly. He requires absolute discipline and as the result receives the greatest respect. He has not hesitated to praise the prisoners for good work done. On the other hand, he has allowed no relaxation of absolute discipline.

As the result there has been a minimum of difficulty and the prisoners have retaliated, acting as good soldiers. It is believed that the smooth operation of the camp, as regards the relation with the prisoners, is entirely the result and is the credit of this attitude of the Commanding Officer. Incidentally the prisoners seemed happy and many were observed singing while going to and from work.[102]

Meanwhile, the hard-core Nazis were busy holding weekly indoctrination classes and threatening, beating, and in a few instances murdering those who were disloyal or too collaborative with the American authorities. "I remember this. Comrade is dead," said Anton Kuehmoser, at a reunion of former Fort Leonard Wood POWs in September 1993. The disgust was evident in his voice as he tapped the photo of a casket holding a POW. Kuehmoser said that the man was stabbed to death after twice failing to show up for the Nazi meetings. "It was a demonstration," he said; "After two warnings they do a 'holy ghost,'" a night beating where a pillowcase or sheet was thrown over the prisoner's head so he could not identify his attackers. "Someone comes in and stabs him and nobody knows who did it."[103]

The Nazis who ran the camps exerted their influence in a number of ways. An inspection report in May 1945 noted that they went so far as to censor the reading material of other prisoners. "Reading matter seems much more acceptable in the branch camps than at Fort Leonard Wood," wrote a Swiss visitor to the camp, "since the leading prisoners at Fort Leonard Wood interfere with the distribution of anything which does not appeal to them and even threaten fellow prisoners who insist upon reading magazines or papers of which they, the leaders, do not approve."[104]

Camp inspectors were careful to avoid blaming a giant brawl that took place at the camp in November 1943 on political strife, though it most likely played a part. However, as a result of it, nine POWs ended up under arrest and another wound up in the hospital, where he later died of his injuries. One of the Germans received a fifteen-year sentence at hard labor for his role in the violence, a prison term that a review board eventually reduced to a year's confinement.[105]

In another instance of violence within the camp—again, with nothing in the official accounts linking the incident to political turmoil—German POW Wendelin Schiller was murdered on September 25, 1943. Fellow POW Hans Fiedler was ordered to stand trial before a general court-martial, charged with premeditated murder by striking with a club.

Fiedler was found not guilty of the charge but was sentenced to fifteen years at hard labor. Prisoners convicted of such crimes typically served their sentences at the disciplinary barracks at Fort Leavenworth, Kansas, and the end of the war and subsequent return of their fellow prisoners to Europe did not nullify their punishment.[106] A January 1944 visitor noted the presence of considerable political friction among groups of prisoners at the camp and predicted that the conflict would only increase with time:

> The spirit of the prisoners is not good, due to the friction between various factions among the prisoners. There is apparently no answer for it except closer supervision by the American authorities. The belief is that this tension among the prisoners will increase as the war goes against the Germans.
>
> The feeling is that the non National Socialists [non-Nazis] will more and more tend to express themselves as against the strict internal control maintained by the militant National Socialists in the camp. This calls for first-class officer administrative personnel.[107]

In May 1944, the camp administration penned up a group of the worst agitators in their own area of the camp to minimize their disruptive influence on the rest of the prisoners. The camp commander ordered a section of Compound 3 to be fenced off and in there placed 380 noncommissioned officers who refused to work, among other misdeeds. These men were not allowed to mingle with other prisoners, they did their own cooking in this camp within a camp, and they attended shows and movies separate from their fellow Germans.[108]

Within a year, however, these problems straightened themselves out. An inspection report made by members of the Swiss Legation cited the influence of the spokesman as the chief reason for the improvement. At that point almost all the prisoners were employed, with 90 percent working at the Army post and 10 percent in the POW camp.[109]

Naturally, from time to time other misbehavior occurred among Fort Leonard Wood POWs. For instance, fourteen prisoners were on disciplinary

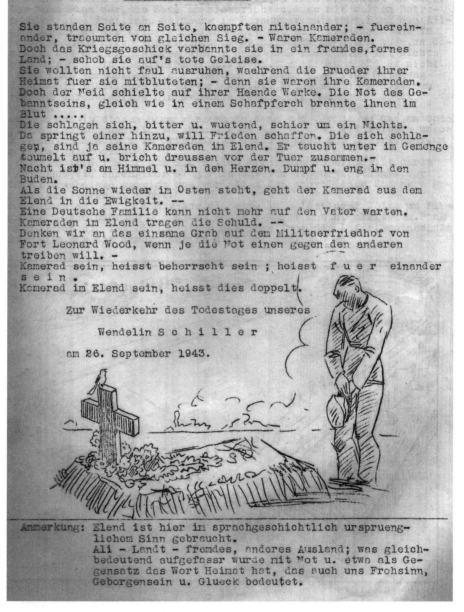

Kameraden im Elend.

Sie standen Seite an Seite, kaempften miteinander; - fuerein-
ander, traeumten vom gleichen Sieg. - Waren Kameraden.
Doch das Kriegsgeschick verbannte sie in ein fremdes,fernes
Land; - schob sie auf's tote Geleise.
Sie wollten nicht faul ausruhen, waehrend die Brueder ihrer
Heimat fuer sie mitbluteten; - denn sie waren ihre Kameraden.
Doch der Neid schielte auf ihrer Haende Werke. Die Not des Ge-
banntseins, gleich wie in einem Schafpferch brannte ihnen im
Blut .....
Die schlagen sich, bitter u. wuetend, schier um ein Nichts.
Da springt einer hinzu, will Frieden schaffen. Die sich schla-
gen, sind ja seine Kameraden in Elend. Er taucht unter im Gemenge
taumelt auf u. bricht draussen vor der Tuer zusammen.-
Nacht ist's am Himmel u. in den Herzen. Dumpf u. eng in den
Buden.
Als die Sonne wieder im Osten steht, geht der Kamerad aus dem
Elend in die Ewigkeit. --
Eine Deutsche Familie kann nicht mehr auf den Vater warten.
Kameraden im Elend tragen die Schuld. --
Denken wir an das einsame Grab auf dem Militaerfriedhof von
Fort Leonard Wood, wenn je die Not einen gegen den anderen
treiben will. -
Kamerad sein, heisst beherrscht sein ; heisst f u e r einander
s e i n .
Kamerad im Elend sein, heisst dies doppelt.

   Zur Wiederkehr des Todestages unseres

     Wendelin S c h i l l e r

   am 26. September 1943.

Anmerkung: Elend ist hier in sprachgeschichtlich ursprueng-
          lichem Sinn gebraucht.
          Ali - Landt - fremdes, anderes Ausland; was gleich-
          bedeutend aufgefassr wurde mit Not u. etwa als Ge-
          gensatz das Wort Heimat hat, das auch uns Frohsinn,
          Geborgensein u. Glueck bedeutet.

"A German family can no longer wait for their father," reads the memorial page for Wendelin Schiller in the POW camp newspaper. Courtesy of Franz Engelmann.

punishment in January 1944 for simple refusal to work.[110] Later, in May 1944, the camp administration had to contend with a much larger group's refusal to work as well as the ongoing theft of clothing by POWs from the post laundry. An inspection report detailed these disturbances:

> From February 1 to date, seven thefts of clothing, usually from the laundry, were punished variously by the prisoners being restricted to compound labor for a week, forfeiture of part pay, restricted to short terms in the guard house, etc....

> In general, disciplinary measures were such as were calculated to induce the men to return to work. In each case, this seems to have been the result.

> During this period, an even larger number (108 prisoners) received disciplinary treatment because of unsatisfactory work. Some were removed from detail; others forfeited part of their pay. Some forfeited their right to canteen purchases for a few days, and some were restricted to the guardhouse.[111]

Poor-quality work or slowdowns in production were common problems, but the War Department made progress toward solving them when it issued a 1944 directive tying prisoners' pay to their output. The regulation was intended to be used whenever production or piecework could be easily measured, and the normal standard was for prisoners to accomplish at a minimum two-thirds of the work regularly required of civilian employees. "This measure created some discontent among the prisoners at first, but this discontent is now diminishing," wrote one observer of the Fort Leonard Wood operation. Prisoners working in the laundry, for instance, on one of the three daily shifts of seventy men, now had to meet certain standards. A prisoner operating a stream presser had to iron twenty pairs of trousers each hour, and a group of six POWs ironing sheets were expected to turn out twenty-eight hundred sheets each shift.[112]

Of course, in a camp housing five thousand young men, other problems were bound to arise. As an example of the wide range of misbehavior in which the prisoners engaged, in April 1945, camp records listed twenty-four disciplinary cases among the prisoners. An inspection report read like a rap sheet as it provided the details for these misdemeanor problems:

Thirteen of these were for refusal to work and obey orders of officers; four for laxity of work; three for theft of clothing or beer; three for hiding out when supposed to report for duty, and one for writing forbidden notes to a civilian employee.

Their sentences have been, almost without exception, confinement for three to 30 days, on restricted diet; occasionally at hard labor, with full ration.[113]

Prisoners filed complaints about work conditions—most unfounded, such as pinsetters' fears of being hit by flying bowling pins—with visiting inspectors from time to time. "Some of the bakers complained that there was a 24-hour shift in the bakery," wrote one State Department visitor to the camp, "but their complaint was not taken seriously by the Swiss representative when he was reminded that there were three shifts of these workmen and none were required to work regularly at night.[114] Complaining, it seems, was in most cases offered in the same vein from which the escape attempts originated. There was never much expectation for success, and mostly it was just another way to pass the time and create some diversion for men trapped in a boring environment.

Re-education and Reorientation Program

In the spring of 1945, Fort Leonard Wood, like other camps in the United States holding German POWs, was the scene of an ambitious re-education program that intended to promote the virtues of democratic society, Judeo-Christian values, and free political expression and to combat the influence of the Nazis who frequently terrorized the camps.

A special officer called the assistant executive officer—in the case of Fort Leonard Wood, Lieutenant Perry Georgiady—was responsible for carrying out the program at each camp. The assistant executive officer oversaw the printed and visual media available to the prisoners, monitored the content of the classes in the education program, and kept his finger on the pulse of prisoner political sentiment.

A May 1945 status report to the director of the POW Special Projects Division, the group that was responsible for the re-education program, highlighted Georgiady's work and noted the progress being made among the German prisoners at Fort Leonard Wood. "The assistant executive officer has improved camp facilities for the prisoners of war and obtained the media necessary for the reorientation program," noted the evaluation of Georgiady's work. "Many American newspapers, magazines, and other periodicals are prominently displayed in the canteen and also are available in the reading rooms. Lieutenant Georgiady is enthusiastic about his work and he has managed to foster considerable interest among the prisoners of war in our program."[115]

As part of the strategy to confer authenticity on the program, to plan credible activities, and to offer material that would be appealing to POWs, the Special Projects Division tried to make things seem as "German" as possible. Because of this, Georgiady benefited especially from the assistance of two enlisted men assigned to work with him, Sergeant von Halle and Sergeant Kassel. "Both men are German refugees and have shown themselves to be competent and intelligent," wrote an inspector from the Special Projects Division after a visit to Fort Leonard Wood. Because of their good work, the inspector recommended that at least one of the men be able to attend the Orientation Conference for POWs conducted by the Special Projects Division at Fort Eustis, Virginia, and the camp commander agreed.[116] The conference provided intensive instruction on democratic principles, civics, and history and often provided an inroads for participating POWs to hold positions in the postwar German or interim government.

One aspect of Georgiady's work was to coordinate "sponsorship" of the program with a nearby university. This sponsorship program was based on the assumption that a rigorous and high-quality educational experience would be more convincing to POWs as to the excellence of American higher education and would be more likely to engender enthusiasm about the possibility of earning college credit for themselves through the program. "We lined up all the universities that we could get our hands on—and there were many," said Maxwell McKnight, who headed the Special Projects Division. "Where there was a camp, we got a university that normally had a German department, and we arranged for the university to send its German-speaking head of the department and to open up its literature collections."[117]

Because of the secrecy still shrouding the program, some universities were understandably hesitant to sign into a commitment about which they had only the most general information. The Army originally recruited Washington University in St. Louis to be the sponsoring institution for the new education program for POWs at Fort Leonard Wood. Georgiady visited the university on several occasions in the winter and spring of 1945 and met with a number of university officials to detail as much of the top-secret program as he could and to discuss what participation would mean for the university, particularly in terms of its accompanying responsibilities as a sponsoring organization.

"The university fully understands the relationship between the prisoner of war camp and the university and how it can be of service," wrote Georgiady to the Special Projects Division. "The university also understands that it is not necessary to make frequent visits to the camp and that the Assistant Executive Officer [Georgiady] will maintain liaison with the institution. It was fully understood by the university that expenses incurred in the program would be payable by prisoner of war funds."[118]

Even though coming to an agreement was a slow process, it looked like everything was a go for the partnership between Washington University and Fort Leonard Wood. "The reason we have done very little about this until recently is that we have been unable to secure any definite information about what is expected of us," wrote Stuart A. Queen, acting librarian at the university, about the school's decision-making process. "However, on January 11, Lieutenant Georgiady visited Washington University and explained to us a concrete basis for cooperation. We are, therefore, now ready to proceed with definite plans."

Washington University went so far as to designate a lead person for the project, Professor W. B. Bodenhafer, who was appointed by acting chancellor H. B. Wallace to "carry on negotiations and subsequent dealings between the Fort and the University."[119]

Despite this promising start, Washington University administrators ultimately backed out of the sponsorship. Like the leadership at a number of other institutions, they were hesitant to become involved in something they were unable to learn enough about to feel as if they could make an informed decision, especially given the amount of criticism the POW program was receiving from politicians and in the press.

"The real reason for the university declining the sponsorship is that it questions the aims of our educational program, which is of a classified nature and could not be revealed," wrote Georgiady in a memo. "More so, the conservative element of the school fears unfavorable publicity. Recent articles appearing in publications regarding 'coddling' and 'prisoner of war muddle' are for the most part responsible for this attitude."[120]

Following Washington University's decision to pass on the sponsorship, Georgiady suggested the University of Missouri as an alternative, and the Special Projects Division moved quickly to involve the university in the program. An inspector of the camp seemed to refer to the pending sponsorship when he wrote in March 1945 that Missouri "is ready to begin a library loan service and upon approval of a new relationship this and other services can be initiated," with these "other services" most likely a veiled reference to the re-education program. Indeed, the University of Missouri signed on and assisted in furthering the educational activities at the camp by providing suitable books and outlines for courses of study, as well as technical assistance to instructors.[121]

To visitors from the Swiss Legation, who may or may not have been aware of the true nature of the Intellectual Diversion Program at that time, Georgiady's efforts seemed appealing to the prisoners. "Both in the quality and quantity of reading materials offered as well as in the courses of study provided," noted the Swiss rep, "the prisoners have responded in a very gratifying manner to the efforts of Lieutenant Perry M. Georgiady, in charge of Intellectual, Athletic and Other Diversions."[122] Georgiady reported that eleven hundred copies of novels published as part of the *Bucherreihe Neue Welt* (New World Bookshelf) series had been sold. These paperbacks, put out by the Special Projects Division as part of the re-education program, were available for $.25 in the canteen and featured prominent authors that portrayed free and democratic societies in a positive light. Georgiady noted that because of the demand for the books, thirty more copies were bound in hardback and placed in the camp library to ensure availability.[123]

In addition to fostering alternatives for study, recreation, and entertainment, the assistant executive officer and other members of the Special Projects Division staff also tracked the political currents running through each camp as closely as possible. In particular, they looked to the prisoner selected by his fellows to be the camp spokesman as an important sign of their political temperament. A Special Projects Division report detailed one visiting inspector's opinion of the camp spokesman and the reaction he engendered in his compatriots at the Fort Leonard Wood POW facility:

Captain [Walter H.] Rapp was accompanied by the camp spokesman on his tour through the compound and he was impressed by the liberal attitude and political views of that prisoner of war. The spokesman appeared to be extremely well liked by the other prisoners of war. He greeted and shook hands with each of his comrades as he escorted Captain Rapp through the compound. That prisoner of war was a large exporter in Hamburg some years ago and he appeared to be an intelligent individual.

It is considered clever subterfuge for prisoners of war to tell the American authorities, "I never like the Nazis, I never was politically interested," but the cooperative attitude and unimpeachable conduct of that spokesman made it evident that he was sincere in making that statement.[124]

The spokesman's role was an important one, for he represented the prisoners to the camp administration. Via his contacts with the visiting inspectors from the various neutral agencies such as the Swiss Legation and the International Red Cross, he had a direct connection for communication to the German high command back home.

Mail Service

The usual complaint about mail service so prevalent in other camps was not absent in Fort Leonard Wood. "Many of the prisoners have received no news from home for the past five or six months," wrote a Swiss inspector. "They show some anxiety and even go as far as making some criticisms on the subject."[125] However, the German POWs automatically assumed it was pure malice on the part of the U.S. authorities causing the lack of mail and did not consider that perhaps a failing Germany could be the reason for the delayed or nonexistent postal service.

"The standard complaint heard on all sides is of the failure to receive mail from overseas. For the most part the prisoners are unwilling to believe that there could be any disorder or disruption of German prisoner of war mail facilities," wrote an exasperated camp inspector after being drowned by lamentations about the poor mail service. "They appear to believe that their failure to receive mail is chargeable to the action of the American authorities, although they have been repeatedly informed to the contrary by the camp authorities and the Swiss authorities."[126]

By May 1944, as a result of increased efforts by the Swiss Legation, the Red Cross, and other organizations to remedy the problems associated with the exchange of mail between the countries, this situation had been rectified to a large extent. "The incoming correspondence has greatly improved, some 23,000 letters having been received in April," noted a visitor from the neutral Swiss government. "Only one prisoner was found to have been without mail in this last shipment.[127]

V-E Day Disturbances

With the looming collapse of Germany, the PMGO feared a large-scale uprising coinciding with the surrender of the Third Reich. Assistant provost marshal general Bryan requested that the POW Special Projects Division, the unit responsible for the prisoner re-education program, monitor the situation to prevent what he called "Hara-Kiri activities" in the POW camps.[128]

Accordingly, Captain Rapp, the Special Projects Division officer, wrote Bryan from Fort Leonard Wood to update him on the status of the POW camp at the installation. "In the opinion of the Post and Prisoner of War Camp Commanders of this station, there is no evidence which supports possible disturbances or mass suicides by German prisoners of war on or about V-E Day," wrote Rapp. "The Post and Camp Commanders feel confident that military authorities within this command are fully capable to deal with any disturbance or case of violence against military authorities which might arise in connection with V-E Day."[129]

Camp officials at Chesterfield, one of the branch camps operated by Fort Leonard Wood, feared similar disturbances. The Reverend William Gabler was a local chaplain who ministered to the German POWs at the floating camp on the Missouri River at Chesterfield. Gabler remembered going to the houseboat one Saturday night in the spring of 1945 to conduct services, and he saw at first hand the measures the Army had taken to prevent any mayhem. "During the service, I noticed that everything was being lit up outside the place," said Gabler. "I continued my service and as soon as I finished the commanding officer came in from his quarters and pulled me aside. 'Do you want a gun?' he asked me. And I said, 'For what?!'"

The officer told Gabler that they had received a report that Germany had surrended. While they weren't sure if it was just another rumor, or if it was an accurate report this time, they weren't going to take any chances. "'We've got a couple of men on the boat that we expect to make a break for Mexico,' he said," recalled Gabler. "'So everything is lit up and we won't be going to shore for a while because we don't want you to be in the line of fire when you get off in case anything happens.'"

Gabler told the officer that he didn't need a gun but that he would wait as long as necessary to see what would happen. After the service, the men normally stayed and listened to the radio, playing cards and socializing in the room where the service had been held. Gabler and the officer lingered just outside the door and listened. "The fellows had the radio on and they got a news report—special bulletin—and just that quick they turned it to another station," said Gabler. "By the time they actually heard the announcement, it had already been declared a rumor."[130]

Ultimately, there was no large-scale uprising when Germany's surrender was announced. For POWs who had been keeping abreast of the developments and especially those captured in the last days of the war who knew how poorly things were going for Germany, the news was no surprise.

POW Fritz Ensslin was at Jefferson Barracks when the announcement of Germany's surrender was made. "I will never forget the day of the victory. We had the chance to view the world's largest fireworks show over St. Louis, and could heard President Truman's speech over KWK radio from St. Louis," he recalled.

Jefferson Barracks was a huge post used to process troops, and Ensslin worked in the mess hall serving meals to the thousands of soldiers returning from overseas and being discharged from the St. Louis installation.

"Many of the GIs spoke to us by saying, 'Deutschland kaputt, Hitler kaputt,' and similar statements. Meanwhile we learned how to shun rather than provoke unnecessary arguments, but some insisted on an answer," recalled Ensslin. "'We conquered Germany. What do you have to say about that?' We almost all had the same answer. 'It's okay, but the worst is yet to come, namely the Soviet Union.'"

That invariably fired up the American GIs. "Oh, that's typical Nazi propaganda, conquered and still arrogant," Ensslin recalled the GIs responding. "We are going to beat the militarism out of your bones, you Nazi bastards."[131]

Like Ensslin, most prisoners just went quietly about their work in the months after Germany's defeat, perhaps more than anything relieved that the danger was over for their families and hopeful that perhaps they might get to go home.

End of the Camp

As the fall of 1945 rolled into winter and turned into spring 1946, Fort Leonard Wood POWs were increasingly anxious to return to Europe. The POW camp newspaper was filled with articles about the various possibilities for governance in postwar Germany, the practical effects of Germany being divided into four zones of administration, and many simple, sentimental pieces about what it would be like to finally return home. For most of these men, though, home was still a long way away both in terms of time and distance. Both Edmund Koga and Paul Schanze, like many other German POWs, would be waylaid by the British and French governments, who required them to work rebuilding those countries generally for another year or more. Schanze was forced by the French to work in a coal mine, until deteriorating health caused by malnourishment and conditions in the mine put him in the hospital. After a French doctor declared him unfit for work, he finally arrived home December 23, 1946, a year and a half after the end of the war in Europe.

Paul Schanze. Courtesy of Paul Schanze.

This marathon of misery experienced by the German POWs after their release from U.S. custody stands in sharp contrast to how quickly the camps packed up once the prisoners were gone. For instance, at Fort Leonard Wood, as at many other camps, because of the several months' advance notice of the impending closure received by the camp administration, the doors of the internment facility often literally closed on the heels of the last groups of prisoners to depart from the installation, a quick and simple last page to this chapter of history.

"Since The Provost Marshal General has advised that all prisoners of war at Fort Leonard Wood, Missouri, are being placed on movement order with readiness date of 20 April 1946, and has advised that these prisoners will not be replaced," wrote Lieutenant Colonel N. J. Safourek from Seventh Service Command headquarters in Omaha, "it is desired that planning action and such immediate action as is appropriate in connection with the closing out and disposition of the prisoner of war camp, together with operating personnel, supplies and equipment, be initiated without delay."

Upon receipt of these instructions in March 1946, Fort Leonard Wood officials began the process of turning over excess food, clothing, and vehicles not needed for use of the camp and prepared a list of buildings, structures, and equipment on site so planning could begin for their reuse, relocation, sale, or disposal. Officers and enlisted men who were "rendered excess" by this discontinuance were to be separated if they met the eligibility requirements for leaving the service; transferred within the organization if needed and an authorized slot was open; or reported available for reassignment to the Seventh Service Command headquarters. Additionally, reminded the headquarters memo, "prompt action will be taken to cancel any leases which may have been executed in connection with the establishment of branch camps."

The first outbound groups of prisoners left Fort Leonard Wood as early as March 6, heading for California in anticipation of an eventual return to Europe via a long boat trip that took them through the Panama Canal. The camp closed completely with the departure of the last group of prisoners who climbed aboard a waiting train on May 20, 1946, bound for Camp Shanks, New York, and their eventual return to Europe.[132]

And with that, this chapter of history at Fort Leonard Wood was closed. An inspection report summarized the experience of most of the five thousand plus Germans who had been housed there during its years of operation:

> From every viewpoint, this camp may be said to be well administered. Military courtesies are strictly observed; the discipline seemed good; the treatment of the prisoners is humane and their morale as good as can be expected of men behind wire fencing.[133]

At the same time that the POW camp was being dismantled and the prisoners shipped elsewhere, Fort Leonard Wood itself was shut down as an active military post. With the cessation of war, it simply was not needed in its role as a training facility. A caretaking crew of about fifty stayed on site to secure the grounds and to provide the most basic maintenance to allow continued use of the post for summertime training purposes for National Guard units. However, when the Korean War erupted, the base was reactivated as a training post on August 1, 1950, and was made a permanent military installation shortly thereafter, thanks in part to the efforts of U.S. Congressman Dewey Short. Today, Fort Leonard Wood is a significant military facility, turning thousands of recruits into soldiers each year as one of the Army's basic training posts in addition to being the home of the Army's Military Police, Chemical, and Engineer Corps. Little remains from the former POW camp, although the post museum has re-created a POW company area in one of the few remaining World War II–era barracks left at the post. Visitors can walk through and see how the POWs lived and what their barracks looked like, complete with lumpy Army matresses, wool blankets, and a collection of 1940s pinups and little swastika flags tacked onto the walls.

POWs work in the Camp Crowder motor pool. Courtesy of Missouri State Archives.

Facing: Soldiers of Headquarters Company 800th Signal Corps Battalion sit down to Thanksgiving dinner. Courtesy of Camp Crowder Collection, Crowder College.

Chapter Six

Camp Crowder

ROM THE OUTSIDE, THE POW CAMP AT CAMP CROWDER appeared to be a model camp, with hardworking, "cooperative" German prisoners. In truth, lax conditions prevailed, and a handful of Nazi thugs attempted to rule the camp through terror and intimidation. These men threatened the other prisoners, promising punishment, even death, to those whom they saw as "disloyal" to Hitler.

For a former Luftwaffe pilot named Hermann Half, the decision to skip a celebration organized by the Nazis could have cost him his life. "On April 20, Hitler's birthday, the whole camp went up to the football field and raised a big Swastika flag and sang songs," said Half. "I laid on my bunk and didn't go." This action caused the Nazis to question Half's allegiance, and suddenly the man feared for his safety. "It was very dangerous. I heard my name mentioned a few times," said Half. "There was one fellow, he had a French name—Boulanges—who established a kangaroo court. They were going to hang people, our own prisoners, if they didn't shape up, and I was worried. Believe me, I lived in fear."[1]

Camp officials and visiting inspectors did not see these dark currents under the surface of what appeared to be a harmonious, peaceful group of soldiers content to sit on the sidelines while the war played itself out. "This is one of the best-disciplined camps which I have seen in any service command. The prisoners are working well. Their individual and collective behavior is all that could be desired," wrote Verner Tobler, a visiting representative of the Swiss Legation. "They do not have a single complaint. There have been no courts-martial and no escapes. The morale of the camp was outstandingly good."[2] While Half made it out of the camp without being harmed, this contrast between the outward appearance of Camp Crowder and reality defined an almost schizophrenic existence that lasted throughout the camp's operation.

History of the Installation

According to historian Kay Hively:

When Camp Crowder was located just outside of the City of Neosho, Missouri, it changed the lives of many people. People who had lived in the area for generations gave up their homes and farms; the economy of the area changed so drastically that it would never seem the same again; young men from every corner of the nation came to the Ozarks as soldiers and not only touched the native residents but were touched by them; in short, this very rural area quite literally moved into a modern sophisticated world that was almost alien before.[3]

With war looming on the horizon, brand new military reservations were being created by the week, it seemed. Seventh District congressman Dewey Short, a man of considerable persuasiveness, began massaging every influential contact he had to land a camp in his own southwestern Missouri district. His efforts eventually paid off.

In February 1941, a board of Army officers investigated a number of sites for additional Army cantonments. They examined highway access, rail facilities, and existing water supplies and finally settled on a location in the far southwest corner of the state, which in their opinion offered the best combination of all factors. The site was immediately south of the tiny Ozarks town of Neosho, which hunkers down seventeen miles south of Joplin, twelve miles east of the Oklahoma border, and thirty miles north of the Arkansas state line.

In early May, six men arrived in Neosho and arranged for temporary work space in the municipal auditorium. Within two weeks seventy-two workers and nine field survey crews were hard at work. Naturally, this activity caused quite a stir in Neosho. Up to this point, there had been no formal announcement of an Army post coming to Neosho and no land officially designated as an intended site for the facility, though it would be hard not to place its general location given the small army of surveyors traipsing through the woods with maps, marking stakes, plumb bobs, and tripods.

The U.S. Federal Court on August 18, 1941, granted permission for the government to take possession of some eighty-nine hundred acres of land for immediate use in building the first stage of the camp. Residents of this area were notified they had to leave their property, and people living on several tracts in the areas designated first for construction had to clear out within ten days. All farmers in the area were told to harvest what crops were ready and to take with them any buildings they desired.[4] "The right of Eminent Domain was declared and the price offered for property may or may not have been fair. Sentimental value was not one of the equations considered when they transferred ownership," said Jim Herrin, whose family's farm ended up untouched, just outside the camp boundary. "Most farms belonged to families for generations and were not for sale at any price."[5]

Those who were removed from their properties left both willingly and otherwise. A number of farmers protested this action, and at one point the government threatened to relocate the camp to another area unless those affected ended their demands for what the government characterized as exorbitant land prices. That claim was just a bluff, because by that point Camp Crowder's creation was a foregone conclusion. Said resident Pauline Freund, "The farmers sent letters and telegrams to their Congressmen and Senators but it was like whistling in the wind. About all we heard was there was going to be an army camp built here, whether we liked it or not.[6]

This governmental steamrolling fostered resentment among residents that remained sixty years later. Charles Lowrey recalled, "I felt the farmers in the Crowder area were treated badly. Most of the land was bought for $50.00 an acre or less. We had no choice but to sell.... They destroyed many crops when the surveyors trampled through our fields.[7]

As the government's land-taking activity continued working toward the camp's original planned size of 66,500 acres, area residents grew somewhat disillusioned about the project. "The citizens of Neosho are hostile," reported an article published by the *St. Louis Globe-Democrat*, "because the government gave local residents no say in taking their land and offered ridiculously low compensation."[8] Said resident Les Bond, "We lost our place to Mr. Dewey Short's 'gift' to Southwest Missouri. He thought the army camp was just what we needed to make our life complete. He had not gotten many votes from our family in the past, and this good deal didn't change my parents' position on his reelection."[9]

Farmers trying to unload livestock and equipment got almost nothing in return, for their neighbors in the same situation were of course not ready buyers. "We sold all our machinery and cattle [at auction].... Everything...went except some furniture, but of course most of the buyers were neighbors and friends in the same situation, no place to go," recalled Freund. Thus her family had no work on the farm, but they could not leave because the government had not yet paid them for their land.[10]

A big photo spread in *Life* magazine, though bringing considerable publicity to the area, portrayed area residents in a negative light. Springfield newspapers followed up with "an equally confident assertion that the town was isolationist," implying that they were being both hardheaded and ungrateful for looking this "$30,000,000 gift horse over with a critical, not to say, disillusioned, eye."[11]

On August 18, 1941, the same day as the federal court's decision granting the government license to gobble up large chunks of farmland for the new post, Tarlton-MacDonald Construction of St. Louis was named the general contractor for the Camp Crowder construction project. The company immediately came to Neosho to set up offices in the National Guard armory and to tackle the first stages of the massive project. Within a month, almost 750 people were on site, including 643 men performing construction and 81 civilian guards keeping watch over the facility.[12]

The camp was originally going to be called Camp Cockrell, in honor of former U.S. senator Francis Marion Cockrell, who served from 1875 to 1905 and was candidate for the Democratic presidential nomination in 1904 as well as a Confederate general during the Civil War. That moniker, announced September 9, 1941, lasted only two weeks. On September 24, workers at the camp learned that the installation would be called Camp Crowder, named for the late major general Enoch H. Crowder. Crowder, a Missouri native, was a West Pointer who eventually earned a law degree while serving as a professor of military tactics at the University of Missouri between 1885 and 1899. That degree eventually propelled Crowder to the role of judge advocate general of the Army in 1911. Among other accomplishments, Crowder drafted the Selective Service Act during World War I and also served as provost marshal general during that conflict, bearing responsibility for the military police and POW operations in the conflict.

With the initial groundwork laid, construction activity mushroomed at Crowder, and the number of workers at the camp swelled. A bus line to carry workers from Joplin was approved on September 27, and by the end of the month more than forty-four hundred men swarmed the facility. Even with all this work taking place and Army personnel beginning to arrive, including Lieutenant Colonel George Teachout, the first commanding officer of the installation, the camp's exact purpose had yet to be revealed.

The next month, however, Lieutenant Colonel Robert A. Willard of the Signal Corps finally confirmed the main purpose for Camp Crowder's creation: a massive training center for the Army Signal Corps.[13] "Activity at the site was near a frenzy, especially in the eyes of the local citizens who had come to realize that they were moving from a slow, rural way of life to one of camptown uproar," wrote Kay Hively in her history of the installation, *Red, Hot and Dusty: Tales of Camp Crowder*. "A check of police guards on October 14 showed that during the 24-hour period ending at midnight of that date, 10,561 cars passed in and out of the campsite."[14] Hively described the frenetic activity taking place at Crowder during this construction phase:

> By October 18, 639 buildings had been staked out for construction and 220 buildings were actually under construction. Over 15,000 feet of permanent railroad track had been built, 53,000 cubic yards of dirt had been moved, 10,000 feet of sewer line had been laid, 12,000 feet of electrical distribution lines installed and a temporary water supply for drinking and concrete mixing was in operation. Also by that time there were 9,788 persons employed.[15]

One of the obstacles workers had to contend with during the construction period was the mud that was everywhere. Just under ten inches of rain were recorded in October 1941, more than three times the normal precipitation. A favorite joke at the time, according to former Crowder soldier Lieutenant Colonel Leo Riegel, was about a soldier driving down one of the muddy roads at the camp. The soldier spied an officer's cap lying in the mud alongside the road and stopped to pick it up. When he lifted the cap, he jumped back, startled to see an officer buried up to his neck in the mud. Astonished, the soldier asked, "May I give you a lift, sir, or help you in some way?" The officer replied, "No thanks, soldier. I'm OK on my horse."[16]

With the great amount of work to be done at Camp Crowder, the number of civilian employees continued to grow at an astounding rate. By November 1, 1941, some 13,181 people were working at the camp, and by December, this number grew to a total of 16,356. Another vehicle check showed 21,288 cars passing through the gates on November 28, 1941. At the period of peak construction in January 1942, 20,543 men would be engaged in building this camp.[17]

The increased traffic caused by the project would be one of the biggest problems encountered by area residents. Elected officials drafted a bevy of new city ordinances regulating parking and driving, and the state highway patrol established a headquarters in Neosho complete with shortwave radio equipment to coordinate and expedite traffic flow.[18]

With these many headaches came boomtime profits, however. Men were working six days a week, ten hours per day, trying to get the camp finished by the February 1942 deadline. At hourly wages ranging from $.80 up to $1.50, plus time and a half for hours worked over eight per day or on

CAMP CROWDER

229

Saturday and Sunday, the weekly payroll at Crowder was approximately $625,000 for the last week of November 1941.[19]

Finally, after months of nearly round-the-clock work, the first troops to be housed at Camp Crowder arrived on the afternoon of December 2, 1941. "I remember the first company of soldiers who arrived at the new post," recalled Jim Herrin's older brother, Charles. "They were unloaded at McElhany, having arrived on the Kansas City Southern Railroad and marched down 71 Highway to Cockrell Drive, which was the Camp's south entrance. This was quite exciting and very impressive. Mud was ankle-deep in the camp because almost no streets had been constructed at the time."[20]

The Pearl Harbor attack followed almost immediately after the arrival of the soldiers, and the pace of the work went into overdrive, if such a thing was possible. Everyone at Camp Crowder, soldiers and civilian workers alike, knew events had taken a dramatic turn for the United States, and their efforts, whether in pouring concrete or training for war, were now extremely important. "We're in it now and if the boys who will use the camp need it, we'll build a road to Hell or a bridge to the Moon," said one of those tired and dirty men who had put in sixty hours that week and would probably work another sixty more if they let him.[21]

Lyon Gate was the main entrance to Camp Crowder. Courtesy of Missouri State Archives.

These men saw their work almost as an attack on the enemy positions of complacency and unpreparedness. That grim determination drove them to reach new levels of productivity and achievement. Crews were pouring a concrete road at a pace of about sixteen hundred feet each day. Men laying a gas line into camp were putting down ten thousand feet per day, while welders turned out as much as two thousand feet of pipe every twenty-four hours.

Indeed, this effort to build Camp Crowder showed the spirit and fire of the American people when united for a common task. Construction of the camp took just over eight months, a remarkable accomplishment. Perhaps most amazing, given the long hours, the mud, and the incredible pace of the construction activity, the "safety record of the workers at Camp Crowder was probably the best ever established on any War Department construction job of such magnitude."[22]

Work crew at Camp Crowder. Courtesy of Camp Crowder Collection, Crowder College.

The formal dedication of Camp Crowder took place on April 12, 1942. An estimated sixty thousand visitors turned out to hear Missouri governor Forrest C. Donnell give a formal address and to tour the facilities of the new installation. Three other speakers appeared, including Neosho mayor Glen Woods, Newton County presiding judge Guy Everhard, and McDonald County presiding judge I. M. Wiles.[23]

Home to the Signal Corps

At Crowder, young men in the Army Signal Corps were put through two weeks of basic training on drill and ceremony, marksmanship, military courtesy, and other rudimentary tasks. After those two weeks, the new soldiers attended one of the Signal Corps specialty schools, which also operated at Camp Crowder. These schools provided instruction in a number of areas, such as aircraft warning, message procedures, and telegraph printer operations. Additionally, the Signal Corps trained its own personnel to perform general support activities such as automobile maintenance and cooking. Upon completion of one of these advanced courses, GIs were sent immediately to active Signal Corps units to begin their service.

In its role as a main Signal Corps base, Crowder was also home to a training and breeding center for pigeons used to carry messages in wartime. The birds came in handy on other occasions, as well, such as when frustrated GIs used a pigeon to relay their need for a spare tire from fifty miles away. Parked on the side of a road with a flat tire on their jeep, the soldiers were glad to have that little bird when considering the prospect of a very long hike for help.

The men assigned to the main pigeon unit at Crowder, the 282d Signal Pigeon Company, probably got more than their fair share of ribbing from other GIs, but this incident, plus the fact that they used pigeons exclusively to communicate with the main camp when out in the field on maneuvers, convinced most servicemen at the camp of the birds' worth. At the end of the war, nearly all the birds at the camp as well as thousands of others sent from the battlefield were declared surplus and were put up for sale for $25 for five pairs of the pigeons. The new owners of the birds were given a certificate of service as well as a note of their loft location, so if the pigeons opted to return to Crowder instead of their new home, they could be returned to the proper person. After a year of trying to get rid of the birds, the Army had sold just over fifteen hundred pigeons and still had seventeen thousand birds left— more than twelve thousand at Crowder alone. The Army gave up trying to sell the fowl and started giving them away instead, just to be rid of the flock.[24]

Housing Shortage

With twenty thousand construction workers, engineers, surveying staff, inspectors, and support personnel, plus military men and their families, pouring into the Neosho area by the trainload, decent housing stock was soon in short supply. The Federal Works Agency performed a survey of residential rental rates and found that monthly rent shot up 11.4 percent just in the period between December 1941 and April 1942. People were forced to take up residence anywhere they could, including dilapidated tourist cabins and even some renovated farm buildings such as chicken coops and milk barns.[25]

Two Lutheran pastors who came to Neosho to survey the community to assess the prospects of starting a church found it a hopeless task because of the great numbers of people stuffed into every sort of structure. "Canvassing is difficult under the congested conditions in Neosho," wrote the pair in their report. "Since hotels and rooming houses are crowded, and many residences have room renters, it is difficult to locate all of the people."[26]

Dorothea Driscoll was married to a serviceman stationed at Crowder and recalled what it was like to live in those conditions. "We lived at Melton's Cabin Camps, R.D. No. 2, Neosho. There were twenty-three families living there from all walks of life. We all had one thing in common and lived more or less day-to-day," said Driscoll. "We made our little one-room cabins a home away from home and kidded about such things as having running water, but we had to run for it."[27]

Jim Herrin and his family lived in a stone house just west of Crowder's south entrance and saw at first hand the effects of the housing shortage. "Many of the workers slept in their cars or in cracker-box contraptions on the back of pickup trucks. Shacks began appearing everywhere. People rented rooms in their homes to construction workers. Mom rented a bedroom to two men, and a man from Sulphur Springs, Arkansas, rented the front porch to sleep on," recalled Herrin. "Two couples rented a small building in which we raised baby chickens. Any place with a roof was eventually called home by someone. Things you wouldn't think of were in short supply. We had an outdoor toilet and so many strangers using it, we almost had to take a number to use it ourselves.[28]

The spiraling rent and food costs put a pinch on many people, as times were tight and a GI's wages never went far for a young family. As the wife of a Crowder serviceman so poignantly stated, in many cases "the wolf and the stork worked in the same neighborhood."[29]

Other prices jumped as well, noted one of the Lutheran ministers. Grumpy about his meager wages, the man sat down at an old typewriter and pecked out a fourteen-page manifesto that he titled "Report on Inadequate Financing of Neosho Missionary" and sent to church headquarters in St. Louis, trying to justify an increase in his pay. According to a local dry-goods merchant, wrote the pastor, prices for clothing had jumped from 20 to 50 percent, depending on the specific item, and he estimated that the overall cost of living was up at least 50 percent.[30]

Neosho Support of Servicemen

Though having thousands of people pouring into once-quiet Newton County required major adjustment for many of the residents, they opened their hearts and homes to the GIs and their families and made a special effort to welcome them. The "Gray Ladies" of Camp Crowder—so named because of their gray and white uniforms with the Red Cross insignia—were a corps of nearly sixty women who started volunteering at the camp hospital in September 1942. These ladies spent at least a half day each week at the hospital, talking with the sick soldiers, playing cards and checkers, and helping them to write home, as well as reading letters and newspapers to them. They also acted as chaperones at the dances, bringing the girls out to the camp from town and returning them home afterward.[31]

Newton County Masons established the Masonic Service Center to take care of the needs of soldiers and their families who were often many miles from home. The services offered to the soldiers were often simple, but for those trying to adapt to new surroundings, any help made all the difference. The center arranged for a soldier's wife to be met at the train station, helped at the holidays with wrapping and shipping gifts to a soldier's family back home, and arranged for area families to open up the dining table for a Camp Crowder GI who longed for a home-cooked meal and simple social interaction. During its most busy times, the center assisted seventeen hundred soldiers a day.[32]

Recreation for the Soldiers

Donald Halbedl, a Crowder GI, recalled the challenges posed by trying to find something to do. "Trying to get off post into Neosho or Joplin meant being on long bus lines both ways only to find a town full of soldiers," he said.[33]

One alternative to heading into town was to wait for the entertainment to come to Crowder. "Bus Loads of Girls Coming to Big Dance," read the headline above a *Camp Crowder Message* article that described an upcoming event at the post field house. Ladies were trucked in from Joplin and other local areas for the four-hour event, which featured comedy and musical offerings interspersed with the sounds of the Ted Weems Orchestra, "for years, one of the nation's top musical entertainment organizations."[34]

The buses running twenty-four hours a day operated by the Joplin Public Service bus line offered transportation to those GIs who wanted to get away from the post. Neosho resident Thelma Slankard recalled the throngs of GIs who poured into the once-quiet town each weekend from the post, which averaged some forty thousand soldiers at any given time during the war. "It was something else. It changed our lives. We had to become accustomed to hearing sirens all night long and seeing the sidewalks on the square literally spilling [their] overflow into the streets as soldiers came in on Friday and Saturday night looking for friends, fun and a chance to get away. To say the least, it was something else."[35]

"Defense money is flowing at a rate this little town never dreamed of back in the days when it was primarily an agricultural community," noted an article in the *St. Louis Globe-Democrat*. "Merchants report their business has in most cases increased 50 to 75 percent. Some have doubled their business and there is scarcely a restaurant in town that has not been bought and sold one or more times at a handsome profit." Jim Herrin noted what a boon this was for area businesses: "There was a desperate need for large quantities of food. Many small grocery stores came into being. They were stocked wall to wall in the morning and everything was sold by evening. Restaurants were so packed you had to wait in long lines to be served."[36]

To provide recreation for the GIs, the city of Neosho received an $85,000 grant from the Federal Works Agency in April 1942.[37] The money was used to ensure bored soldiers did not get into trouble. The community would not succumb to corruption or other vices, vowed Police Chief Joe Thurman: "Boom or no boom, Neosho is going to stay clean."[38]

Herrin recalled that problems did spring up in the area, however: "All this money and all these people created an impossible job of maintaining law and order. Drunks and prostitution gave law enforcement agencies a big headache. Portable trailers were set up for brothels and were almost impossible to control."[39]

However, there was much uncomplicated and wholesome fun to be had in southwest Missouri. On May 10, 1943, twenty-year-old GI Mort Walker, future *Beetle Bailey* comic-strip artist, arrived at Camp Crowder. He described his efforts to find something fun to do:

> When we got a pass, we would take a bus into Neosho and walk around in the park. Or we'd go to the USO in Joplin and dance with the local girls. The "War Moms" of Monett had a big dinner for us one night. The first home-cooked meal we'd had in months. Afterwards we took some of the girls to a place called Westport and danced till the wee hours.

> I had an adventure once when I rented a horse which hadn't been out of the barn all winter. The minute I got on him he took off running at full speed, sliding across the paved roads with sparks flying from his shoes and barreling down unpaved roads, flying across ditches...and all I could do was hang on and yell, "Whoa, dammit!..."

> I have used Camp Crowder (along with Fort Leonard Wood where I was stationed after Washington University) as a background for Beetle Bailey. Of all the camps I was in, it seemed most typical.[40]

Unlike Walker, who found fame later through his comic strip, actor Burgess Meredith was already a celebrity when he arrived at Crowder. His stay was short—only three days—as the government changed its plans for him after reassessing where his services might be most valuable. After working until midnight the night before to shoot the final scenes for the movie *Street of Shadows*, Meredith was inducted at Fort McArthur, California, and sent to Crowder to begin basic training at the Signal Corps Replacement Training Center. Meredith arrived on Thursday, March 5, 1942, and by the following Sunday, March 8, was back on a train to Moffett Field, California, having been reassigned to the publicity arm of the U.S. Army Air Corps to better make use of his fame and on-screen talents.

The *Camp Crowder Message* described an interview conducted with Meredith about his impressions of the Neosho post:

> "What do you think of your new home here at Camp Crowder?" asked one reporter from the public relations office.

Glancing down at his ponderous, mud-besplattered army shoes Burgess drawled, "Well, I'd say what would be very nice in camp right now is some good, green grass...."

"Yep, when I write the folks back home, just think I'll say, 'Don't send cookies, send grass seed.'"[41]

Camp Crowder service club. Courtesy of Camp Crowder Collection, Crowder College.

Another person of note stationed at Camp Crowder was Klaus Mann, son of the German writer Thomas Mann. The younger Mann, who was a sergeant with the 825th Signal Repair Service Company, had been editor of *Decision* magazine and had written two well-received books before joining the Army. Along with composing a regular column for the *Message*, Crowder's camp newspaper, in September 1943 Mann used his cosmopolitan background to organize a collection of items donated by nearly one hundred celebrities that was exhibited at the camp and then auctioned off to help fund the war bond drive. Mann had personal connections to most of the contributors, a list that included some of the most famous artists, writers, and celebrities of the twentieth century. The *Message* publicized the event:

A display of autographed books, signed photographs and original manuscripts and drawings contributed by nearly 100 celebrities will be exhibited this evening and Friday and Saturday nights in the Blue Room of Service Club No. 2....

Included in the collection are contributions from Wendell L. Wilkie, Walter Lippman, Pearl Buck, Albert Einstein, Upton Sinclair, John Steinbeck, Thomas Mann, Clifton Fadiman, Franz Werfel, Thornton Wilder, Igor Stravinsky, Charley Boyer, Edward G. Robinson, Katherine Cornell, Helen Hayes, Katharine Hepburn, Marlene Dietrich, Hedy Lemarr and many others.

Certainly Mann wanted the auction to do well, but no one could ever have anticipated the astounding price the items would bring. One W. T. Grant paid $1 million to secure the entire batch of items offered at the auction for the library of the University of Kansas City.[42]

GI Sports

Like GIs everywhere, servicemen at Crowder played sports in their free time. Hively noted that:

> Possibly the first soccer ever played in Neosho was played at Camp Crowder. Many of the men stationed there came from the East where soccer was more common and many of the athletes were professional or semi-professional players. In 1943 Pfc. Johr Nugent, a native of Scotland who had played in international competition and for the Chicago Bricklayers, and Pvt. Joe Echino, who played with the Brooklyn Hispanos, were heavily involved in the sport as officials.[43]

Basketball was a popular pastime as well, and the Neosho High School gymnasium and then the Camp Crowder field house hosted innumerable contests between Crowder teams, who played against each other, college squads, and other military teams. Regular opponents included the Drury College Panthers and GIs stationed at the massive O'Reilly General Hospital, both in Springfield, Missouri, as well as servicemen squads from Fort Leonard Wood and Jefferson Barracks. Additionally, Crowder GIs played softball, baseball, and other sports against an array of teams from area towns as

Camp Crowder WAC basketball team. Courtesy of Camp Crowder Collection, Crowder College.

well as high-school squads. After the arrival of female soldiers at Camp Crowder in November 1942 when the first members of the Women's Army Corps (WAC) were sent to the installation, women's teams formed as well and often accompanied the men's team for a double-header against the host group.

Because of a draft that took every able-bodied man in the country, just about every professional or semiprofessional league in the United States found a number of its players among the GIs at Crowder. Those who made their living in any number of athletic pursuits, including baseball, football, track and field, hockey, ice skating, pool and billiards, table tennis, rodeo, golf, volleyball, boxing, wrestling, horseshoes, basketball, bowling, soccer, and weightlifting, could be found at Camp Crowder continuing their athletic passion in their free time, honing their skills and teaching their sport to others.

Even the drama of professional wrestling attracted the interest of Crowder servicemen. In January 1943, the reigning world light-heavy-weight champion, Billy Raeburn, traveled to Neosho to take on Sergeant Eddie Williams, a former professional wrestler who was attached to the Quartermaster Corps at Camp Crowder. More than three thousand GIs stomped, hooted, and whistled as Williams was defeated by the champ in a two-out-of-three-falls bout.

Entertainers also made the rounds, providing diversion for Crowder GIs during free time. Buster Crabbe, the famous swimmer and movie actor, was the first of a number of stars who would appear at the camp. Crabbe visited Crowder on February 21, 1942, but was able to stay only about ninety minutes. Wrote historian Kay Hively, "It was noted in the camp newspaper that Crabbe was scheduled to be called into service the following summer."[44]

Benny Goodman brought his swinging orchestra to Neosho in September 1942, packing the house as he and his musicians played the biggest hits in America for soldiers and their dates. GIs packed the dance floor to the sounds of "One O'Clock Jump," "Stompin' at the Savoy," and other tunes.

Heavyweight boxing champ Joe Louis visited Camp Crowder on December 8, 1942, as part of his tour of military bases around the country. Louis dropped in on men in the hospital, gave a talk on physical fitness, and boxed in several exhibition matches with Crowder champions, all of whom were soundly beaten by the hard-hitting Louis.[45]

Cary Grant drew huge crowds during a four-day visit in March 1943. Grant performed two shows a night as well as a Saturday matinee. When not performing, he toured the camp; ate with the soldiers in the GI mess halls; visited the hospital, classes, post clubs, and recreation rooms; and joined the trainees on bivouac, winning over just about every soldier in the camp with "his presence and friendly attitude."[46]

Outdoor Fun

Soldiers who preferred outdoor entertainment found plenty of opportunity around Crowder, such as fishing in the clear, spring-fed Ozark creeks and lazy rivers in the area. Several of the streams on post, such as

Entertainment at Camp Crowder. Clockwise: Ray Anthony and his "Talk of the Town" band played the field house, May 1946, courtesy of Missouri State Archives. Joe Louis sparred with PFC Booker T. Laster on December 16, 1943, courtesy of Missouri State Archives. Hollywood actors Richard Webb and Ronald Reagan, courtesy of Camp Crowder Collection, Crowder College. Cary Grant "enjoying'" chow in the GI mess, courtesy of Missouri State Archives.

Elm Springs, were stocked with game fish, which were pursued even by patients from the hospital during their recuperation. The only problem was a shortage of equipment, because few GIs thought to stuff a pole or tackle in their duffel bag when shipping out for boot camp. Members of the conservationist organization the Izaak Walton League came to the rescue when they agreed to meet up with servicemen each Sunday, providing equipment and expertise for a day of fishing or hunting.

Although fishing wasn't allowed at the Neosho National Fish Hatchery, it was the source of the fish used to stock area streams, including Shoal Creek and Indian Creek. Hatchery manager Aurum Balch issued GIs an open invitation to visit the seventeen-acre facility, which the *Message* described as being "laid out in a very leisurely and pleasant fashion, with ponds, fish troughs, shady walks, picnic grounds and a white clapboard house from which Mr. Balch directed the destinies of his fish."[47]

Additionally, because of the previous agricultural use of the land on which the camp now sat, blackberries and strawberries grew in abundance. The May 31, 1945, edition of the *Message* detailed some of the goings-on when berries were in season:

> It has been the custom here at the camp to capitalize on the berry crops in order that local mess halls may take advantage of them. For the past three years, a special "Strawberry Map" has been circulated showing the patches allotted to each unit. The ASFTC, for instance, has over 40 acres of strawberry patches out in the field training area.[48]

Creation of this map showing assigned strawberry territory was the single most important thing post authorities could have done to maintain peace at Camp Crowder, for strawberries were serious business. The *Message* detailed the zeal with which units guarded their particular plots:

> There is more diplomacy and protocol involved in a single Crowder strawberry patch than in the entire Department of State. Every unit must protect its rights for when one of them has a particularly lush growth there is liable to be a certain amount of brigandage on the part of unscrupulous G.I.s from other units.
>
> The areas, therefore, are jealously guarded. South American countries may get excited over boundary disputes but their wrath is gentle and child-like compared to that of a master sergeant from the Second Army who has discovered intruders from the TRC in "his" patch.[49]

Establishment of the POW Camp

Nearly two full years after American GIs first arrived at Camp Crowder, soldiers of another nationality came marching in. Citing the need for an expanded number of stateside POW facilities to hold the ever-increasing number of POWs from the European theater, the government was opening new POW camps at a rapid clip. Crowder was an ideal choice given its Midwest orientation and relatively isolated placement. Additionally, because the POW camp was placed on an existing military facility, the government could avoid the hassle and expense of securing space through seizure of private land and relocation of the people living there.

One concern, though, was the effect of having German POWs colocated with American trainees. Officers who served in the POW administrative effort knew how well the POW operations went in other parts of the United States. Cordial relationships between the prisoner population and the camp administration, substantial interaction between POWs and GIs on post, and prisoners enjoying fair amounts of freedom was the norm. The officers feared that seeing Germans relaxing happily or playing soccer could engender conflicting emotions in the recruits about the men they were supposed to go kill on the other side of the ocean. One commanding general of an infantry replacement training center said, "We must treat the German prisoners of war interned at military stations as a brutal, treacherous group, or we should keep them out of sight of our trainees."[50]

The first residents of the new internment camp at Crowder were scheduled to arrive in early October 1943. Naturally, the sizable civilian and military contingent located at the base was curious about the group. The speculation about the coming POWs grew to the level that the 566th Military Police Escort Guard (whose motto was, "Treat prisoners as you would wish to have our soldiers treated") issued guidance to the camp community about the incoming Germans:

> There is much curiosity about the Prisoner of War Camp. It's a natural American trait. But several points must be remembered by camp personnel. Through international agreement, these prisoners are fed and housed with care equal to that of the U.S. soldiers guarding them....

> Don't try to take advantage of a situation which might allow you to converse with the POWs. Just as our men, unfortunate enough to be in the hands of the enemy, would resent the stares of their captors, so must we respect the feelings of these men under our care.

As a word of caution, don't ever walk between the guard and the prisoner he is watching. If you walk by the place where the prisoners are working, take your curious looks, see that they are men like you and I, and move on. When the guard is off duty, he'll be glad to answer any question he is permitted to answer.[51]

Arrival of the Prisoners

Workers finished the stockade on October 1, 1943, and the POW camp commander, Major Francis Judkins, arrived at Camp Crowder October 4. Just two days later, October 6, 1943, the first group of 443 prisoners came rolling in. Almost all the men in that first group were captured in North Africa in the period around May 10, 1943, as part of the massive surrender of the Afrika Korps. Given that the POW installation had a single thousand-man compound, the first group did not occupy even half of the available space. Even though things were generally peaceful within the new camp, the prisoners were still separated as far as their political temperament could be discerned. The bulk of the prisoners were Germans and were housed in one area of the internment camp, while a smaller group of twenty-four prisoners—Austrians and others "not politically amiable toward the main compound," including "convicts, socialists, and political prisoners"—were quartered in a separate area. This smaller group did not remain long at Crowder and was shipped on November 10, 1943, to a Pennsylvania camp designated especially for these types of prisoners.[52]

Almost immediately upon arrival, Germans at Crowder beset the internment area with plans for improvement and vigorous activity to match. Within a month, the POWs laid out boundaries for a number of planned gardens and planted flowers all around the barracks. This industry was noted by Howard Hong, a delegate from the international committee of the YMCA. Hong had been at the POW facility at Camp Clark in Nevada, Missouri, when he decided to stop by the newly opened Camp Crowder, which was about sixty-five miles south of Clark on U.S. 71. Hong noted that "in spite of the newness of the camp, a surprising amount of work has been done within the camp: roads built; drainage ditches dug and lined or tiled and plans laid for the athletic field.... There is a tremendous left-over lumber pile, and the men will have sufficient material for barracks furniture or for their day room and theater."[53]

Things were bustling in those early days as both prisoners and camp administration became adjusted to their new home and worked to establish their routine and to improve the facilities at the camp. The Germans set about building a sports field and created a smaller field inside their compound for soccer and volleyball. "They will soon have a magnificent playing field," observed one visitor to the camp.[54]

Despite the attention given to this work both inside the compound and out, including road building, landscaping the camp, and sorting and stacking the giant pile of lumber, prisoners were eager to begin classes and to establish a library. Hong noted the need for books and instructional material and worked to arrange an interlibrary loan program with Charles H. Compton and Louis Nourse, librarian and assistant librarian, respectively, of the St. Louis Library, "provided we can make practicable arrangements for censoring." Hong reported that any material the YMCA could send would be helpful and eagerly received.

Prisoners crowded the Sunday morning worship held during those first weeks. Hong noted a "remarkable interest" and reported that the Lutheran chaplain, an American named the Reverend Robert M. Jank, had counted 134 at the first service and 170 the following week. Catholics managed a turnout of 120 at Sunday mass, despite a complete lack of hymnals, music, and prayer books.

Naturally, starting a camp from scratch meant that the stocks of musical and theatrical equipment and instruments had to be acquired, but Hong noted that the prisoners were so busy they hadn't noticed. "We have a good opportunity to help here at the very outset," he wrote. "I made arrangements with the local USO to secure a good used piano and bill us. The camp will pick it up."

Hong wrote that though the men had found some entertainment with a table-tennis table and one lonely ball, both provided by camp commander Judkins, additional supplies for arts and crafts could also be put to good use, though the POWs had not yet found themselves with enough vacant hours to think to ask for such free-time paraphernalia. "There are some artists in the camp, but their recent arrival and lack of paints, etc., has prevented their working. Wood carving has also begun somewhat with the help of chisels sent in by the camp engineer," wrote Hong. "All in all the camp has really nothing for recreational activity. The men have been so busy they perhaps have not felt the need, but it is immediate."[55]

The tenor in these early days at Camp Crowder was encouraging, and both Judkins and Hong noted the importance of getting the camp started on the right foot and continuing the momentum through the weeks and months to follow. Hong wrote, "A fine spirit seems to exist in this camp, through the interest and efforts of the commanding officer and his staff and the cooperativeness of the men. If we can help them in the early weeks of the camp there is a possibility of extending the good beginning into the [continuing] activities that will have a great significance to the men as individuals and as a community."[56]

First Impressions

When an eighteen-year-old conscript private named Karl-Heinz Richter stepped off the train at Camp Crowder in September 1944, it marked the last leg of a very long trip from the European battlefield. Richter was captured by a Canadian outfit in August 1944 outside Falaise, France, and subsequently handed over to the British. They sent him to England with other injured POWs for treatment of shrapnel wounds in the back and arm. After medical personnel declared him fit for travel, Richter and other POWs shipped from England to Glasgow, Scotland, where they received word of their next destination: the United States.

Karl-Heinz Richter. Courtesy of Camp Crowder Collection, Crowder College.

"We were taken on a huge boat, and altogether we were about 500 POWs and a couple of hundred GIs, which we assumed were going home. On September 16, 1944, we came to the Hudson River in New York, where we were put on a train and the trip started," wrote Richter in his recollections of the journey. "We traveled for 5 days, which gave us the opportunity to see the United States. We traveled through NY to Cleveland, Chicago, St. Louis, Springfield, and on September 21, 1944, the train stopped in NEOSHO, MISSOURI."[57]

The new arrivals marched from the depot in Neosho to the military installation. "It was very well lit, and there was a lot of twisted barbed wire, towers, and armed soldiers," recalled Richter. "We all thought, 'Oh God, this is where we are going to live!' But...we walked right past it." The Germans were marched farther on into the Camp Crowder installation, until they came to the site of the POW camp. "We finally came to another wired, well-lit enclosure, but it did not have as much barbed wire and fewer armed guards," said Richter. "The door was opened, we walked in and we were greeted by our comrades from the Afrika Korps, also prisoners. They had been in Neosho since 1943! When we saw them, our hearts lightened considerably."[58]

POW Hermann Half had a similar first impression of Camp Crowder. Famished from the lack of food over the four-day trip from their port of arrival in the United States, the Germans complained to the guards as the troop train clattered over the last few miles of tracks. "Don't worry," the guards told them as they neared the camp, "you'll soon have more food than you know what to do with."

What the guards said was true. When the Germans arrived at Camp Crowder they found themselves with a meal that surpassed any expectation. "It was just unbelieveable what we had to eat. It was Christmas in September. They cautioned us all the time don't eat too much so we didn't get sick because, you know, we had been hungry for so long," said Half. "We had steaks, we had turkey, we had pork chops, we had everything. And they served us, the Afrika Korps, and there were white linens on the table. It was just unbelievable. On each bed they had placed cigarettes, soap, and towels."[59]

Camp Appearance

Early comments about the appearance of Camp Crowder and the surrounding areas were not positive. "The country is hilly, badly eroded, and...cannot be said to be fertile or suitable for raising such standard crops as wheat, corn, etc.," wrote Charles Eberhardt of the State Department on a visit in November 1943. "Apparently there never have been forests of any great extent and at present the area is sparsely timbered, principally with scrub oak."[60]

Even though Crowder looked like a typical POW camp, with guard towers, barbed-wire fencing, and patrolling dogs, prisoners benefited from the forethought of the engineers who had created it. While no trees remained too close to the fences or in other places where they might pose a security risk, between fifty and one hundred trees were left standing between the buildings, which not only added considerably to the appearance of the facility but also provided much-needed shade to the barracks. In southwest Missouri, the average daily temperature in July is a warm 86.5 degrees, so these trees were of enormous benefit. Also, part of the POW camp stood on the grounds of an old apple orchard, so in addition to providing shade, the trees offered fruit to hungry soldiers.[61]

The POWs at Camp Crowder worked hard to improve the appearance of the camp. To complement the existing greenery, the Germans set about planting Bermuda grass throughout the stockade, including the two sports fields, and the grass grew surprisingly well in the poor soil. The men cleared the area of rocks and used them to line the walkways around the camp and planted numerous flowers and shrubs around the grounds. Additionally, noted a State Department inspector, the "prisoners have already performed a most commendable feat of beautifying the premises by riprapping the shoulders of the gutters and grading"—lining the ditches and gutters with loose rock.[62]

Just a week after his arrival, German POW Robert Belser wrote his wife, Else, and told her about the new camp:

> This newly built camp surrounded by bushes and trees, including even fruit trees, will be our new home for some time to come. Here at last we no longer sleep on the ground, but have a good roof over our heads, comfortable beds to sleep in, plentiful, well-appointed meals, and also good treatment. We also have a canteen where many things can be obtained which we had to forego for so long. We can go out to work every day and a sports field is being developed. There are many additional plans for the improvement of the camp and the surrounding grounds.[63]

Interior of POW barracks, Camp Crowder. Notice the prisoners' "mascot" "standing at attention." Courtesy of George Kelly.

Karl-Heinz Richter agreed with Belser's opinion of the camp and recalled the positive first impression he had of Camp Crowder in September 1944. "Each building held 50 men. The beds, tables and chairs were wood," commented Richter. "There was plenty of space for any luggage we had brought with us."[64]

Crowder's German POWs lavished the same sorts of attention on the interior of the barracks as they did on the outside. A December 1943 inspection report by the PMGO elaborated on the prisoners' work inside the barracks. "This camp was also unique in the interest which the prisoners have taken in decorating the interior of their barracks. Tables and benches have been made so that there will be one for every three bunks. Artificial flowers have been made and placed in vases to decorate the tables," wrote the inspector. "Attractive drapes have been put on the windows and the barracks are scrupulously clean. All in all this camp had the appearance of being a model one."[65]

Because of all this work, in less than a year the camp took on the appearance of "a charming village, with gardens, roads, houses covered with vines and flowers," according to a visitor from the International Red Cross. Prisoners constructed an outdoor covered bandstand and even created a *biergarten* as a comfortable place to socialize, complementing it and other little nooks around the camp with benches and tables for more intimate visits.[66]

Miniature village constructed by Crowder POWs. Courtesy of George Kelly.

Another feature of the camp was a model village constructed by the prisoners in the space between two barracks. "We built a miniature flour mill, blacksmithy, lumber mill, a church, each with moving parts. The saw sawed, the bells chimed. It was run by water-powered electricity. All the wires were underground," said Richter, who was involved with its creation. "All the street lights worked, a water-wheel turned, and an electric train ran." Prisoners installed tiny bells in the church tower that could ring to call the faithful to worship, typical of the many clever and intricate details they incorporated throughout the miniature landscape.[67]

Food

One of the nice things about moving into a brand-new POW camp was that most of the equipment and furnishings were of recent vintage. Paul Schnyder, a visitor from the International Red Cross to the installation just a month after its opening, noted that the kitchen in the POW mess had a Frigidaire and plenty of dishes, silverware, and glasses. The prisoner soldiers gave these items a workout once they tasted the food served at the camp. As always, it seemed the "foreign" cuisine served in the camps was a grand improvement on the ordinary American fare. Schnyder reported that the men "received the same food as the American soldiers, but as there are several excellent cooks among them their cooking is very much better."[68]

Gerhard Frenkel sent a letter to his family in Thüringen, Germany, a week after his arrival at Crowder, describing the kinds of food available to the prisoners at the new camp, items that had been scarce in Germany for some time. "You need not worry about me at all, I am very well off here," wrote Frankel. "The food is excellent, and it is as plentiful as it is varied; above all it consists of such rare things as fresh meat, vegetables, fruit, milk and even eggs!"[69]

Often, the selection and amount of food available was literally overwhelming to newly arrived POWs who had endured months of malnourishment on the battlefield. "We were so surprised to see so many things to eat on the table," said Karl-Heinz Richter of his first meal at Crowder. "We had so much to eat! We all ate so much that many of us had big stomach aches."[70]

Charles Eberhardt of the Department of State expressed his satisfaction with the Thanksgiving dinner in 1943, which he enjoyed in the prisoners' mess. Eberhardt "had his Thanksgiving dinner among the prisoners and found it to be the same as that furnished in the officers' mess or in the station hospital." He included a copy of the menu, which noted a sumptuous spread of shrimp cocktail, roast turkey with dressing and gravy, buttered asparagus, mincemeat pie, and fruitcake. The menu (from the station hospital) also listed an array of choices with which one could top off the meal—coffee, candy, nuts, cigars, or cigarettes. "The food is ample, well-prepared, and the prisoners themselves are excellent living examples of its quality," wrote Eberhardt upon a return trip to Crowder in April 1944. "They have all gained in weight and none could justifiably make any criticism of food with which they are furnished."[71]

Herman Half, a German pilot, was held at Crowder for two years, beginning in 1944. Half always said the best he ever ate in all his life was in Crowder, said his son, Herbert Half. "He said he really liked it there."[72]

Recreation

Even after three months at the camp, little was to be found in the way of instruments, stage props, or other equipment for orchestra or theater activities. This lack of necessities did not stop the Germans from preparing for the day that equipment would be present. Using wood from the scrap lumber pile looming over the Crowder landscape, the men built a stage in a building intended for use as a visitors' center. The POWs planned two Christmas plays, writing the scripts and hoping for timely receipt of wigs and dresses that had been ordered with the help of Chaplain John H. Plueger and the USO officers in Neosho.[73]

By April 1944, the situation was much improved. Three pianos were purchased, and the prisoners accumulated enough instruments and music that they were able to put together a combination band and orchestra. By the end of summer, two full orchestras were in place as well as several choirs. Karl-Heinz Richter noted how participation in these "extra-curricular" activities grew rapidly, saying, "With one thousand men, we started forming musical groups.... There were three professional musicians, and with their guidance, we formed a symphonic orchestra, a band, and a popular music band. We also formed a theatre group."[74]

Prisoners were able to roll out a new play almost every two weeks, and a rented projector allowed the showing of two movies to the internees each week as well. Continued work on the erstwhile visitors' building transformed it into a full-blown theater, and many decorations were added to enhance its appearance. Sculptors and painters were given room to practice their craft and a great number of prisoners enjoyed woodcarving and other handiwork during their free time. Several exhibitions of art and crafts were staged, with the YMCA providing small prizes for the best pieces in each category.[75]

Camp Crowder POWs were wonderfully creative both in using materials available to them and in improvising to create furniture and other items to beautify barracks living. Prisoners pulled the springs from an old automobile bench seat salvaged from the camp dump, installed them in a wood frame hammered together by POW craftsmen, and covered it all with cloth purchased from the canteen to make a cozy overstuffed couch.

The sports program saw similar improvement after numerous donations of gear from the International Red Cross, the YMCA, and other organizations. Verner Tobler of the Swiss Legation and Charles Eberhardt of the Department of State visited that month and commented on the marked improvement in athletic equipment and facilities. "Three bowling alleys have been constructed and are most popular; a boxing arena has been built in the open air; and a gymnasium with punching bag and other up-to-date paraphernalia is maintained in one of the barracks," wrote Eberhardt. "Fist ball [volleyball] and tennis are also popular outdoor games."[76]

Camp Atmosphere

Camp Crowder was an extremely well run camp in many respects. A unique spirit of friendliness and cooperation existed between the POWs and camp officials. A cable from the Swiss interests who visited the facility called it a "splendidly conducted camp," marked by "perfect harmony between war prisoners and camp director." The Swiss representative noted a spirit of camaraderie was pervasive and the "maintenance and health conditions were first-rate," giving visitors an excellent overall impression.[77]

Having served as assistant executive officer of the greater Camp Crowder prior to assuming command of the POW camp, Major Judkins had personal knowledge of the installation's administrative staff—a great advantage to him in helping to avoid the pitfall befalling many POW camp commanders whose facilities were located on a larger military base: the issue of micromanagement of the POW installation by the post camp commander or a lack of cooperation and support from him. "Being adjacent to or a part of Camp Crowder, there might seem to be divided authority," wrote Eberhardt, who had firsthand knowledge of the frequency of these problems and how difficult they could be to resolve, "but certainly no evidence of any lack of thorough cooperation between the two organizations was discernible during this visit to the camp."[78]

Judkins was a skilled administrator and took great pains to get to know his camp staff as well as the prisoners. He visited the compound several times a day and was "respected by all the compound leaders." Additionally, wrote Eberhardt, Judkins "also [knew] most of the [German] men, who seem unanimously to respect and esteem him."[79]

One of Judkins's key strategies for gaining POW cooperation was to be permissive in allowing the prisoners latitude to create an environment unlike a typical POW camp. "Major Judkins...[is] very much interested in making this PW camp unique in respect to services rendered to prisoners," wrote B. Frank Stoltzfus, a visitor from the YMCA. He described the appearance of the camp, portraying it as a pleasant and charming place:

> Brown buildings, rather than black; guard houses small in size; streets laid out in small-village fashion; fruit orchard; much green grass, flowers, young trees and shrubs; freshly painted patches here and there on windows or doors, on garbage barrels, on miniature fences; private dens (tiny little painted one-room huts); private drinking haunts for still larger social groups scattered about, each having peculiar architectural design and paint to suit the fancy; two bowling alleys, covered from the cold, with stoves to warm them.[80]

Inspectors saw this as a positive sign. "The Commandant of the camp knows how to win the prisoners' respect. He treats them well and goes to a good deal of trouble for them," added another visitor, Paul Schnyder of the International Red Cross. Schnyder's impression was consistent over time as well. In a follow-up visit to Crowder nearly a year later, in August 1944, he called the camp "undoubtedly one of the best in the United States."[81]

Herb Half recalled the story of an incident that his father, Herman Half, loved to share and that illustrated the trust between guards and the internees. "The American GIs were playing poker one night, and they had a hot game going. They had been playing for a couple of hours and were running low on beer, but didn't want to interrupt their game. 'Hey Half,' one of the guys said to my dad, 'could you go get us more beer?' With that, the guy tossed my dad the keys to the truck so that he could go and get them some more beer. And he did it. Got the beer and came right back."[82]

The praise for Judkins flowed in from all sides, and U.S. officials held the same view as the neutral inspectors. "This is an outstandingly good camp. It is certainly one of the best I have seen in any service command," commented Parker W. Buhrman from the U.S. Department of State. "The camp is well ordered and unusually well administered. The Camp Commander merits the highest commendation."[83]

While the positive relations and the liberties granted to the internees created a pleasant atmosphere, they also set up the camp as a prime target for the impending tempest over the issue of POW coddling. To the dismay of Judkins and the others who worked so hard to foster a positive and productive atmosphere (as evidenced by the relative lack of visible political turmoil to the outside observer and extremely high rates of participation in the POW work program), Crowder was held up as a prime example of excessively soft treatment by those demanding much harsher treatment of POWs.

For instance, a small zoo maintained by Crowder POWs drew much attention from critics. Prisoners created a "miniature zoological park with bird house and tiny fountain, love birds, parrots, quails, guinea pigs, white mice, rabbits, snakes, alligator, monkeys; pet cats, dogs tied and untied, delightedly playful, a pet pig brought from another camp, [and] two goats," wrote an astonished YMCA inspector.[84] This zoo would be the focal point of criticism leveled at Judkins, that he was being lax by allowing POWs to keep these animals. But POWs keeping pets was not uncommon, noted Judith Gansberg in *Stalag, U.S.A.* "Soldiers seem to have a talent for picking up stray animals, and German soldiers are no different," wrote Gansberg. "Many kept pets at camps. Later, upon repatriation, some fought—unsuccessfully—to take their pets with them. Camp zoos were populous and often attractive additions to the compounds."[85]

These POW pets stayed behind after the war, and at least one area family benefited from them. Growing up, Frieda Betts and her four siblings lived ten miles southwest of Neosho, and during the war her father, Fay Kessinger, oversaw a crew of POWs who collected trash from the camp. His job there provided the family with some unexpected treasures—a cast-off dictionary, ladies' shoes that fit her mother—that ordinarily they wouldn't have seen in those tight days. Another time, Kessinger carted home a wooden suitcase that still had pinup photos pasted inside the top cover by the original owner. The best thing her father ever brought home, said Betts, was a dog of the prisoners that they couldn't take back to Europe.

The dog was a just a little black thing, and the prisoners called it Lumpe (pronounced LOOM-pee), which was an ideal description for the dog, from both the German *lump*, meaning "rascal," and *klump*, "dirt clod" or "lump of coal." "Lumpe had only been around men, so Dad was afraid of what it would be like around us. He tied Lumpe to a tree and there he stayed for several days. We kids sort of eyed him and stayed beyond the end of the rope," recalled Betts. "But one day our brother George, who was maybe four or five, went out, untied the rope, and said, 'Lumpe, let's go for a walk.' Needless to say, he had done this without permission and when Mother looked out and saw the empty rope she nearly had a heart attack, but when George and Lumpe came back, that was it."[86]

Canteen

Major Judkins made every effort to provide as many items for the POW canteen as regulations allowed. He knew the positive effect it had on prisoner morale, which was confirmed by a December 1943 visitor from the PMGO who noted "the availability of articles sold in the canteen has increased the prisoners' incentive to work by a hundred percent."[87] Another advantage Judkins recognized by having a canteen lined with desirable goods was that funds generated from POW labor would be put to good use. All profits generated by the canteen were put back into the camp and allowed for the purchase of much-needed recreational equipment, textbooks for classes, and books, magazines, and newspapers to line the barren shelves of the camp library.

Anton Muhlberger mentioned the canteen in a letter to his family in Germany. His words convey the popularity of the canteen and how having the opportunity to purchase items there motivated the prisoners to participate in the labor program. "You do not need to send me anything. We get everything we need because we are in America! Besides that, we can go to work and use the money we earn to buy anything we want, from beer to chocolate in the camp canteen," wrote Muhlberger. "As you can see, I am well off, and you need not worry about me in the least."[88]

With its wide selection and the camp's prosperous POW population, the canteen made a lot of money. Four weeks of sales in April 1944 totaled approximately $21,000 and generated $3,400 in profits to be used in camp via the prisoner fund. Judkins noticed that the canteen generated a profit of over 16 percent. This seemed perhaps a bit steep to him, given that the POWs had no other shopping options. Also, this rate of profit meant the camp POW fund was soon awash in excess money, and prisoners were buying items such as sports equipment frivolously just because the cash was available. Charles Eberhardt of the Department of State mentioned to Judkins that plans were being considered at other POW camps whereby the profit margin on goods sold in the POW canteen would be held at 7 percent, and any surplus funds in the POW account would be held for the prisoners until repatriation or for other POW expenses that may arise.[89] This cap on profits was eventually enacted at Crowder and elsewhere, and while the POW fund still burgeoned with canteen profits, it wasn't as excessive as before.

A minor snafu on the part of the PMGO and higher-level authorities caused major prisoner dissatisfaction in October 1944. Officials decided that POW canteens should no longer be independently administered and instead should fall under the auspices of the centralized post exchange authority, a change that occurred at all camps, not just Crowder. This change caused problems in the supply chain, and suddenly the various forms of tobacco offered were in short supply, angering cigarette-loving prisoners. Swiss representative Verner Tobler, who visited Crowder that month, blasted this decision:

> The post or service command apparently have lost sight of the fact that the prisoner of war canteen is highly useful as a morale building factor, particularly in work camps. There is every reason in work camps to place as wide a list of commodities as possible at the disposal of the Camp Commander for use in encouraging the prisoners to work. There is obviously no purpose in the prisoners working if there is nothing in the canteen to buy....

> The canteens were well supplied with noncritical items. The prisoners were anxious to work and draw their entire compensation because they could buy certain things that had some intrinsic value or worth. Now they are being arbitrarily cut back to where the prisoner of war canteen has very little interest to the prisoners. Consequently, it adversely affects their working morale.[90]

Tobler accused the post exchange administration officers at several camps of having the attitude that POW canteens were entitled to little or no consideration in the allocation of goods, a situation in which the POW camp commander would be "gravely handicapped in the handling of his prisoners." Eventually, this too would be straightened out, and Camp Crowder POWs would be once more working and smoking happily.

Mischief

Working in the motor pool provided prime opportunity for POW mischief, said German prisoner Hermann Half. "We would go into the motor-pool on the weekends and take out vehicles. There was never anyone around and the keys were there," said Half, who believed that the camp administration knew about it but chose to look the other way. "They never said anything. We had a lot of people working there, and so we all learned how to drive. We knew how to put the key in and turn it on. We drove around the base and it was nice to go out and have fun."[91]

Willie Huffman, Challis Elliff, and an unidentified man, all civilian workers at Camp Crowder. Courtesy of Carson Elliff.

Though apparently driving for legitimate work-related reasons, a POW in an Army truck hit another vehicle in August 1945. Willie Huffman, a civilian worker at Camp Crowder, was driving on post with his son, Everett, when the POW ran a stop sign and smashed into the side of his car. The incident eventually involved everyone from Crowder's commanding general to Dewey Short, U.S. representative for the area.

Huffman wrote in a letter to Short: "I had started home from the Post Engineer [office], going north on Daniel Boone Street [and] a German prisoner was coming from the east driving a government truck. He run the stop sign and hit my car—bent the frame, bent axle, broke one headlight and tore off the left fender." At the government's request, Huffman had gotten estimates from three mechanics for the repairs, with the lowest coming in at just over $200. "A party told me they would settle with me to fix my car at the time, but now claims it was as much my fault as it was the German prisoner's fault, and I would appreciate it very much if you could help me get the money to fix my car."[92] Short asked Brigadier General Charles M. Milliken, the commanding general at Crowder, to help, and the damage to Huffman's car was paid as promised.

Crowder POWs found that their work at the camp gave them other opportunities to get into trouble. Huffman's son, Everett, also worked at the camp and had a good friend there named Challis Elliff. As a foreman at the camp, Elliff supervised a number of POWs, including one named Heinz Brick. Elliff and Brick came to be good friends, so much so that when departure loomed for the POWs, Brick presented Elliff with a souvenir portrait photo of himself, made after hours in the Camp Crowder studio, which was run by another POW. Sneaking into the studio with the POWs' mascot under his arm, a little dog of questionable lineage, Brick posed in his POW work uniform for the portrait. His eyes gleaming with impish intent and the dog with its paw in Brick's hand, Brick recorded for posterity the fun that could be had as a POW with a mind for mischief.[93]

Other misbehavior took place when POWs who worked as cooks and kitchen police in mess halls around the base found the opportunity to play peeping toms when they finished work and marched back unattended at night to the POW compound. Their route took them past the housing area for the Women's Army Corps (WAC) soldiers. "Finally one time somebody figured out there was a ladder for a fire

Another POW working in the Crowder photo studio likely made this portrait of Heinz Brick and the POWs' dog on the sly. Brick gave this photo to his friend Challis Elliff. Courtesy of Carson Elliff.

escape that went up to the second story where the WAC's shower room was. So every night when it was dark they went by there and climbed up and they watched," said POW Hermann Half. "The officer of the WAC told Judkins that the POWs were climbing up the ladder and looking in the shower room. He told her, 'No way, my prisoners would never do this' and she said 'Okay, the next time I'll call you and you'd better come over right away.'"

Just two days later the woman called. Judkins grabbed two MPs and raced over in a jeep and found the POWs up on the fire escape looking into the window. "The MPs were pounding on the ladder, 'Come down, you guys! Come down!' and they didn't even hear it. They had to climb the ladder and pull them down," said Half.

For punishment, the POWs got three days in the guardhouse with a restricted diet of bread and water. "After the first night, Judkins came over and asked, 'How did you spend the night? Was it cold?' and they'd say, 'Yes sir, it was very cold,' and so he gave them blankets," said Half. "The second day he came and said, 'Are you hungry?' 'Yes sir, we are very hungry,' and he said 'Okay, come on out.' It was very funny."[94]

Members of the Women's Army Corps in a Camp Crowder mess hall. Courtesy of Camp Crowder Collection, Crowder College.

Labor Program

Ample opportunities for work existed at Camp Crowder and the surrounding areas, and almost all the German prisoners participated. POWs worked in the quarry, on road-building crews, in camp stock rooms and warehouses, in brush-clearing details, or in the post laundry. Only a month after arrival, some 318 prisoners were working outside the compound, 40 were engaged inside the stockade, and about 40 worked in the hospital, serving as orderlies or kitchen police. Out of a total of 419 POWs (which included 17 prisoners who were in the hospital and a handful of others unavailable for labor because of minor maladies), this meant that more than 95 percent were engaged in the labor program, an extremely high rate of participation that continued throughout the camp's lifetime.[95]

"The vicinity of the American military camp has the advantage of providing work for the prisoners," wrote Paul Schnyder of the International Red Cross during his November 12, 1943, visit. He noted that the Germans were engaged in the following jobs:

Grading and earthwork outside the camp	17 men
Sewers	12 men
Soil erosion	10 men
Timber	57 men
Quarry	30 men
Wood sawing	19 men
Ditch draining	13 men
Light road repairs	6 men
Warehouse	9 men
Warehouse No. 1927	10 men
Laundry	51 men
Military Police	3 men
Studio	1 man
Camp's roads	15 men
Janitors	2 men
Spokesmen	44 men
Miscellaneous	19 men
Total	318 men[96]

During this 1943 visit, Charles Eberhardt found a few minutes to chat with the foreman of the rock quarry. The man "expressed his special pleasure and satisfaction over the work which the prisoners were performing," and it seems that the Crowder prisoners performed equally well in whatever area they were assigned.[97]

There was plenty to be done, as Crowder was a post that was only a couple years old and its mission to support the training of forty thousand GIs offered myriad tasks and projects to tackle. "Services of the prisoners of war were utilized in a host of jobs—in warehouses, the laundry, bakery, repair shops and motor pools, and—to the joy of many a buck private in the U.S. Army—as KPs, firemen, orderlies, janitors and other details," wrote the *Camp Crowder Message* in a piece describing the various tasks employing the German internees. "Officials estimate that the savings to the government by the use of PW labor aggregated about $38,000 a week during the period the Crowder compound was in operation."[98]

Charles Dunn was a painter and carpenter at Crowder from the time the camp opened. He supervised a crew of workmen, including two Austrians about eighteen years old named Karl and Adolph. "They said they were forced into the German Army and surrendered to the first soldiers they encountered," said Dunn's daughter Betty Reid, who met the prisoners when she went with her mother to see her father at the camp. "I remember that when we were introduced to them, they bowed and clicked their heels together. I was age 17 and to me they were The Enemy. But father was very fond of them and tried to explain that they were caught up in unfortunate circumstances and were no different than us."

"When the time came for them to return to Austria, they thanked father for being so good to them," recalled Reid. "They had enjoyed the white bread, the fruit and all the food they had never had in occupied Austria." Naturally the men missed their families and wanted to be home, said Reid, especially one who was due to be married. "Karl was engaged," recalled Reid, "[and my] mother and my aunt gathered and made lingerie for the bride and mailed her a large package," unaware, perhaps, that this fell outside the traditional categories of "postwar aid" sent by the United States to Europe.[99]

POWs working for the post engineer. Courtesy of Missouri State Archives.

Newly arrived POWs at Camp Crowder were surveyed about their educational background and civilian and military vocation, and from this information, work assignments were made, said POW Karl-Heinz Richter:

Most of us were put to work serving the U.S. troops that were being trained at Crowder. We were truck drivers, kitchen workers, bakers, refrigeration chamber workers, butchers, launderers, supply area people where uniforms, shoes and food were dispersed. We POWs with special skills were in motor pools where we repaired cars and trucks were maintained.

Because of my electronic training, I was put into the motor pool. I was there with an older U.S. technician #5 where we turned motors. It was a beautiful and interesting job for me. I am sorry to say it ended when the war ended. Then mechanics were not as much needed as during the war, and in the fall of 1945, the motor pool was closed.[100]

Though not a soldier at Crowder, James Osborn saw life from both sides of the fence. Osborn was first an American POW in Germany and then saw the Germans at Camp Crowder when he worked at the camp as a civilian employee in the motor pool. Osborn served in the Army Air Force until he was shot down over Austria by the Germans in July 1944 and was placed in a camp run by the Luftwaffe, the German air force. During the next several months, Osborn spent time in several German camps. The situation was increasingly desperate during those last months of the war, and the American POWs were moved west, walking for "days on end" to keep ahead of the advancing Russians.

Osborn and six other Americans slipped away from their captors at one point and were on the run for eighty days. Eventually the men made it to Allied territory in eastern Germany. The date was April 26, 1945, and Osborn weighed less than a hundred pounds. He had walked some eight hundred miles since his escape.

After a stay in a hospital in France while he recovered from his ordeal, Osborn was shipped back to the United States and arrived at Camp Myles Standish, Massachusetts, where German prisoners were working in the cafeteria. "Once we got there, they said, 'please don't rough up any of these PW's because of what happened to you,'" said Osborn. "'It just causes trouble when people do that. The last time one of you guys came through, he gave them such a hard time we couldn't get them to come out of the barracks.'"

In January 1946, Osborn ended up at Camp Crowder, where he worked as an expediter in the motor pool, scheduling maintenance and repair of vehicles through the shop. A large number of German POWs worked in the area as mechanics, and the scene was ripe for tension. "I had some bad feelings after my experience," said Osborn. "It took me a while to get over it. At first, you know, if I heard German being spoken, it made my hair bristle." One could hardly blame Osborn if he had a great deal of anger built up inside toward the German POWs because of what he had experienced at the hands of their fellow countrymen. "I didn't have any hard feelings toward them individually, though I had been treated pretty rough," said Osborn. "They were actually curious as to how I had been treated. When I told them the story of how I was captured, held as a prisoner and then finally escaped, they thought I was exaggerating. Unfortunately it was all true."

Osborn said that though he didn't hold any anger toward them collectively, his experiences made it difficult to have the same sort of carefree, unburdened relationship with the Germans that other GIs enjoyed. With the exception of interaction required by their work, the prisoners kept to themselves and Osborn didn't go out of his way to be friendly with them.

"I never harbored ill will toward them as an entire race," recalled Osborn. "But there were individual guards in Germany who I would happily have strangled if I had the chance."[101]

Although many other workers at Camp Crowder enjoyed the contact with POWs, Verla Mooth, a civilian employee at the post, was deeply resentful of the Germans' presence. With a brother in Europe flying bombing missions over Germany, a brother-in-law who was wounded in the Pacific theater, and a new husband who daily faced the potential of being sent overseas, to Mooth these Germans represented the very embodiment of those who wanted to harm her loved ones.

By December 1944, Mooth was in her third year of working at the post, and her duties in the quartermaster's office included calculating the rations needed for the POW camp based on prisoner population. By this time, news services were carrying accounts of the treatment of American POWs in Europe, and Mooth described her feelings toward the Germans at Camp Crowder as she daily ordered the food to sustain these enemies:

> As more and more stories of the way our POWs were being treated came over the radio, I grew to resent what they were receiving. Several of the POWs had been assigned to work in the warehouses, and I would encounter them being marched back and forth as they passed our office. The "goose step" and stiff backs of the Nazi-style of marching seemed arrogant and defiant to me. I had always had a loving and compassionate nature, but the longer the war lasted, the more bitterness and hatred I felt toward our enemies.

On Christmas Eve morning, Mooth's boss came out and asked for everyone's attention. The German POWs had been saving part of their rations for the past two weeks, he said, and they had made coffee cake and apple strudel for Christmas. They wanted to bring these at 10 A.M. as a gift of appreciation for the kindnesses they had received from the Americans. Mooth described how the scene played out as a German POW came to present the desserts the prisoners had baked for the Americans:

> At 10 A.M. the coffee was boiling when two guards and a young POW drove up to the office. The guards marched in the prisoner who carried two large pans of coffee cake and strudel that smelled delicious. In German they instructed the prisoner to place the pans on a desk that had been cleared off to act as a table. They ordered the POW to stand against the wall, facing my way. Cake and steaming cups of coffee were

passed around and the guards were invited to share. Everyone in the office took some, but I refused to partake. I could hear my co-workers say how delicious the pastry was. But I glared at the prisoner to let him know how I felt.

As the minutes passed, it became harder for Mooth to continue to be so defiant. She noticed how young the prisoner looked:

He was shy and had his head down. I had noticed he was very blond and had china blue eyes. He was only a boy; I would guess he wasn't more than 17 years old. Whiskers had scarcely started to form on his face. I started to think about how awful it would be if my brother were captured and how lonely he would be on Christmas Day. I wondered if this young prisoner had a family in Germany he was thinking about. Did he have sisters, or even a sweetheart? He had not started the war! *Hitler* had started the war.

My heart began to soften just a little. After all, the angels had sung "Peace on Earth" that first Christmas. *Maybe I should have a piece of cake and a cup of coffee*, I murmured to myself.

As I got up from my desk and got a piece of apple strudel, I saw that the young prisoner was watching me. He smiled faintly and I smiled back. Then I saw him raise his arm and brush away a tear.

My heart felt much lighter. I had been judging an entire race by the evil of a few. I knew in that moment that I had just received the most priceless Christmas gift—the ability to forgive.[102]

Expansion of the Labor Program and the Camp

An inspector from the PMGO, Captain Robert B. Heinkel, noted that the thousand-man compound at the POW camp was only half filled, and there was much more work that could be done, in "the Quartermaster laundry, warehouses, rock quarry, repair shops, utility work, clearing the drill fields of loose rock and many other jobs found on a fairly new post to improve its appearance and utility." He estimated that around one thousand prisoners could be employed. Heinkel suggested Camp Crowder, with its long list of waiting tasks, be filled to capacity at once and recommended the transfer of German POWs from Camps Phillips and Concordia, both in Kansas, as well as from the pool of available workers at Camp Clark, seventy miles to the north of Crowder. All three camps had more POWs than could be used on labor projects in their immediate areas, and the need for more workers at the Neosho base was great.[103] The transfer recommended by Heinkel was accomplished in relatively short order, as January 1944 saw the arrival of some 575 German POWs sent to Camp Crowder from Fort Leonard Wood.[104]

Because of increasing numbers of prisoners being sent to the United States, as well as the continued need for workers at the sprawling Neosho post, the government announced plans to expand the POW camp at Crowder in spring 1945. The proposed expansion would double the size of the internment camp, adding a second thousand-man compound to the one already in place. The new compound was situated about one thousand feet from the existing POW facility and was an area formerly used by American soldiers. It incorporated existing structures that were "superior to those existing in the first compound." One thousand prisoners from other U.S. camps arrived to fill the second compound on April 27, 1945, bringing the total interned at the camp to two thousand German POWs.[105]

With the arrival of the new prisoners, a number of new musical and theater activities began, both to occupy the time of the recently arrived residents and to take advantage of the gifted POWs lurking among them. YMCA representative Howard Hong noted that in addition to the two popular orchestras found in the first compound, others were added, including a guitar-mandolin orchestra and one focused only on classical works. "Much talent is being unearthed," wrote Hong, "and local sources are expected to be adequate to supply a minimum need for instruments."

Of course, once they got a look at the advanced athletic program organized among the "old" Crowder prisoners in Compound 1, the new POWs in Compound 2 were eager to begin their own sports program. They were nicely outfitted with four sets of sports equipment kits provided by the PMGO but lacked a place to play. "The main need, therefore, is the leveling of an area set aside for soccer, etc.," wrote Hong. "The men are eager to begin grubbing at it."[106]

Indications of Nazi Presence

With the addition of these new prisoners, it took some time to build up the camp library to meet POW demand. At the end of November 1943, only sixty or seventy books were on hand. By April 1944, more than eleven hundred donated or purchased books, most of them German-language, crowded the shelves. Prisoners subscribed to the usual collection of

English-language newspapers from St. Louis and New York, as well as a number of magazines. One periodical the men flatly refused to have anything to do with, one inspector noted, was the New York–based German-language newspaper *New Yorker Staats-Zeitung*, because of its "rabidly anti-Nazi" content.[107] Of the English-language papers, the POWs told a State Department representative that they favored *The New York Times* and *The Christian Science Monitor* because they considered them the most balanced and the least anti-Nazi of any of the U.S. papers they received.

Though relatively subtle, this dislike of anti-Nazi material pointed to the Nazi presence in the camp. It showed up in the prisoners' religious activity as well. The initial spiritual fervor prisoners displayed during the first few weeks of the camp disappeared rapidly, and it wasn't long before the "remarkable interest" shown in religion in the fall of 1943 became no interest at all. By summer 1944, the Protestant chaplain had completely given up trying to have services. The American Catholic chaplain doggedly continued to give Mass despite the paltry number of prisoners who showed up. By October 1944, the chaplain had been transferred from the camp, and religious services at Crowder had stopped completely.[108] "The religious aspects of the camp—what can and also what cannot be seen from the outside—indicate a seriously abnormal state of things," wrote B. Frank Stoltzfus of the International YMCA in an account of his visit to the camp in November 1944. "The several PWs with whom I talked about this agreed that it was something clearly wrong when only 20 Catholics meet [for] spiritual comfort and when only 2 or 3 Evangelicals congregate for devotion."[109]

This atmosphere of religious antipathy was clearly attributable to the Nazi presence in the camp, an irony given Crowder's otherwise seemingly well deserved reputation for having a peaceful climate and an environment of remarkable cooperation, and especially in light of the high rates of participation in the POW labor program. Of course, disinterest in worship services does not necessarily indicate anything on its own; however, the flagrant flouting of traditional ceremonies that took place at Camp Crowder in favor of a celebration of national and Nazi spirit revealed the true nature of some members of the camp's population, including the POW spokesman and compound leadership.

Charles Eberhardt, who visited Crowder in April 1944, documented what happened when a German POW died in the camp hospital as a result of shrapnel wounds received earlier during the fighting in North Africa:

> The prisoners glory in the fact [that there is no visible interest in religion] and assert that they are 100 percent Nazi. With this attitude

goes one of scoffing at Christianity.

During the last two days preceding the death of the patient referred to above, the American Chaplain at the request of the patient ministered to him frequently. When arrangements were being made for the funeral, the camp spokesman Ludwig Krause presented himself and, stating that acting on behalf of the fellow prisoners, he would take charge of the ceremony.

He further stated that he and his companions did not pray to the same gods as the Americans and Russians and they would conduct their own ceremony in their own way.[110]

At the Krause-led funeral, an open-air ceremony conducted on a stand built especially for the purpose, the spokesman gave a short talk, two poems were recited, and two marching songs were sung by the entire funeral party. Three volleys were fired over the casket, and the remains were shipped to the POW cemetery at Camp Clark, for there were no burial grounds at Crowder. In addition to the POWs present, a number of the camp staff attended the funeral, including the commanding officer Judkins, nine American soldiers, and Lieutenant John Plueger, the Lutheran U.S. Army chaplain who had ministered to the man before he died.[111]

Despite the apparent presence of a good many Nazis in the camp, the prisoners were cooperative and the atmosphere was in most cases pleasant and relaxed. Eberhardt wrote of this phenomenon in a report of his visit:

There has been little or no open friction at this camp between Nazi and anti-Nazi elements; in fact the camp spokesman, Ludwig Krause, insists that the camp is one hundred percent Nazi. Others who know the camp well are skeptical on this point and feel that the minority of anti-Nazis are discreet and know enough not to air their own views too freely.[112]

Of course, had he heard this opinion issued by the State Department representative on conditions at Crowder, POW Hermann Half would have strongly disagreed. Half drew the attention of Nazis at the camp when he skipped the Hitlerfest celebration on the soccer field. He found himself in deeper trouble when they learned Half's wife and brother-in-law back in Germany were actively opposed to the Nazis and that Half's brother-in-law had been meeting once a month in secret with those planning an alternative form of government to Nazi rule.

POW funeral at Camp Crowder, April 1944. Courtesy of Missouri State Archives.

German POWs standing at attention at an April 1944 funeral. Courtesy of Missouri State Archives.

A man named Boulanges led a group of fanatical Nazis at Crowder, said Half, and being on their bad side was dangerous. These men held secret midnight courts and threatened those who were "disloyal" with violence, including beatings and murder by hanging if they didn't shape up. Half was at the top of their list. He was careful to watch his back and not get into situations where he was physically vulnerable to attack. Half's salvation came when the camp administration identified the Nazis and shipped them to another camp specifically designated for these hard-core cases. "When Col Judkins found out what was going on, he transferred out Boulanges and a few of his friends," said Half. "The whole camp was relieved."[113]

This was the irony and the dilemma at Camp Crowder. Other than a few overt cases like this one, the prisoners for the most part behaved themselves and worked hard, regardless of their political disposition. The few noted disciplinary cases almost always involved a POW private disrespecting a German NCO or a prisoner who didn't feel like working on a particular day. Usually, a bread and water diet for a day was enough motivation to rectify the situation.

If there were problems, they usually flew below the radar of camp administration and outside inspectors, who saw Camp Crowder as a peaceful, hardworking camp. There were only a couple incidents that came close to qualifying as a mass disturbance. The first came when a number of POWs refused to undergo required inoculations, the same series of shots administered to a group of American GIs immediately ahead of them in line at the clinic. The prisoners were given tags and cards to present for the inoculations, which suddenly were "lost" when it was time for the shots. The heavy-handed solution to quelling this revolt was to simply close the sports area to all activity until the lost certificates were found and all POWs agreed to be inoculated, which happened almost at once.[114]

On another occasion in spring 1944, POWs notified the camp administration that they intended to observe April 20, Adolf Hitler's birthday, as a holiday and would not be working that day. Major Judkins told the men that the U.S. Army observed only one holiday a year and that they would be treated the same way. If they wanted to celebrate Hitler's birthday by staying home from work, he said, their party would be in the guardhouse with a special banquet of bread and water in honor of the event. Prisoners went to work that day as always and moved the activities marking the occasion to the evening. April 20 came and went with no disruption, though much murmuring occurred among the prisoners.

At the same time, the POWs were preparing for the arrival of May Day. There was a buzz among the prisoners about a strike to take place on May 1 in honor of the workers holiday celebrated by socialists, labor unions, and the like in many countries outside the United States. Again, Judkins averted trouble by promising appropriately "severe" measures if there were acts of disobedience. The soccer field would surely be closed to the men, and more ominously, Judkins threatened some with removal to the POW camps at Fort Leonard Wood, or Alva, Oklahoma, where conditions were much more strict. That was a real threat; there was a unique atmosphere at Camp Crowder, a remarkable environment of mutual respect and cooperation and a notable lack of visible turmoil. Despite the homesickness and the fear of violent Nazis, the prisoners at Camp Crowder found much to like in life as a POW.[115]

"They were a proud bunch," said Herman Martinelli, an American GI who attended Signal Corps training at Crowder in 1945 and stayed on through the next year to work in the out-processing center. "When they went from their compound to work, they'd march in cadence, goose-stepping down the street. It was really impressive—the sound of their boots on the pavement. Whomp! Whomp! Whomp!"[116]

"I hesitate to think what might happen to their minds and hearts if suddenly they should have orders to move to another camp," wrote B. Frank

Stoltzfus, a visitor to the camp in November 1944. "Both Sgt. Armbuster, the German spokesman, and the canteen manager, Sgt. Frenkel, often repeated their admiration for Major Judkins in particular. They pointed out to me the open gates leading out, although there were guards about."[117]

Most of the time, the situation at Camp Crowder was so serene that even the once-stringent security measures were relaxed. MPs who originally trained and utilized sixteen guard dogs, both attackers and trailers, cut that number in half. "There has been no need for their services as there have been no escapes and no known attempts to escape," noted a State Department visitor in April 1944. The number of guards in the towers was also cut in half, so only one man stood watch from each point, where two were previously mandatory. By August 1944, prisoners were working wholly unguarded outside the POW complex in the Camp Crowder confines. They went freely about their tasks in the motor pool, laundry, and warehouses.[118] "The camp commandant trusts the prisoners and gives them much responsibility," wrote Paul Schnyder of the International Red Cross. "This system works perfectly for the commandant obtains excellent cooperation."[119]

Although things in the camp generally were good, the POWs were still human, which meant that they liked to gripe, almost as a form of recreation, and would do so to anyone who would listen. These complaints were sometimes valid, sometimes not. During an April 1944 visit, POWs complained to representatives of the Swiss Legation and U.S. Department of State that things got monotonous for prisoners assigned to a particular task for any length of time. They wanted more variety in their work and surroundings. When Major Judkins heard this, to the amusement of both inspectors, he told the prisoners that he was not running a "tourist agency" on their behalf and that they would have to accept the work as it was assigned to them.

Other POWs griped that the comforters on their bunks badly needing washing. These prisoners were told that the comforters—the same kind as were used by U.S. troops—were made from material that could not be simply thrown in the laundry, but they would receive the special dry cleaning they required in due time. Significant issues, indeed, these challenges facing the prisoners.[120]

Classes

By April 1944, seven months after the arrival of the prisoners, classes at the Crowder POW camp were underway. An internee who was an influential and highly respected educator in Germany prior to the war was selected to direct the schools in the camp, and he quickly put together an ambitious curriculum of courses in basic and advanced English, elementary and higher-level math, stenography, history, and various technical subjects. The director of classes told the State Department's Charles Eberhardt that 55 percent of the Crowder POWs were enrolled in at least one course.[121]

By late summer 1944, contact was established with the University of Chicago for assistance in offering POW instruction. The curriculum expanded accordingly, and courses in accounting, German, and Latin were added as well as a practical mechanics course for which the prisoners bought a motor to take apart and put back together. In addition to the classes, POW instructors held forth once or twice a week on various areas of personal expertise, offering lectures on such diverse topics as natural history; anatomy; Julius Caesar's history of the Gallic War, *De Bello Gallico*; and a discussion of the seventeenth-century play *Tartuffe* by Molière.[122]

School was held in the former guardhouse, as the lack of disciplinary problems meant that the space was almost always unoccupied. Working during their free time, the prisoners actually transformed the building into a top-notch modern educational facility, centrally heated with three classrooms equipped with chalkboards with indirect lighting, a typewriter, and a mimeograph machine, as well as private rooms in which the full-time teaching staff lived.[123]

With the introduction of the top-secret POW re-education program, the list of classes offered at Camp Crowder was expanded yet again. Although language courses such as French and Russian were added to the curriculum, in accordance with the Special Projects Division's aim of changing German opinions of democracy and the United States, most of the classes offered at the camp were focused on English and American history. Nine Americans served as part-time instructors, including the assistant executive officer, who taught one of the American history courses as part of his duties of overseeing the reorientation of German prisoners through the intellectual diversions program. Ten German instructors were also on the "faculty"; five of these taught full time, and five taught part time.

Escape

As at other POW camps in Missouri, the escape rate at the Neosho base was low. However, in May 1944, two Crowder POWs, Gunther Schmidt and Lothar Schedlbauer, decided to do some sightseeing and left the camp when the guards weren't looking. The men were on the run for two days, and patrols made up of 150 Crowder GIs and members of the Missouri State Highway Patrol scoured the area, searching primarily around the towns of Ritchey and Grandby, fifteen miles east of Neosho. The men were captured in McDonald County, however, south of the camp, when they showed up at a quiet country farmhouse and banged on the door, asking for food. The farmer called the authorities, who quickly dispatched a party to bring the men back to camp. The two returned to Crowder, ready to escape the chiggers and ticks and to resume their life of mess-hall chow and comfortable barracks bunks.

In May 1945, another Crowder duo, Hermann Heitmann and Karl Leininghaus, escaped from the POW camp and were recaptured early the next morning in Springfield by a city policeman. These men again offered no resistance and even mentioned that they were glad to be going back to camp, remarking that spending a single "very wet night in the open" was enough for them.

Another POW who wanted to escape decided that there had to be a better method than jumping fences or burrowing out. He had plenty of time to consider these options while confined in the stockade, so on the day of his escape, his plan was in place and virtually foolproof. He slipped undetected from the stockade into the supply warehouse and outfitted himself with a complete U.S. Army uniform. The POW strolled confidently through the camp grounds, only to be seized by the first guard to see the handsome "GI" wearing a uniform matched with a hat usually issued only to members of the Women's Army Corps.[124]

Family Ties

In one of the more unusual events involving POWs at Camp Crowder—and one that showed the U.S. government's willingness to make accommodations for the benefit of POWs where the security risk and expense were minimal—officials at the Security and Intelligence Division of the PMGO permitted the transfer of internees from one camp to another to allow a father and son to be housed together at Camp Crowder.

Private Gerhard Heyde came to Camp Crowder on January 17, 1944. His father, Willy Heyde, was also a German POW and was housed at Camp McAlester, Oklahoma. The elder Heyde requested a transfer so that the two might be reunited, and the government approved this action, as neither prisoner was disruptive nor identified as being a political agitator. The prisoners involved were responsible for covering the cost of the transfer, including transportation, meals, and other expenses for themselves and the guards who accompanied them while in transit. Gerhard and Willy were reunited at Camp Crowder on March 21, 1944. Costs for Willy Heyde's trip and that of the guard who accompanied him were covered by Gerhard and two of his friends, Willy Meyer and Heinrich Hamann, who each contributed $10.84 to allow father and son to reunite.[125]

A transfer of prisoners was repeated in December 1944, after the PMGO approved a request by Crowder POW Karl Wippich to have his brother Fritz transferred from the POW camp at Fort Custer, Michigan, to the Missouri facility so that the two could be together.[126] "I have received information that my brother, Gefreiter [Private] Fritz Wippich, is also in the United States as a prisoner of war," Wippich wrote in a letter to Judkins on November 29, 1944. "Since I have not seen him for several years, I would like to be with him again very much."

This family reunion cost the Wippiches $64.70, which included $35.83 for the guard's round-trip transportation and $19.87 for the prisoner's one-way ride, $6.00 for six meals for the guard, and another $3.00 for Wippich's three meals while en route.[127]

A third request of this nature involving Crowder prisoners was denied by POW authorities. German POW Josef Vietoris requested that his brother Hans Vietoris, housed at the camp in Hearne, Texas, be allowed to transfer to the Neosho base. The request was denied because Hans Vietoris was considered a noncooperative prisoner and had shown himself to be a disruptive influence on several occasions. The PMGO, however, left open the possibility for a future transfer. "In the event German prisoner of war, Hans Vietoris, becomes a cooperative noncommissioned officer prisoner of war by his future conduct," wrote the PMGO, "this office will approve the transfer provided all other conditions are met."[128]

In addition to reuniting family members, the United States was marrying people. German POWs held in the United States were legally able to wed their sweethearts back home in absentia, through the practice of proxy marriages that were arranged on an infrequent basis through official channels. Often big "wedding receptions" complete with food and music were held at the POW compounds, where the newly married couple—minus the bride—was honored. A notary public was on duty at Camp Crowder who performed "commendable services" in certifying signatures, principally for the process of proxy marriages, wrote Charles Eberhardt of the Department of State in November 1943.[129]

Judkins Criticized

The good times couldn't last forever at Camp Crowder, especially when others in the higher-level POW camp administration caught wind of the unique arrangements Major Judkins made with the prisoners to secure their cooperation in promoting a peaceful camp environment and their participation in the work program. Judkins's first major run-in came when Captain Walter Rapp of the POW Special Projects Division visited Camp Crowder

April 27–28, 1945, to discuss with Judkins the top-secret reorientation program being phased in at POW camps across the United States.

Rapp wanted to hear from Judkins about the progress made in the re-education of the Crowder prisoners, as well as to evaluate the work of Captain Robert W. Shaw, who was assigned to Crowder as the assistant executive officer, the dummy title given to the officer at each camp specifically in charge of the re-education program. Rapp considered Shaw "a man with exceptionally good cultural and educational background, and one who is capable of being an excellent assistant executive officer" and knew that Judkins was not allowing him to operate in the role that the re-education program intended. Judkins wanted no part of any such discussion with Rapp and resented Rapp's presence at the camp. Judkins was openly hostile toward Rapp and told him at their very first meeting it was inconceivable that a "visiting fireman" from Washington had to scrutinize his camp because there had never been any trouble.[130]

Whether Judkins did not understand the purpose and nature of the re-education program or did not agree with its intent and methodology is not clear. What is known, however, is that Judkins gave Rapp as little chance to explain why he was there and what the program was about as he gave assistance and cooperation to Captain Shaw, who was supposed to be overseeing the program. Rapp noted in his account of the visit that Judkins told Rapp that he was tolerating Shaw only because he was ordered to do so by Major General Brehon Somervell (commander of the Army Service Forces, and one of Judkins's bosses) and that Judkins hindered Shaw's work in every way possible. "Without a doubt Major Judkins has made it difficult, if not impossible, for the assistant executive officer to perform his duties with any hope for ultimate success. The Commanding officer gave Captain Shaw a direct order to keep out of the compound," wrote Rapp. "It is unfortunate that the initiative and efforts of Captain Shaw have been hampered by the shortsighted and unmilitary attitude of the camp commander."[131]

The men struggled to have a civil conversation. Rapp attempted to explain that his sole reason for visiting was to offer advice and assistance in the promotion of the Intellectual Diversion Program, but Judkins persisted in badgering the man with questions wholly unrelated to the matter. "Captain Rapp had no success in explaining his position as the camp commander insisted on asking questions concerning camp operations," noted Rapp, writing in the third person. "When Captain Rapp was unable to answer or stated that he had no authority to answer such questions, Major Judkins used Captain Rapp's behavior as irrefutable evidence that there was no necessity to visit this camp."[132]

Then, whether out of anger over his treatment in Neosho or in genuine concern for Camp Crowder and the prospects for success of the Special Projects Division (which Judkins wholeheartedly opposed), Rapp wrote two sentences that would damage Major Judkins's efforts to promote harmony at Camp Crowder and indeed his personal vision and strategy for himself as a leader. "It was most evident that Major Judkins had only one concern and that was to avoid trouble with the prisoners of war," charged Rapp in his report. "He frankly admitted that he would lean over backwards to accomplish that end."[133]

These were explosive words. At the same time of Rapp's visit, a national controversy raged in the press, in Washington, and around kitchen tables in homes across America about the perceived soft treatment of prisoners being held here. Images of Nazi POWs living a life of luxury and ease, enjoying recreation and rich foods forbidden to ordinary citizens, were portrayed in the press in contrast with the harrowing experiences endured by POWs in Nazi Germany. Rapp's accusations were about the most serious he could make against a commander of a POW camp, and he was well aware of the implications.

Rapp proceeded to compile a lengthy list of evidence to prove Judkins was coddling the prisoners to keep them appeased. He sent the damning information directly to Washington. Rapp went into great detail to describe the scene at the camp:

> Numerous pets and all the necessary housing facilities were found in compound one. There were eight fat pigs who are fed the garbage from the mess halls. Upon questioning by Captain Rapp, the spokesman admitted that a pig had recently been slaughtered to augment the normal subsistence of the prisoners....
>
> Almost every barrack had an elaborate outside aerial. Those aerials could be used for short wave reception, since each one was constructed around a mast from eight to twelve feet in height. Flourishing flower beds, trellises, small ponds filled with fish, sprinkling fountains, and ducks swimming about, all contributed to make the camp seem more like a sanitarium. Through landscaping, the beautification and construction of special shacks, stables and other facilities, the camp commander has made every effort to keep the boys happy in order to avoid trouble.[134]

Rapp's report ran counter to accounts from previous visitors to the camp, who had praised the camp and the commander's handing of its residents. Reasonable disciplinary measures with clearly communicated standards became "coddling" in Rapp's eyes, and where others saw an amiable relationship between Judkins and the camp spokesman, Ludwig Krause, Rapp saw the commander being manipulated by a crafty Nazi. In the report of his visit, Rapp accused Judkins of violating several War Department directives rather than risk upsetting the prisoners. As evidence, he cited the introduction of *Der Ruf,* the national German-language camp newspaper put out by the Special Projects Division:

> [Judkins] had refused to allow *Der Ruf* to be placed on sale in the canteens. The spokesman had complained about the contents of the first issue of that magazine and demanded that its sale be discontinued or he could not guarantee tranquility in the camp.

> Major Judkins immediately complied with that demand by ordering the assistance executive officer [Shaw] not to put succeeding issues of *Der Ruf* on sale. The camp commander informed Captain Rapp that he was extremely annoyed because the War Department did not consult him prior to the appearance of *Der Ruf.* He further stated that if his opinion had been requested he would have replied, "The paper isn't worth a damn."[135]

Judkins only allowed *Der Ruf* to be placed on sale in the canteen after the service command headquarters directed him to do so, starting with the release of the fourth issue.

Additionally, Rapp noted, Judkins did not put other magazines and newspapers on sale in the canteen that had been directed for use as part of the re-education program by the provost marshal general. Judkins's response was that he ordered such material placed directly in the barracks and given to the barracks' leaders so as to assure its equitable distribution, an action that played right into the hands of the Nazis who controlled the camp, said Rapp:

> That procedure has made it possible for the spokesman and his friends to control the circulation of all magazines and newspapers and to dispose of all reading material which is not approved by them. The prisoners of war who do not fall into line with the spokesman's political views can read only what is allowed to filter through to them.[136]

Rapp also claimed that Judkins made no effort whatsoever to segregate the most active Nazis from the rest of the prisoner population. In fact, they held leadership positions within the internal POW hierarchy. The compound leader, chief interpreter, and director of studies were all extremely militant Nazis, said Rapp, who described the men as "young, aggressive and overbearing" and noted that they did not miss a single opportunity to criticize and condemn the United States while talking to Rapp. Judkins had secondhand knowledge of these attitudes but told Rapp that he would not take any action against the men, as he had no evidence to back it up. Rapp blasted this lack of active assessment of the political temperament of the POWs at Crowder and noted that these avowed Nazis were in fact put in charge of in-processing the one thousand new prisoners who had just arrived, allowing these men the opportunity to assess each new POW for his loyalty to National Socialism. "The newly arrived prisoners of war were processed by other prisoners under the supervision of a few enlisted men," wrote Rapp. "The strong-armed Nazis had an excellent opportunity to look over the new arrivals from France, size each one up, and if necessary, indoctrinate each prisoner before he could step out of line."

Ultimately, the POW spokesman was the one really running the place, Rapp said. "The camp commander has made every effort to coddle the prisoners of war and make them feel at home. He has used every means to win their whole-hearted cooperation and good will, even to the extent of sacrificing the integrity of his own personnel," said Rapp. "It is at once apparent to even the most casual observer that the camp spokesman wields a big stick and he is able to tell the camp commander what to do."[137]

According to Rapp's account, the ordinary GIs working at the camp deeply resented these conditions and only the prisoners and Judkins were happy with the way things were run. Rapp said that both enlisted men and officers substantiated the information he received about Judkins's administration. Rapp asserted that one enlisted guard told him, just before they went into the POW compound, "I guess, Captain, you and I might just as well go inside and have the prisoners guard us, then we could live the life of Riley."

Even Lieutenant Colonel Frakes, commanding officer at the POW facility at Camp Clark, chimed in with criticism of his own. Frakes was "aware of the deplorable conditions" at Camp Crowder, wrote Rapp, and Frakes believed that the situation should be reported to the provost marshal general. "During a recent visit to Prisoner of War Camp, Camp Crowder, Missouri," Rapp quotes Frakes as saying, "I saw the most clear evidence of pampering, coddling and fraternization that I have ever seen in any prisoner of war camp." Frakes was both disgusted and infuriated, said Rapp, by the complete lack of discipline among the prisoners and the obvious control of the camp by the POWs rather than by camp authorities. "The only difference between the prisoners of war and the American guard personnel stationed at Camp Crowder is that the prisoners are not able to obtain three-day passes to go home," said Frakes, who worried what would happen were the conditions at Camp Crowder brought to the attention of such high-profile commentators as Walter Winchell or Drew Pearson. "There'd be hell to pay," said Frakes, if these prominent and influential men who were already vocal in their criticism of the POW situation in the United States found out about the *biergartens* and bandstands and everything else the prisoners were enjoying at Camp Crowder. Frakes concurred with Captain Rapp on the need for a complete investigation of the conditions at the camp.[138]

How is it that a camp which was continually being praised in official inspection reports by both U.S. and international agencies as one of the best in the nation was suddenly condemned as the perhaps the worst example of how to run a POW camp? How is it that an administration ceaselessly lauded for the peace and tranquility it fostered both among the prisoner population and in relations with the camp administration, and the 95 percent participation rate it garnered in the POW labor program, could be suddenly criticized for creating a den of Nazi activity? The many activities and simple but unusual comforts were not done in order to pamper the prisoners, asserted Judkins. Even an inspection report made by the neutral Swiss Legation in March 1945 noted that the activities Judkins allowed were undertaken "with the understanding that the continuation of such privileges was contingent upon the continued cooperation of the prisoners."[139] These actions described as coddling, said Judkins, were done using prisoner labor and scrap materials and at no extra cost to the government. It was all done for the sake of maintaining good relations in the camp and high participation in the labor program. Judkins continually pointed to the unparalleled number of working POWs and the fact that there were few disciplinary problems as evidence that his approach, though unorthodox, was highly effective.

Judkins's response when asked by Captain Rapp if he as camp commander approved the menagerie of animals housed in the POW zoo underscored most clearly his reasons for allowing prisoners to have these unique privileges. "If you let the prisoners have this kind of stuff you are sure to avoid trouble," said Judkins, "and we are working the prisoners very hard on this post."[140] Judkins's philosophy of running the camp was based on two principles. First, he let prisoners be creative and allowed them leeway to do what they wanted in their free time as long as that privilege was not abused. Second, he gave them any opportunity to work and then to spend the money they earned. Letters from Crowder POWs to their families reflected the effectiveness of Judkins's approach from the prisoners' perspective. "We are living in nice barracks and all the furnishings are first class. There is also enough work for us to do, and the treatment and food is good. Therefore, dear parents, you do not need to worry about me," wrote POW Horst Bieler to his family in Leipzig, Germany. "There is also a canteen where many good things can be obtained, especially sweet things. Smoking supplies are also available there."[141]

Another POW, Gerhard Richter, wrote to his wife about the prisoners' opportunities to enjoy themselves during their free time. "We also have plenty of entertainment," he wrote. "There is a sportsfield and a social hall where there are plenty of games available."[142]

Karl-Heinz Richter described the positive impact that Judkins's approach had on the POWs most clearly:

> Our life in camp, as we were well-treated and cared for, gave us comfort. The commanding officer, Major Judkins, got us the instruments. He allowed us to have pets. Dogs, cats, birds, rabbits and guinea pigs! The freedom we were given was so good!...
>
> Speaking to other POWs that were stationed in the U.S., I discovered that some prisoners of war in the U.S. were not always treated as well as we were at Crowder. I thank Major Judkins for being the humane man that he was to all of us Germans.[143]

Judkins also asserted that his style of running the POW camp was done with the complete approval of the post commander. While this was true, particularly with Judkins's friend and former boss Lieutenant Colonel Teachout who was in charge of the post from April 1942 to July 1944, a new commander, Brigadier General Milliken had only recently assumed command. Milliken said that he was unfamiliar with the operations of the POW camp but promised to look into the matter.

Others in the chain of command claimed similar ignorance of conditions and practices at the Crowder POW camp. In addition to reporting his concerns to the PMGO in Washington, D.C., Rapp reported them to the Seventh Service Command in Omaha, Nebraska. Officials of that headquarters, which oversaw the operations of Crowder's POW camp, were appalled, said Rapp. "Although they could offer no explanation as to why such conditions had been allowed to exist," they assured Rapp "that immediate corrective action would be taken."[144]

In the end, it is not clear what effect Rapp's allegations had on the atmosphere at Camp Crowder and on Judkins's style of administration. Judkins remained in his role as POW camp commander and was promoted from major to lieutenant colonel immediately on the heels of this incident. No further mention of these problems was made by U.S. inspectors, and the other visitors to the camps—the normal rotation of Red Cross, YMCA, and Swiss Legation representatives—continued their usual unstinting praise for Judkins and the atmosphere of the camp. "Discipline appeared excellent and morale appeared to be very good," wrote Karl Almquist of the YMCA after a visit in September 1945. Guy Metraux of

Lieutenant Colonel George Teachout, commander of Camp Crowder. Courtesy of Camp Crowder Collection, Crowder College.

the International Red Cross Committee paid a call to Crowder in mid-October 1945. "This is an outstandingly good camp as has been previously reported. The camp is well ordered and well administered," Metraux wrote. "There was no evidence of tension within the camp, yet military courtesies are strictly observed and considerable freedom of movement within the camp was permitted."[145]

Closure of the POW Camp

Beginning in February 1946, U.S. authorities at Camp Crowder began to ship the German POWs to other U.S. camps as the first step in the process of returning them to Europe. The last group finally left May 7, 1946. Departing prisoners bundled their possessions in barracks bags slung over their shoulders, taking with them the clothing issued during their stay in the United States, various other personal effects they had accumulated, their bedding, and a maximum of four cartons of cigarettes. Sixty-five pounds of baggage were permitted for each enlisted prisoner, with officers being able to bring home 175 pounds, though none came near that upper limit, said post officials. Each POW also carried a military payment order that would be cashed out upon arrival in Germany for the funds they had accrued in camp accounts through their monthly allotment and earned from the POW labor program.

The *Camp Crowder Message* captured the scene the day the last prisoners left:

> A locomotive whistle cutting through the night air Tuesday signaled not only the departure of another troop train from the post, but also the closing down of Crowder's prisoner of war camp after two years and seven months of operation.
>
> Aboard the train were 212 German prisoners, headed for repatriation back in their homeland. They were the last remnants of the 2,000 PWs who had been confined at Crowder during the war years.[146]

Neosho had changed forever when the U.S. government established Camp Crowder in 1941 on the southern edge of town. The town swelled from a population of 5,000 to over 20,000 during the construction phase, then stabilized at a level around 10,000 people while the camp itself, a U.S. Army Signal Corps Training Center, flooded the streets and shops of Neosho with its average on-post population of 40,000 uniformed men and women. From 1941 to 1946, some 300,000 servicemen and women passed through its gates. The impact of Camp Crowder's establishment can only be matched by the impact of its closure. The millions of dollars spent locally by the government and soldiers disappeared almost entirely when World War II ended.[147]

By 1946, the government was selling off $7.5 million worth of surplus fixtures and equipment from the site, as noted in an article in the *St. Louis Globe-Democrat*. "Equipment to be offered includes office, store, warehouse, restaurant, barber shop, beauty shop and service station fixtures. Also included is household furniture, such as curtains and Venetian blinds, and woodworking, gymnasium and athletic equipment." World War II veterans had top priority for the sale of goods, which lasted eight days.[148] Whole buildings were dismantled and hauled off for use elsewhere, including most of the POW barracks. Declared surplus, the barracks, plumbing fixtures and all, were transferred by the War Department to the War Assets Administration for disposal. Nearly fifty of these buildings, prefabricated and easily disassembled and moved, went to the University of Missouri campuses at Columbia and Rolla as well as other colleges, where they housed student veterans arriving for school.[149]

Jim Tisoto was one of the servicemen who returned to school after the war. He and literally thousands of other former soldiers used the GI Bill to fund their education and flooded campuses across the United States starting in the fall of 1945. At the University of Missouri–Columbia, Tisoto lived in one of the former POW barracks that had been moved there. "There were four students to a room, and every pair of rooms shared a common area. Two more rooms meant that there were sixteen of us in each one of these buildings," said Tisoto. "I must say that they were darn nice accommodations considering all the places they were putting people back then."[150]

Another structure torn down and rebuilt in another location was the Officers' Club, leveled by the Federal Works Agency in November 1947 and then shipped to Central College (now Central Methodist College) in Fayette, Missouri, for use as a student recreation center.[151] The remaining buildings stayed on site and were leased for grain storage, the raising of broiler chickens, and many other purposes.[152]

In the years after the war, various proposals were floated for the camp, including a massive state institution for the senile to be located in the twenty-seven-hundred-bed hospital. Those discussions became pointless, however, when Crowder was reactivated in 1951 to serve as a reception center for the Korean War and for use after the war as a military prison until the post was closed again in January 1958.[153]

Following the second closure of the camp, conversation again turned to possible uses for the site. State representative Robert E. Young of Jasper County proposed that the state take over Crowder for use as a badly needed hospital and school for the mentally retarded. That idea was squashed, and the government began selling off land occupied by the camp. The original owners purchased some of it, but much went to investors and others wanting to farm or build homes in the area. Community and business leaders used other parts of the camp to create an industrial park, and yet another section of the installation became the home for Crowder College after the University of Missouri accepted the title to 634 buildings and 9,570 acres for the purposes of establishing a vocational school.

Additionally, a sizable part of the former post was turned into a wildlife preserve administered by the Missouri Department of Conservation, open for hunting and other outdoor pursuits. Finally, a small area continues to be used by the Missouri National Guard, and a mock POW camp has been built on the site for training MPs.[154]

German POWs living in barracks on the Hellwig Brothers farm near Chesterfield, Missouri, march into the mess hall for supper. The letters "PW" are stamped prominently on the rejected GI clothing they wear. Photograph by Post-Dispatch *staff photographer, March 27, 1945.* St. Louis Post-Dispatch *News Research Department.* © *1945,* St. Louis Post-Dispatch.

Chapter Seven

St. Louis–Area Branch Camps

AS THE SHORTAGE OF ABLE WORKERS GREW more intense in early 1943, government officials hatched a plan to create so-called branch camps, smaller operations located apart from the main camps that put the prisoners where their work was most needed.

Being away from the main camp was often a nice change of pace for both prisoners and guards, and relaxed conditions at the branch camps sometimes turned into such easygoing situations that without the uniforms, it was unclear who was supposed to be guarding whom. Sometimes this laissez-faire environment caused difficulty for those who were serious about sticking to regulations.

Gene Enchelmaier, who lived in the area of the Chesterfield, Missouri, branch camp west of St. Louis, remembered when local farmer Phillip Meyer earned the ire of the guards one day when returning prisoners he had hired to the camp, which was located at the Hellwig Brothers Farms in the Gumbo Flats. Meyer, who tilled acreage in the area of U.S. Highway 40 and State Highway 141, just east of the Chesterfield valley, was very tired one night as he and the prisoners were coming in from the field. Enchelmaier recalled:

> Meyer was so tired that he didn't feel like driving the men back to the camp. He took one of the German POWs, put him behind the wheel of his truck and told the man to take the others prisoner back to Gumbo and then to return again in the morning. That guard was really beside himself when they [the prisoners] pulled into the lane.[1]

There were other reasons to try to leave the branch camps, too. Verna Hellwig, who was married to George Hellwig, youngest of the four Hellwig brothers whose farm

281

housed the camp, recalled that the family suspected one of the prisoners was sneaking out at night.

"Bill [Hellwig, the oldest brother] lived right there and some days his daughter would come out and find her bike in a different spot than where she left it the night before," said Verna Hellwig. It wasn't until Bill Hellwig was driving one night and spotted the white "PW" on the man's uniform reflecting in his headlights, the cyclist's legs pumping the pedals of a little girl's bike down the road for yet another romantic liaison, that they knew for sure what the man was up to.[2]

"Certainly it was possible to disappear out of the camp without being discovered for a night. But I don't know anyone who made a custom of doing so," recalled Walter Minning, a POW at the Chesterfield camp. "Somebody having a girlfriend, that I only knew about in one case. Naturally, he couldn't stay out more than just that one night."[3]

In Missouri, most branch camps were established to support agricultural operations and, in many cases, were created expressly so that POW labor could satisfy seasonal labor needs. Examples of these types of work include picking cotton in the Bootheel, detasseling corn stalks in central and southeast Missouri, and harvesting potatoes in the areas near Independence, which at the time was home to some of the nation's leading potato producers. Branch camps provided much-needed labor for a short-term but intensive phase of activity that normally lasted only up to two months, depending on the specific crop. Other camps provided longer-term support to agricultural activity not so seasonally driven. Prisoners at the branch camp in Louisiana, Missouri, worked at the Stark Bro's Nursery and Orchards pruning trees, tending to seedlings, and performing a dozen other tasks. Prisoners at the Hellwig Brothers Farms near Chesterfield worked year-round as well. Whether tending to vegetables in the vast truck-farm operations in the rich loam of the Gumbo Flats or working on farms or in greenhouses and nurseries in Des Peres, Kirkwood, or other St. Louis suburbs, the prisoners were kept remarkably busy.

Despite the emphasis on satisfying agriculture's need for farm labor, several other Missouri branch camps were established specifically to place POWs where there were industrial labor needs. Prisoners in Hannibal, Missouri, for instance, worked on a short-term project sorting shoes in the Bluff City Shoe Factory, while downstream their interned compatriots in St. Louis helped assemble truck bodies and facilitated the repair and shipment of replacement parts for military vehicles. On the western side of the state, prisoners worked in cold-storage plants in the Kansas City area, as well as at the U.S. Gypsum plant on the north end of town.

The most unusual type of branch camp was the boat camps, floating operations where prisoners lived on "quarterboats" equipped with bunks, a kitchen, and a latrine. The men, usually captured Navy personnel, performed dredging operations and other river work in conjunction with the Corps of Engineers. Additional POWs stationed at the boat camps stayed in these floating barracks only at night; they came ashore during the day for levee-repair projects and work in boat yards along the rivers.

Boat camps were located on the Mississippi and Missouri Rivers at St. Louis, Chesterfield, Gasconade, Glasgow, Grand Pass, and Washington, Missouri, and official inspection reports noted how these Navy POWs appreciated the chance to work on the river. "The beauty and fascination of flowing water is, of course, not wasted on seamen. They like to be here rather than in a land camp," wrote Howard Hong of the International YMCA, who visited virtually every Missouri camp, both on land and on water.[4]

Branch Camps Background

In January 1943, the War Department, the PMGO, and other agencies responsible for overseeing the POW program in the United States knew that they had a ready pool of labor in the 175,000 POWs held in the United States. They had decided early on, however, to locate the camps as far away as possible from settled areas for security reasons, and that meant that the POW labor could not be easily accessed.

While there were, in fact, limited opportunities for POWs to be engaged in agricultural labor in the areas immediately surrounding the big camps, most of the work was seasonal and required extensive use of limited transportation resources. Additionally, a number of prisoners could be utilized in capacities related to the actual operations of the main POW camp, but that number was usually only a small fraction of the three thousand to five thousand men held in most of the camps. Having large groups of unemployed, inactive POWs together created a volatile situation, reported the inspector general, who surveyed POW work utilization in the stateside camps in 1943. The situation prompted an urgent recommendation that something be done to occupy the prisoners and, at the same time, remedy some of the pressing labor issues facing the nation.[5]

The inspector general's report showed that because of the camps' isolation, only about 40 to 60 percent of the POWs available for work were actually engaged in any type of employment, and of this group, only a fraction was taking part in truly useful activity. Of those working, about a third were engaged in the maintenance of the larger military posts where they were housed, another third were involved in POW camp administrative operations, and the rest worked in agricultural operations and other miscellaneous projects. The report declared that the POW camps were for the most part too big, too elaborate, and in perhaps the worst locations for maximum use of the prisoners' labor.

The PMGO sought the input of other government agencies, including the War Manpower Commission and the Department of Agriculture. The PMGO wanted to work cooperatively with them to identify possible work projects near established camps, and it asked that they suggest sites for new camps with nearby projects on which prisoners could be employed and that they identify areas where internees could be used to help meet seasonal farm demands. The responses to these requests started the branch camp program.[6]

The branch camp program took full flight after a key August 1943 agreement was hammered out between the War Department and the War Manpower Commission. This agreement provided specific guidance on the POW labor program to both camp commanders and prospective employers and eliminated the existing bureaucratic vagueness that previously hamstrung widespread use of prisoner labor. The agreement finally nailed down important details, including the exact types of work for which prisoners could be used; established the priorities for use of prisoner workers; and provided instructions to contractors on how to determine the cost of POW labor.

By June 1944, nearly three-quarters of all eligible prisoners were working, and by April 1945, that percentage had reached nearly 90 percent. That increase is directly attributable to the activation of many new branch camps and a greater focus on transferring prisoners within and between service commands to put them where their labor was most needed.[7]

Support of Branch Camps

For several reasons, untangling the connections between the main camps in Missouri and the branch camps they supported can be a confusing process. First, not all main camps supported branch camps. Camp Crowder, for instance, operated no side camps because of its relatively late date of establishment and its enormous appetite for labor generated on the post itself, where supporting forty thousand GIs consumed all POW workers available. After the arrival of German prisoners in August 1944, Camp Clark became another main camp that supported no branch camps.

Although the first internees at Camp Clark, Italian prisoners of war, had been assigned to distant camps in Springfield and Kansas City during their relatively short stay at Clark, those operations ended once the facility became chiefly a punishment camp for the most hard-core Nazis. A few short weeks each summer provided exception to that generality, when Clark's cooperative POWs picked potatoes in Atherton and Orrick, Missouri.

Additionally, some Missouri branch camps were sponsored by main camps located out of state. Fort Riley, Kansas, was responsible for the operations of camps at Liberty and Lexington, Missouri, and Iowa's Camp Clarinda oversaw the Missouri POW camps at Hannibal, Independence, New Madrid, and Orrick, as well as those at Marston, Lexington, and Liberty for a time. This overlap in operational responsibility between Fort Riley and Camp Clarinda for the Lexington and Liberty camp administration was common. The amount of labor available at a given base camp, coupled with the specific need for workers at a given location, meant that a main camp might operate a seasonal branch camp one year and not the next, when another main camp might send POW workers to that location. The POW camp at Fort Leonard Wood, for instance, sent its POWs to work at the branch camps at Independence, Liberty, Orrick, and Marston, which as noted above were all operated at other times under the supervision of other main camps. Essentially, the POW camp commanders in Missouri and neighboring states worked with a higher-level coordinator, the commander of the Seventh Service Command in Omaha, Nebraska, to allocate available POWs from the main camps to the branch camps, making best use of the prisoner labor pool.

The main Missouri camps supported work at branch camps in a number of other states as well. In addition to spawning five auxiliary camps in Missouri, the five-thousand-man internment facility at Weingarten oversaw the operations of branch camps in Kansas, Iowa, and Colorado. In time, the primary purpose of the main camps evolved into operating and supporting the various branches grafted around the state, serving, in essence, as a central distribution hub, shipping prisoners around as dictated by the need for labor.

Colonel H. H. Glidden noted exactly how far the Weingarten camp's reach extended through these branch camps in his discussion of the operation with the *Ste. Genevieve Herald* in April 1945. "The administration of the Italian PW Branch Camps, of which there are eight at the present time, continues to be one of the main functions of the base camp at Weingarten," said Glidden. "All branch camps are located in areas where civilian labor shortage is critical. These PW's thus engaged are helping very materially to alleviate the present manpower shortage in the Seventh Service Command."[8]

Fort Leonard Wood sponsored fifteen branch camps, including four boat camps, two branch camps at other Missouri military installations (Jefferson Barracks in St. Louis and Sedalia Army Air Field), and nine other camps scattered around the state, to provide work for a number of agricultural efforts.

It is difficult to compile an exhaustive list of Missouri's side camps because of their sheer number as well as the brevity of their operation; many existed only for a couple weeks to provide seasonal agricultural labor. The difference between a temporary encampment that provided short-term labor and a formally established branch camp grows blurry at times in the memories of local residents as well as present-day historians. In addition to the "official" list that shows twenty-four branch camps in Missouri, at least a dozen more sites can be counted by those who lived nearby, even if the camps' existence cannot be corroborated by government reports, local newspapers, or other sources.

Housing

Housing at branch camps was determined by whatever was available. Depending on the time of year and the length of the prisoners' stay at a particular location, standard Army field tents were frequently used along with temporary structures—prefab shelters that could be set up and torn down quickly at sites that would be around for several months or over a winter period, such as was the case of the camp near Sikeston, Missouri. Once a location for a new branch camp was identified, advance detachments of POWs, living under field conditions, prepared the site, including creating necessary roads and fences and erecting tents or snap-together barracks. One group of POWs from Fort Leonard Wood, designated especially for this task, crisscrossed the state in the summer of 1945. Starting June 20, these fifty prisoners spent ten days in Independence preparing the branch camp site for the main group of POWs coming to bring in the potato harvest. Then, they traveled to Orrick for four days to repeat the task. Next, they moved on to Marshall, Missouri, for another two weeks (July 7–24, 1945) to set up the site there. After the two weeks at Marshall, they went back to Independence for ten days starting July 25, 1945, and then on to Orrick from August 4 to 15, 1945, to tear down the camps they had just set up a couple weeks prior when the work at these locations was done and the prisoners had moved out.[9]

Otherwise, prisoners often inhabited any suitable structures found nearby that could be adapted to meet basic housing requirements and the approval of the PMGO, as well as the visiting inspectors from the Swiss government and other organizations. Prisoners stayed in a turkey house at a camp in Liberty, and at Louisiana, a place called "the finest branch camp in the nation," they lived in barracks recently vacated by the National Youth Administration, a work-study program originating in the Great Depression that provided part-time jobs for those aged sixteen to twenty-five who wanted both to work and to continue their education.[10]

Many prisoners as well as American servicemen enjoyed the chance to work at the branch camps. The pace was slower, the structure less formal, and the security even more relaxed than at the main POW installations. The small-town setting of most of the branch camps afforded more opportunity for interaction with local residents, and POWs at branch camps across the state frequently attended movies, swam in the municipal pools, and attended church services in the towns where their camps were located.

Of course, there were disadvantages as well. Access to chaplains and immediate medical care was not as convenient as at the main POW camps, where the POW chapel and the station hospital were often just down the street. Less variety in recreational opportunities existed as well; a smaller and more remote branch camp couldn't match what a big camp offered in terms of sports, music, theater, library resources, and camp educational programs. Also, the auxiliary camps sometimes got slighted when it came time to dole out equipment. "A small branch camp's needs are equal to those of a half-compound," wrote Howard Hong, "but when a base camp is short of things or just close to filling its minimum needs, the branches often do not receive a share."[11]

"We had considerably more possibilities for recreation at Fort Leonard Wood than at Chesterfield," recalled German POW Walter Minning. "There was soccer, handball, ping-pong, a library and often also movies. In Chesterfield, however, only ping-pong."[12]

Both POWs and American personnel assigned to a branch camp might occasionally feel neglected by and isolated from the camp administration, which sat ensconced in the middle of the main camp hubbub, seemingly less focused on the goings-on at the branch camps. The POW spokesman from the main camp wasn't able to visit often and the newspaper published by prisoners at the main camp was often outdated by the time it could be trucked out to the branch camp.

The result of this isolation was that the prisoners housed at branch camps formed unusually close bonds both with one another and the

American guards who lived alongside them. Al Griego worked as a guard at the camp at Louisiana and recalled the close friendship that developed between himself and the prisoners, particularly a trio named Rudy, Hans, and Fritz. "I enjoyed working with them. The ones we had, they were a really good bunch of boys, they were all friends of mine," said Griego. "I would consider myself one of their boys."

Griego said that the Stark Bro's Nursery's regular employees liked working with the Germans as well and that the feeling was mutual. The prisoners were good workers, he said, noting "if I had a business, I wouldn't mind having a bunch of people like that to work for me."

The extent of their fondness for one another was displayed when Griego decided to marry a local girl he'd been dating. On Griego's wedding day, the prisoners baked him and his new bride a giant wedding cake in a tub from the camp mess.[13]

Prisoners working on the rivers shared the quarterboat accommodations with their captors and frequently ate meals together in a combined mess. Griego, for instance, also worked as a guard on the floating camp at Washington, Missouri. Here, about a dozen German prisoners lived on a houseboat and worked repairing levees near the town. Because of limited space on the boat, the guards and prisoners ate together, and their sleeping quarters were also in close proximity. The boat had a room for free-time relaxation on its lowest level, and Griego recalled an incident when some of the guards talked him into putting on some boxing gloves and going a couple of rounds with one of the prisoners. His sparring partner was a "little bitty German," but the POW proved tough competition. "That man put nothing but leather on my face," Griego recalled. "He had me coming and going."[14]

Internees at other branch camps saw their American captors sleeping in the same type of musty canvas tents and using the same field showers and latrines. The setting encouraged the smaller groups of prisoners to form much more intimate associations with one another. Imagine, for example, the difference in ambiance between just a hundred prisoners staying at what is now Van Meter State Park in Saline County, Missouri, working together to detassel corn, and five thousand men jammed into the Fort Leonard Wood POW camp. In the branch camps, prisoners also got an up-close look at the real America—not how Hollywood depicted it or what it looked like through double-wire fencing back at the main camp. Branch camp POWs ate with farmers and their families and played with their "hosts'" children during breaks from work. They saw residents welcome the sight of a truckload of singing POWs as they rolled through town every morning on the way to work. The prisoners took those American images back to Europe with them.

St. Louis–Area Branch Camps

Walter Winchell must have had it in for Missouri. First, the prominent radio commentator stirred up the Camp Clark "loving cup" controversy, which flooded Lieutenant Colonel Frakes's office with misguided letters from across the United States from those enraged at the way he was "indulging" the German prisoners housed there. Then, Winchell turned the searing focus of his nightly national broadcasts on the national security "danger" posed by the German POWs in Chesterfield in the Missouri River bottoms west of St. Louis.

Winchell fired off a "Flash!" to his 20 million listeners that "Mr. and Mrs. America" were in danger because the Weldon Spring Ordnance Works was located "adjacent" to a POW camp. "Nothing is to prevent them from blowing up the Weldon Spring plant," said Winchell during this broadcast, implying that all the prisoners had to do was climb over a fence from their home on the Hellwig Brothers Farms and they could take over the facility. At that time, Weldon Spring Ordnance Works was the largest TNT manufacturing facility in the world, with more than one thousand buildings and a peak employment of 5,200 devoted to the operation of twenty explosives production lines. In Winchell's magnificent, malicious way of blasting the government's supposed laxness on security, he had Americans on edge as they waited for the coming explosions. What Winchell conveniently failed to mention, however, was the wide Missouri River, nearly twenty miles of ground, and a small army of determined guards that separated the POWs from the Ordnance Works. Nonetheless, the hornet's nest was disturbed.[15]

"Within fifteen minutes of the broadcast, the phone started ringing and ringing," said William "Bill" Hellwig, whose family owned the land on which the Chesterfield camp was situated. It was the press, and they all wanted more information. "They wanted me to comment on it and to know what in the world was going on. Of course, I couldn't say anything, and told them that they had to talk to the government men, that it was their concern."[16]

Editors at the *St. Louis Globe-Democrat*, in all likelihood knowing that Winchell's allegations were nothing more than an attempt to boost ratings, sent reporter Beulah Schacht out to investigate the accusations. Schacht wrote that instead of the hair-raising trip promised by Winchell, the scene at the camp housing the Germans "was about as melodramatic as a trip to the Zoo":

> It was a very peaceful scene. In the barnyard a half dozen "supermen" were kicking a soccer ball around and cheering each other in German.

Just to the left rear of the house was a clothesline and one of the POWs was hanging up his weekly wash and shaking the wrinkles out of a pair of dungarees in the warm March sun.

They looked at us and we looked at them.
"Pretty easy job?" the photographer called to the sentry.
"Purty monotonous," came the curt answer with a distinct Arkansas accent....

The Lieutenant appeared and he was very upset over Winchell's Sunday night broadcast, but he couldn't say anything because it was against regulations to open his mouth.[17]

Schacht and the *Globe-Democrat* conceded that though Winchell's warning, in theory, was valid, it was an unlikely possibility. "We don't deny that those POWs could break away from their camp, swim the swift Missouri River, shinny [*sic*] over at least two 8-foot barbed-wire fences and find exactly what they are looking for on a dark, 17,000 acre reservation," wrote Schacht, "but they'll have to be bigger 'supermen' than they've proven to be thus far."[18]

Lieutenant Colonel S. C. Schubart of the Weldon Spring Ordnance Works chimed in with his assessment of the security measures in place. "I have inspected the prison camp," said Schubart. "I know that while the boys there are not under armed guard every minute of the day, a roll call is taken at least twice a day and they have never made attempts to escape or cause trouble."

Chesterfield Camp

The Hellwig Brothers Farms—operated by William, Henry, Walter, and George—had only been in business in Chesterfield for a couple years when war broke out. Established in 1937, the farm grew fruit and vegetables, including great quantities of spinach and cantaloupe, which were marketed to both the United States and Canada. Following the nation's entry into the war, the government sought a number of locations for internment camps, and the Hellwig brothers entered into a contract with the government for one of these facilities on the grounds of their six-hundred-acre farm in the Gumbo Flats area of the Missouri River bottoms.

The first residents of the internment camp at the Hellwig Brothers Farms were not actually soldiers at all. They were one hundred "relocated" Americans, some of the thousands of U.S. citizens of Japanese descent who were interned because of the government's suspicion about their allegiance to the United States following Japan's attack on Pearl Harbor and the United States' entry into World War II.

"It sounded like the government was worried about these people on the West Coast sending information to the Japanese," said Verna Hellwig. "They had a number of suspicions, including that they were signaling Japanese aircraft by the way they were hanging their laundry out and stuff like that."

Hellwig remembered going to downtown St. Louis to pick up several of the arriving Japanese Americans from Union Station to bring them back to the Chesterfield internment camp. "I waited at the curb outside until they came out to meet me. They got into the car and just like that, we had a flat tire. There we were, stuck in the middle of Market Street in downtown St. Louis, and with no jack in the car," said Hellwig. "One of the Japanese went to a nearby filling station and came back with a jack and we fixed the tire and went on."[19]

The Japanese Americans had stayed at the relocation center for less than a year when the Army decided that the Hellwig farm would be an ideal site for a POW camp and better used for that purpose. The Japanese Americans were removed from the camp, and the first group of prisoners, Italians, arrived to take their place.[20]

"Labor was very scarce because everyone was being taken for the war so my brother, Bill, sent an application to the Federal Government asking for help," said George Hellwig. "So in 1944, they sent us Italian prisoners."[21]

These sixty-five Italians, all POW officers from Camp Weingarten, were under the command of a Bronx-born Lieutenant Curley. The Ascension Parish history notes that Curley's first stop was at the nearby Ascension Church to visit the pastor there and to arrange for the spiritual care of the prisoners and the twenty American GIs who would guard the POWs.[22]

The prisoners and American servicemen, most of whom were Catholic, began coming to seven o'clock mass each Sunday at the Ascension Parish. Every Sunday, Army trucks pulled up to the church, and the soldiers, both American and Italian, jumped down from the back, fell into formation, and marched into the sanctuary. "One of the first things the Italians did was to ask permission from the American Officer to give the Priest a party," noted the parish history. "It was a real party. Refreshments consisted of home-made cake and coffee."[23]

A unique project of the POW labor program in the Chesterfield valley occurred later when the Ascension Parish engaged two Austrian POWs from the Hellwigs' farm to paint the outside of the church building, an episode noted in church history:

> Help was then so scarce and the stucco needed painting so bad that Father asked Lieutenant Schiavoni, a Catholic boy, if he could let him have two of the Austrians. These men were so happy to be painting a Catholic Church that tears actually fell from their eyes when they arrived to work.

> It was a most unusually hot summer and Father called a break about every hour for a cool drink and a rest. At each rest period they always spent a few minutes praying in our little Church.[24]

It was through events such as these that area residents were exposed to the prisoners. Motorists passing on nearby U.S. Highway 40 could clearly see the POW camp and the men working in the fields, which attracted a considerable amount of attention. Roger Gerth remembered riding past the camp on several occasions as a five-year-old with his father, who, like many other citizens, was quite curious about the men housed there. "My dad would actually pull up close to the entrance of the camp and we'd sit and watch the POWs for a minute or two," said Gerth. "After a bit, the guard would come out and signal to us to move along."[25]

Three large buildings—a barracks, a mess hall, and a latrine—dominated the camp's skyline, but it was the sprinkling of dainty cabins all around the camp that really stood out. "The camp appears more like a tourist camp than a prisoner of war camp," noted one inspector, "since most of the housing facilities were built for transient family laborers and are of the cottage type."[26]

The Hellwigs enjoyed having the Italian prisoners at their place, though they didn't stay very long—"just a few weeks," recalled Henry Hellwig. "They were loving people, very nice. On Easter, they invited my husband, me, and our daughter to their dinner," said Verna Hellwig. "They baked so many things, and had so many courses—it was a delicious meal and a wonderful event. And those men were so happy to see my two-year-old daughter, they just passed her from one to another the whole time."[27]

The next residents of the camp at the Hellwig Brothers Farms were Germans from Fort Leonard Wood, who arrived at the end of April 1944. These 109 Afrika Korps troops stood out, too, in the minds of the Ascension parishioners, who again tried to minister to the prisoners. This time, however, parishioners remembered this group of prisoners for their unfriendliness and lack of desire for spiritual care.

The Reverend John F. Godfrey, pastor at Ascension, wrote to Monsignor John Cody of the St. Louis Archdiocese to tell him of the complete rejection he experienced when he attempted to say Mass for the newly arrived prisoners. Cody advised Godfrey in a letter of reply that the prisoners' response to his efforts was to be expected:

The experience you have had, of course, is not new to me as we have had considerable trouble at Fort Leonard Wood from whence these prisoners came.... The Gestapo is quite well at work in these German Prison Camps and Catholics have actually been forbidden under pain of death to confess to an American Army Chaplain.

At Fort Leonard Wood we solved the question by having a German Prisoner of War priest to care for these prisoners but, because of the scarcity of German priests, it is impossible to supply them for all the German Prison Camps we have in America.

It may be interesting for you to know that the German Government "kindly" permitted two chaplains for every division of 20,000 men, one Catholic and one Protestant.... What a difference between the men of the two allied governments, Germany and Italy.[28]

The prisoners were brought to Chesterfield for their labor, of course, but it took the farm foremen a while to get the prisoners up to speed on the variety of tasks associated with work on a truck farm. During the month after their arrival, Colonel Andrew Duvall, commander at Fort Leonard Wood, told General Paul Clemens, his boss and commander of the Seventh Service Command in Omaha, that things weren't going so well with the prisoners at the Chesterfield camp. "The ones at Chesterfield are not doing very good work. We are getting a complaint on them," advised Duvall in a three-way conference call. "They are not picking as much spinach or whatever it is as the Italians did." The commander of the POW camp at Fort Leonard Wood, Lieutenant Colonel William S. Hannan, pointed out that bad weather may have played a role, and the branch camp commander, Lieutenant F. J. Schiavoni, said that he thought the situation would be resolved as the prisoners grew more familiar with the work.[29]

This matter highlights one of the few bumps in the POW labor program—how to provide training to people who often didn't speak English. "In many areas, the effective use of prisoners of war was hindered by their lack of skill, aptitude and experience for the type of work demanded," note Army historians George Lewis and John Mewha. "The prisoners performed most effectively on jobs that required a minimum of training and skills, and where the routine of the job did not require repeated explanation and interpretation."[30]

A variety of techniques were employed to show the prisoners just how they were supposed to perform a specific task. In some cases, pictures were prepared for use in training, while in other cases, POW group leaders were given a day's instruction on topics such as how to pick corn. These men then taught the other POWs the proper way to perform the task. In still other cases, training sessions featured movies in the prisoners' native language, and job aids were provided to the prisoners for ready reference. For instance, to help educate prisoners working in midwestern cornfields, an illustrated sheet with instructions in German called "Snap Sweet Corn Easier and Faster" was mimeographed and handed out to farmers using POW labor, and a movie on sweet-corn snapping with a German-language soundtrack was shown at training sessions for POWs. "Such training efforts paid rich dividends in increasing the productivity and skill of the workers," write Lewis and Mewha, "as well as in reducing the needed amount of supervision and on-the-job instruction."[31]

German POWs outside the mess hall at the Chesterfield camp. Courtesy of Terry Culver.

Walter Gerst was a ten-year-old when the German POWs came to Chesterfield. Like many other neighboring farmers, Gerst's family hired POWs from the Hellwigs' camp when extra help was needed. "We had a few of the prisoners working for us in our fields," recalled Gerst. "I'd drive the tractor through the fields while the men picked up cantaloupes and loaded them on the trailer." After working with the men all day, sometimes Gerst's imagination would get the better of him. The boy seized on a comment frequently made by the prisoners and worried about it until he was sure it was going to happen. "Because I had blue eyes and blonde hair, they would tell me that I would fit right in in Germany. They told me that when they left, they'd take me with them," said Gerst. "After a while, I was afraid they'd come after me one night and the next thing I'd know, I'd be in Germany."[32]

Shifting Population

After the departure of the Italians in April 1944, only German prisoners lived at the Chesterfield camp until its closure March 31, 1946. But both the nationality and the political temperament of the internees varied considerably over time because of prisoners transferring back and forth between the branch camp and the base camp at Fort Leonard Wood. Because of these transfers, based largely on labor needs, the original bloc of enthusiastic Afrika Korps Nazis that made up the entirety of the Chesterfield camp began to dissipate, replaced by other Germans less persuaded of the joys of National Socialism, as well as a handful of Austrians who resented Hitler's annexation of their country through the 1938 Anschluss. Enough new POWs transferred into the Chesterfield camp by December 1944 that prisoners began to demonstrate a previously unseen interest in religious activities. The Reverend Edward A. Bruemmer, a German-speaking priest who was based at St. Mary's Hospital in Richmond Heights, Missouri, was assigned to serve as auxiliary chaplain. He reported that of the sixty-five men at the Chesterfield camp during the slower winter months, forty of them were Catholics and came to Mass on Christmas Day. Though this increased interest was encouraging, none went to confession or received the Sacrament. "It seems they will not confess to a priest they have just met, and are very suspicious of everyone," wrote Bruemmer to Monsignor Cody of the St. Louis Archdiocese. "While this is understandable, it will take some time to bring them around."[33]

In time, the entire contingent of proud Afrika Korps troops moved on to other camps, replaced by Austrians. The new Austrian prisoners were ardent anti-Nazis transferred from the main camp at Fort Leonard Wood to Chesterfield after the branch camp was designated by the camp administration a haven for those who opposed the Third Reich. This segregation ensured their safety, noted a visitor from the Swiss Legation in May 1945. "Branch Camp #1 at Chesterfield is made up entirely of 136 strongly anti-Nazi Austrians who have their own newspaper and who are rendering service which is highly satisfactory and much appreciated by their employers," wrote the Swiss inspector. "These Austrians are greatly disliked by the rank-and-file Nazi of the main camp, at whose hands they would almost certainly suffer violence were they not furnished the protection of a separate camp such as Chesterfield."[34]

The nature of the change was reflected in a letter written by one POW to another interned at a different Missouri camp, which was printed in the *Chesterfield-Herold* camp newspaper. The letter both provides interesting insight into life at the POW camp as well as underscores the fear prisoners felt about being perceived as disloyal by fellow Nazi prisoners:

When we arrived at Camp Chesterfield on January 2, 1945, we found a small, clean camp with very nice quarters.... After three weeks work began. We cut trees along the Missouri River and removed brush. Later I helped a farmer to harvest corn. Everywhere I enjoyed my work. We get along well with the farmers. We all work well and we have developed a good relationship with them.

Our free time is always filled with many educational activities. We study the English language a lot. Wednesdays, we watch movies. We also study U.S. history, world economy, and have discussions about politics, war, and the future of the world. We can talk freely without fear of getting our heads bashed in.... I hope now, since the nationalism is destroyed, that we will have a better Germany.[35]

Chesterfield Boat Camp

About a year after the initial group of German prisoners of war arrived at the camp on the Hellwig Brothers Farms in April 1944, another camp was set up nearby. This was Chesterfield Camp Number 2, a floating camp established on a Missouri River houseboat moored near Centaur, Missouri, a tiny community about four miles south of the Hellwig Brothers Farms. The prisoners at the boat camp were mostly sailors and were used for levee work and other projects in the area.

Bob Leiweke, whose father was the postmaster for the clutch of houses at Centaur, was ten years old when the German boat camp was tied up to the bank just a couple hundred yards from his house. Some of the sixty prisoners living on the three-story houseboat were assigned to a project in the little town. "The men—and I'd say there were about twenty of them—worked for at least a month tearing down this huge building," said Leiweke, pointing into a patch of overgrown brush across the road from his house, where a lumberyard once stood. "They hauled all the wood from it out to University City, where they used it to construct an ice-cream plant."

Even though Centaur at that time was still a "backwards little place," as Leiweke said, noting that electricity didn't arrive there until 1946, he didn't recall any particular fascination with the presence of the foreign men in their community that summer. Like many Missourians, to him, the prisoners "were just there." Said Leiweke, "They'd come off that boat and work all day. At night they'd return to the houseboat. We really didn't think too much about it."[36]

Ascension parishioners recalled the men of the boat camp as being hardened Nazis, uninterested in their efforts to reach out to them. The Reverend William Gabler, a pastor who ministered to the Protestants on the boat, recalled his concern for possible Nazi intimidation of the prisoners who wanted to come to church. He remembered one time an eavesdropper tried to listen in on a conversation he had with one of the men on the boat. "I was talking with one of the men, and suddenly I felt a shadow," said Gabler. "A man on the level above us was leaning over, trying to listen in."

Gabler mentioned this incident to the American officer who commanded the boat camp, speculating that one of the Nazis had surreptitiously tried to find out what he was doing. "'That's one of our men,' said the captain," Gabler recalled. "The man was a plant, an American who could speak fluent German, living among them and pretending to be a POW so that he could find out what the Nazis were up to and help us keep an eye on them."[37]

Perhaps the temperament of the prisoners on the boat, like that of prisoners in the land camp, also changed over time as different men rotated in and out, but the Ascension Parish account of the German internees on the boat as being hostile to religion is at odds with the notes kept by auxiliary military chaplain Edward Bruemmer. Bruemmer went each Sunday to the Missouri River bottoms to say Mass for the German prisoners.

Bruemmer noted in his monthly activity reports to the St. Louis Archdiocese that in February 1945, eighteen sailors from the houseboat were trucked to the Chesterfield camp for Mass. The next month, he went to the boat camp to say Mass for the German prisoners, as well as their American captors. "All Catholics attended," noted Bruemmer on his visit March 21, 1945, "including American soldiers stationed there."[38]

The floating POW operation was docked at Centaur for a relatively short period of time—from February 1, 1945, until May 25, 1945. After that, the sailors pulled up the mooring lines, and the boat went upriver to Washington, Missouri, where it stayed until early September 1945, and the soldiers did the same sorts of work on levee repair and erosion control. After the summer on the river in Washington, the boat camp went to Glasgow, where it stayed until being deactivated on January 31, 1946.

Conflict

As it turned out, it wasn't just Nazi intimidation that challenged Bruemmer's ministry to the Chesterfield POWs. The height of the summer melon harvest had the men working in the fields from sunup to sundown, which made it difficult to find time to hold Mass. Bruemmer went so far as to accuse the Hellwigs of intentionally obstructing his efforts to hold services at the camp.

The problem first arose one Sunday morning in early May 1945 when Bruemmer drove out for Mass at the Chesterfield camps. Bruemmer's normal practice was to say Mass at 10 A.M. each Sunday for all who were interested. He could tell something was different, though, as he entered the gate of the camp that particular morning. The place was quiet, and there was not a prisoner to be seen. He found one of the Hellwig brothers and asked him where the prisoners were. Neither Bruemmer's account nor other archdiocesan reports say which brother it was, but only William and Henry, the two oldest, were running the Hellwig Brothers Farms at that time. The brother told Bruemmer that the prisoners were out working, and, indeed, Bruemmer confirmed that just fifteen minutes before Mass was to begin, "Mr. Hellwig took almost all of the Catholics away in a huge truck…to work in the spinach fields." Bruemmer's notes indicate that he was somewhat taken aback, and he asked Hellwig for an explanation of this action.

"While he was very respectful, it seems he did not think it necessary for them to attend Mass, because 'you can worship God in your heart,'" wrote Bruemmer to Lieutenant Schiavoni and to Monsignor Cody. "Of course, you and I know that the U.S. Government wants every prisoner to have the opportunity to worship God according to his belief."[39]

Further, Bruemmer reported that Hellwig told him that with the onset of the melon season, the prisoners would be needed all day, every Sunday, from 7 A.M. on, making it virtually impossible for Bruemmer to hold Mass at the Chesterfield camp. Bruemmer protested, to both Hellwig and Lieutenant Schiavoni, as well as to officials at the St. Louis Archdiocese. These complaints apparently had some effect, as both Schiavoni and Hellwig agreed to forego their much-needed labor for a period of several hours and promised that the men would not have to work on Sunday mornings so they could attend Mass.

However, the very next weekend, as Bruemmer pulled into the camp, he saw a cloud of dust rising off in the distance as another big truck loaded with prisoners drove toward the fields. Ninety men had left the camp for work just as Bruemmer arrived.

The priest was baffled by this action. Though he knew that the contract the Hellwigs held with the government said they could work the prisoners fourteen hours a day, seven days a week, Bruemmer was surprised that Hellwig and Schiavoni seemed to go back on their promise. In trying to explain for himself and for Cody what may have driven this action, he raised some serious concerns about conditions at the camp:

> Mr. Hellwig, it seems, is a shrewd businessman, who has some odd power over the soldiers and Lieutenant Schiavoni. Although I have little respect for his intelligence, in matters that pertain to human psychology, he holds the whip over the prisoners by giving them extra vegetables for their meals, if they do what he says. And the prisoners have no rights at present, as the Geneva Convention is being ignored and supplanted by arbitrary rules.[40]

Bruemmer urged immediate action from Cody and raised again the specter of maltreatment at the camp, pointing blame at both the Army and the Hellwigs for creating a situation where prisoners could work on Sunday instead of attending Mass, as he thought they should:

> I am convinced that this laxity on the part of the Army, and greed on the part of the Hellwig brothers should not be tolerated. At present, the food is inadequate to nourish men who work as hard as these prisoners do, and the fact that arrangements are being made to prevent them from attending Holy Mass makes my blood boil.

> The prisoners want to be good Catholics, but this spirit of indifferentism, a typical Protestant attitude, should be stopped.[41]

During a subsequent hour-long meeting on the subject with Schiavoni and Hellwig, Bruemmer said both tried to "pass the buck, the same old Army game...and assured him that it would not happen [again] and it was all through a confusion that they were taken away last Sunday." The men were not being forced to work, said the pair; a choice was clearly offered to the prisoners: work in the fields or attend Mass.[42]

In Bruemmer's world, this practice of offering a choice between worship and work was unacceptable. He would rather the entire camp be idle during the time of those Sunday morning services so that there would be no conflict in the minds of the prisoners. Bruemmer told Hellwig that Hellwig's way forced the prisoners to make a difficult decision:

> When you ask for 90 men at 10:00 o'clock on a Sunday morning, you are telling them to choose between the worship of God and your farm labor. You are placing religion in a bad light, although you protest that you want them to worship God. Until you show me that you

mean what you say, by promising that the prisoners will not be asked to work on Sundays between the hours of 9 and 12, I cannot believe that you want them to worship God.

When some men work and other go to Mass, you are creating a bad morale in the camp, and causing trouble for the Church. Before you took them out to work during Mass, the attendance was almost 100 per cent. And it is still that, when you leave them here. Most of the men in this Camp are Catholics, and it is my duty to protect their interests, and their right to attend Mass.[43]

Surprisingly, and much to the credit of the branch camp commander and the Hellwig brothers for their flexibility and desire to go beyond what was required of them, Hellwig and Schiavoni promised that no prisoner would be asked to work in any manner between the hours of 9 A.M. and noon on Sundays. The prisoners would go to work early, have the time off to attend worship, and then return to the fields, allowing them to both go to Mass and still put in the fourteen-hour days that the Hellwigs needed during their busiest time of year. If this promise was violated, Bruemmer threatened, Cody would take the matter up directly with Colonel Andrew Duvall, overall commander at Fort Leonard Wood.

"Oh, yeah, that guy [Bruemmer] was going to report me to the government," remembered William Hellwig in a later interview. "He thought I was taking the prisoners away, making them work when they wanted to go to church instead. Really, that wasn't up to me, it was the Army's concern, and in any case, it was the Germans who mostly weren't so interested in going to church. They'd have rather worked."[44]

Nothing more was written about this dispute, and Bruemmer noted smugly in his notes that the prisoners were happy and grateful to him for "untangling what had been to them a mysterious action on the part of Hellwig and the Army."[45]

Looking at these incidents from another perspective, it seems that in Bruemmer's zeal to minister to the prisoners, he obstructed the Hellwig brothers' efforts to run their business most effectively at their busiest time of the year. Although there may have been a mix-up about the time when Mass had been scheduled, the rest of Bruemmer's accusations seem wholly unfounded. Certainly his statements implying that the Hellwig brothers were starving the prisoners seem mean-spirited and come close to slander of the Hellwigs' collective character. His comments also run contrary to all other available evidence. The simple fact that the Army, not the Hellwigs, was responsible for feeding the POWs nullifies these charges. Several other independent accounts refute Bruemmer's accusations about the poor quality of food, including inspection reports from that same time and accounts from prisoners who testified about the great treatment and hearty meals they enjoyed while at Chesterfield. "Being at the Hellwigs pleased me much more that being at Fort Leonard Wood. Reason: the food was better," recalled Walter Minning. "At the end of the war the food provided by the U.S. Army was considerably reduced. Since we were in Chesterfield though, permanently there with the civilians, they cared for us with all the necessities."

Also, using volunteer POWs for labor on Sundays was not just a practice of the Hellwigs, noted Minning. He made it clear that prisoners understood that they had a choice between working and participating in worship. "I worked frequently for other farmers," remembered Minning. "I remember especially one Mr. Damado. He fetched us always on Sundays (only volunteers). We cultivated a piece of land for him that he later sold to the state of Missouri."[46]

Other visitors to the camp witnessed treatment just the opposite of Bruemmer's claims, and the Reverend Gabler noted that the Hellwigs fought strongly against the government-directed reductions in the quality and quantity of food served in the POW mess. "At that time [spring 1945] there was a dramatic cutback of rations for the prisoners of war. The Army said that they had to cut back on what the prisoners were being fed, but Hellwig raised Cain about that change. He knew that with the very demanding work they were doing for him in the fields, that there was no way the prisoners could keep up the pace given the cuts in their diet the government was putting in," said Gabler. "Hellwigs were using these men to produce and they were paying for them to produce. You can't expect men to put in a good day's work if they haven't got food in their stomachs."[47]

Gabler said that the Hellwigs' concern for the prisoners' welfare went beyond what was necessary, going so far as to feed the prisoners more than the regulations allowed. "The rules were pretty plain on it. You were not supposed to give these men anything extra, like a sandwich," said Gabler. "They were supposed to just eat the military rations. But most of the people who used these men on the farm, they fed them."

Gabler recalled a time when the Hellwigs tried to put on a nice dinner for the prisoners but were prevented by the commanding officer of the camp, a man who was a stickler for the rules. "One time, Hellwig wanted to butcher a steer and have a big shin-dig for the prisoners, and this guy wouldn't let him," said Gabler. "Hellwig protested it, and when the officer went down to Fort Leonard Wood, they went ahead and did it anyway."

It could also have been that Bruemmer did not understand the "no work–no eat" policy the Army used to motivate prisoners who balked at participation in the labor program. This policy arose out of the early difficulty the PMGO experienced in disciplining prisoners because of the ineffective methods available to them. Prior to October 1943, American authorities were allowed only to "admonish, reprimand or withhold the privileges of the prisoners of war" or could use the military courts to deal with more serious offenses. POWs understandably weren't too concerned about being scolded, and they didn't have many privileges to have withheld. The legal option didn't help much either, as it was difficult and foolish to try to prosecute a POW in a military court for the minor infractions that made up most of an internment camp's problems. The Army knew that the only effective disciplinary measures were those affecting a prisoner's food and his pay, and accordingly, in October 1943, the PMGO reread Article 27 of the Geneva Convention, and after this second look, interpreted it as permitting an interning government to use reasonable means to require prisoners to comply with a legitimate work order. Two Army historians discussed the reasons the government used to support this policy of "administrative pressure" providing the backbone for the "no work–no eat" practice:

> "Administrative pressure" authorized the camp commander to withdraw certain privileges from and to impose a restricted diet on those PW's who refused to obey a lawful order, including a work order. The theory behind this policy was that it was not punishment for any act but was merely an inducement to make the PW's comply with a lawful order or regulations.
>
> It was not imposed for a definite period but only as long as the PW's refused to obey a proper command. The PW's could therefore terminate the pressure simply by complying with the order that they had violated.[48]

This is legalese, to be sure, but the bottom line is that the Army permitted camp commanders to differentiate in the menu offered to prisoners who were complying with orders and those who were not compliant. This occurred quite frequently, as camp commanders used just about every method they could to keep prisoners working, thereby satisfying area agricultural interests and their military higher-ups. For example, Colonel Frakes at Camp Clark allowed the working prisoners to establish a bakery in their compound to bake their own bread, rolls, and other items. This privilege was denied to those who were not good workers. Camp Chesterfield, like every other POW camp, certainly had in its population a number of those prisoners who were determined to cause problems and to complain about the mistreatment they received. It's possible that they might have complained to and manipulated a chaplain with a sympathetic heart, who came out from the city to visit them for a couple hours on Sundays and did not see their behavior during the rest of the week.

Finally, it could be that Bruemmer, discouraged by his lack of success in ministering to the mostly disinterested Germans, exaggerated and elaborated this misunderstanding to make himself look like a hero and to explain away the prisoners' lack of participation in the ministrations he offered.

Further, the Reverend Gabler said that Bruemmer was not popular with the prisoners. Gabler noted that when Bruemmer ate lunch at the Chesterfield boat camp, the man would sit by himself in the dining room and eat entirely alone, sometimes complaining about the racket coming from the kitchen. These actions were in contrast with Gabler, who, in his efforts to connect with the prisoners, usually ate his lunch in the kitchen, joining in and, in all likelihood, even provoking some of the happy din.[49]

Escapes

On two different occasions, prisoners took off from the Chesterfield camp, running as fast across the Missouri River bottoms as they could. An intense desire for freedom drove the attempt by the first pair, who left in the night during a cold October rainstorm in 1945. "Maybe we don't have a chance," wrote Joseph Swoboda and Michele Kunz in a note they left in their quarters, "nevertheless we will try. We say who doesn't risk can't win."

The duo, ages thirty and twenty-seven, respectively, was on the run for ten days, hiding out in fields and living off green corn they picked along the way. Aiming for South America, they made it as far as Waterloo, Illinois, about forty miles away, before hunger and fatigue drove them to surrender. Fred Krewer, superintendent of the Columbia Quarry Company in Valmeyer, Illinois, was driving along Route 3 one night when he saw a pair of hitchhikers on the side of the road. Krewer stopped to pick them up and discovered that his two passengers were escaped German soldiers who wanted a ride back to Chesterfield. "Once he figured out who they were, he was scared that they'd try something on him," said Fred Krewer, Jr., who remembered clearly the night his father picked up the prisoners. "He was able to speak German, and so he just kept talking to them until he could get them to the sheriff's department in Waterloo."[50] After the men were turned over to Monroe County sheriff A. C. Ludwig, Ludwig notified the FBI, which had spearheaded the hunt for the escapees, and Kunz and Swoboda were taken to Jefferson Barracks. The younger Krewer said that the unique way his father met the POWs must have forged some sort of bond between them. Kunz and Swoboda exchanged Christmas cards and other correspondence with his father every year until Krewer's death in 1977.[51]

Henry Hellwig described another instance when a prisoner got away from the Chesterfield camp. "He only made it as far as Babler Park [less than five miles away]. The guy was losing his mind," said Hellwig. "He had heard that the Russians were taking over the zone where his parents lived, and he was fearful for their safety. He was worried so much about it, he was losing his mind."[52]

Bob Leiweke, of nearby Centaur, described the fear that gripped the little communities in the area when they learned "Nazis" were on the loose. People began locking their doors for the first time, and men slept with shotguns ready by the bedside, in case they needed to be called into quick use. Leiweke and his family were driving down a lonely country road in the Wild Horse Creek valley on a dark, windy night when they came upon a solitary sentry, one of the military policemen encamped at Babler State Park, standing guard in the roadway. "As we came on this poor fellow, our headlights shone on him, and you could see his knees knocking together, he was so scared," recalled Leiweke. "Of course, those Germans didn't mean any harm. They just wanted to get out because they didn't want to go back to Germany."[53]

These escapes, coupled with the 1944 breakouts of German POWs at Fort Leonard Wood, raised fears about the loyalty of some members of the German American community in St. Louis. An extensive FBI investigation of alleged ties, however, showed practically no connections between Germany and St. Louis German Americans. Even the most public and well-known group, the German American Bund, a pro-Nazi society of ethnic Germans living in the United States devoted to maintaining American neutrality in the European conflict, dissolved in 1940 and at its peak claimed only two hundred members. Bund members, some of whom liked to don Nazi uniforms and march around giving the stiff-arm salute, limited their activity to distributing literature and apparently never engaged in sabotage or advocated it. During the years of its brief existence (1937–40), the Bund made its headquarters at Camp Deutsch Horst on the Meramec River, where children were taught Germanic language and culture, and a swastika flew alongside the Stars and Stripes. When war broke out in Europe, leaders of the St. Louis Bund returned to Germany, and the movement died out in the area.[54]

FBI officials concluded that these German prisoners acted alone and were unaided by civilians during their escapes. And if further proof was needed, doubters needed only consider the lack of assistance Kunz and Swoboda received during their brief foray from Chesterfield to Waterloo, with eight days on the run and nothing to eat but green ears of corn.

Chesterfield Inspection

Although the branch camps did receive occasional visitors from the neutral agencies charged with ensuring the prisoners' welfare, including the Swiss government, the YMCA, and the International Red Cross, these visits were not nearly as frequent as at the main camps, which seemed to have a group showing up each week to check out the mess hall and talk with the prisoners. Both the camp at the Hellwigs' farm and the Chesterfield boat camp were visited by Howard Hong, a representative of the International YMCA, in December 1944. In his write-up of the trip, Hong noted that the men were receiving movies each week from the main camp at Fort Leonard Wood but were eager to get more musical instruments, books, and other diversionary devices to augment the limited choices at the "almost non-existent store."

The YMCA's mission was to provide materials intended to improve the prisoners' quality of life and opportunities for recreation. Hong fulfilled the mission by leaving a number of diversionary items at Chesterfield, just as he did at most branch camps. He gave the prisoners, among other things, two dozen table-tennis balls, art supplies, books, a harmonica, and a guitar.[55]

Hong returned in March 1945 and observed that in addition to the camp movie series, the prisoners were also receiving the YMCA concert-record series, a series of classical-music recordings. These performances were much enjoyed, but live music performed by a trained musician added another level of enjoyment to the cultural-arts program offered to Chesterfield POWs. "Even better," noted Hong, "will be the music of a concert violinist, who just arrived at camp."

Hong wrote also that prisoners at the Hellwig farm enjoyed access to a swimming pool, a feature not commonly found in Missouri POW camps. It seems Lieutenant Schiavoni took advantage of an insurance requirement that a certain amount of stored water be available at all times in case of fire, and he allowed the POWs to create a swimming pool to be used for that purpose. "This fulfills the demand of the underwriters and serves admirably for other purposes on hot Missouri summer days," wrote Hong.[56]

Work in the City

In addition to working for the Hellwig Brothers Farms and other agricultural operations in the Chesterfield valley, prisoners at the camp were used across the St. Louis area for a number of different tasks.

Otto Deutschmann lived in the Kirkwood/Des Peres area of southwest St. Louis County, and in 1943 he started going back and forth to the Chesterfield camp, fetching prisoners to work in the family's greenhouse and nursery on Manchester Road, near Ballas Road. A failed physical kept Deutschmann out of the service and home in St. Louis "so that he could take care of the girls," said his friends. He'd drive out every day to the camp in the Gumbo Flats and pick up ten or so prisoners in a long-paneled '35 Ford pickup. "It was real relaxed," said Deutschmann. "We'd have pretty much the same bunch every day so I got to know them pretty well. They'd have a guard come along, and he'd put his gun away and go snooze somewhere or just sit and gab with us."[57]

That scene played out countless times across the St. Louis area, as the Chesterfield prisoners were hired out to work for many of the region's farming families. Ruth Cummins's father, Walter Steiner, used three or four of the German prisoners on an as-needed basis, much to the delight of Cummins's aged grandmother, who could speak the prisoners' native language. "She was almost blind and would sit and talk German with them on their lunch break," remembered Cummins. "She enjoyed it very much, and of course, we kids thought it was really neat that she could talk with the POWs."

Cummins, who was six or seven years old at the time, remembers her mother preparing the prisoners' food with the same care she gave to her husband's meals. "She'd cook German-style food like they would have had at home," said Cummins, who remembered her own little-girl shyness and intense curiosity about the men from the POW camp. "They really enjoyed it and seemed to be happy to be out working, not like you'd think prisoners would be. They probably felt comfortable because of the neighborhood and the people."[58]

C. R. Wagner also hired Chesterfield prisoners. He spoke German and came from a distinct German background, so the four prisoners who worked for him for a year really felt at home. "My father could speak it passably and it served them well day to day," said Ross Wagner, who was a boy when the men were working on his family's farm. "However, when they needed to get into the technical details of a matter, then they'd go and get my grandfather," for whom German was his first language.

Wagner had a farm in Sappington and also bought fruit and vegetables from area truck farmers and resold the produce at a location on Gravois

Road in Sappington, as well as at St. Louis's Produce Row, at that time located at Washington Avenue and Third Street, near the foot of the Eads Bridge. Beginning in the fall of 1944, the prisoners helped him clean up a long-neglected farm he had purchased on Sappington Road, trimming trees on the site as well as pruning an overgrown grape arbor. They turned their attention to a creaky old barn on the property and spent several months remodeling it, using the family's pooled ration for tin to get enough from Edward Eime's hardware store in nearby Concord Village.

In the winter, Wagner kept the prisoners busy doing things to help prepare his business for spring. "They spent a lot of time busting up these larger crates that fruit like apples and oranges were shipped in so that the wood could be reused," remembered Wagner. "They'd remove the nails and cut the slats into shorter pieces to make baskets, bushel boxes, and berry trays for use with other fruits and vegetables in my father's commission house."[59]

Working with those prisoners for that length of time, Wagner and his family became close to the four prisoners who worked for him each day, particularly an Austrian named Nikolaus Pascher. Wagner and Pascher exchanged letters after the war, and when Pascher mentioned in 1947 the difficult time he and his family were having in Vienna because of the still strongly felt effects of the war, Wagner and his family started sending them packages of clothing and food. "Our joy was very great to receive these packets. I don't know how I can thank you for all of these precious items that you have sent," wrote Pascher in early 1948, after three boxes were received. "Mrs. Wagner, how could you have known that my wife had no coat? You don't know what a service of love you have done. For my wife, who had no winter coat at all, it is like this fell to us from heaven."[60]

Ed Kusmec and his family lived in the same general vicinity as the Hellwigs, and ten-year-old Kusmec and his brother helped out in the summertime, working in the fields and at the roadside stands that dotted the area, selling vegetables to passing motorists. "One day, one of the prisoners cut a swastika into a really big pumpkin," recalled Kusmec. "He didn't dig really deep into it, just below the outer orange layer where the color gets much lighter so you could see it really good." Kusmec's brother, with entrepreneurial wisdom far beyond his years, hauled the pumpkin up to the road and plopped it prominently front and center of the family's vegetable stand, where it could be seen by one and all. "People would notice that pumpkin with the big swastika on it, and they'd start asking questions," said Kusmec. "They'd want to know all about the prisoners of war, and pretty soon they'd start buying."

The process of picking the produce was another interesting sight, said Kusmec. Two tractors pulled a pair of farm wagons through the fields as the men loaded them with watermelons, pumpkins, or cantaloupes, depending on the time of year. "The prisoners would all line up at one edge of the field, and somebody would blow a whistle," said Kusmec. "The men would pass through the field, picking all the fruit and then stop when they came to the other edge of the field. The tractors pulling the wagons would cart off the fruit, and the men would march to the next field down, where they would sweep through again."[61]

Because of the relaxed relations among the German POWs, guards, and local residents, several people living in the area recalled seeing prisoners frequently working alone, unguarded on solitary assignments well away from the camp. June Stapleton grew up near the farm of Harry Hoffmann, whose property sat near the present-day intersection of Des Peres Road and Barrett Station Road. Hoffmann owned a telephone company that provided service to the residents of that rural area. Stapleton remembered that a single prisoner stayed with them on the farm to work in Hoffmann's fields. "He was a slim fellow in his younger twenties," said Stapleton. "No one was afraid of him. We'd see him all the time out working when we'd cut through Mr. Hoffmann's fields."[62]

German POW workers at the Wagner farm in Sappington, Missouri. Courtesy of Ross Wagner.

Robert Weiss was fourteen when he first encountered the German prisoners. His family lived on a five-acre plot of ground next to the Hellwig farm, and his mother worked for a Dr. Courtney, an orthodontist with a practice nearby. "Whenever Dr. Courtney needed something done on his place, the Hellwigs would send over a couple of the prisoners to take care of it, whether it was tending to his yard or doing some other kind of odd jobs around the property," said Weiss.[63]

Eventually, George and Verna Hellwig moved into a farmhouse across the street from the Chesterfield camp. There was little housing available, even on their own farm, so they temporarily lived as renters on the second floor of this house. "The American soldiers who ran the camp lived in a two-story farmhouse that was on our farm," said Verna. "When they were closing the camp, they had the prisoners paint the house and fix it up for us, because we were going to move in after they left." The Germans apparently had free rein in choosing the colors they used, said Verna. "They painted the molding and trim with a variety of colors in the European style," she chuckled. "In places it almost had a 3-D effect, and it took some getting used to."[64]

In a scene reminiscent of Floyd Fadler's pub-crawling bus down at Weingarten, Missouri, Roice Jones remembered POWs gathering each Saturday afternoon at the Countryside Inn, a cozy little tavern-restaurant combination on Schoettler Road, between Conway and Olive Street Road. "They would bring up five or ten of the German prisoners on Saturday afternoons because that place had the coldest beer in town," said Jones, who worked there as a teen. "Those prisoners would sit and drink beer, talk German with the old-timers, and have a little party. It was like they were free. They didn't have a guard with them—usually it would be the head laborer from the farm that would take them there."[65]

Working with local farmers in the St. Louis area provided POW Walter Minning the excuse and the opportunity to have a wonderful reunion with some old friends. Writing from Fort Leonard Wood, he told his parents that he was being held in a Missouri POW camp. Upon receipt of Minning's letter, they sent him the address of a former neighbor, William Bühning, who had immigrated to the United States in 1927 and was living in the St. Louis area. Minning contacted his "dear uncle" Bühning by mail, and Bühning wrote back at once to his "nephew." This ruse of being related was necessary, for contact with those in the United States other than family was generally prohibited for German POWs. Minning recalled the first time he saw Bühning face-to-face. "In 1946, when I got to Chesterfield, the possibility of us meeting became very favorable, and it played out like this—one Sunday afternoon I was called by one of the fellows with the words, 'Come up to the gate; your uncle is there,'" said Minning. "And in fact, my new uncle William Bühning was there. The guard was as good as nonexistent, so that I could go all the way up to the road and talk with him undisturbed."[66]

Bühning told Minning that there was a good possibility he could get him out of the camp under the pretense that Minning would do some work for Bühning. As it was early in the year, the Hellwigs didn't need as much of the prisoners' labor, and so the POWs were available for anyone who wanted to use them. A few days later, Bühning called the Chesterfield camp and told them that he wanted to get a German prisoner to work for him and inquired if Minning was available. "Why Minning?" he was asked, and Bühning responded that he had heard the man was a good worker. The plan succeeded, and Bühning came to get the POW he had hired. "He picked me up and took me to Kirkwood, where we spent a beautiful day. All of his friends and acquaintances who had come from Germany were there," recalled Minning. "He had a full house. Here I spent a full day with a family for the first time since I became a POW."[67]

Deactivation of Chesterfield Camp

By spring 1946, the prisoners were eager to return to Europe. "There is a general anxiety to go home, but morale is still excellent," wrote the Reverend Bruemmer, who still ministered to prisoners at the camp. Their departure would come soon, and the Hellwigs said farewell on March 31, 1946, to the prisoners who had worked with them for the past two years. Even on the POWs' departure, the Hellwigs' consideration and courtesy toward the prisoners—Bruemmer's allegations notwithstanding—cemented in the minds of the prisoners the Hellwigs' compassion and humanitarian concern, and it was clear the Hellwigs were going to miss the Germans. "At our departure from the Hellwig vegetable farm, he gave us several large sugar melons," recalled Minning, who returned to visit Henry Hellwig in 1984. "Then he made a somewhat melancholy reminiscence of all his memories from the past [couple years]."[68]

The prisoners returned to Fort Leonard Wood, where they remained for the next ten days, helping to pack up and close down the internment camp there before being shipped to Liverpool, England, via Camp Shanks, New York. Minning arrived in Liverpool on May 9, 1946, and worked there exactly a year before receiving his freedom on May 8, 1947.

Jefferson Barracks

As the POW population increased at Fort Leonard Wood, camp officials worked with their Army counterparts at Jefferson Barracks to establish a branch camp at the St. Louis installation. The old post, a major induction and training center during World War II, was perched on the banks high above the Mississippi River a few miles south of the St. Louis City limits. The post was established as a frontier garrison in 1826 and named for Thomas Jefferson, who died on July 4, 1826, a few days after troops of the First and Fourth Infantry Regiments encamped at the site. It was the Army's first permanent base west of the Mississippi.

From its early use as a cavalry post, Jefferson Barracks evolved into a center where modern war-fighting technology was developed and honed.

It was here that the first successful parachute jump took place in March 1912, and in 1940, Jefferson Barracks became the nation's first Air Corps training base. Additionally, Jefferson Barracks served as one of the largest induction stations in the United States, processing hundreds of thousands of American men and women into the Army during the World War II years.[69]

The great number of troops passing through Jefferson Barracks, combined with the needs of the training units stationed there, led to the opening of the POW branch camp there on May 16, 1944, with 150 German prisoners from Fort Leonard Wood. The POWs, who lived in former Civilian Conservation Corps barracks, performed the same sorts of work supporting the installation's operations as their counterparts at other large Missouri bases that were home to large numbers of GIs, such as at Camp Crowder and Fort Leonard Wood. The men worked in the supply warehouses, the post laundry, and clothing- and shoe-repair shops and had general maintenance and upkeep duties around the post grounds.

The number of German POWs at Jefferson Barracks hovered around 144 through the months of June and July 1944, but the population grew rapidly as prisoner work opportunities were expanded. Forty-eight new prisoners arrived in August, and in September another 167 Germans arrived, which swelled the count at the branch camp to 359 men. In October 1945, at the peak of the camp's nearly two-year period of operation, just under 500 Germans lived and worked at the post. "I was the supervisor in the Salvage and Excess Clothing and Equipment warehouse, and we usually had six or eight PWs working there each day," recalled Doris Kresyman, a civilian who supervised POW workers. "They worked sorting and patching clothing and shoes. A big truckload of shoes would come in, and they'd dump the load out on the ground. Those prisoners would sort the good ones out to be fixed, and the rest would be recycled for scrap."[70]

Through this sort of daily contact, German POWs working at Jefferson Barracks seemed to develop the same sorts of friendships with supervisors as those developed at other camps. Among the information at the Jefferson Barracks museum relating to the internees is a copy of a hand-lettered sympathy card for an American coworker signed by eighteen prisoners. The caption reads, "We, the P.O.W. of Jefferson Barracks Bldg #40, wish to express our sympathy of the sudden death of your mother in law, Mrs. Wilson." Another scrawled note is the address for a departing POW, Heinz Altner, at the POW camp at Wirral-Cheshire, Great Britain, presumably the man's next destination.[71]

Of course, life for prisoners at Jefferson Barracks was not without occasional friction. A dispute involving one POW at the quartermaster warehouse who refused to go to work swelled into a four-day walkout involving every prisoner at the camp and finally required the Fort Leonard Wood base camp commander, Lieutenant Colonel William Hannan, to intervene. Although the exact reason for the incident remains unknown, on Wednesday, January 17, 1945, the aforementioned prisoner refused to work. U.S. authorities promptly threw the man in the post guardhouse on a restricted diet of bread and water. That punishment prompted twenty-three more Germans who worked in the same area to walk off the job, vowing not to return until the first man was released. Those prisoners, too, were placed in the guardhouse.

Once word got out among the POWs about what had happened in the quartermaster warehouse, the situation grew more inflamed. Via their camp spokesman, the Germans requested that the twenty-four men already in confinement not be punished. When this proposal was rejected, the remaining four hundred prisoners went on strike. The guardhouse couldn't hold every German POW at Jefferson Barracks, so when the strike entered its third day, Saturday, January 20, the men were confined to their compound, all on a restricted diet and loss of canteen privileges. "More than 300 Germans prisoner of war sat sullenly in the compound at Jefferson Barracks today after another breakfast of bread and water," read an account in the *St. Louis Post-Dispatch*. In that same article, camp authorities talked tough about their response to the prisoners' calls for release of those already confined to the guardhouse. "Prisoners of war are in no position to make demands of the United States Army," said a statement released by post headquarters, "and none of them will be released from confinement or the restricted diet until all of them agree to return to work."[72]

Evidence of the degree to which U.S. authorities were reliant on prisoner labor to operate Jefferson Barracks (and just about every other military post) can be seen in how the government had to scramble to make up for the loss of that labor. Officials pulled American GI jailbirds out of the post's Army Rehabilitation Barracks, a punishment center for those convicted of military-law violations, and used them alongside other active-duty personnel taken from their regular work to fill in for the prisoners. These substitutes stepped in on construction projects, in the post laundry, and in warehouses and other facilities where loss of POW labor had had the greatest effect. "The strike definitely does not put us behind the eight ball," said one Jefferson Barracks official who was determined to maintain a brave face, "but the Nazis are putting a crimp in all work details.[73]

German POWs working in the Jefferson Barracks motor pool, November 1944. From left: Franz Teufel, Karl Bergmann, E. Witthe, E. Zrink, Paul Rahn, S. Koch, H. Hulboon, and D. R. Chromy. Courtesy of Terry Culver.

By Sunday, January 21, Lieutenant Colonel Hannan was involved. Hannan knew these Germans well from their time at Fort Leonard Wood, and he was eager to break the impasse and get the men back to work. Hannan and the POW spokesman conferred at 1 A.M., and on their mutual agreement that the authorities would take no further disciplinary action against the prisoners if they immediately returned to work, the strike was called off.[74] Post headquarters announced emphatically that the prisoners had "gone back to work, no concessions having been made to them." The prisoner whose confinement in the guardhouse sparked the whole disturbance remained there, and authorities promised to hold him there until his punishment was complete.[75]

Prisoner Life at Jefferson Barracks

Being at the Jefferson Barracks POW branch camp didn't feel much different from Fort Leonard Wood or one of the other large base camps. It was big, with many soldiers, both American GIs and German POWs, and a great variety of work. The typical branch camp, on the other hand, was much smaller, usually more isolated, and generally devoted to just one type of labor. German POWs enjoyed the convenience of "post life" enhanced by Jefferson Barracks' location at the doorstep of a major city. The modern post hospital doled out treatment to sick or injured prisoners, and balm for the soul was available at weekly Protestant services conducted by a Concordia Seminary professor, George Schick, or at Catholic Mass, led by Father Preus of Saint Louis University. Despite the efforts of these men, attendance was paltry, perhaps indicating an active Nazi component within the camp. Each service averaged only twenty out of four hundred men, which when combined barely reached the 10 percent mark of the camp's population.

Doris Kresyman recalled a couple incidents that support the suggestion of a strong Nazi presence. "Oh, there were some mean ones [at Jefferson Barracks]. The prisoners would beat up anyone they saw as being pro-American, and several times they [the government] had to move some to Chesterfield to protect them," said Kresyman. "There was one little guy, short with horn-rimmed glasses, and I remember he played the violin really well. He always spoke well of America, and because of it, [the Nazis] broke his knuckles. After that he was shipped to Chesterfield."

The Germans did not limit their hostility to those they considered cooperative with the Americans. An American GI, Helmuth Schulz, was assigned to go to St. Louis in September 1945 to pick up a group of Italian POWs and bring them to the camp at Weingarten, stopping for lunch at Jefferson Barracks on the way back. He recalled what happened when his Italian charges encountered the Germans at Jefferson Barracks: "I was somewhat disturbed inasmuch as the German prisoners of war were working there as cooks and related work, and they displayed their resentment to waiting on the Italians. Here again I was glad I could speak German, and all turned out well," said Schulz, who berated the Germans for harrassing the Weingarten POWs. "They resented the Italians because Mussolini entered the war later when things looked bad for the Germans in the old country, yet he wanted a piece of the pie in case Germany could still win."[76]

Although prisoners were mostly indifferent to religious activity, the camp educational program had many participants; nearly three-quarters of the camp enrolled in classes. Offerings included the usual battery of language classes, plus math, history, literature, shorthand, and veterinary medicine.[77]

A workshop offered opportunities for painting and carving, and the men were particularly active in music and theater. This program really took off when prisoners managed to secure a juke joint of their own, as noted by a camp inspector in December 1944:

> To accommodate the large groups of music makers and theater players, an unused warehouse outside of the stockade has been opened for use at specific times. Authorization has been secured, happily, for the moving of some old CCC building to be located inside the stockade when it is enlarged to provide needed room. The CCC buildings will constitute a theater and a music hall.

> *Stille Nacht, Heilige Nacht* ["Silent Night, Holy Night"] sent to all camps by the YMCA, will be the first play presented in this branch camp. All concerned were greatly pleased to receive copies of this original Christmas drama. Musical activities are circumscribed by lack of instruments, but L. Wood just authorized local purchase of instruments up to a certain dollar figure.[78]

Jefferson Barracks National Cemetery serves as the final resting place for two of the German POWs, as well as the five Italians who were buried at

Nazi POWs stand at attention as burial service is read at the funeral of Gustave Pfarrerr, a POW who was buried at Jefferson Barracks National Cemetery. October 24, 1944. Photograph by staff photographer, St. Louis Post-Dispatch, *1944.* St. Louis Post-Dispatch *News Research Department. © 1944,* St. Louis Post-Dispatch.

*Nazi salute given by German POWs at the funeral of Gustave Pfarrerr, a POW who
was buried at Jefferson Barracks National Cemetery. Men in uniform in foreground
were pallbearers. October 24, 1944. Photograph by staff photographer,* St. Louis Post-
Dispatch, *1944.* St. Louis Post-Dispatch *News Research Department. © 1944,*
St. Louis Post-Dispatch.

Camp Weingarten, whose remains were transferred after that camp closed in
October 1945. These men lie buried in the same row, interspersed with
American veterans and surrounded on all sides by former GIs.

Little is known about *Oberfeldwebel* (Sergeant) Max Suemnick, who
died June 29, 1944, while a prisoner in the United States. However, his
companion buried exactly five feet to his right, Corporal Gustave Pfarrerr,
left a bit more history. Pfarrerr, who died October 21, 1944, was thirty-five
and had been captured at Anzio, Italy, where he lost his right arm. Pfarrerr
was on an Army train en route to an Oklahoma hospital when he fell ill
near St. Louis. He died in the post hospital at Jefferson Barracks.

At the funeral, his fellow POWs and countrymen held at Jefferson
Barracks mustered in formation in front of a coffin draped with a large
swastika. A German officer "expressed the hope that the body, now resting
in a foreign land, might some day be taken back to the home land."[79]

Closure of Jefferson Barracks

The Jefferson Barracks branch camp was deactivated March 30, 1946, and the final group of 346 prisoners was sent back to Fort Leonard Wood for eventual repatriation to Germany. At the same time, the Jefferson Barracks military installation was winding down its service as an active-duty post. The government tore down or sold a number of buildings, including twenty-three that went to the city of St. Louis to be used as housing. Holding 8 families each, the set of structures provided living space for 184 families. Finally, after 120 years of service, the historic installation on the Mississippi would serve only as a limited training area and administrative headquarters site for several National Guard and Army Reserve units. The sprawling national cemetery remains, with its rows of identical white headstones. The rest of the property was transformed into a St. Louis County park. Bikers and joggers use trails that wind through the park, mostly unaware of the history that lies underneath their feet, and of the fact that they tread on the same ground walked by Zachary Taylor, Ulysses S. Grant, Jefferson Davis, and of course, some five hundred German prisoners of war.[80]

St. Louis Ordnance Depot

In close proximity to the camps at Chesterfield and Jefferson Barracks, St. Louis had two POW camps actually within the city limits. One was a floating boat camp, tied up on the Mississippi at the foot of Arsenal Street. From there, fifty German soldiers emerged each morning and performed work on the levees in the immediate vicinity. This Fort Leonard Wood branch camp was relatively short lived, operating only from February 23, 1945, until June 10, 1945.

The other was located at the St. Louis Ordnance Depot at Broadway and Humbold Avenues in the city's north-side Baden neighborhood, between the Mississippi River and the Calvary and Bellefontaine Cemeteries. Opened in March 1944, this branch camp was both larger and of a longer duration than the boat camp. During the sixteen months of the camp's operation, both German prisoners from Fort Leonard Wood and Italian POWs from Weingarten were housed at the facility at various times but in separate sections when both groups were present.

St. Louisan Mark Orlando remembered going by the camp and seeing the prisoners outside. "You'd take the Broadway streetcar and get off there at Humboldt and walk down a hill to the Mississippi. There was a ferry there that would take you out to Mosenthein Island for fifty cents, and people used to go out there to swim," recalled Orlando. "Right there on Broadway, on the right hand side, about a hundred yards down, was the camp. We used to pass it. They had two compounds there, and the Italians were closest to the fence. The Italians would be out in the compound, playing soccer or sometimes volleyball, and of course a pretty girl would walk by the camp there, and they'd throw the ball out over the fence into the street."

Orlando was watching all this one day when he was thirteen or fourteen years old, and he saw one of the prisoners lifting up the fence like he was going to crawl out underneath. "I pointed this out to the guard, but he waved it off," said Orlando. "He knew the prisoner was just going to go out of the bottom of the fence and fetch the ball and come right back in."

Orlando and his friends would hang around the camp occasionally and chat with the guards on the way to their swimming spot. "One of them told me, 'Those Italians are a lot friendlier—you don't have to worry about them,'" recalled Orlando. "But the Germans—the guard told me that originally both groups had been housed together until one day when they played a soccer game. The Italians had won, and the Germans got mad, and they had a big fight. That's why they had to separate the two groups."[81]

Dell King also grew up nearby, and he was a regular presence at the camp as well. "We'd walk down there almost every Saturday," said King, who was about twelve at the time. "We'd give them cigarettes, and they'd trade us Hershey bars for them."

When they weren't trading goods, King and his friends enjoyed provoking the soldiers. "These Germans would walk around outside in their uniforms and boots," said King. "We'd stand there at the fence and holler '*Achtung!*' and stuff like that at them. I think those fellows would have strangled us if they got the chance."[82]

Work at the Depot

The Ordnance Depot was a major hub for repair, reconditioning, shipment, and distribution of Army vehicles, parts, and certain munition types. "All the manufacturers would ship their parts into the depot," said Phil Kratzert, an inventory specialist at the facility. "We'd store the items, track them, ship them out as needed, and then order more when we got low so that there was always enough on hand. We had every type of part you could imagine."[83]

Prisoners at the depot loaded and unloaded train cars, built crates used for shipping the various replacement parts, and prepared vehicles for transport and repair. The prisoners' work was valuable to the government, but frequently the issue was raised whether or not their efforts violated what was considered "permitted work" under the Geneva Convention. In addition to barring any work under dangerous conditions, the Geneva

Convention also prohibited prisoners from performing any tasks that would directly and exclusively benefit their captors' armed forces in military operations. For example, using POWs to work with batteries that could be used in a variety of civilian and military vehicles was allowed, but requiring them to repair tank plating or make ammunition was not. Because of the nature of the activity at the depot, Army officials were particularly vigilant about making sure this rule was clearly understood and practiced. Nonetheless, questions sometimes still arose. For instance, even after Italy aligned itself with the Allies in October 1943, Italian prisoners at the St. Louis Ordnance Depot who worked on Army rolling stock complained to a visiting inspector that their tasks were in contravention with the Geneva Convention guidelines. "We assured them after an inquiry that no machine passing through their hands would carry arms or munitions," wrote Guy Metraux from the International Red Cross, who visited the camp in January 1945.[84]

Joe Rice worked at the St. Louis Ordnance Depot after his graduation from McBride High School, from 1942 through the fall of 1944. He started in the office but soon moved into the warehouse and worked as a storekeeper, sorting parts and placing them in specific storage bins and locations. Although the Italian POWs worked mainly unloading boxes from the cars that sat on a railroad siding that snaked through the facility, at times they worked with Rice in other parts of the depot. "I got pretty friendly with them," said Rice, who bought himself a little Italian dictionary and phrasebook to help with conversation. "We'd talk every day."

On many summer Sundays, Rice took the launch out to Mosenthein Island to swim and picnic. "We'd walk by the depot, my friends and wife and me, and the prisoners would just hoot and whistle at us," said Rice. "I worked with a bunch of them, of course, so they were hollering at me just like they'd holler at any one of their buddies who'd be passing by."[85]

Unlike Rice, Kratzert had little contact with the POWs because of his job, which was located in a different part of the facility. On one occasion though, Kratzert and his coworkers did socialize with the German POWs. "It was Christmas time, and we were getting ready to have a little party at lunch time," said Kratzert. "Somebody said, 'Hey, why don't we include the Germans?' so we invited them over. We played records and everybody sang and danced. It was a real nice time."[86]

Recreation

At first, like at any other start-up branch camp, prisoners at the St. Louis Ordnance Depot were fairly famished for diversion. The first crew of Weingarten POWs who arrived there in the spring of 1944 had nothing to occupy their time in the off-hours. "Within the past week I have been consulting with two of the colonels in charge of the Prisoners of War at the Army Depot in Saint Louis, and we have been trying our best to work out a feasible method of giving these poor men some recreation," wrote St. Louis monsignor John Cody to the Reverend John O'Hara, military ordinariate of the Catholic Church in New York. "There are 170 of them quartered in barracks at this depot, but there is not a shade of recreational facilities for these men and there is no place where they could even have movies. The men are quite discontented."

Army officers created a plan to bring the men twice a week to the nearby Baden Theater for movies, but Cody was skeptical of this plan and anticipated hostility from people in the area. "I fear difficulties on the part of some of our hot-headed citizens who are opposed to Italian as well as German prisoners," wrote Cody, who also expected problems of another sort within the depot itself.

Italian prisoners wearing appropriate ID badges were free to come and go within the depot, moving through different parts of the facility as required by their job. Many civilians, including women, worked there, and Cody was concerned about the possibility of romantic intertwinings occurring as a result of that interaction. Interestingly, he points to the women at the depot as the source of the problem, portraying them as schemers intending to ensnare the helpless POWs through their feminine wiles. Cody wrote:

> I must say truthfully that the men [POWs] at this Army Depot seem to understand full well the Army regulations forbidding them to associate with the American girls who are employed there. Fortunately for me, both the Colonel in charge of the Depot and Major Cavanaugh, who is the Security Officer, have issued stringent rules to the girls forbidding them to talk with the prisoners. Of course, when they are free to go and come in accordance with Army regulations, there may be some possibility of unwarranted alliances being established between the prisoner and some of these girls, whose morals, I regret to say, are not always the highest.[87]

With the creation of the Italian Service Units (ISU) in March 1944, which put cooperative Italian POWs in special military units under the control of the U.S. Army, prisoners at the St. Louis Ordnance Depot suddenly began to feel like regular soldiers once again. This program, designed to provide whole blocks of Italian troops to work in quartermaster, transportation, and other service and support roles on a number of U.S. military posts, called for them to receive uniforms identical to those of American soldiers with the exception of a green oval-shaped "Italy" patch on one shoulder. They were to be treated much like GIs. The prisoners who signed up for the ISU program were paid at the same rate as U.S. privates and could even get weekend passes.

The ISU program was started almost simultaneous with the kick-off of the branch camp at the St. Louis Ordnance Depot, and after just a couple of weeks, the Weingarten prisoners there were sworn in as members of the ISU. Though this group would work at the depot just a few more weeks before being transferred out to attend a "basic training" course in their specialized branch of service, their status as members of the ISU gave Cody a double dose of worry. Now, instead of just worrying about the prisoners being hassled at the movie theater or consorting with women at the ordnance depot, suddenly he had 170 men with the freedom to take on the town every night of the week and an unrestrained two and a half days each weekend. Cody quickly organized programs for the men in conjunction with the Catholic Church and called upon the faithful of the city to open their homes to these men for the sake of providing wholesome entertainment and Christian influence in a city filled with temptation. "We plan to bring them each weekday evening to our National Catholic Community Service Club and thus to place them in contact with the Catholics of the city," Cody told O'Hara. "Two of the Italian parishes have offered to organize programs so that these men can be invited to homes where we know they will be in good hands."

Cody oversaw the planning of a number of outings for the prisoners, including trips to the Fox Theatre on North Grand Avenue, a priest-led weekly tour of places of interest in the city that began at the St. Louis Cathedral, and every-Sunday expeditions to the Hill neighborhood for Mass at St. Ambrose Parish and dinners with Italian families living nearby. Nevertheless, he was still worried, as he told O'Hara: "I might say in general, Your Excellency, that the men are very happy in their new-found liberty but the problem of recreation, that is, wholesome recreation, is of some concern to me," wrote Cody. "I have done everything possible to keep them from falling into the hands of the undesirable who are, alas, only too often anxious to take in these men."[88]

Cody's concern about the Italian POWs and the corrupting influences that could befall them did not last. The Italians at the St. Louis Ordnance Depot who had enrolled in the ISU departed for transfer to other stations at the beginning of May 1944, bidding farewell to those who had been such gracious hosts.

In a letter to Harry Arthur, manager of the Fox Theatre, Cody forwarded a note of thanks from the Italian prisoners and expressed his own appreciation for Arthur's help in making possible the POW visits to that splendid facility. His gratitude to Arthur was indeed the same deep appreciation he felt toward all those who went out of their way to make the Italian POWs feel at home in a strange city and to keep them out of trouble. "I can assure you that your generosity and kindness to them will long remain a lasting memory, and I also wish to assure you how deeply I personally have appreciated your generous cooperation," wrote Cody. "At the time we came to you to ask your assistance, I can tell you confidentially that we were well close to serious difficulties at the Camp due to the utter lack of recreational facilities. The men enjoyed their visits to the theatre immensely and each and every one of them asked me to express the deep appreciation they feel towards you personally and towards the Officers of the Organization."[89]

The prisoners sent to replace the departing POWs also came from Camp Weingarten but had not volunteered for the ISU when the opportunity was offered. Being "nonparticipants" meant that they were considered regular POWs and therefore not entitled to the same privileges as their predecessors. With the arrival of the new group of Italian prisoners, again the attention turned to bolstering the recreational opportunities at the camp because the new men did not have the same freedom to leave the premises as the first group. With the passage of time, Army officials secured equipment for the POWs, and a small library was established with books brought by the prisoners and augmented by *The New York Times* and *Il Progresso Americano* newspapers that arrived each day. In their free time, the prisoners enjoyed use of a billiard table, a small bowling alley, and a soccer field established next to their barracks, and they saw three movies a week shown inside the compound. By January 1945, an inspection report noted, "material conditions at the camp [were] excellent from all points of view."[90]

Eventually, the Catholic Church resumed hosting visits by POWs to the Hill, an effort that had a tremendously positive effect on the interned Italian prisoners. "Through the gracious cooperation of Colonel Glidden, Commanding Officer of Camp Weingarten, I obtained permission to take these prisoners to Saint Ambrose Catholic Church in an Italian quarter for Mass on Sunday, and after Mass we took them to a large Italian restaurant where a dinner was served to them by a committee under the guidance of Fathers Lupo and Palumbo, pastor and assistant at Saint Ambrose Church," wrote Monsignor Cody.[91] The *St. Louis Post-Dispatch* confirmed these outings, reporting:

> A large group of Italian prisoners of war attended special services yesterday at St. Ambrose Catholic Church in the "Hill" district and were given breakfast afterwards at Rufferi's restaurant. The church was closed to the public during the mass and military police guarded all entrances.... A crowd outside the church watched the prisoners enter and leave but there was no demonstration. No one was allowed to speak to the prisoners and the throng simply looked on curiously.[92]

The men at the St. Louis Ordnance Depot continued their work until that POW camp was closed at the end of August 1945. At that time, the 216 POWs left at the camp, all Italians by that point, returned to Weingarten to be repatriated to Italy.

POW field hands. Courtesy of National Archives.

Chapter Eight

Bootheel Camps

THE DOMESTIC LABOR SHORTAGE in the United States hit every area of agriculture hard, but no farm industry was affected more than cotton growers. Their work was particularly labor intensive, and when the opportunity came for contracting POW labor, they were especially pleased.

In the fall of 1944, several camps sprang up to work the cotton harvest in Missouri's Bootheel, where the eastern edge of the Ozarks melts away into the broad flat floodplain of the Mississippi River. Beginning in late summer 1944, POWs were living and working in the fields near six little towns in far southeast Missouri: Charleston, Kennett, Malden, Marston, New Madrid, and Sikeston. Some camps were short lived, such as the one at Malden, which operated just more than two months. Others turned into semipermanent operations, including the one at Sikeston, which was open from November 1944 through August 1945. First started as an initial run at corn detasseling in the fields of the C. F. McMullin Estate, a hybrid-seed corn producer, the prisoners then picked cotton there and at other farms in the area, as well as working in a nearby cotton-oil mill. Another relatively long-running camp was at Marston, located between Portageville and New Madrid, where 425 German POWs from Camp Clarinda, Iowa, performed a variety of farm labor between August 1944 and February 1946.

The process for setting up each camp was the same. Once the arrangements for the camps were made in terms of government contracts and other necessary agreements, an advance party of POWs and American GIs went to the site and erected tents, fencing, and lights in preparation for the arrival of the main body. For example, Lieutenant M. L. Reiss and several Americans traveled from Weingarten to Sikeston in September 1944 to finalize details of the branch

camp going up there. The hundred or so Italian officers and enlisted POWs who volunteered for the cotton-picking detail would live in huts from Jefferson Barracks, and Reiss and the other GIs supervised a crew who set up the shelters and fencing needed for the camp.

Religious Life

As a great many of the prisoners sent to these Bootheel branch camps were Italian Catholics from Weingarten, the St. Louis Archdiocese was vigilant in ensuring that the men received proper opportunities to attend Mass. Monsignor John Cody tried to make sure that as the southeastern Missouri branch camps kept popping up and disappearing, the local parish priests would be available to minister to them.

More than 300 Italians "just moved in," wrote Cody in a letter requesting the designation of the Reverend C. P. Lyon, a pastor in Wilhelmina, Missouri, as auxiliary chaplain to the camp at Kennett. He sent off a similar letter asking the Reverend S. P. Stocking, pastor at St. Eustachius in Portageville, for help in ministering to the 450 prisoners located at the camp at Marston, four miles north of Portageville, noting that the government anticipated at one point bringing as many as 700 more. Cody also called on other priests at Bootheel parishes in Charleston and Sikeston to conduct services for the prisoners at camps located nearby.[1]

Charleston and Kennett

In Charleston, the four hundred Italian prisoners from Camp Weingarten were housed on the grounds of that city's National Guard Armory during their stay from October 1944 through the end of the year. Originally, the Army intended for the prisoners to live in a tent city on the lot directly west of the armory, but when the tents and other equipment failed to arrive on time from Kansas City, the POWs set up sleeping quarters in the armory's auditorium, and other portions of the building served as the mess hall and administrative offices.[2]

A committee of Charleston-area farmers led by A. J. Drinkwater, Jr., Clifford Vowels, and E. L. Brown, Jr., secured the POW labor for the cotton harvest, posting a deposit of $700 as an advance against anticipated wages and $2,000 in cash to defray the cost of a bathhouse and to pay for fence posts, wire, light poles, and other equipment required to secure the camp. The committee hired J. W. Barron as full-time manager of the venture and set about divvying up the manpower, allocating 320 prisoners to farms in Mississippi County and the remaining 80 to neighboring Scott County. Area farmers could apply for POW labor as long as they met a number of requirements adopted by the committee and, instead of an hourly rate, paid for the amount of cotton picked by the prisoners at a rate of $2 per one hundred pounds, about what an average man picked per day. Conditions imposed by the committee for hiring prisoners included hiring a minimum group size of ten POWs, posting an advance deposit equal to one day's picking, and providing all necessary equipment and transportation between the farm and the prison camp.

Charleston residents galled by local food shortages apparently complained to the camp commander that the feeding of the prisoners was causing the rest of the town to do without. The complaints were enough that the commander found himself on the front page of the *Charleston Enterprise-Courier*, trying to explain that the camp was not responsible for any bare shelves in the grocery store. "Other than the materials used in construction of the camp the only items which have been purchased thus far on the local market are bread, fresh milk and ice," the commander was quoted as saying in the article, which was intended to "correct certain misinformation currently coming from residents of the Charleston community." The prisoners at the camp and their American guards also lacked the scarce items, just as the locals did. "For the last five days due to the local shortage, this camp has been entirely without fresh milk," the commander continued. "All other supplies are secured from the nearest commissary and canteen, which is at the Malden Air Base."[3]

The POW camps in little towns all over the Bootheel gave southeastern Missouri residents many opportunities to interact with prisoners. Carl Williams of Kennett was about twelve when the Italian POWs came by his family's lumber mill to pick up a load of sawdust. "They were getting it for their jumping pit out at the camp, where they'd do long jumping and high jumping," said Williams. "You'd see them out there playing sports, and they looked like they were having a good time, laughing and joking, not like whipped dogs or anything." His family owned property adjacent to the camp, and Williams walked by the front gate on his way home from school. "The camp was out on the edge of town. It was still in the city limits but there wasn't much but vacant lots around it," he said.[4]

The Dunklin County Farm Labor Board, led by Earl Jones, Kimble Swindle, and Fred Chailland, organized the effort to bring the prisoners to Kennett. Residents first learned of the plans for the camp in an article that the *Dunklin Democrat* ran on August 17, 1943, titled "War Prisoners to Be Available Here." At a minimum, said the piece, three hundred prisoners, and possibly more, were coming from Weingarten to work in the cotton harvest. "The main difficulty standing in the way of bringing the prisoners to this county to supplement the local labor which is insufficent to properly harvest the large crop, which is estimated at 80,000 bales," said the paper, "is the manner of housing the group of prisoners together with the army personnel, which of necessity must accompany the group."[5]

Jones, Chailland, and Swindle surveyed available sites and settled on the property adjacent to the Williams place. Kennett resident Sue Gill recalled:

> We lived about four blocks from where the camp was, and it was at the east end of Second Street where it now runs into Chance. From there on east, there was nothing.... When you passed that you were out in the country. I was just a little girl but we would venture over on our bicycles, would watch through the fence as the prisoners played volleyball.

Gill said that she was too young to have gone there to flirt with the prisoners, but she observed that the Italians were in fact "good-looking people." She remembered, "They would call to the people [passing by], you know, say something to them, but I don't know anyone who could understand them."[6]

Shirley Davis was eight years old, playing hopscotch out in front of her house on Cedar Street, when the trainload of prisoners came rolling into town. "I was a very nosy child, and I liked to watch the trains, and the train was moving slowly as it headed southward. There were lots of voices, and so I ran down to the end of the street to watch the train," said Davis. "As the train came by all of these soldiers [POWs] had moved to the windows, and they were hanging out of the windows, and they were waving and hollering and smiling and laughing. It was a foreign language, and I couldn't understand what they were saying." As Davis waved at the prisoners, suddenly she felt a yank on her shoulder. It was her mother, who was furious at the little girl. Davis was in serious trouble, said her mother, for being "friendly to the enemy."

"But I knew that was not true. I knew they were not enemies because I had seen enemies in the movies and they did not laugh. They were not friendly. These men were laughing and shouting greetings at me and waving," said Davis. "And I knew they couldn't be the enemy because enemies didn't do that. Enemies went around looking serious and using their boots to knock down doors."[7]

Grover Wicker, who worked as a farm manager at the Cotton Exchange Bank, knew quite a bit about the agricultural operations in the area, and so he was put in charge of operations of the Kennett camp. Wicker's daughter Pauline was about twenty-two years old at the time, and she recalled the prisoners fishing in a drainage ditch that ran alongside the camp. "They would hook these little-bitty fish out of there, maybe only three or four inches long," recalled Pauline (Wicker) Burns. "Then the Italians would take them back to the camp and fry them up."

Burns also remembered a strike of sorts that took place at the camp. "One day they decided that they weren't going out to work, that they had had enough," said Burns. "Well, my daddy told the cook that if the prisoners were going to take the day off, so could he. So they didn't get any breakfast. The same thing happened at lunch and at dinner. By the next morning, they were good and ready for breakfast and ready to go back to work."

For a smaller camp, and one relatively short lived, the Kennett camp had a fair amount of drama packed into its few weeks of operation. "Another time four of the prisoners decided they were going to bust out of there. They had relatives in Chicago and were going to head that way," recalled Burns. "Instead of traveling north, they went south, going in absolutely the wrong direction." The men stayed off of the highway but got wet and cold wading through the diversion channels that crisscross the area, routing runoff from river-bottom farmland into the nearby Mississippi River. "It gets kinda swampy down that way they were headed, and I think those fellows got a little scared," said Burns. "They finally went up to a man's house near Rives, Missouri [about ten miles south], and knocked on the door. They were cold and hungry, so he took them in and fed them, then called my daddy and called the sheriff, who went and got them. I think they were glad to get back to the camp."[8]

Residents recall mixed reaction to the prisoners. Kennett endured the same lack of basic foodstuffs that other area communities experienced, and there was some discontent toward the Italians, who residents felt were partially responsible for the shortage. Others felt a sort of empathy for the prisoners, knowing that they had been caught up in something beyond their control.

Sikeston

In Sikeston, Italian prisoners had similarly frequent contact with townspeople, as they were allowed to use the municipal swimming pool twice a week, attend Mass at St. Francis Xavier Church on Sundays, and regularly take in movies at the Malone Theater.

The first murmurings about the possibility of establishing a camp at Sikeston came when the Reverend John O'Neill, pastor of St. Francis Xavier, presumably acting on behalf of local agricultural interests, wrote to Monsignor Cody of the St. Louis Archdiocese in October 1943 to ask about the possibility of obtaining POW help for farm labor. Cody referred O'Neill to Colonel Glidden, commander of the camp at Weingarten. Glidden sent the priest a packet of information, everything needed to facilitate the process, including the forms necessary for applying for POW help through the War Manpower Commission, which was responsible for determining labor needs and allocating prisoners accordingly. Glidden wrote, "We will be very glad to do everything we can to assist you in this matter. The Prisoners of War are anxious to go to work and we want to do everything we can to assist in relieving the labor shortage."[9]

This need for labor in the Sikeston area eventually led to the establishment of a camp at the C. F. McMullin Estate, an eight-thousand-acre farm outside of town. There, in July and August 1944, Italian prisoners tried to master the finer points of detasseling: lopping off the pollen-laden plumes from the tops of corn plants to allow pollination with other varieties in adjacent rows to produce hybrid seed. It took a while to get the prisoners up to speed, recalled Marilyn Grant, whose father, Elmer Grant, Sr., managed the farm. "Those first three days in the field were pretty rough," said Grant. "The interpreters they used didn't know farm work, so they had difficulty explaining the details of the detasseling process."[10]

Initially, the Sikeston prisoners were only going to be used for a few weeks during that summer for the work in the cornfields at the McMullin Estate. Accordingly, their lodging at the camp, which was based in a grove of trees adjoining the home of William "Bill" Pratt six miles north of Sikeston—an area also known to some as Grant City—was simple canvas tents with wood floors. By August 1, 1944, the detasseling was done, and the prisoners had returned to Weingarten.

However, with the need for additional labor and the positive results of this first experience, farmers in Sikeston and areas beyond clamored for more help from the prisoners. In mid-September, a party of POWs returned to Sikeston to tear down the tents and erect basic wooden barracks. The approaching winter and the likelihood of a long-term presence of POWs at the Sikeston camp prompted the Army's decision to fit the barracks with heat and running water. POWs working with American GIs under the supervisor of Weingarten's post engineer, Major Max Adams, put together the prefab wooden barracks. The rest of the men arrived not long after, bringing the total at the Sikeston camp to one hundred Italian officers. About forty of this group continued to work on the McMullin Estate, bringing in its cotton harvest from seven hundred acres; another thirty POWs went to work for Pinnell Hunter on acreage owned by S. L. Hunter and Sons Farms; and the remaining thirty checked in at the Sikeston Cotton-Oil Mill, the first time the prisoners had worked in a plant in southeast Missouri.[11]

Sikeston's Judy Bowman was about five years old the first time she encountered the prisoners. One day when the prisoners were swimming, lined up inside the fence surrounding the pool, waiting to enter the water, she ran up to investigate. The men, who missed their own families terribly, were charmed by the little girl. "All of a sudden, the prisoners were reaching out through the wire, poking their hands out because they wanted to pat my head or feel my cheek," remembered Bowman. "Of course, I didn't know what they were doing, that they just wanted to touch a little girl, and I was terrified by all of these prisoners trying to grab me." Bowman fled back home, upset by what had occurred at the pool. "My mother wiped my tears and explained to me what had happened. They just missed their own children so much that seeing a little boy or girl reminded them of home," said Bowman. "My mother took me back each week that summer to visit with the prisoners."[12]

Ann Clark was also growing up in Sikeston at the time and remembered the town's interest when the POWs went to swim in the Sikeston pool. "Everyone went to see it, the adults, kids, everybody—it was quite a show," she remembered. "The men seemed to have a ball, and they really swam beautifully. The pool had a three-meter springboard, and some of the prisoners were quite good divers."[13]

Residents recalled only one incident involving the Sikeston POWs that prompted some alarm. One day, one of the prisoners snuck away from a work detail and hid in the house owned by Bill Pratt. Whether the prisoner was motivated by loneliness or boredom (as suspected by those who recalled the event) or had more sinister plans in mind, he didn't harm or threaten the woman living there, but he scared her nevertheless. "He was a young Italian lieutenant," said Marilyn Grant. "My dad didn't think he had any ill intent but it sure caused a big hoo-ha."

As a result of the incident, authorities at the Sikeston camp instituted much stricter rules regarding the treatment of prisoners and the manner in which they could interact with locals. This outraged the other prisoners, but their anger was not directed at camp officials, rather toward the disobedient prisoner. They blamed him for ruining the camp's easygoing atmosphere marked by trust and friendly relations with local residents. "The other prisoners were really upset," said Grant. "They were incensed that their privileges had been canceled and that the good treatment they had experienced was put in jeopardy by this fellow."[14] Because of the animosity toward this POW, soon afterward the Americans running the camp "had to send him away to protect him from the other prisoners," said Joy Corbin Ghersi, whose father, E. L. Corbin, supervised POWs working on the McMullin Estate.[15]

One of the Italians held at Sikeston, Felice Ghersi, actually returned to southeastern Missouri after the war, obtained American citizenship, and began farming in the Sikeston area in 1958. Ghersi had been part of the large contingent of Italians held at Camp Weingarten after capture in North Africa in 1943. He disliked the monotony of the main camp and so when the opportunity arose to work at one of the side camps, the officer volunteered. He was one of several hundred sent to work near Sikeston. In an interesting twist of fate, Ghersi came back because of a romance that developed long after the war between himself and Joy, whose father had been Ghersi's supervisor at the camp. "My father was the plant breeder and sales manager at McMullin estates," said Joy. "During the war there was a terrific shortage of men to do the farm work, so the POWs were really needed. During the off-season, a team of four prisoners helped my father with his work."

Ghersi was one of the POWs who worked especially closely with Corbin, and the Corbin family developed a friendship with Ghersi and the others, even inviting them into their home for meals. Though Joy, then twenty-two years old, lived in Sikeston, she and her future husband never actually met. She worked in town, and her path never crossed with the man who would become her husband.

After Ghersi wrote to Corbin, Joy replied, and thus began an eight-year correspondence. On a trip to Europe in 1955, Joy stopped off in Italy to visit Felice and his family. She said, "When we met, we more or less decided we would get married." Because of the difficulties of life in Italy even a decade after the war, the two decided to make Sikeston their home. Joy returned to the United States and flew back to Italy a year later for their wedding, which took place at the Turin City Hall. Being married didn't mean being together, however. Because of red tape and delays in getting a visa, it took two years for Ghersi to rejoin his wife in the United States.

When Ghersi arrived in 1958, he moved into the Corbin farmhouse with Joy, her mother, and her father. Ghersi was already in his fifties and had only limited (POW) farming experience, but he successfully took to his new way of life. Ghersi was recognized twice for his farming skills by the local farm-service group and by the University of Missouri, honors that were meaningful to him.

Surely the gentle Italian officer never imagined that he would be returning to the place where he was a prisoner. But the friendship of his boss during the time of his stay in Sikeston started the process that would bring him back to America. "Now, it is the same for me to live here as it would be to live in Italy," said Ghersi, now deceased, in a 1982 interview. "This is my home."[16]

Marston

Like other Bootheel farmers, New Madrid County cotton growers were excited about the prospect of bringing in POWs to help with the crop. Led by growers Arline Avery and Albert Beis, the New Madrid County Extension Service and the New Madrid County Farm Labor Association stepped up to sponsor the camp at Marston to bring much-needed labor to the area to pick cotton. Though the cotton was ready for harvest, only 20 percent was picked at that point, so the coming POW labor was extremely helpful. The prisoners, all enlisted German soldiers, originated from the main camp at Clarinda, Iowa, although control of the branch camp would soon be transferred to Fort Leonard Wood, which was much closer to the camp. An advance party of fifty POWs bunked down in the Marston high school gym while they worked to prepare the campsite in late September and early October 1944, erecting fencing, latrines, and sturdy square tents with wooden floors for housing in anticipation of the larger group. Approximately four hundred POWs ended up at the camp, which was built in a grove of trees on the Charles Pikey farm on Highway 61 near Conran, Missouri, about eleven miles south of New Madrid. When the camp was ready and the rest of the POWs arrived, they started picking cotton, bringing in some 500,000 pounds during the first month alone. Later, when the cotton crop had been brought in, the prisoners chopped cotton stalks in preparation of the next year's crop and labored in the soybean-oil mill in nearby Portageville.[17]

POW field hand bundles saplings. Courtesy of National Archives.

Army officials, after months of accusations that they were coddling the prisoners, took members of the press on a tour of the Marston camp in March 1945. They trotted the newsmen around in the mud to show them that, contrary to popular perception, the prisoners were not living the high life and free to come and go at their pleasure.

Colonel Andrew Duvall, commander of the main camp at Fort Leonard Wood and sponsor of the auxiliary camp, led the tour. Duvall pointed out that even though the Army's shortage of manpower necessitated that the

POW field hand prepares row crops. Courtesy of National Archives.

prisoners were guarded only loosely, the security level was sufficient to prevent almost every problem, and they experienced a low rate of escape. The barracks area was constantly watched, and a system of roving guard patrols and periodic field checks of the POWs working under a civilian foreman kept tabs on the men out working in the fields.

Duvall also pointed out that prisoners were not receiving the same lavish menu that early on had provoked the press's criticizing of the Army. Food shortages affected everyone in the country that spring, and Duvall emphasized that the prisoners' food was rather similar to what civilians were eating. Dinner that night for the prisoners was pancakes with scrambled eggs and bacon—a fine meal but nothing particularly rich. Gone were butter and milk, said Duvall, and POWs got meat but once a day.

Cigarettes were also limited in the camp canteen, and prisoners griped to the newsmen (with rather convenient timing, in the Army's opinion) that they had recently been without tobacco for three weeks. Though the Army's rebuttal of the charges of coddling that plagued the POW program was long overdue, hosting these type of visits for the press made it possible to present a more accurate picture about life in an internment camp.

Another question Duvall received during the press tour came from the POW camp spokesman and was so appropriate in its timing that it seems prearranged. The spokesman asked Duvall about the possibility of getting some shrubs as well as more shovels to improve and beautify the camp area. Duvall parlayed the opportunity this question provided into a demonstration for the press that the Army was not going out of its way to be soft with the prisoners. With the newsmen standing around scribbling every word in their notebooks, the colonel told the prisoner that if the Germans wanted shrubs, they could go dig them out of the woods or else buy them with profits from the canteen.[18]

Rolf Wunderlich was twenty-four when he was captured by General Patton's army in Italy, flushed out of a barn at gunpoint by a bunch of GIs in June 1944. Transported by truck and boat, Wunderlich ended up in a big camp near Naples, Italy, where he waited with other groups of prisoners until a group of twenty-five hundred was moved to the United States in August. Wunderlich was one of those for whom the trip across the Atlantic was rather enjoyable. "We were allowed to stay on the forecastle (the front part of the vessel) from dawn until dusk, which was extremely kind and generous. As a matter of fact, I got a feeling I never had before: enjoying the sunny side of life as a tourist."

Guarded by destroyers watching for submarines and balloons designed to entangle low-flying aircraft, the convoy carrying Wunderlich and the other POWs safely crossed the ocean and arrived at Newport News, Virginia, on September 18, 1944. From there, Wunderlich rode a train to Camp Clarinda, Iowa, where he stayed just long enough to learn that he was headed for southeastern Missouri. "We arrived at Marston from Clarinda (via St. Louis–Hannibal) about the 10th of October, 1944. The Camp, U.S. Army tents, was being erected. Some 50 prisoners had been sent down some days before to prepare the camp. The tents were set on a wooded floor and intended to accommodate four men each. They were connected by boardwalks which were indispensable when heavy rainfall occurred," recalled Wunderlich. "In addition to the tents, a messhall was constructed, made of corrugated sheet metal. There was also a shower and, last but not least, a toilet (I believe, an eight-seater)."

Since Wunderlich could speak English and was handy with a typewriter, he served as an office clerk. The other prisoners, of course, were at Marston to work in the field, and they left early each day. "After breakfast the working details went out in the morning, which means they were picked up by the farmers," he remembered. "One major problem was that the access road to the camp entrance often was so wet and muddy that trucks got stuck. During rainy periods work in the cotton fields was impossible, so the men had to stay in the camp."

Wunderlich mentioned that some of his fellow prisoners were former Afrika Korps soldiers. True to form, their pride and confidence in German superiority caused some friction in the camp, with both the farmers as well as the more recently captured German prisoners who knew how poorly the war was actually going for Germany. "Sometimes POWs refused to board the trucks [after they had been driven down the muddy lane coming into the camp], alleging they were not clean enough. Sometimes they 'went on strike' because they did not get enough potatoes," said Wunderlich of the Afrika Korps men. "They still believed in the final victory and were fanatic. When we told them that the war had virtually been lost because we had seen the bombed cities in Germany and knew that the German troops were in retreat on all fronts, they threatened us with murder and assassination."

Other than these conflicts within the camp and worries about people back home, life in the camp was pleasant enough, said Wunderlich. Prisoners worked and earned money to save or spend. The canteen was well stocked with cigarettes, soft drinks, soap, socks, and even radios for POWs with enough coupons in their wallets to afford them. He recalled the going rates for various items: $.05 for soap, $.10 for a chocolate bar, $.15 for cigarettes, $.35 for a pair of socks, and $6 for a wallet.

Wunderlich enjoyed good relationships with the U.S. personnel assigned to the camp and recalled riding regularly with Corporal Bob Rath into Portageville or Marston to pick up the mail or run other errands. "I remember Christmas 1944 when we received a message from Sikeston that an Army Jeep had engine trouble. So I went...to Sikeston to tow the stranded vehicle back to the camp," remembered Wunderlich. "It was for the first time in my life that I saw nearly a whole city festively illuminated by thousands of colored lights. During all those war years no lights had been allowed in Germany for fear of enemy air raids."

Despite its relative isolation, prisoners at the Marston camp showed remarkable industry in the cultural arts. The camp's musical inventory included four violins, an accordion, a piano, four trumpets, and a drum set. A twenty-five-member choral group gave concerts and performed at weekly church services that YMCA inspector Howard Hong called "the main event" for the camp during a March 1945 visit. Both Protestant and Catholic services were held in the mess hall, and attendance averaged seventy and one hundred men for worship, respectively. "As a rule, the prisoners dressed up on Sunday for the church service held in the camp," said Wunderlich. "They held their clothes in good condition and liked to use some aftershave to smell good."[19]

The usual sports held the prisoners' enthusiasm, though classes also competed for their attention during their free time. For a branch camp, the Marston school was broad and well organized, offering weekly lectures in astronomy, letter writing, hygiene, rural life, the Rhineland, and more.[20]

As the POW program wound down in the early spring of 1946, the GIs and POWs at the Marston camp began the process of dismantling the operation. By February 1946, only 70 prisoners were left of the 425 who once were there, and at the end of that month, the camp closed completely. "Some of us had tears in our eyes when we left the camp site aboard a bus. After losing the war, we didn't think that we would be able to come back to America," said Wunderlich. He eventually made more than twenty trips to the United States in the decades after the war, including several jaunts back to Marston and the greater Portageville area.[21]

From Marston, the Germans traveled to Fort Leonard Wood, where they stayed only about three weeks before packing up again. At the end of March 1946, they climbed onto a troop train heading west, to the port at Oakland, California, where Wunderlich and his companions boarded a ship and sailed south to the Panama Canal. They steamed through the locks and up the other side, eventually landing at Liverpool, England. Wunderlich spent another year working as POW in Scotland before finally being repatriated in 1947.[22]

POW Paul Markl sketched this scene of life at the Orrick camp. Courtesy of Dagmar Ford.

Chapter Nine

Kansas City–Area Camps

L IKE ST. LOUIS, WHICH HAD FIVE BRANCH CAMPS within the greater metropolitan area, Kansas City also had a number of installations housing POWs. Prisoners detasseled corn, dried alfalfa, and dug potatoes, doing whatever American farmers needed in the field. Several of these camps were short lived, including the ones at Lexington and Orrick, Missouri, which operated for just a period of weeks at certain times of the crop year. At Orrick, 351 German soldiers from Fort Leonard Wood arrived on July 12, 1945, and worked for barely a month before packing up and moving out again.

Other camps provided workers for more industrial purposes. The POWs at the camp in Riverside, Missouri, located just north of downtown Kansas City, worked in cold-storage plants, while prisoners in north Kansas City worked at the U.S. Gypsum Company facility. Regardless of where they were placed, the prisoners significantly eased the labor shortage in Missouri.

Atherton and Orrick

One of the earliest POW work programs was in Jackson County. The prisoners had been in Missouri for only six months, since December 1942, and up to that point the government had used POWs for few projects outside its camps. So it was national news in 1943 when the government announced its decision to use POWs for contract work in the Kansas City area. The June 29 *New York Times* reported, "Camp Clark officials report that 250 Italian prisoners of war have contracted to dig potatoes at Courtney and Atherton, Mo., where 1,000 acres and 1,200 acres, respectively await harvest labor."[1]

The Missouri River bottoms on the eastern end of Jackson County from Courtney to Orrick were a major source of potatoes from the mid-1920s to the mid-1950s. The rich, sandy soil deposited by the river proved ideal for potato growth, yielding three hundred to four hundred bushels per acre of Irish Cobbler, Red Triumph, Warba, and Pontia potatoes. Growing potatoes was a risky proposition, though, as entire crops could be wiped out by floods or ruined by drought. The drain on manpower during World War II also complicated the process, leaving few people to undertake the labor-intensive work.[2]

A combination of misfortunes hit potato growers in 1943. An early flood wiped out about half the acreage used for growing potatoes, and there were so few people to harvest the 1,060 salvaged acres that boys and girls, some as young as eight years old, worked in the field to save the remaining crop.[3] Given this scenario, it was a godsend when the Jackson County Potato Growers Association learned that they could hire Camp Clark prisoners to help with the harvest. An advance party arrived from Camp Clark in June 1943 to prepare the campsite on the J. W. Adams farm near Atherton, located north of Independence. The rest of the prisoners arrived not long afterward and stayed for approximately three weeks until the work was finished. In total, POWs working in Jackson County picked almost fifty thousand, one-hundred-pound bags of potatoes that year.[4]

During the same period, Camp Clark officials brought 250 Italian prisoners to a camp established at Orrick, located just ten miles east of the Atherton camp on the other side of the Missouri River. Captain Fred Mealy and a company of MPs had escorted the prisoners from Nevada, Missouri, and secured them during their stay at both branch camps. The spokesman for both POW camps was Sergeant Mario Corradi, a thirty-five-year-old former professor of agricultural economics at the University of Turin. Corradi, who split time between the two camps, noted in a July 15, 1943, inspection report that he was "highly satisfied with all the features of the camps" and praised conditions at both locations. Especially touted was the branch camp mess. Rolf Roth, visiting inspector from the Swiss government, described the mess in his report: "The kitchen, which is ample and very well run, is equipped with a large wooden icebox in which there were large quantities of meat, watermelons, milk, vegetables, a variety of fruit and a huge tray of frogs which the prisoners had been permitted to catch in nearby streams." Roth also observed that the 250 Italian POWs at Orrick daily consumed in excess of 125 pounds of noodles. The Italians were also inclined to such habits as "grinding up good steak for meatballs to go with their pasta."[5]

The Italian prisoners' work on the Adams farm and others began in June, according to Adams's son Frank. "Between 250 and 300 of the prisoners came out," he said. "Our family was one of five growers in the immediate area, and the group was split up so that we had about 50 men each."[6]

The work itself occurred within a basic but arduous process. A potato digger mounted on a tractor brought the potatoes to the surface. Potato pickers would follow along behind, rooting potatoes from the soil one by one, shaking off as much dirt as possible, and placing the potatoes into wire baskets. The pickers would then dump the contents into one-hundred-pound burlap bags, sew the bags shut in the fields, and load them onto a truck for transport.

"The glamorous macho job of the season was 'bucking sacks,'" said Gale Fulghum, who picked potatoes in Jackson County as a teen. "This entailed loading the filled one-hundred-pound bags cab-high on a flatbed truck, hauling them to the railroad loading station, and loading three hundred of them into a stifling-hot freight car."[7]

Production at the Adams farm and other farms in Jackson County proved substantial. Onetime Potato Growers Association president H. S. Mann estimated that the potato growers would produce between 1,000 and 1,200 carloads of potatoes from the 2,500 acres under cultivation.[8]

Frank Adams believed that the prisoners, who were housed in tents inside a nearby five-acre pasture ringed with barbed-wire fencing, enjoyed the work.

This POW crew bucked one-hundred-pound potato sacks from field to truck to rail car. Courtesy of Twylia Brand.

"They were good workers and glad to be out in the fields," he said. "They were especially happy to be in the U.S. and not in North Africa any more."[9]

An Italian POW interned at the Atherton camp confirmed that he, at least, liked being in the United States and was particularly glad to be at Atherton. "I am thirty-three years of age, but since I have been here I feel ten years younger," he said. "If [my family] only knew how satisfied and fine I feel and how well we are treated they would have little cause to worry about me."[10] Official inspection reports also assert that the Italians, all volunteers for the assignment, enjoyed being part of the potato harvest. "The prisoners are literally delighted to have this opportunity to be removed from the compound and to be allowed to engage in paid work," wrote a visiting camp inspector in July 1943. "The health and morale of the prisoners are very good indeed."[11]

The Italians enjoyed their free time as well, said Adams, noting that he could often hear shouts and cheers at night as the prisoners engaged in different athletic contests. "They had boxing matches and put on some shows," he recalled. "One of the men had been an opera singer in Italy, and he sang for the others."[12] The boxing, incidentally, was not just for fun and exercise. The Italians took it seriously, holding bouts each night and awarding prizes to the winners.

In addition to the boxing matches, prisoners played soccer, volleyball, and card games, and spent time reading and writing letters. Also, the Italians attended Mass every Sunday. Inspector Roth reported, "Bishop O'Hara of Kansas City has shown much interest in the welfare of the prisoners, and the Reverend Father Anzon and Father Henessy of a nearby Catholic diocese visit the prisoners regularly at frequent intervals. Mass is held in the camp every Sunday and the prisoners enjoy complete freedom in the exercise of their religion."[13]

These branch camps, some of the first established in Missouri, had a positive impact on local agriculture and paved the way for the expansion of the branch camp program. Nonetheless, one short-lived incident of organized resistance popped up that first summer at the Orrick camp. Fifteen Italian prisoners refused to go into the fields one day. A visitor to the camp wrote of the incident, "They had stated that they are not skilled farmers, that the work was too strenuous for them and that the temperature was unusually high."

In response, the authorities forced the prisoners to perform work at an adjacent lot near camp. There, they cleared weeds at gunpoint. This punishment was enough to prompt the POWs to change their minds, and they worked in the fields for the rest of their brief stay. Other prisoners who had stayed on the job attributed the problem to the misery the defiant ones felt after learning Allied air attacks had hit their hometowns.[14]

Although POW labor provided needed help with the harvest, some members of the county Potato Growers Association griped about the muddled process of contracting POW labor from the government. In the beginning of the arrangement, the government had tried to charge the growers for transportation of the prisoners to and from Nevada, for the prisoners' rations, and for their housing expenses throughout the camp's operation from July 1 through July 21. However, after the harvest, association president B. F. Larkin challenged the government's demands. He considered the $4,100 bill sent to the growers outrageous, and he complained to U.S. representative C. Jasper Bell, arguing that the government would have paid the prisoners' board had they been housed anywhere else. In a letter, Larkin wrote, "You can easily see that this ration cost could have made our total cost very excessive should we not have been fortunate enough to have the kind of weather that permitted harvesting of potatoes steadily through out the period. With a few days' rain we would either have had an exorbitant expense amounting to about $300 per day or would have had to return the prisoners to Nevada and have lost our potato crop."

Larkin added that while the weather had cooperated in the last season, no guarantees about the weather or other variables existed for future seasons, making this arrangement extremely risky for potato producers. He wrote, "The negotiation of such a contract [in the spring of 1943] was interpreted by many of our growers who needed this labor as writing a blank check to the federal government. The results of having to enter into such a confusing and uncertain agreement with the federal government caused many growers who

Above: POWs in Atherton loading sacks of potatoes on a train. Courtesy of Jackson County Historical Society.

Below: POWs with two Atherton girls, Marian Van Tuyl and Martha Ann Lewis, outside the co-op grocery store. Courtesy of Twylia Brand.

needed this labor to refuse to become a party to such a contract. If we expect maximum production in 1944, such a procedure must be eliminated because this appears to be our only source of labor to save our crops."

Finally, noted Larkin, the potato growers felt they had paid too much for the prisoners' labor. Though the prisoners had filled fifty thousand bags of potatoes, the association calculated that POWs were only 30 percent as efficient as civilian pickers, and the cost per bag for POW-picked potatoes was almost 20 percent higher.

Essentially, Larkin argued that the government needed to work quickly to make sense of the contracting process and to resolve the disparity in cost between POW labor and local labor. Under the constraints imposed by the government, the outlook for the 1944 growing season appeared bleak to potato growers. They faced a choice between having no labor at all, effectively dooming their crop, and having to hire inefficient, overpriced labor through the government.[15]

In response to the letter, Representative Bell delivered a copy to Provost Marshal General Allen Gullion. Having Bell as a friend in Washington paid off for the Jackson County potato growers. Gullion alerted Bell to a new agreement between the War Department and the War Manpower Commission. Put into effect just weeks before, it set the price to contract prisoners at a rate equal to prevailing local wages. Gullion wrote, "It is believed that under this new arrangement, which went into effect on 17 September 1943, the Jackson County Potato Growers Association will have no difficulty in negotiating an equitable contract for the harvesting of their 1944 crop." The agreement also made the Army responsible for the prisoners' mess, meaning any delays in harvest would not result in additional room and board expenses for the potato growers.[16]

With the cost problems with the government resolved, the Jackson County Potato Growers Association arranged for POWs to work in the fields the next year. The 1944 camp was set up just southwest of Atherton on the Ed Watson farm, near the intersection of U.S. 24 and Blue Mills Road. This time around, German prisoners came in to help with the potato crop. Residents noted the difference in temperament between the Germans and Italians. Area resident Gale Fulghum said that in contrast with the Italians, the "Germans…were all business. They were members of the elite Afrika Korps. Some were 'dyed-in-the-wool' Nazis and many were outwardly arrogant."[17]

Potato grower Bill Mann recalled what tended to happen when workers discussed news of the war with the German POWs. "When we showed them headlines of the Allies push ahead, they wouldn't believe it. 'Propaganda! Propaganda!' They would shout and stomp their feet on the paper."[18]

Relations with farmers were bumpy at first. A newspaper headline, "Nazis Arrogance Irks Atherton," reported that Germans had been whistling at local girls. Additionally, the prisoners ambled around Atherton, "even entering residential yards on occasion." Some Nazis within the POW population "stirred up trouble in the fields," and the Germans "got the idea they weren't going to put out too much," according to one local resident. Army officials began to recognize the problem and returned the offenders to the main camp in exchange for more cooperative prisoners.[19]

Some of the trouble caused by the more defiant prisoners became evident after their departure. In October, three months after the Germans had left, Atherton farmer Claude Griffin discovered something as he cleaned the fence rows around his field. Pulling away weeds and brush, Griffin found about fifteen bushels of potatoes the Germans had thrown into the weeds rather than harvest properly.[20]

Other incidents also caused a stir. One of the Orrick POWs could not be found and later turned up at the home of Lucy Dillen of Excelsior Springs, Missouri, some ten miles north of Orrick. Dillen had answered a knock at her door one hot summer day, August 10, 1944, and found a man wanting a drink of water. The man had been hiding in the woods all day, and after requesting a drink from Dillen, he asked to be taken back to Orrick.[21]

By the third year, all was nearly routine for the Atherton and Orrick camps, although the government still seemed to waffle on its plans at almost every turn. For example, when the potato growers requested 880 POWs for the 1945 crop, the government answered that it couldn't commit to specific numbers, sometimes saying that it couldn't guarantee any prisoners at all.

L. L. Shaw, vice president of the Potato Growers Association, noted his exasperation to Representative Bell over the government's policies:

> The owner of the site is demanding that the producers either engage the site immediately and pay him or definitely tell him that they do not want the site so that he can convert the property into some pro-

POWs in Atherton on the south side of the co-op grocery store. Courtesy of Twylia Brand.

ductive use. You can readily see that the Potato Growers with no more assurance than they have for getting prisoner help hesitate to pay out several hundred dollars for this site.[22]

The Army also was wavering on other issues. It changed its position several times on who was responsible for providing housing to the POWs. The growers expected the Army to provide tents, as before. However, the government argued that the farmers needed to cover such accommodations. Again, the growers turned to their representative in Washington. "You will recall that we mentioned to you that in two of the past three years [the government] alarmed us about the tentage situation but in each case they worked it out and finally secured the tents without any effort on our part," wrote H. S. Mann to Representative Bell in April 1945. "This year they definitely leave it as our responsibility."[23]

President Harry S Truman visiting Camp Crowder. Courtesy of Missouri State Archives.

That summer, prisoners arrived and were housed once again in standard Army field tents. Their compound included the usual two messes, a kitchen, a canteen, an infirmary, and several latrines and shower facilities. The men arrived at the beginning of July and worked for a month or so until the end of the potato harvest, then returned home. The Associated Press reported on July 31, 1945, that the 350 German POWs posted at the Orrick branch camp had finished their work and awaited new assignments before their impending return to the base camp.[24]

Germans at the Atherton camp received a special visitor one day: President Harry S Truman, who hailed from nearby Independence. Atherton prisoner Walter Meier said, "One day we were told to stay in camp and not go to the fields because we were going to have one of the greatest visitors in the United States to see us. It was President Truman, and we shined up our shoes—really. He only spoke about a minute, but he said, 'The war is over and you'll be going home soon.'"[25]

Liberty

The camp at Liberty, Missouri, in Clay County sat on a former turkey farm two miles south of town, about two miles east of the intersection of present-day State Highways 210 and 219. There, Leon and Harriette Miller lived on, and operated, the Desert Gold Turkey Farm. Business was good, and in 1942 the facility expanded when the Millers built an immense egg-laying house for turkeys. The Millers believed that this new laying house could provide as many as thirty thousand turkey eggs a year.

Tucked next to a bluff to protect it from north winds, the brand-new laying house was 650 feet long and 35 feet wide and offered turkeys the latest conveniences and luxuries, including heat, running water, and windows. "The building was painted white, and looked as nice as any building on the farm, or any building in the community, for that matter," said the Millers. The fifty rooms gave turkeys plenty of privacy, and a larger room in the center was used for feeding and egg handling.[26]

The turkeys barely had time to get used to the new laying house, however, when they were relocated to other quarters. After just a year, the War Labor Board approached the Millers about using the laying house for an entirely different purpose. Labor was in short supply, and the government sought a place to house POWs, who would help with the harvesting of potatoes, tobacco, hay, and vegetables along with other agricultural tasks.

In a 1990 recollection of the POW camp that operated on their farm, the Millers wrote:

> [The government] explained the great need for a place to house our prisoners of war and to make a work camp for them in the Kansas City area. The prisoners would be able to help farmers as well as help in many vital places. We didn't think we had a choice. The need was great and we felt like we wanted to do our part in the war effort. We made plans immediately to buy our needed baby turkey poults from hatcheries.[27]

So the turkeys moved out, and the prisoners came in. The latter included some six hundred Italian POWs from Camp Clarinda, Iowa. Twelve men slept in each of the fifty rooms in the laying house, and the center room became the POW mess. After a few months, the Italians left and six hundred Germans from Fort Leavenworth, Kansas, took their place.

While the camps in nearby Atherton and Orrick were set up to provide labor for the potato harvest, the Liberty installation was a true work camp, assigning prisoners to any farmers that needed help. On July 12, 1944, the *Kansas City Star* announced that the German POWs in Liberty were available for labor if farmers contracted them that same day. Contracted prisoners were dispatched in groups of ten, and farmers requiring fewer numbers had to co-contract with their neighbors. Available for all types of farm labor through December, the Germans could, according to the article, "build fences, clear timber or do any kind of seasonal work." The prisoners went out accompanied by one American guard and a German foreman.[28] Liberty POWs participated in the seasonal potato harvest, but their work took them other places as well. The Millers said, "Some were sent to Orrick, Missouri to work for W. J. Small Dehydrator Co. [drying alfalfa], other to paper box companies in Kansas City, to the Kansas City Stockyards, apple picking near Independence, and many other places that were desperately needing help of any kind."[29] Other prisoners at the Liberty camp planted trees along roadways in the area. Their efforts can still be seen on the north side of Highway 10, now Route H, where trees stand in semicircle formation.[30]

The variety and amount of work supplied by prisoners helped those who contracted them, but the relationships often rankled organized labor, which took exception, in particular, to POWs working in American factories. One of many disputes occurred over German POWs working at the U.S. Gypsum Company plant in north Kansas City. Joseph Appelbaum, regional director of the United Gas, Coke, and Chemical Workers Union, expressed his opposition in a telegram to Representative Bell:

> American workers at this plant have refused to work with Nazis. Plant is shut down. Several incidents have occurred between American workers and Nazi prisoners of war. To avert serious catastrophe, American workers removed themselves from plant. Effect of situation—American workers being discriminated against in favor of Nazi prisoners of war. Army officials claim they are powerless to act.... War Manpower Commission in this area claims it is up to the army and they are powerless to act. Respectfully urge you take action which results in removal of Nazi war prisoners from this plant.[31]

The telegram came when Congress was out of session. Bell's secretary, Vernon E. Moore, responded to Appelbaum in a letter. He wrote, "I have checked with War Department officials in charge of the use of prisoners of war, and in view of the lack of complete information from you regarding the matter, they suggested you take the matter up direct with the Seventh Service Command of the Army at Omaha.... The Commanding General there would have the power to cope with the problem adequately and because any appeal from here would have to be cleared through him."[32]

Congressman Roger Slaughter echoed the union's concern, demanding a full report from the War Department and the War Manpower Commission on the reasons for employing the Germans at the plant.[33] However, the objection soon faded away and received no further mention. It remains unknown how the issue ultimately was resolved, but prisoners soon left the Liberty camp and their assignment at the factory.

Life at Liberty

The Liberty camp experienced the usual amount of mishaps, misbehavior, and mischief. On one occasion, the guards thought one prisoner had escaped, when he merely had been left behind during an off-site work detail. Scouring the countryside for the missing man, they found him walking down the middle of a gravel road, grumbling to himself as he tried to find his way back to the camp in time for dinner.

Another time, a young German POW accidentally ran his hand through a power saw. The guards took him to Kansas City for treatment. From the top floor of a Kansas City medical building, the prisoner looked out over the city in bewilderment, discovering that he had been misled by German propaganda. "We were told Kansas City had been bombed," said the prisoner, who couldn't understand why he was seeing so many undamaged buildings.[34]

Liberty residents described other contact with prisoners. Shirley Dauzvardis gave an observation of the prisoners she saw at the Desert Gold Turkey Farm. "I felt sorry for them being locked up, but after all, they were Germans—Hitler's soldiers," said Dauzvardis, who as a teen frequently rode past the Liberty camp. "I had the impression that they were being treated humanely and I was glad of that. In fact, I think I was proud of that."[35]

Elvin Frevert ran the local hardware store in the Liberty town square. Frevert spoke German fluently and, on occasion, was called out to the camp to interpret for the guards. "It was usually a case when there was a disagreement or where somebody was sick," said son Jerry Frevert, who continued in his father's footsteps and operated the True Value Hardware Store in Liberty. "They needed someone who could understand when the POWs described specifically what they were experiencing, who could figure out the severity of the illness, or interpret the actual location of what it was they were suffering from."[36]

Phillip Miller, one of Leon and Harriette Miller's five boys, recalled being out with the prisoners and how they loved to sing and play with him:

They looked liked they were cloned—blond hair, blue-eyed...real physical specimens. I learned how my name should sound in German. "Phillip Muller, Phillip Muller, How are you today, Phillip Muller?" and they'd throw me around like a sack of sugar to each other.[37]

The morning the POW camp officially was deactivated, Leon Miller took his four oldest boys to the camp to say good-bye to the prisoners. His wife, Harriette, recalled the scene of the prisoners' departure:

These two years had brought some strong friendships between the guards, prisoners, and our family. Our daughter, Marty, and our youngest son, Jack, sat with me on our swing on the screened in porch, waving good-bye to the men...many truckloads of prisoners and guards passing through our yard. They were on their way to their homes at last.[38]

Riverside

In April 1944, Camp Clark authorities established a short-lived camp for Italian POWs in Kansas City. These prisoners were initially registered guests at a city hotel, where military police had established secure quarters for them. Shortly after that, however, the prisoners moved to housing at another site, a former racetrack in Riverside, Missouri, just north of downtown Kansas City. Prisoners at Riverside likely were unaware that their temporary home was part of the legacy of Tom Pendergast, the notorious political boss of Kansas City who placed Harry S Truman on the road to the presidency. Pendergast, whose association with Truman later embarrassed the president and nearly ruined his political career, had run Kansas City on a trifecta of graft, violence, and vice. He essentially had turned the municipal government into his personal moneymaking enterprise.[39]

The track was a popular place, attracting daily crowds of seventeen thousand people, especially when paired with the Cuban Gardens, a nightclub and casino on private grounds nearby. Horse racing wouldn't be the only thing to draw attention to the track, converted in the spring of 1944 to house Italian POWs. Based at this camp, Italian POWs worked a variety of assignments in the area as hired labor for local farmers. The mere curiosity of the POWs' presence and their amiable nature attracted the attention of local residents. "We'd go down and talk to the prisoners," recalled Vernon Davis, who lived nearby. "A lot of them could speak pretty good English. And they liked it here because they knew they weren't getting shot at."[40]

One of Davis's neighbors ran a gas station. The man was of Italian descent and could speak the language. On Sundays he and Davis would take candy bars and cigarettes down to the camp. Another neighbor sometimes brought her three kids, and Davis recalled them all standing at the fence. "The guards never gave us any trouble," said Davis. "They just let us stand and talk to those boys. It wasn't much of a job for them, and I think they were glad to have a little distraction too."[41]

Dorothy Day lived near the racetrack and remembered an altercation between her father and the POWs. The prisoners were hauling a truckload of garbage and other trash down present-day Green Mills Road. They began unloading trash into the creek that ran next to Day's house and under the road. Day said, "When my father saw the men dumping the trash off the bridge into the creek, he hopped right up and told them to stop. Then he made them climb down into the creek and pick up everything that had already gone in there."[42]

For religious services, prisoners at the Riverside Racetrack were bused five miles down the road to Holy Rosary Parish on East Missouri Avenue in Kansas City. The parish, staffed by Scalabrini priests assigned to minister to the Italian immigrants in the area, had supported the Italian POWs since their arrival in Missouri, sending radios and other items to Camp Clark for enjoyment. Having the chance to see the POWs in person, parishioners welcomed them eagerly.[43] Angelo Bongino, who attended the church as a child, said, "There were these fellows getting off the trucks in these old gray suits and talking to people in the language and listening to Mass, some of which was in Italian for their sake. That's about the closest war ever got to here."[44]

The Italian POWs lived among this welcoming community until May 1944. With their departure, the Riverside camp closed.

Aerial view of the Gasconade boatyard. Courtesy of Kansas City District Corps of Engineers.

Chapter Ten

Central Missouri Camps

THE ARMY ESTABLISHED BRANCH CAMPS for POWs in several central Missouri towns in 1944 and 1945. The men were used primarily for agricultural labor, but a detachment of German prisoners from Fort Leonard Wood also worked at the Sedalia Army Airfield in support of military operations. The Sedalia men performed general upkeep and maintenance of the grounds, soil erosion control, road maintenance, and repair on the installation. Although Sedalians initially protested the Germans' presence to Governor Forrest C. Donnell, airfield commander Colonel Jerome McCauley described the prisoners to the *Sedalia Democrat* as "men who have been found to be of good behavior and not trouble makers, desiring to work where ever they are sent."[1]

The Germans arrived 139 strong at Sedalia Army Airfield in May 1945. They worked under the supervision of U.S. Army captain John P. Kaysen. Another shipment of prisoners from Fort Leonard Wood roughly doubled their numbers to 300 in July, but the population dropped back to 150 in September. Ninety men returned to the Fort Leonard Wood main base in February 1946, and the remaining 60 departed when the Sedalia branch camp closed on March 8, 1946. Sedalia Army Airfield is now Whiteman Air Force Base, named for Pettis County native Lieutenant George Whiteman, a pilot killed in the Japanese attack on Pearl Harbor.[2]

Fulton

Other camps operated in central Missouri. The Italian prisoners sent to work for the Missouri Hybrid Corn Company in Fulton during the summers of 1944 and 1945 made a big impact on the residents there. Although they worked in the cornfields of Boone and Callaway Counties, the prisoners lived in nearby Columbia, Missouri. Some of them resided in the Sigma Phi Epsilon fraternity house on the University of Missouri campus, and former POW Vincenzo Mancuso remembered prisoners sleeping in dormitories at Stephens College, an all-female school, during the summer recess. The next year, the men lived at the edge of Fulton in an old National Youth Administration (NYA) camp on U.S. Highway 54.

Missouri Hybrid Corn Company in Fulton.
Courtesy of Karen Price Myers.

The decision to bring the Italians to Fulton resulted from the appeals of Ernest Wagner, general manager of the Missouri Hybrid Corn Company. Wagner was an expert in the hybridization of seed corn. Heading into the spring of 1944, Wagner knew he had a serious problem. Labor had been hard to find the year before, and the situation had only grown worse. The detasseling process was labor intensive, requiring hand-cutting of the pollen-laden plumes from the tops of certain rows of corn. Wagner feared that there wasn't enough labor in central Missouri for the several thousand acres that grew his company's corn. Typically, some three hundred to four hundred men and boys had worked each year during July and August to carry out the detasseling work, and the war had drained the supply of able-bodied men.[3]

When Wagner heard that the government was making prisoners available for agricultural work, he saw a potential solution to his problem. He made an inquiry in the spring of 1944 and began seeking a site to house the prisoners. Although it seemed an unlikely option, the most suitable and available housing was in nearby Columbia. The war had depleted the student population at the University of Missouri, leaving many residences empty. On July 10, 1944, Wagner entered into a four- to six-week lease with Edith Simon of Columbia for use of the Sigma Phi Epsilon fraternity house. Rent for the property was $100 a week, and Wagner wisely included a provision that allowed him to terminate the lease should a general crop failure make use of the house unnecessary.[4]

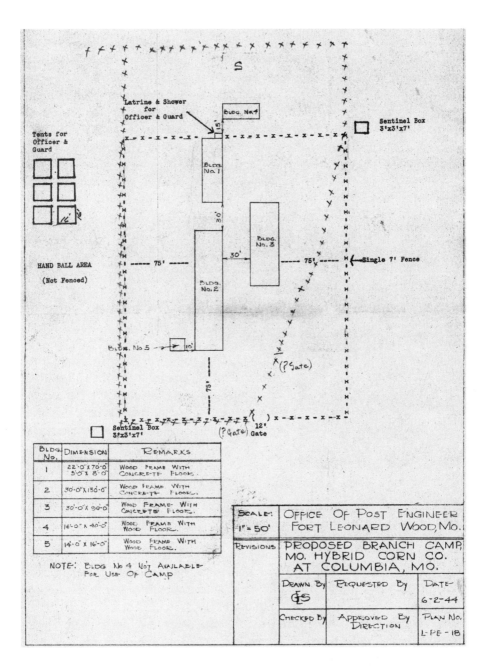

Tents for
Officer &
Guard

HAND BALL AREA

(Not Fenced)

Latrine & Shower
for
Officer & Guard

BLDG. No. 4

Sentinel Box
3'x3'x7'

BLDG.
No. 1

BLDG.
No. 3

BLDG.
No. 2

←──Single 7' Fence

BLDG. No. 5 →

X(?Gate)

Sentinel Box
3'x3'x7'

(?Gate) Gate

12'

BLDG. No.	DIMENSION	REMARKS
1	22'-0" X 70'-0" 5'-0" X 8'-0"	WOOD FRAME WITH CONCRETE FLOOR.
2	30'-0" X 136'-0"	WOOD FRAME WITH CONCRETE FLOOR.
3	30'-0" X 90'-0"	WOOD FRAME WITH CONCRETE FLOOR.
4	16'-0" X 40'-0"	WOOD FRAME WITH WOOD FLOOR.
5	14'-0" X 16'-0"	WOOD FRAME WITH WOOD FLOOR.

NOTE: BLDG No 4 Not Available
For Use Of Camp

SCALE: 1"= 50'	OFFICE OF POST ENGINEER FORT LEONARD WOOD, MO.
REVISIONS	PROPOSED BRANCH CAMP, MO. HYBRID CORN CO. AT COLUMBIA, MO.

DRAWN BY GS	REQUESTED BY	DATE 6-2-44
CHECKED BY	APPROVED BY DIRECTION	PLAN NO. L-PE-18

The plan for the Fulton branch camp housing in Columbia, summer 1944. Courtesy of Western Historical Manuscript Collection, Columbia, Missouri.

The Italian prisoners, all of them officers from Weingarten, arrived on July 10 and began working in the cornfields at once. Farm trucks and buses carried the prisoners to their work assignments on private farms contracted to grow hybrid seed for the Missouri Hybrid Corn Company. The impact of their work was immediate. "Hybrid Corn Company Has Its Best Year," claimed the headline in the *Fulton Daily Sun Gazette* on August 10, 1944, and the article that followed estimated that forty thousand bushels of seed would come from the sixteen hundred acres worked by the Italians. "The Missouri Hybrid Corn Company of Fulton, with the aid of a large number of Italian prisoners of war, has completed the job of detasseling its corn and Ernest Wagner, manager of the company, said Thursday that this will be the best corn the company has had in its seven years of operation." Wagner praised the work of these men and said that without their help, the company would not have completed its work.[5]

Ernest Wagner, general manager of the Missouri Hybrid Corn Company. Courtesy of Karen Price Myers.

The Italians' presence in Columbia attracted considerable attention and curiosity from residents. The men were a regular presence at Sacred Heart Catholic Church and even performed as a choir there on several occasions. However, their attendance at the church seems to have ended after some members questioned the appropriateness of having "enemies" there.

Prisoners also attended social events, including movies at the Hall Theater in Columbia. Residents remember the POWs marching into a designated seating section. Columbian Marion McGee Guffey was at the movies one night with the prisoners. She hadn't realized their presence, though, until they departed. "One evening in the movie theater," said Guffey, "in the middle of the movie—it was dark, it wasn't intermission—all of a sudden two or three rows of men stood up all at one time and walked out. Of course it was unusual…I suppose that they left during the movie to cause least commotion rather than getting mixed up with the crowd if they left at the end."[6]

One visible spot occupied by the POWs was their exercise and recreation area on the former university golf course adjacent to Maryland

Italian POWs in a cornfield outside McBaine, Missouri, during the summer of 1944.
Courtesy of Karen Price Myers.

Avenue. This area allowed room for the men to play soccer and other sports and also provided the easiest avenue for public contact.[7] Columbia resident Francis Pike said, "I remember going by and seeing them there. I guess my son was four years old then. So I took him around and they wanted to talk to the 'bambino,' that's what they called him."[8] Resident Jimmy Hourigan said, "People on nice days would take them cookies and cake and hand it to them. And see, most of them could speak English real well, too."[9]

Donovan Rhynsburger, longtime professor at the University of Missouri, went out of his way to check up on the Italian prisoners during their stay in Columbia. Earlier, he had met some Jamaicans living in Columbia, workers imported by the American government to ease the labor shortage. He'd been struck by how lonely they seemed, being in a strange place far away from home and family. "Don was a person of considerable civic enterprise and love of people," said Loren Reed, a colleague of Rhynsburger. "He did any number of things to ease the plight of the Italian prisoners."[10]

Rhynsburger's wife, Peggy, described his friendship with the POWs: "He found out that most of them were professors, musicians, and artists. So he asked what they would like to have. Well, we had a wonderful selection of records. So they said, 'Bring us opera, bring us this.' Don would take those over and visit with them." In the course of his visits, Rhynsburger grew fond of the educated Italian officers. Peggy said, "All these prisoners had degrees and spoke four and five languages. There was an artist in the group. He wanted some sepias, to paint, so Don took him some, and he painted the prettiest little landscapes of what he could see."[11]

A good portion of the prisoners' work occurred in the river-bottoms cornfields around McBaine, Missouri. In the area was a Campfire Girls facility, Camp Tepeetoto, and Rosemarie Berry, a twelve-year-old camper, remembered the Italian POWs passing by on trucks en route to daily work assignments. "Every morning these prisoners of war would come on the gravel road that ran right through the middle of the camp," said Berry, recalling the surprise of the campers upon seeing the POWs. "There were no guards in the trucks and they wore beige work uniforms."[12]

The prisoners seemed to enjoy the work and living conditions in Columbia, and several developed personal ties to Wagner, later sending him cards and letters from Weingarten and other branch camps. The Italians thanked Wagner for his kindness and expressed hope that they would see him again. Several thanked Wagner for a souvenir he had given them to remember Missouri. POW Giuseppe Grondona wrote Wagner several times after his return to Weingarten from Columbia, even sending him a note at Christmas. In one letter, Grondona wrote, "After a month spent in your farm picking up tassels on the field corn, I am here to P.O.W. Camp Weingarten. I am very glad to say you that my health has plentifully regained with that life out of door. Here I am studying and I spend all my time enclosed in my barrack."[13]

Another POW, Francesco Borelli, wrote from Sikeston in December 1944. Borelli apparently found Sikeston less appealing than Columbia but was vague about his dissatisfaction. He wrote to Wagner, "I remember always your good advises and I think to your kindness especially now that we are in other side of your country and with persons not like you are. However, I worked two months in the cotton field and now I pick the seed corn; this work will last maybe until February and after I hope to stay here again.... I think that if it'll be possible, we'll be very glad to come back with you in your fields next year."[14]

American authorities helped reinforce positive impressions of the Columbia camp. In fact, Weingarten commanding officer H. H. Glidden wrote to Wagner saying that the Italians would line up to volunteer for a repeat assignment with the Missouri Hybrid Corn Company.[15]

Moved to Fulton

The prisoners' work for the Missouri Hybrid Corn Company went so well that Wagner requested their return the next summer. Because he knew the prisoners so well, and to avoid having to train a new crew, Wagner specifically asked for the return of the same group. In January 1945, Wagner wrote Glidden about the possibility:

> We are beginning to formulate our plans for our 1945 crop. We hope to again secure the services of the Italian officers. Naturally we desire to have as many of the ones who were with us last summer as possible.... This may be going at this through improper channels, but we are wondering about the chances of securing help similar to that used last summer.[16]

Glidden told Wagner first to apply to the local county agent, Harold Slusher, for a certificate of need. Next, Glidden said that while the Italians would be pleased to return, "when we mentioned the suggestion to them, their first reaction was to the effect that they would be in Italy by then."

A return to Italy, however, wouldn't occur until September 1945. Glidden told Wagner that, in any case, plenty of Germans within the Seventh Service Command were available for labor. Glidden wrote to Wagner, "Naturally they would have to be housed in a different manner under existing regulations. A stockade would have to be built around any buildings utilized or tentage if they were housed in tents."[17]

Wagner continued making arrangements for the coming season, and in April he secured housing for his anticipated POW crew at a former NYA camp outside Fulton. The Fulton Board of Education had taken over the recently vacated grounds and agreed to rent Wagner five dormitories—starting in July—to house one hundred POWs for six weeks at $100 a week. The dormitories were single-story, wood-frame structures. Inside were four large rooms, two lavatories, and a common area. Four dorms were used for housing; the fifth was used as an office, storage, and administrative area. The total area taken by the camp would end up about three hundred by four hundred yards. The prisoners to be housed there that summer would have neighbors: a teen recreation center.

In correspondence with Wagner, an Army representative told him everything he would have to provide at the new Fulton facility. Lieutenant Colonel William S. Hannan, who coordinated the request on behalf of the Omaha-based Seventh Service Command, provided Wagner with a thirteen-point list of everything from sentry boxes to showerheads that Wagner would need for approval of an on-site camp. Hannan wrote, "This information is furnished so that you may plan accordingly, but you are advised not to expend any funds until the project is approved by the Seventh Service Command."[18]

Wagner noted all the demands while awaiting approval for the project. "Clean buildings and put up screens," he jotted on a piece of paper. "Build fence and sentry box on north end...Brooms and mops...Garbage disposal."[19]

Neither the government nor Wagner was concerned about residents' reaction to locating the POWs in Fulton. The positive experience the previous summer was one factor; the other was an informal survey conducted by Captain Burton Marston during an inspection of the proposed site in May. Marston wrote, "Contacts were made with several leading businessmen of the city of Fulton, including the one newspaper editor and it was found there is no objection to having the camp in the community."[20]

In June, the Missouri Hybrid Corn Company entered into a contract with the War Department for the use of POW labor and sent a check for $2,300 as a down payment, along with the certificate of need from the War Manpower Commission. The total amount due at the end of the summer, less the down payment, would be $9,240 for 2,310 man-days of work, which worked out to a $.50-per-hour cost to the company. The POWs received $.10 an hour, and the government pocketed the rest. In June 1945, assistant provost marshal general B. M. Bryan told the House Committee on Military Affairs that through their use of POW labor, "contractors have paid into the United States Treasury $22,000,000 in cold cash."[21]

As the time drew near for the prisoners' arrival, Wagner was a bit anxious. Wet weather during the spring had stretched out the planting phase. This delayed and extended the detasseling process. Wagner noted that because only a few acres would be ready at first, it would be "a gross waste to put all of these men in the field at one time." He requested that the government provide only fifty men the week of July 10 and then double that number the next. He wrote, "If you could make any provision in the contract wherein some allowance could be made for this, it would be highly satisfactory from our standpoint."[22]

It looked increasingly unlikely that the officers who had worked the previous year could return. Captain Marston, POW labor officer at Weingarten, wrote:

Because of the experience [the officers] had in detasseling the corn last year, I realize it would have been more acceptable to you to have the Italian Officers, however, they are out of the picture and I believe it will be necessary to use enlisted men for this purpose. I believe with the use of additional guards, these men can accomplish the work satisfactorily although it will require more and closer supervision.[23]

Even though Wagner knew he faced the prospect of working with an inexperienced crew, he still hoped to return some of the Italian officers from the previous summer to supervise and instruct the enlisted POWs. He even offered to make any special arrangements to get them, a testimony to his respect for the men's abilities and work ethic. Only three weeks before the POWs' scheduled arrival, Wagner wrote:

> Since these men will all be enlisted men and will be no doubt inexperienced, we are wondering if it would be possible to get three or four of the officers that worked for us last summer to act in the capacity of foremen. We would be very happy to get any of these which you think could serve in this capacity. However, the men who actually were serving as foremen last summer are Diego Guala, Francesco Biancheri, Cosimo Fiei, and Amilcare Cellai. We would be willing, if possible to get these men, to meet any special requirements as to quarters.[24]

Marston replied with news that the request could not be fulfilled because, with the exception of one officer, the rest were still at the Sikeston camp. Marston also noted that "both Colonel Glidden and Captain Pontrelli (the Stockade Officer) feel that having Italian officers on duty at your camp along with the enlisted men would create a situation that would be difficult to handle and that the camp might not work as smoothly as would be desired."[25]

The impending start of camp left Wagner no time to dwell. Months of preparation and planning had come to an end, and the prisoners would appear in a matter of days. "Prisoners of War Arrive Monday," read the July 16, 1945, headline in the *Fulton Daily Sun Gazette*. It continued, "100 Italians Will Work for Corn Company, to Live at NYA Center."[26]

A convoy of dusty Army trucks rolled into Fulton with Marston in the lead vehicle. Fifty Italian prisoners from Weingarten climbed down and began unloading equipment and gear. They took a few days to get settled into their quarters at the camp and then moved into the fields. As requested by Wagner, fifty more prisoners arrived the following week to join them.

Shirley Payne was a senior in high school in 1945. She and other Fulton teens often talked with the POWs when they went to Teen Town, the youth recreation area in another section of the former NYA camp. "We'd go to the courthouse and get on a bus that would take us out to Teen Town for dances," Payne said. "We'd get there and walk right over to the fence and talk to the Italian prisoners. It seemed as natural as could be, and no one

thought anything about it. There wasn't anything scandalous or daring about it. They just seemed glad to talk to us."[27] On several occasions, Pat Humphries joined the flock of girls at the fence. Humphries said, "We didn't relate to them as the enemy. They just got pulled into the war, just like everyone else."[28]

Ultimately, the work went as smoothly as it did the year before. After a couple days of learning the process, the new prisoners became adept at pulling tassels off the corn to be hybridized (leaving every fourth row to pollinate the other plants). Soon, life in Fulton fell into an easy rhythm of work-play-sleep. Each morning, transport vehicles carried the men to the fields. The prisoners returned in the evening for dinner and then relaxed the rest of the evening. The next day the process repeated itself, and so it went until the Italians finished their work and left Fulton in mid-August.[29]

After the intensive work of detasseling was finished, Wagner wrote a letter to the commanding officer of Weingarten, Frank Kingsland, who had replaced the transferred Colonel Glidden. Wagner wrote:

> We wish to express our most sincere appreciation for the help of the Italian Prisoners of War with detasseling corn, and for the excellent cooperation of the American personnel. It would have been impossible for us to have accomplished this detail of work without the help of the above mentioned men. We assure you these men performed in an exemplary manner and caused the job to be well done, for which we are indeed grateful and thankful.[30]

This year's POWs also stayed in touch with Wagner after their departure from Fulton. Several letters arrived while the men still lived in the United States, but the floodgates opened upon their return to Italy in September and October. Many of the letters asked that he send aid to their families in impoverished Italy. Other prisoners expressed the desire to return to the United States to work for Wagner. In November 1946, Nicodemo Calla wrote, "I am in Italy from September 1945 and I am without work. As you told me, I should like to work in your property, I am glad to return if you can do it for me."[31]

Another former Italian prisoner considered leaving his home country and bringing his family to the United States, as the result of a direct proposal from Wagner. Carmelo Amadio wrote from Italy in September 1946, "I have more than once and most seriously thought over your proposal of coming over with all my family. However for the time being, I think it wise to carry on with my military career, also owing to my children being so young.... In fact, if it were just me, I would not hesitate a single moment to sail with the first liner and come over, knowing how life in your country is like."[32]

Plenty of other Italians asked to come as well. Former worker Anthony Troia wrote, "You have too much house empty. I can come all my family to live by you, take off of this bad life of poverty where I have neither land, house nor work."[33]

Another former POW, Bruno Balocco, offered Wagner a clever business proposal:

> Thinking of what you said, [concerning] to be able in the future to begin a relation with you and your Firm...I allow myself to address this letter to you in order to ask if you are willingly to start a business relation between you and me about the importation in Italy of "Missouri King" hybrid corn. I am sure, about what personally I saw during my sojourn at Columbia Mo., that your corn will be able to interest our farmers, and, with your help, it will not be difficult for me to have a success on our market.... I am well introduced by the most important Italian grain merchants, where I have many friends.[34]

Although it doesn't appear that Balocco ever sold Missouri Hybrid Corn in Italy, Wagner kept the letter with the man's proposal, so he may have given it some thought.

Marshall

The area of Saline County around the town of Marshall, Missouri, saw both Italian and German POWs at different times during World War II. The Saline County Hybrid and Crop Production Association enlisted the POW laborers, and like other hybrid corn growers in Missouri, used them mainly for detasseling for a short period in the summer. The five hundred Italian POWs from Camp Weingarten who worked in Marshall in 1944 lived at the present-day site of Van Meter State Park, while the 1945 German camp was set up where Marshall High School now stands.

Harold Swinger of the Swinger Hybrid Corn Company was one of the area farmers who used prisoners for farm labor. One day, the Italians who worked for him announced that they did not want to enter the fields again. This caused mild panic, because timing was crucial to the detasseling process. Any significant delay meant the hybrid seed corn would be ruined—pollinated from renegade cornstalks in adjacent rows.

Swinger and his partner Mr. Stackhouse plotted strategy to address this problem. The two met with the Italians and hashed out a work-for-wine swap. The Italians agreed to the exchange, so Swinger and Stackhouse went to the liquor stores in town and bought every last bottle of wine they could find. The Italians went to work, and, at the end of the day, Swinger handed over their pay.[35]

Jim Shultz, who grew up in Saline County, described the disposition of the prisoners as they did their work: "Every morning they'd come through on the trucks going to the fields singing 'Ama Polla.' They were handsome young men, and the women just loved them and their singing."[36]

Walter Meier was part of the detachment of German POWs who came to Marshall in the summer of 1945. The prisoners received as much supervision as POWs at other branch camps, which meant that they went almost completely unguarded. Meier recalled the behavior of one guard in particular: "He would hang his rifle up in a tree and sit under it and sleep all day. He'd always tell me if I saw some officials coming to wake him up. I liked him. He never gave us any trouble, and we never gave him any."[37]

Meier considered his experience at Marshall a positive one. "It was good to get to Marshall," said Meier, who enjoyed his time there because he could work closely with area farmers. "In other camps I had been isolated except for the guards. But here we had our first connection with farmers…it was important to be so close to the American people."

Meier, who developed an especially close friendship with local farmer Oliver Marshall, recalled the mid-Missouri families he worked for and with: "We were treated really fair. I would tell you a lie if I say something different. There was so much courtesy to us we couldn't even dream of it. The camp in Marshall was the first time I realized the graciousness of the American people."

While in the field, Marshall taught Meier and the other prisoners how to roast ears of corn. "The rations were a little skimpy," said Marshall, "so one day I gave them a big pot and showed them how to roast ears of corn. And pretty soon, every day you would see one of the prisoners going out into the field with a sack to bring back corn to eat. Then they caught on real fast and started bringing salt, pepper, and butter to the camp."[38]

Rosati

Fort Leonard Wood officials opened a side camp at Rosati, Missouri, in August 1944 to provide temporary workers for the grape harvest. Rosati was the closest of Fort Leonard Wood's branch camps, located only forty miles or so east of the post. Rosati was once known as Knobview, but after forty Italian immigrant families bought a 120-acre tract of land from the Frisco Railroad in 1898—to create a foothold for their "colony"—the name changed. It honors the Italian-born Bishop Joseph Rosati, who became the first bishop of the Diocese of St. Louis in 1829, and it reflects the community's unique Italian identity.

The Italian immigrants living in Rosati had come from northern Italy via Arkansas, where malaria and other hardships led them toward opportunities in Missouri. Many of the Rosati immigrants worked on the railroad and farmed, growing tomatoes and keeping herds of cattle. They also planted grapes, and the combination of good soil and careful attention produced a consistently fine product. More than four hundred acres soon were devoted to growing grapes, and the aggressive Knobview Fruit Growers Association, formed by the Italians in 1920, used the Frisco line to ship their product in bulk across the nation. Growers tallied a major success in 1922 when the Welch Grape Juice Company bought eleven carloads of grapes. This marked the first step in a business relationship with Welch that lasted until the 1980s.[39]

The Welch Company crushed the grapes from Rosati growers and then shipped the juice to a plant in Springdale, Arkansas, for processing. In 1943 the Welch Company bought the Bonded Winery #80 from R. M. Cardetti and began processing grape juice in Rosati as well. With so many men off at war, Welch suffered from a dearth of workers, so the company applied to Fort Leonard Wood for prisoners to help with the 1944 fall grape harvest. Subsequently, the Rosati branch camp was established. Sixteen POWs arrived in August 1944 to set up a compound to house 130 German prisoners.

Monsignor John Cody of the St. Louis Archdiocese described arranging for the POWs' arrival to military ordinariate John O'Hara: "Within two weeks a side camp of German prisoners will be established at Rosati, and we are reliably informed that there will be about 130 prisoners there. As about half are Catholics, we have made arrangements with Reverend Cornelius A. Moynihan, pastor of St. Anthony's Church at Rosati, to celebrate Mass for these men on Sundays."[40]

The prisoners set up camp in a compound adjoining the Welch facility, and young Leo Cardetti, son of onetime winery owner R. M. Cardetti, remembered the Germans' presence in the town. He said, "I can remember serving Mass for Father Moynihan every Sunday in a large tent inside the compound. The prisoners were all young men and seemed happy. I clearly remember them marching double-time in ranks up and down the road in from of the church. They sang in their native German as they marched."[41]

Cardetti recalled the contribution that the men made to the grape harvest at Rosati: "They were a fine group of people, awful trustworthy.

They worked picking and processing the grape. You know there were no mechanical pickers at that time. Back then, a mechanical picker was a person with snippers."[42]

Cardetti had the opportunity to talk with the prisoners on occasion. He said, "I asked some of them why they supported Hitler and found that it was like situations in many countries. Hitler had brought them out of poverty which followed the First World War, put them to work and convinced them that 'the good life' was possible. It was difficult for them not to follow, or to see the bad parts of Hitler's policies."[43]

With the grape harvest finished, the camp was deactivated in October 1944, and the Germans returned to Fort Leonard Wood. Although having the German POWs at Rosati led to no documented nationality-based conflicts, it would seem that the Italian Americans at Rosati would have had a special interest in Missouri's Italian POWs because of their common ethnic background. In an interesting footnote, Moynihan wrote Cody asking for a letter of introduction to Weingarten commander Glidden. Apparently some discussion took place in Rosati during the fall of 1943 about bringing Italian POWs to Rosati for "colonization."

Cody complied and sent a letter to Glidden introducing both Cardetti and Moynihan's friend C. B. Michelson. Cody wrote, "I have known Mr. Cardetti for some years and in his capacity as the Italian promoter of the Italian Colony at Rosati. I know him to have won the esteem and respect of the parish priest and the people of that district. They are interested in discussing with you a Colony Project of the Italian Prisoners of War."[44]

Although no documentation exists of any meetings that included Michelson, Cardetti, and Glidden, it is possible that they met to discuss bringing Italian POWs to Rosati. However, no POWs from Weingarten ever came in any official capacity. When this proposal appeared in October 1943, Italy had only just surrendered as part of the Axis powers, and U.S. officials possibly had reservations about bringing Italian POWs to Rosati. Additionally, though it remains unclear exactly what Cardetti and Michelson had planned, the POW work program was still in its infancy, and U.S. authorities remained apprehensive about establishing branch camps at all. Thus, it seems doubtful that Glidden and his bosses at the Seventh Service Command in Omaha would have approved any such proposals that came forward.

Gasconade Riverboat Camp

Once host to a POW camp, the Corps of Engineers shipyard on the Missouri River still operates in Gasconade. During World War II, six hundred people worked there around the clock. Located near Hermann, the twenty-nine-acre boatyard, with its collection of red brick and frame buildings, served as a crucial service and construction site for the landing craft eventually used to storm Normandy.[45]

Both Italian and German POWs worked at Gasconade, although not simultaneously. Housed on a quarterboat moored on the Gasconade River, the men worked as laborers in the boatyard, painting barges, doing repairs, running errands, and handling other low-level tasks.

Orville Clifton worked with a construction crew at the boatyard, pouring concrete floors and performing similar duties. POWs worked with his crew, delivering the freshly mixed concrete in wheelbarrows. Clifton described one memorable incident that resulted from this work:

> There was an older guy who was the foreman of the POWs. One time he told this little guy to take a wheelbarrow full of concrete up this wooden plank to where we needed it. I could see that this little guy was going to have trouble because the concrete was so heavy and the plank was kind of steep. Well, wouldn't you know it, he got about halfway up the plank and the whole thing dumped over off the side because he was just too little to manage it.[46]

Everyone had a good laugh about the incident, said Clifton, and they refilled the wheelbarrow with concrete and went on with their work. Another American, George Johnson, also remembered the Italians fondly, saying, "We weren't supposed to be too close or friendly with them. But I'd sneak down from the office where I worked down to the storeroom to talk to them."

As at other camps, POWs were eager to share with their American coworkers. Johnson recalled going down to the POW quarterboats to eat. "The Italians would invite the Corps of Engineers workers down for meals," Johnson said. "Their coffee was like syrup, it had so much sugar in it."[47]

After the Italians returned to Weingarten, about fifty-five German POWs came from Fort Leonard Wood to take their place. American worker Morris Pearle, who dealt with personnel and radio operations, described these prisoners as "harder to get acquainted with," saying, "it's not that they were rebellious, just more distant."[48]

Both groups of POWs had a fair amount of freedom, including the privileges of fishing and of taking a rowboat up and down the Gasconade River on the weekends. Clifton said, "They really didn't have to guard them at all. They weren't in a chain gang, and it wasn't a jail with bars on the windows. It was just like a barracks but it was a floating deal. At most maybe they had a bed check at night."[49]

Other POWs worked on road crews outside the boatyard, recalled Merlin Walther, who was thirteen or fourteen when the prisoners were there. "The POWs mostly worked on the all-gravel state and county roads and the town streets, maintaining rights-of-way, cleaning ditches, repairing ruts, etc.," said Walther, who would watch wide eyed whenever the prisoners stopped in on breaks for ice cream in his father's general store. "There would be about ten POWs in each work crew and one guard with a rifle with them."

Boatyard supervisor Elwood Massey was friendly with Walther's parents, and Massey invited the boy to visit with the POWs in the boatyard. "Usually I would visit in the evenings when they would have movies. Some of the movies were in German and some in English," said Walther. "The Germans would try to speak some English to me and I would try to use what little German that I knew how to speak to them."

The other boys in the town were flabbergasted to hear of Walther's adventures. They constantly asked if he was scared of the POWs. "The first time I was asked that I was quite surprised," said Walther. "What was there to be scared of? Being scared never entered my mind."[50]

The Color Guard marches at O'Reilly General Hospital. In the background is the Pythian Castle, used as a service club for enlisted men. Courtesy of Evangel University Archives.

Chapter Eleven

Other Major Missouri Camps

T HE BOYHOOD HOME OF MARK TWAIN added 265 residents in September 1944, when the POW camp at Clarinda, Iowa, opened a side camp at Hannibal, Missouri. The camp was a temporary gain, however, as it operated just six weeks.

Hannibal

The POWs had come to tackle the massive task of sorting 2 million pairs of old Army shoes at the Bluff City Shoe Factory. The Army had collected the shoes from around the country and sent them to Hannibal for sorting. After POWs did the sorting, civilian employees repaired the salvageable shoes for shipping to European refugees. According to a U.N. official, more than 126 million pairs were needed in France, Greece, and other countries no longer under Nazi control.[1]

To house the prisoners at Hannibal, Army officials created an enclosure inside a ballpark, Clemens Field. Canvas tents spread out in orderly rows from home plate all the way to the outfield. The decision to locate the camp at the field had caused some consternation among Hannibal residents; the previous spring, the town had allocated $2,500 to buy equipment and hire coordinators for an ambitious sports and recreation program. The field hosted a softball league and other athletic activities for more than two thousand youngsters. When the government announced it would use the field to house prisoners of war, William B. Spann and the other members of the Hannibal Citizens' Committee filed a petition against the decision with the Committee on Military Affairs of the U.S. House of Representatives. The petition argued that the government's decision would reduce recreational opportunities in town and would endanger residents.

The protests failed to stop the project but perhaps alerted the Army to resistance to the prisoners' presence in the community.[2] As a result, Army officials took steps to reassure Hannibal residents that the situation was only temporary and that the prisoners posed no threat to safety or jobs. Articles in the *Hannibal Courier-Post* promised that twenty-five U.S. soldiers would guard the prisoners at all times. The newspaper also pointed out that the shortage of civilian labor, along with the pressing need to have the shoes exported by winter, made prisoner labor necessary at the factory, the only facility in the country devoted exclusively to repairing shoes.

Colonel C. J. Blake, commanding officer of the Kansas City quartermaster depot, worked for the agency that helped coordinate the project. He addressed the reservations held by people in Hannibal: "You and I would not think much of these shoes, but to the poor people of these liberated countries who are barefooted, these shoes will look mighty good. It is my understanding that most of the shoes to be sorted are going to Greece, a country whose people fought valiantly in the present war."

Because of the strong objections to the use of POW labor by unions in other places, Blake actually visited the Bluff City Shoe Factory to assure workers that their jobs would not be affected. Blake told the workers, "You people and the International Shoe Company are not directly involved.... I want to make clear that the work done by these prisoners of war will in no way affect a single job in this big plant. As you can well imagine, these prisoners will not be at all familiar with the complicated business of making shoes."

Blake told employees about successes with POW labor in other parts of the country and said that American GIs on the front lines would support putting the prisoners to use. Blake said, "Every man on the fighting front would say, 'Sure, we took him out of the fighting, now you people use him for all he is worth.'" Blake closed his speech by asking the workers to put aside the labor disputes plaguing the plant, for the sake of the country:

> You will all agree with me that the full enthusiastic and patriotic prosecution of the war until the actual moment of defeat of not only Germany, but Japan, as well cannot be questioned. We must do everything within our power to accomplish our part in winning the war. We must not stop production in this factory for a single hour unless it is absolutely necessary. If we do so, we will be sabotaging America, and more specifically, we will be betraying our own flesh and blood in the fighting services.[3]

Despite the Army's concern, Hannibal residents and factory workers, as it turned out, readily accepted the Germans. Don Smith, who grew up in Hannibal, recalled, "There was almost no fear or resentment with these prisoners. People hated the Japanese because of their sneak attack and the difference in race, but there was no similar feeling toward the Germans."[4]

Before long, the Army stopped using trucks to shuttle prisoners to work. Smith and others remembered the prisoners marching each day from the ballpark to the shoe factories. According to some accounts, Hannibal residents would toss the prisoners rolls and vegetables as they went by.[5]

Because of the openness with which the community received the prisoners, after just a couple weeks, one of the Army officers proposed taking the POWs to watch a Hannibal High School football game. Though the community raised no apparent objection, the plan was called off. Someone pointed out that War Department policy prohibited taking prisoners to public gatherings unless required by their work.[6]

From time to time, the language gap caused some problems for the Hannibal prisoners. On one occasion, POWs requested raw sausage, a traditional Teutonic treat. The government denied the request, however, citing concerns about trichinosis. When the U.S. officers tried to explain the dangers of uncooked pork, the Germans misunderstood and thought they had been fed contaminated or wormy meat.[7]

Although no incidents of food poisoning occurred, one prisoner did die during the brief stay in Hannibal. On the morning of September 29, 1944, a German prisoner returning to his barracks found Josef Gapp, age forty-two, dead in his bed. He had just eaten breakfast and had announced he was returning to his bunk because he wasn't feeling well. Gapp apparently died of heart failure, so coroner William M. Smith determined an inquest unnecessary. U.S. officials took Gapp's remains back to Camp Clarinda for burial the next day.[8]

On the whole, the POWs' time in Hannibal was uneventful, and after the six weeks, the Germans completed their work as planned and returned to Iowa.[9]

Louisiana

Apple lovers might not know the name Stark Bro's Nurseries and Orchards, but they certainly recognize the popular varieties Red Delicious and Golden Delicious. Stark Bro's, one of the oldest and largest nurseries in America, introduced these varieties in 1893 and 1914, respectively.

During World War II, Stark suffered from the same labor shortage as other agricultural concerns. Stark, based in Louisiana, Missouri, needed people to work in its orchards to bud, graft, prune, and tend to the plants and trees of every variety. So when the government began making POW labor available, orchard management seized the opportunity.

The first prisoners who came to Stark were Italians from Camp Weingarten. They arrived in August 1943 and moved into a recently vacated National Youth Administration (NYA) camp, which had closed a month before because of insufficient funding. The quarters, considered top-notch for a branch camp, formerly accommodated 260 young men and women who had participated in the NYA work/study program. Buses carried the prisoners from their camp to Stark Bro's, and employees rode along.[10]

Louisiana residents found the Italians a happy bunch, and townspeople enjoyed hearing the men sing as they marched to St. Joseph Catholic Church on North Third Street. Singing took place inside the church, too; in 1944, a POW choir performed two hymns for a packed house at Easter Sunday mass. The prisoners also attended movies at Clark Theater, where a block of seats in the center section was held for them. Area kids scrambled to sit near them, fascinated by their foreign language and appearance.[11]

Residents enjoyed frequent interaction with the prisoners because of the size of the town, the degree of freedom enjoyed by the prisoners, and the large number of residents employed at the nursery. Robert Cadwallader and his friend Edward got to know the prisoners after camp guards started inviting them into the compound. During these visits, the prisoners showed the boys how to make kites, and Robert won an award for the best kite at a Cub Scout competition. Other traces of the prisoners' influence appeared in the boys' lives. One night after dinner, while Robert was doing the dishes, he took the just-washed silverware, wrapped it in a towel, and began to shake it. When his mother asked what he was doing, he told her "this is the way the Italians do it." Perhaps the biggest impact the presence of the Italians made on the Cadwalladers' household was when Robert came home one day with a large dog. The POWs had kept the animal as a pet, and, with their departure right around the corner, they gave the dog to their young American friend.[12]

Lucille Carroll Keith grew up in Louisiana and spent summers working at the orchards. Although she did not work with the prisoners directly, she received a special memento from one of them. Keith said, "I did not know any of them personally, but the grandfather of a boy I was dating was over the shipping sheds where some of the prisoners worked. He passed word to me that one of the prisoners liked to paint with oil, and if I had a picture I would like the boy to paint, he would have it done for me."

An Italian POW created an oil painting from this photograph of Lucille Carroll Keith. Courtesy of Lucille Carroll Keith.

Keith provided a black and white five-by-seven portrait photograph, and the man transformed it into a twelve-by-eighteen color painting, signing his name in the corner. Keith said, "He had not seen me in person, so I guess he made me look Italian. Painted my hair black and my face darker like an Italian—yet the painting looks just like the original—just the coloring changes my appearance, so I was shocked when I saw it." Keith still has the photograph and painting, and she gave duplicates to her children. "I thought it made a great war souvenir all these years."[13]

The Italians, whom Leone Cadwallader called "wonderful...polite and mannerly," stayed at Louisiana until the end of April 1944 before returning to Weingarten.[14] The *Louisiana Press-Journal* noted, "The Italians apparently were well-pleased with the work and living conditions here."[15]

Following the Italians' departure, Germans from Fort Leonard Wood came to replace their labor. This group of sixty-three arrived on May 16, 1944, and picked up where the Italians left off. According to former prisoner Franz Engelmann, "The accommodations were better [at Louisiana], with three men to a room. Although there were no partitions or doors, it was definitely livable." He praised the mess facilities, too: "It was a good kitchen, with a dining room. The guards sat on the left side and we sat on the right."[16]

Although Stark Bro's employees considered the Germans better workers on the whole, several described the Germans' demeanor as "sullen and resentful." George Minnehans, a civilian employee at the Stark Bro's print shop, was particularly fond of two Germans who worked for him, but he remembered troublesome ones as well. One of them seemed to go out of his way to provoke Minnehans. Minnehans said of the man, "[He] was just a short little guy, bow-legged and ugly as heck. That guy would try to run into me every chance he'd get. Just like that, he'd be walking and would just try to bump into me. It was like he had an attitude. 'You can't do anything to me,' just like that."[17]

Because of such contrary—and in some cases surly—attitudes, the guards watched the Germans more carefully. The effort proved imperfect, as two of the prisoners, Christoph Illhardt and Bruno Renkel, managed to escape one night. Nonetheless, to the authorities' credit, a patrol caught the prisoners less than an hour later.[18]

Relationships with the Germans

Of course, opinions differ among people, and though some considered the Germans distant and unfriendly, guard Al Griego had a more positive impression. Griego often ate with the prisoners in their mess, and some of the men tutored him informally in conversational German. Also, Griego "hired" a couple of the prisoners to iron his uniforms and to keep his quarters clean, paying them in cigarettes for their services.

Griego said those prisoners "treated Louisiana and the guards like their home." He added that when the POWs learned that they would be sent back to Europe, some wanted to stay in Louisiana.[19]

The Germans also received compliments for their effort in beautifying the former NYA camp that was their home. The Reverend August Reyling, who drove each week from Quincy, Illinois, to say Mass at the Louisiana camp, observed, "[W]hat was once a field of rank weeds is now a well-planned tract of lawns and blooming flower beds."[20]

Franz Engelmann remembered having good relationships with his supervisor at Stark Bro's, where the prisoners shipped out young trees as part of the company's mail-order operation. In the fall, the company sold the young trees directly to customers on the nursery grounds. "We had to fill orders," said Engelmann, "and I was allowed to work directly selling trees to the customers. I enjoyed that very much."[21]

Coddling at Louisiana?

By 1945, a national debate was brewing over alleged coddling of POWs. An incident at the Louisiana branch camp brought the debate into sharp focus, notably through an April 1945 letter written by C. D. Hicks to Colonel Harry A. Vaughan, military aide to President Truman.

Hicks, a St. Louis railway magnate, and his wife had taken a Dr. Velarde, the owner of a large collection of orchards in Mexico, and his wife to the Louisiana camp. The purpose was to show Velarde how the Stark nurseries used the railroads and to pave the way for better cooperation between the American and Mexican railroads. What Hicks observed that day disturbed him. Hicks wrote:

> I have read and heard so much [negative press] about the freedom, the care and the coddling of German war prisoners in this Country that I have not given credence to them until [this] experience.... [W]e have all learned so much about the factual atrocities in Germany on prisoners of war and others, that I think it is really high time that we find out just how much we are actually coddling the German war prisoners and the laxity in which they are guarded.

As Hicks and his party walked through the packing sheds, he noticed that only one guard watched the Germans, who worked throughout the nursery complex. Hicks claimed that the Germans were "standing around as much as they were working."

Hicks also claimed to sense hostility from the prisoners as his group toured the facility. He wrote, "When we went through these sheds observing the methods of packing the small fruit trees, it was necessary to go in and among these war prisoners. While I do not understand German, the expressions on their faces and the tone of their chatter among themselves were all unmistakable. The manner in which they glared and stared at Mrs. Velarde and my wife and the meaning it reflected was so obvious as to be almost insulting."

At one point on the tour, Hicks's group traversed a courtyard between several sheds. Hicks observed the prisoners standing around unguarded and seemingly intent on intimidating the group as they passed through: "[T]hey took deliberate pains to move around when we came out of the buildings and to walk slowly back and forth right in front of us with their unmistakable scowl, chatter, and so on." He also noted the lack of any barrier—guard, fence, or other obstacle—that would prevent the prisoners from escaping.

Whether it was out of dismay at the perceived soft treatment of the prisoners, anger at the hostile attitude toward his guests, or genuine concern for the potential political fallout for the government, Hicks worried about what he'd seen and about the response it would provoke if revealed to the public. He imagined something on the scale of the Walter Winchell radio broadcast that put the spotlight on the POWs at the Hellwig farm in Chesterfield.

Hicks wrote, "Of course, if this thing would happen to get into the papers and become public, the War Department, Commanding Officers, Stark, and everybody else would deny it. They would immediately establish protective measures and then invite the newspaper reporters to come out and make a personal investigation, which is more or less what happened in connection with the expos[é] of the prisoners of war near Gumbo, Missouri."[22]

The reply to Hicks was immediate. It was sent within a week and included an informal investigation of the situation at the Stark Bro's nursery (perhaps indicating how seriously the War Department took the issue). Vaughan had appointed Lieutenant Colonel B. W. Davenport, an assistant to the chief of staff of the War Department, to compose the reply. It explained the philosophy behind the POW work program and evaluated its operation in places such as Louisiana.

Davenport testified that the prisoners sent to work at these smaller camps were thoroughly screened. He also said that appropriately trained American troops guarded the workers, at a ratio of one guard for every ten to fifteen workers. The current security plan provided for a sufficient number of guards without tying up excessive numbers of U.S. soldiers needed elsewhere.

Davenport continued, "Other means of promoting security and effecting apprehension of prisoners are employed, such as roving patrols and perimeter guards. Roving patrols circulate over a wide area and patrol all highways in the vicinity where prisoners are employed." Ultimately, Davenport asserted, the prisoners were not an escape risk, and he cited the escape rate for POWs at 4.5 per 1,000, virtually identical to the rate in the federal penitentiary system. Not a single act of sabotage was tied to an escaping POW, wrote Davenport, who noted that POWs provided work simply too valuable to the nation to dismiss: "Prisoners of war have harvested crops that otherwise would have rotted in the field for lack of harvest hands, and have processed tons of foodstuffs. It is believed that the results of their work have been so beneficial to our war effort that the War Department's policy in taking this 'calculated' risk about which Mr. Hicks writes is fully justified."[23]

The branch camp at Louisiana closed permanently on March 31, 1946, when the last group of German POWs housed there returned to Fort Leonard Wood. Recalled Franz Engelmann, "One of the owners of the nursery was the governor of Missouri [Lloyd Stark]. He visited us often and was very satisfied with us. At our departure after two years at the camp, he expressed his praise and thanks for our work."[24]

The returning Germans stayed at Fort Leonard Wood for just a matter of days before that camp closed, and they moved on to other camps as part of the process of eventual repatriation to Germany. Engelmann said, "We departed in May 1946 on a Liberty ship in the hopes of going home.

Sorry—after a twelve day trip we disappointedly reached the harbor town of Liverpool, England. There the provisions were for us just like at the end of the war in Louisiana. The English sure had a big palace for the king but mighty little in the way of food. After a year, in May 1947, by ship we finally went back home."[25]

Springfield: O'Reilly General Hospital

During World War II, Springfield, Missouri, was home to O'Reilly General Hospital, a massive one-hundred-acre medical complex at the intersection of Glenstone and Division. With war looming on the horizon in January 1941, Army officials began planning for a major military hospital in southwest Missouri. Numerous new bases were going up in the area, including Fort Leonard Wood and Camp Crowder, and the existing Camp Clark, in Nevada, Missouri, had plans for expansion. All these posts offered fairly comprehensive medical services, but an advanced-care facility was needed for the treatment of long-term illnesses and injuries experienced by GIs and their dependents.

The Army's Seventh Service Command Headquarters in Omaha, Nebraska, had the responsibility of selecting the site for the medical facility. After the competitive selection process was announced, some thirty cities lined up to bid on the giant federal project and the money and jobs it promised. John T. Woodruff, a member of the Springfield Chamber of Commerce, led the search for a suitable tract of land to offer the government for the facility. One hundred acres were needed, and the committee

O'Reilly patients recuperated through physical therapy, including this bike-riding exercise. Courtesy of Evangel University Archives.

identified the Glenstone Municipal Golf Course as the most likely location. The tract was relatively flat and offered substantial undeveloped acreage on three sides for any possible or necessary expansion.

Springfield's network of transportation routes was another significant feature. In addition to the famed Route 66—which connected the city with Fort Leonard Wood and Jefferson Barracks to the east and Tulsa and Oklahoma City to the west—another major blacktop highway, Route 65, ran through the Springfield. It offered direct links with many of the region's other major cities. Additionally, McCluer Field, Springfield's first airport, was just a half mile east on Division Street, and the Frisco Railroad and the eleven bus lines running into the city provided a multitude of transportation options.

On January 29, 1941, the Army told Springfield officials that the hospital was theirs if they could provide the land to the government at no cost. The Chamber of Commerce immediately negotiated the purchase of the golf course for $70,000, and by February 17, Springfield businesses and residents had raised the money. A Valentine's Day announcement declared the hospital to be named in honor of Major General Robert Maitland O'Reilly, the surgeon general of the Army from 1902 to 1909 and an individual "of masculine courage and feminine sensibilities."[26]

Survey work on the site for the hospital started February 21, 1941, and construction began in April, using plans that originally called for 91 build-

The wards of O'Reilly General Hospital were connected by enclosed walkways, allowing one to traverse the entire complex without ever going outside. Courtesy of Evangel University Archives.

ings and a 1,000-bed capacity. The work finished on schedule by August 24, 1941, and the complex was officially dedicated November 8, 1941. Initial staffing included 73 officers, 120 nurses, 500 enlisted men, and 500 civilian employees. These numbers climbed rapidly, as the hospital soon expanded to include Smith Park and another fifty-three-acre plot owned by a lodge called the Knights of Pythias. Construction on these additional tracts eventually increased the capacity of the medical facility to nearly 5,000 beds and 240 buildings.[27]

A hospital the size of O'Reilly required thousands of military and civilian staff. In addition to the doctors, nurses, medics, and other GIs, the hospital employed almost 1,200 southwest Missouri civilians as postal clerks and carriers, ambulance drivers, secretaries, guards, cooks, and the like. Hundreds more volunteered, including the Red Cross's Gray Ladies, who read and played cards with recuperating GIs. Other volunteers signed up to be drivers for the Red Cross Motor Corps, which took patients on recre-

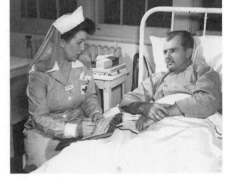

One of the Red Cross "Gray Ladies" visiting with a recuperating soldier at O'Reilly General Hospital. Courtesy of Evangel University Archives.

ational trips. A fourth group that served at O'Reilly included, of course, POWs, who worked in a variety of roles in and around the hospital complex.[28]

The first group of POWs at O'Reilly comprised Italians from Camp Clark in Nevada. The *Springfield Leader and Press* reported this development with an article headlined "O'Reilly Gets Gang of 'PW's.'" The article said, "Sixty Italian prisoners of war in special convoy from Camp Clark in Nevada, arrived at O'Reilly General Hospital today where they'll be used on a labor gang. The prisoners will keep grounds and roadways in repair and be housed at hospital quarters."[29]

Highway patrolmen escorted the prisoners from Clark and, as a precaution, stood by at the hospital on the day of the transfer. The extra security proved unnecessary. All prisoners assigned to the O'Reilly detail showed themselves reliable and, in fact, earned the freedom to roam their area of the hospital complex. These men worked only briefly at O'Reilly before their home at Camp Clark became a pen for troublesome Nazis and the Italians there moved to other camps. The Army replaced them with POWs from Weingarten, who arrived in spring 1944.[30]

POWs worship at a Christmas service with O'Reilly GIs. Courtesy of Evangel University Archives.

Another group of prisoners spent time at O'Reilly in August 1943 but not as workers. Fourteen German prisoners needed treatment and received it within a special ward established especially for them. Despite the attention provided, the Germans proved difficult. Tina Gold, who worked at the Springfield hospital, said, "Because of the truly hostile nature of this particular group of German prisoners, they were not allowed out of their area unguarded. In fact, I don't think they even let them ever get out of bed without somebody watching them." Gold recalled how the men made things difficult for the staff assigned to treat them: "These guys were fanatical Nazis, Hitler all the way. They would try to spit on the medical personnel working in their ward, and it got to the point where the female members of the staff wouldn't even go in there anymore."[31]

This attitude contrasted with that of the Italians, who worked in and around the hospital virtually indistinguishable from most of the American employees. Two favored Italians—Andrino, called Andy, and Giovanni, called Johnny—worked for Gold, who ran the testing laboratory for vaccinations and other medications. Gold said, "We used quite a bit of sheep's blood in our testing because of its similarities to human blood. We kept two sheep, Penelope and Valentine, and Andy and Johnny would draw their blood for the tests." At times the scene at the lab resembled a rodeo, according to Gold: "Andy would sit on the sheep and Johnny would lift its head to draw blood from the neck."

Gold considered the work of these men valuable, as it allowed the lab to carry out tasks critical for the hospital. The Italians performed just about every function necessary in the "animal house," as Gold called the lab. "Those guys washed windows, kept the cages clean, did basic diagnoses of diseases, and prepped the animals for tests," Gold said. "It didn't take them long to learn all about keeping lab animals."

With the end of the war in 1945, the Italians at O'Reilly began to transfer back to Camp Weingarten in preparation for eventual return to Italy. Gold kept up with her POW workers for a year or two after the war and then fell out of touch. She said, "They were marvelous men. Great help in the laboratory but also just great people to be around."[32]

Several of the O'Reilly nurses recalled the Italian POWs flirting with them on occasion. One of the nurses said, "I remember the Italians singing to us in the evenings. They would sit out on the steps with their guitars and their beautiful voices and would serenade us."[33]

During its five years of operation as an active Army facility beginning in November 1941, O'Reilly General Hospital treated more than forty-two thousand injured soldiers and more than sixty thousand GI dependents. O'Reilly closed in September 1946. It reopened two years later as a Veteran's Administration facility. Just four years after that, in 1952, the hospital closed again, this time for good. The Assemblies of God purchased a good portion of the land and buildings for what would become Evangel College (later Evangel University). Even today, the gymnasium, commandant's administration building, Service Club (formerly the Pythian Castle), and Red Cross building serve the university in various capacities. Smith Park was re-created with the rest of the land, and the Army National Guard and Army Reserve assumed the title to the remaining portions of the property.[34]

Even field conditions did not prevent the Italians from making pasta at this Italian Service Unit camp. Courtesy of Pete Puleo, Sr.

Chapter Twelve

Leaving the Camps

T HE MAJORITY OF THE PRISONERS, both German and Italian, held in the United States left America in the fall of 1945 and the spring of 1946. However, the experiences of the two groups were vastly different, both during their final months stateside and upon their return to Europe.

After Italy formed an alliance with the Allied powers in the fall of 1943, more than half of the Italian prisoners left the regular POW camps to work for the U.S. Army in the Italian Service Units (ISU). Under this program, which began in March 1944, some thirty thousand Italian POWs moved to regular Army installations, where they worked in noncombat support roles and were treated the same as American GIs in almost every respect. According to Martin Tollefson, director of the Prisoner of War Division of the PMGO, "As a result of their voluntary entrance into these units, which among other differences required very little guarding, these Italians were given special privileges and performed important work in military establishments which otherwise would have been done by American military personnel and civilians."[1]

Formation of the Italian Service Units

The ISU started when the status of Italian POWs changed, and suddenly it became possible for the U.S. Army to use prisoners in ways previously off-limits because of Geneva Convention restrictions. When the country left the Axis powers and joined the Allies, the Italian prisoners' status was put in flux. This flip-flop began after American forces landed in Sicily in the summer of 1943, and just a few weeks later Italy formally withdrew from the Axis powers and surrendered to the Allies. King Victor Emmanuel had Fascist dictator Benito Mussolini arrested and replaced him with

Marshal Pietro Badoglio, Italian army chief of staff. Badoglio's government operated in the southern part of Italy held by the Allies, while Fascists aligned with Germany continued to jointly control Italy's northern half.

"We learn today that Italy has surrendered," wrote Weingarten POW Aldo Ferraresi in his diary on September 9, 1943. "I see in front of my eyes the thousands of men killed, wounded, missing, from the French border to the mountains of Yugoslavia, from the frozen plains of Russia to the hot deserts of Africa. All this for nothing. And what will happen to Italy? I am sure that the Germans will not go away, and that Italy will again become a war theater!"[2] A month later, on October 8, 1943, Italy officially joined the Allied countries when the new Badoglio-led government declared war on Germany. "Italian Prisoners in Missouri Accept War Declaration Soberly" read the headline in the Associated Press report carried by the *St. Louis Globe-Democrat* on October 14, 1943.[3]

Weingarten prisoners were "rather pleased" about Italy's entrance into the war on the side of the Allies, according to the piece, but they received the news with worries over additional damage to a war-ravaged country. Colonel Glidden, commander at Weingarten, told the reporter that the prisoners under his control thought this was the right thing for Italy to do but were concerned for the people caught in the fighting. "They came from all parts of Italy and are very home-loving fellows. And these prisoners, particularly the officers, are pretty sensible chaps. They are very faithful to their King," Glidden said. "But most of all they are worried about their families, particularly those who come from the part of Italy north of the present battle line. The mail service from their homes is very poor, but they know there is a shortage of food—and they are fearful that the Germans have taken all food in the part of Italy the Nazis hold."[4]

These developments posed a series of difficult questions and provided a dilemma for both the U.S. and Italian governments about the status of Italian detainees at Weingarten and elsewhere. Were they still prisoners, or were they now Allied soldiers, entitled to treatment consistent with that role? Although the Army wanted POWs to remain under tight control, others felt different, including some highly placed officials in the State Department. James Keeley, chief of the Special Projects Division, the arm of the State Department that dealt with POWs, felt there were many benefits to returning at least some of the Italian POWs to Europe at once. "The tales that they would have to tell on their return would, I believe, do much to win general support from the Italian people for our war effort," wrote Keely. "Their tales would, furthermore, filter through into Germany and might have a distinct bearing upon increasing the number of surrenders among German soldiers who might prefer to taste the richness of prisoner of war food in the United States rather than to keep on fighting on German Army fare."[5]

However, the War Department was not convinced that it was a good idea to free the Italian prisoners while the situation was still so fluid. Instead, it favored a plan proposed by the British through which cooperative Italian POWs would organize into military units, supervised by Allied officers but under the direct control of their own officers and NCOs. These units would be used in noncombatant roles to free up Allied troops for warfighting missions. These Italians, like others remaining in the POW camps, would still be considered prisoners, however, and would continue to be "guests" of the Allies until the end of the war. Though it took some convincing, Badoglio, who desired the immediate return of all Italian POWs, ultimately embraced the idea and on October 11, 1943, issued the following proclamation that was posted in all POW camps where Italian soldiers were interned:

To the Officers and enlisted personnel comprising Italian war prisoners of the Anglo-Americans:

In the new political-military situation, arisen because of the hostile German action towards Italy, it is our intention to give the Allies all possible, active collaboration in order to rid our country of German troops occupying our nation.

It is therefore our duty to help the Allies in every way possible, excepting in actual combat. We are to be linked together in activities constituting special services and in work under the command of officers to be designated. In that manner you will collaborate effectively from now on in the fight for our redemption from the century-old enemy as the people in Italy are now doing alongside the Anglo-American forces for the liberation of the Homeland.

Signed: The Marshall of Italy: BADOGLIO[6]

Badoglio's proclamation meant that an immense pool of labor was now available for work previously barred by the Geneva Convention. Article 31 of that agreement prohibited POW work on activities directly related to the American war effort, but because of the "cobelligerent" status now accorded to Italy, the Allied countries could employ volunteer Italian prisoners in many types of work directly related to the continuing U.S. fight against

Germany and Japan. Article 32 of the Geneva Convention, which dealt with the health, personal safety, and well-being of POWs, still applied, however, and precluded their service in combat, on docks, on wharves, or on vessels at ports within the United States, as well as prohibited the prisoners from handling explosives or other dangerous materials. These changes in POW status paved the way for much broader use of the prisoners in service to the United States, and later that same month, Secretary of War Henry L. Stimson began developing plans to organize Italian POWs into Italian Service Units.

In March 1944, the ISU program was formally organized by order of Major General J. A. Ulio. "In order to utilize to the maximum the services of Italian prisoners of war who are loyal to the cause of the [Allies], they will be organized…into service units without arms," wrote Ulio.[7] Naturally, while the Army wanted as many qualified volunteers as possible, it also hoped to spot troublemakers, especially pro-Fascist POWs, and to weed them out. To do so, the Army established a comprehensive screening program under the direction of Captain Paul Neuland, who prior to the war had been an FBI agent investigating subversion and espionage by German and Italian embassy staff in the United States. Neuland and his four-man staff (including an Italian major) visited twenty-five POW camps and spent four months interviewing fifty thousand POWs to assess their suitability for participation in the ISU. Of that total, only three thousand were rejected for service. "Some camp commanders didn't like our having the last say-so, and occasionally vetoed our efforts by assigning men to ISUs against our recommendation," recalled Neuland. "Ironically, nearly every one of them was later returned to a POW camp for misbehavior. Our system thus seemed to have worked well, and it was provably fair."[8]

Internal Conflict

Even though more Italian POWs (75 percent of the total in the United States) volunteered for the ISU program than there were positions available, the decision was not always an easy one for the prisoners, especially as the program was first getting underway. The ISU program and its purposes required some explaining, and even then it was not clear to many POWs what participants would be doing. Some were interested in fighting to free Italy from Nazi occupation. "Even before the declaration of war many of them asked about the possibility of their going back to take up arms in defense of their homes," said Colonel Glidden, but the program had no combat considerations. Others thought the participants would have to fight on behalf of the United States, perhaps in the Pacific, a prospect feared by many.[9]

Ennio Calabresi was a POW at Camp Weingarten until June 1944, when the opportunity arose to join the ISU. He was unsure of what to do and asked many questions about the program. "I certainly didn't want to fight anymore, and neither did my friends," said Calabresi. "When they said, 'Oh no. No more fighting for you,' we all signed up right away."[10]

Italian POWs who considered volunteering for the ISU often felt substantial inner conflict over the decision, and the tension reached its peak when Neuland and his team showed up at their camp to recruit volunteers. Historian Louis Keefer observed that it was then the hard choice had to be made: help the Americans and leave the camp or refuse and stay behind the barbed wire for the duration of the war. "To collaborate with the Allies against Italian and German forces, that is, against our very brothers, the Italians, and against the Germans with whom we'd fought side-by-side only some months before, we would have had to work with those who had been our enemies in a war that wasn't yet over," said Armando Boscolo, who was adamant in his refusal to participate in the ISU. "For me, that would be like being a football player who switches sides when he sees his team is losing, an unheard-of thing, which if it were to happen would result in the player being thrown out as a traitor."[11]

Weingarten POW Aldo Ferraresi ultimately joined the ISU, basing his decision on several reasons, but noted his choice was still not an easy one:

First the proclamation of the King and Marshal Badoglio declaring war on Germany. As a career officer, I followed the King's command without hesitation. Second was my own deep-seated dislike of the Germans, based mainly but not totally on their mistreatment of my father who was their prisoner during World War I.

There was also my personal resentment of the Germans. The few I met in Italy were very arrogant, and when we occupied Yugoslavia in 1941 their comportment and attitudes were again very arrogant. They treated us not as allies but as poor, inferior relatives.

Despite all this, however, choosing sides was not easy: My close friends and I had hours of discussion about the pros and cons of the matter, in order that we would never in the future feel that we had acted hastily.[12]

Another Weingarten POW, Francesco Tarasco, spent hardly any time thinking over the various implications of joining the ISU, and when the opportunity was offered, he signed up at once. "I saw nothing but advantages. It would mark an end to my idleness, and a way to earn some extra money for the future," recalled Tarasco. "I was an educator in private life, not a career officer, so politics was not a factor in my decision. I don't remember any fake promises being made, only that we were to have more freedom and earn more pay, than if we remained strictly POWs."[13]

The War Department directed that all ISU personnel receive $24 per month. One-third was paid in cash and the rest in PX script or for deposit to the prisoner's trust account. Other than the necessity to obtain passes to leave the military post and to travel in the company of Americans, the men in the ISU were not under strict military supervision and were not really prisoners any more in the earlier sense of the word. The soldiers were expected to maintain regular military discipline and good order and to perform their tasks as directed. Any uncooperative or subversive attitudes or serious violations of laws called for them to be sent back to the POW camp. Ultimately, what the ISU offered participants—a combination of greater freedom, better pay, increased responsibility, and less monotonous work, as well as enhanced opportunities to interact with civilians—was a big draw for many Italian POWs.

Colonel Glidden and his staff watch ISU troops pass post HQ in review. Courtesy of Norma Overall Jacob.

In May 1944, the Weingarten POWs who had signed up to be in the ISU transferred out of the camp to go to their new assignments. Dressed in crisp new uniforms, they could almost pass for American GIs. Before their departure, they marked the occasion with a solemn military ceremony, including an inspection and parade complete with an Italian flag. Colonel Glidden and his staff looked on as the Italians marched past their post in review.

Occasionally, strife erupted in the camps because most of the pro-Fascist POWs viewed the ISU men as collaborators and traitors. There were a few accounts of violence and one or two full-blown riots:

Grant Hanna [an American soldier] recalled having to help break up one such riot. He said they fought with such ferocity that it was almost impossible to separate them. The guards, who were allowed to be armed only with billy clubs inside the compounds, were forced to knock them out before they would stop fighting....

There are reports that there was a father and a son who were held in different compounds, because one was a Fascist and the other a King's man.[14]

Because of the possibility of reprisals against volunteers for the ISU, particularly toward those who signed up for the program but remained in the camps because of a lack of assignments, U.S. authorities took pains to separate prisoners based on their interest in being involved in ISU service. For example, a visitor to Camp Weingarten from the Italian embassy noted in August 1945 that three POW compounds were active at the facility. The first compound held 539 officers who had volunteered to join the ISU but were awaiting assignment. The second compound contained cooperative enlisted men who had volunteered for ISU service, including a number who already had been out on ISU assignments but returned because of medical reasons. The third compound contained enlisted men who refused the opportunity to enroll in the ISU, "non-signers" in government parlance.

A State Department representative who accompanied the Italian delegate to Camp Weingarten noted the man's focus on the question of the Italians' status as POWs, particularly those who volunteered for the ISU but were not selected. He felt it was wrong that these men who wanted to work for the Americans were still treated just like any other POW. "It is obvious…that he is deeply concerned regarding the decision of the American authorities to continue to apply the same regulations to Italian prisoners of war as are applied with respect to German and Japanese prisoners of war," wrote the State Department representative. "In this connection he argues that the Italian prisoner of war finds it extremely difficult to understand why he should continue to be treated as an enemy prisoner, particularly when, through no fault of his own, he is not assigned to a service unit or once having served in such a unit, he is released without prejudice and again finds himself subject to the same regulations as are applicable to enemy prisoners of war."[15]

Structure of the ISU

The commander of the ISU program was General John M. Eager, who spoke Italian and served as military attaché at the American embassy in Rome during the 1920s. Setting up headquarters in Fort Wadsworth, New York, Eager was a strong advocate for the welfare of the thirty thousand

POWs under his control and was "often battling his superiors in an effort to improve the lot of his Italian charges."[16]

The basic unit in the ISU program was a company-size group of between 200 and 250 men, staffed by Italian officers and sergeants and supervised by American officers responsible for administration and discipline. Men in the ISU performed quartermaster, transportation, engineering, and other types of support work. Most ISU volunteers went to "basic training" in their area of specialty, lasting from eight to twelve weeks at a number of stateside posts; the length and location of the training was tied to the type of assignment for which the men would be used. Instruction included English classes, familiarization with basic American military customs and courtesies, and classroom and hands-on technical training in their area of expertise. Other Italian POWs who were sent to established service units simply got on-the-job training. By the end of May 1944, some 180 units staffed by 1,046 Italian officers and 33,614 enlisted men were in place, with supervision provided by 234 U.S. Army officers and 1,221 enlisted men. All but four companies that served remained stateside, working in supply depots, hospitals, arsenals, and ports. The four that went overseas were quartermaster units and served in supply depots in Scotland, Wales, Belgium, Holland, and even Germany. The men mostly serviced vehicles and moved fuel from freight cars to trucks.[17]

Corporal Paul Trunzo, an American, was with the 102d Quartermaster Service Company. He recalled the frantic pace of the work: "When we reached Reims [France], the men were put to work transferring war materials from freight cars to trucks. It was terrifically hard work without any let-up, the men divided into two shifts, twelve hours on and twelve hours off." After two weeks of this, the Italians had had enough. They sat down and refused to work anymore, and the American advisers to the ISU company called the men together so the officer in charge, a captain, could talk to them. "He got so mad he didn't wait for the translation, but just started ranting and raving in English," said Trunzo. "Then he pulled his Colt .45 and began waving it around. The men got the message and went back to work."[18]

POW Ennio Calabresi went to Pine Camp, New York, for training in work in a quartermaster unit. "I was there for a month, at driving school, which I certainly didn't need, since I had driven big trucks in Italy before the war," recalled Calabresi. "At Pine Camp I learned to handle the U.S. Army open-sided command car. They had a test where I had to back up into a garage, hook up to a little trailer, and drive away without hitting anything. It was easy."[19]

Frank La Piana was a corporal in the U.S. Army who was involved in the training program for nearly one thousand ISU men transferred from

Weingarten to Atlanta, where a large training center was located. "I went to Atlanta from the Army Specialized Training Program at Georgia State Teachers College in Statesborough, Georgia, where I had studied Italian. They said it was a 'secret mission,' and I volunteered for it," recalled La Piana. "Since my parents had been born in Sicily, I could talk to the men easily. I translated and presented films on fire safety, venereal disease and military courtesy. I also wrote a glossary of terms in Italian called "shop talk" that helped the men with their work on automotive repairs. They were all happy to be out of the war and took training seriously."[20]

106th Italian Company, Engineer Base Depot. Top, left to right: Sargente Antonio Prato, Soldato Umberto Bologhini, Sargente Cesare Marzari, Soldato Vincenzo Bertini. Bottom: unknown, Soldato Gino Pancone, Corporal Pete Puleo, Sr., of the U.S. Army. Courtesy of Pete Puleo, Sr.

St. Louisan Pete Puleo, Sr., was drafted as an infantryman, but in April 1944, when the Army learned of his ability to speak Italian, it promptly put him to work at Camp Claiborne, Louisiana, helping to supervise an ISU engineer unit. "Our company of Italians operated as a community. They were given standard GI clothing and the various supplies they required," recalled Puleo. "For their kitchen, special ingredients were supplied so they could make their own pasta, polenta, pastries and other typical Italian dishes. I couldn't help but put on weight."

In June, Puleo's company was sent to the outskirts of San Bernardino, California, where they worked in an engineer maintenance depot, repairing equipment from the European theater and then shipping it to the Pacific. The Italians working there could get one- or two-day passes and visit San Bernardino and other nearby towns when accompanied by an American. "On several occasions, the Italians were invited to dinners or picnics at one of several Italian wine estates around Asti, California," remembered Puleo. "I would also take two or three guys in a jeep and drive to Los Angeles, where we made visits to the well-known USO, the Hollywood Canteen."

Puleo enjoyed working with the men of the ISU and developed friendships with a couple of them that lasted through the years. He grew particularly close with Sabatino Pasqua, an accountant from Genoa. "We worked together taking care of company clerical matters, which included personnel, postal duties, payroll and other details," said Puleo. "I also shared with him the job of teaching English. We have visited several times since then."[21]

Weingarten POW Aldo Ferraresi went to Florence, Arizona, where he helped organize a new ISU battalion bound for service in Oakland, California. As part of the ongoing effort to recondition equipment used in the war, his platoon's first mission in California was to prepare amphibious trucks for shipment overseas. His men drove the trucks off the railroad cars, applied oil to protect them against rust during the sea crossing, and assembled the tool kits that accompanied each vehicle. "There are ten male civilians, all older men, except for one 18-year-old who will join the army in a few weeks. There are also ten women truck drivers," wrote Ferraresi in his diary. "All of them are very nice and friendly, especially the women who at lunch offer us coffee, ice cream or chewing gum. The women work hard, and I am impressed with how well they drive these oversized trucks."[22]

The mess hall staff from Pete Puleo's ISU group.
Courtesy of Pete Puleo, Sr.

Salvatore Davide, another Weingarten POW, also worked at Camp Knight in Oakland loading ships heading for the Pacific. "Sal worked hard at what they told him to do, but he was really an entertainer at heart. His passion was singing, and always in Italian," said his widow, Annette Davide. "He and the men had a group that entertained at USO shows. They had one ribald version of Pistol Packin' Mamma that always brought down the house. But they also did the very sentimental Italian ballads, too."[23]

Puleo's recollection of taking the ISU men to the Hollywood Canteen is consistent with the recreational opportunities available to the Italians, who had little restriction on where they could go during off-duty hours. Though the camp for Puleo's men at San Bernardino was rather remote, other ISU units were placed at military installations in cities with large Italian American populations, including New York, San Francisco, and, of course, St. Louis. It was in St. Louis that Mario Pertici encountered a pair of ISU men out on the town, wearing uniforms marked with the green "Italy" patch on their shoulders. "I had the pleasure of meeting two fine looking Italian soldiers at 'Momo' Mariani's residence on 4235 Maryland Avenue. The rear of this home had bocce [lawn bowling] courts for entertainment and towards evening dinners were served in the two rooms made available for this purpose," recalled Pertici. "Our family found them very polite and gentle men and were happy that Italy had joined the side of the Allies."[24]

Francesco Tarasco managed to get married in Baltimore while serving in the ISU. Breaking several Army regulations, in 1945 he married his American sweetheart, Elsa, who said it was all done legitimately. "We got our license at City Hall. I didn't lie. When they asked what Francis' profession was, I said 'schoolteacher,'" recalled Elsa Tarasco. "I didn't say 'prisoner,' and they had no reason to ask. We took the license to the priest and he later married us in the big downtown cathedral." The priest knew Tarasco was an Italian POW, but the Army never found out about the marriage. The pair had to wait while the priest verified with Rome that Tarasco didn't already have a wife in Italy, but that was the only delay in their plans. They were reunited quickly in the United States after Francesco's mandatory repatriation to Italy in late 1945. "We took a gigantic chance, because if the army had learned what we had done," said Elsa, "they would have sent him back to some POW stockade."[25]

Coddling and the ISU

Understandably, to the American public, the Italian soldiers of the ISU were no different from the others back at the POW camps. When they saw these men out on the town, going to dances or picnics, or on sightseeing tours, it only fueled the national debate on "coddling." The following commentary appeared in the *Boston Herald* on February 12, 1945:

> The organization of committees to canvass communities for musical instruments, to arrange dances, to furnish the gentlemen who are our guests only by virtue of having shot it out on the battlefield with American kids and lost, with so many hundreds of pounds of Italian pasta, bocce balls, and operatic recordings, to get them out as house-guests, to, after a manner of speaking, reward them, and make heroes of them generally, is a queer way of adding up the score.[26]

Marching behind the Italian flag, Weingarten POWs prepare to depart for service in the ISU. Courtesy of Kent Library, Southeast Missouri State University.

Like so many of the other complaints about coddling, most were made on the basis of incomplete information. Many civilians did not understand the mission and purpose of the ISU and did not know that its participants were indeed different from regular POWs in the privileges and liberties granted them. For instance, when a complaint was raised about POWs from Camp Shanks, New York, traveling some fifty miles to go to church in Bound Brook, New Jersey, the writer assumed the trip was being made at government direction and expense. Actually, because the area around Camp Shanks lacked enough churches to handle all those who wanted to attend, the mayor of Bound Brook specifically invited the men to come to worship in his town, and they traveled there at their own expense.[27]

Ultimately, with the end of the war came the end of the ISU, and after eighteen months of service to the U.S. government, the ISU program was disbanded. The soldiers were returned to the main POW holding camps to await repatriation, which would come in just a month or two. This effectively ended complaints about coddling driven by the ISU's high visibility.

Those Left Behind

If there was any fallout related to the creation of the ISU, it came in the decreased efficiency and morale of the POWs who were left behind in the camps. In many cases, the departure of the men selected for the ISU put those who remained on a downward spiral. Whether through non-signing or the non-availability of slots for those who did volunteer, these men often became even less motivated. When coupled with the disruption in camp life caused by the departure of a significant portion of the camp's population, it set the stage for much time wasting.

Inspector Luis Hortal described the malaise that set in at Weingarten after a good number of the POWs departed for duty with the ISU:

> After the signing [with the ISU], practically all the activities in the officers' compound stopped because many of them were expecting to be sent to Service Units. Though they knew that many of them could not be assigned no attempt has been made to organize any camp program....

> In music and theater nothing has been yet done. There are a few musical instruments, but not enough. Lack of materials is always the reason given for not doing much that is constructive in Italian camps. I would dare to say it is not materials only that is lacking, but men. I would not take any request for musical instruments until they had players for them. Then they can ask for what they need.[28]

Certainly, losing nearly a quarter of the camp's population was a significant event. One of the camp newspapers was called *L'Attesa* (The Wait), and its final issue was released just before many of the men went to ISU training camps and was dated simply "Easter 1944." An editorial in that paper expressed hope for good fortune and merciful treatment by fate and destiny for those leaving camp to join the ISU, as well as acknowledging the continual longing of the Italian soldiers to return home:

> Perhaps, within a short time, we will separate and each one of us will go wherever destiny may lead; another path, other lands, other horizons will open out before our eyes already accustomed to new things for quite some time now....

> During the long journey, our sight will ever be turned toward a land outstretched on the sea, a small land, poor and wretched as no other in the world, but immensely dear to our hearts.[29]

Departure of the ISU

Two months after V-E Day, in August 1945, General Eager prepared a report for distribution by the Office of War Information to the people back in Italy. He knew that the men of the ISU were going home soon and wanted to explain what the program was and what the men had done during their eighteen months in service to the United States. He included a mention of what their efforts meant to the United States:

> To those of you in Italy who have relatives or friends in the Italian Service Units, let me say that...you can be proud of them because they have voluntarily and materially assisted in the defeat of the common enemy, in speeding victory and in driving from your country and the world those evil forces and criminal groups who had gained possession. In America, they have contributed this part to help us in our tremendous and complex military efforts. What they have done in the Italian Service Units should enhance their value to Italy and their families.[30]

The Last Months

With the war in Europe finished and Japan about to fall, many German and Italian prisoners figured their return trip home would come in a matter of days. For the Italians, the process went perhaps as they expected. Just about the same time Eager was writing his tribute to the ISU for the people of Italy, the first major shipment of Italian POWs left Virginia for Naples. This group, 550 officers and enlisted men, set sail on August 9, 1945, on the *Haym Salomon*, with Eager standing dockside to bid them farewell. An additional 15,000 or so ISU men departed by the end of October, and the remaining 15,000 were gone by Christmas. Their departure took precedence over those remaining in the POW camps, whose stay in the United States lasted several months longer. Of those who were not ISU participants, about half went home by the end of 1945, and the rest crossed the ocean during the first months of 1946. The last group of Italian POWs finally departed the United States in March 1946.

Back at Home

Conditions were difficult in postwar Italy, a country ravaged by the fighting. Many POWs returned to find their homes in ruins and family members scattered or missing. After returning to his hometown of Turin, Felice Ghersi, a Weingarten POW who eventually returned to Missouri, wrote in November 1945 to his former manager at a farm in Sikeston, Elmer Grant, Sr.:

I am now back home again, or better to say, among the ruins of my house. This [situation] of mine is not an exception, because here all of the houses that have been left in their feet, more or less are damaged. The worse is the Winter at the door, without coal, with lacking wood, and with the windows without glass; and Winter in North Italy is very hard. However, my people lived in this condition last winter, therefore I'll do as well the same thing.

Moreover the economic and financial situation is very dangerous, the national wealth heavy destroyed, money ran about ninety-five percent out of value, the necessaries insufficient and to an astronomical price.

Although Ghersi saw the damage to his home, he was quietly confident he would prevail through determination, hard work, and, above all, the happiness provided by finding his family intact: "As you see the background is just terrible, nevertheless so great is my happiness for finding my family safe, that the present situation doesn't frighten me, and it doesn't take away my trust in the future."[31]

The conditions were the same for nearly every returning POW. Ernest Wagner, general manager of the Missouri Hybrid Corn Company in Fulton, Missouri, received a passel of letters asking for help, a testament to the difficult situation faced by many, in which poverty, poor health, and lack of food caused much suffering. "It is from the distant land of Sicily that I send you my desperate appeal, certain that your kindness will be great enough to take it into consideration," wrote Giovanna di Micela, the wife of one of Wagner's former workers. "I write you the present letter hoping that some help may reach here from you. I beg you not to be deaf to my prayers and to send me anything you wish, because anything whatever will be for us a great comfort."[32] Another prisoner wrote, "I shall say that I arrived home and found all well and safe, but I found many crises—the whole family barefooted and naked and little to eat.... If you want you can send me some little thing for the children, for all five are naked because here one can't earn anything because there isn't work."[33]

All these pleas must have tugged at Wagner's heart, but the requests for help from his former workers in the cornfields seemed unending, each one more pitiful than the last:

I have been ill for four months and I still am not quite well; I don't have the financial means to obtain the treatments that I need. Although my family has always been very poor, when I was repatriated from the prison camp I found them even worse off than before. I found that my father had died; that there had been no news since 1942 from a brother who had been on the Russian front; that my mother was ill and that I had two more little sisters.

I found our house looted so that I have to sleep on the bed without sheets and I cannot buy any more. My only clothing is my prisoner's uniform, which is completely worn out and I have not the means to have another made. My shoes are worn out and my sisters are as badly off as I am.[34]

Wagner apparently sent items to aid the prisoners or coordinated donations to the Italians from other Fulton residents. In April 1948, di Micela sent Wagner a thank-you letter with another request:

About four months ago I felt it necessary to write a letter to you explaining the very bad conditions here with the hope of receiving some little material aid. Although I did not hear from you, I was happy to receive a man's suit from Fulton, the sender being a certain professor [at Westminster College], Colin McPheeters.

Naturally we are certain that our request to you was indirectly responsible for the gift and we are hoping to benefit perhaps again by the offer of women's clothing (I am tall and robust), because our need is very great. We are infinitely grateful to you and beg your forgiveness for bothering you again with such a plea.[35]

Gradually life in Italy improved, and most of the former POWs settled into a sustainable life with boundaries marked by family, work, and community. A few, such as Giuseppe Zazza and Francesco Tarasco, returned to the United States after marrying American women. After Zazza's return to Italy, he waited a year for his fiancée, Ida, to join him for their wedding that would take place in Rome. Ida stayed in Italy six months waiting for her new husband's visa to be approved so that they could return to the United States together. The clock was ticking, however, as she was five months pregnant with twins. Their efforts to get to the States before the delivery were successful, and their twin boys, Fred and Ettore, were born in America.[36]

Others, such as Giuseppe Zanti, who was interned at Camp Clark and Jefferson Barracks, came back after finding sponsorship from relatives in America. Zanti had an uncle on the Hill in St. Louis who frequently visited him at nearby Jefferson Barracks during Zanti's time as a POW. After the war, the man agreed to sign for Zanti's visa application, testifying that Zanti was a man of good character who could support himself or, failing that, that the uncle himself would provide for Zanti in the United States. Zanti returned to the United States in the early 1950s and lived on the Hill from then on, as comfortable in that Italian community as he was back home in Europe.[37] Other former prisoners sought sponsorship from Americans they had met during their time in the United States. Ernest Wagner received several such requests, and though he offered several select POWs the chance to return to Fulton because of the bond they had formed during their time working for him, none apparently came back to Missouri through his sponsorship.

The immigration to the United States sometimes brought mixed emotions. "Do I miss Italy? Yes, in a way, but in particular, I miss the military career I left in 1947," said Aldo Ferraresi, who married a woman from San Francisco and returned to America in 1947. "I do not regret in any way my decision to come back to the U.S., and I have tried my best to be a good American citizen. I feel I love the U.S. as much as I love Italy. On top of all this I feel that my coming here gave my children a better opportunity for a better life, and that overshadows everything else."[38]

Experiences of the Germans

For many German prisoners, the anticipated departure from the stateside POW camps was prolonged and quite different from the Italians' experience. The first thing that caused discontent among many German POWs was the drastic cutback in rations in the spring of 1945. Driven by the allegations of luxury conditions in American camps—especially when coupled with the horrifying conditions uncovered in German camps liberated by Allied forces and a general food shortage across the United States—the War Department ordered dramatic changes in the POW mess hall menus.

"On May 5, 1945, came a big surprise," recalled Franz Engelmann, who worked in mess halls at Fort Leonard Wood and the Louisiana, Missouri, branch camp. "Overnight the provisions provided for the prisoners' mess hall were drastically reduced."[39]

Portion sizes were cut, and meat became a rarity, served only twice a month. When it did appear on the prisoners' menu, most frequently it came in the form of pork and beef organs such as heart and liver, as well as tripe, neck, and tailbones, cuts not acceptable for feeding to the regular army. Butter and eggs virtually disappeared from the table, as did chocolate, cigarettes, beer, and soft drinks from the camp canteens. The Germans saw it as punishment, that the United States was showing its true face and exacting vengeance on the German POWs now that the war was nearly over and the American POWs in Germany were free. "What was wrong?" asked Engelmann rhetorically. "Germany lost the war, and from then on, the United States was free from the Geneva Convention and could treat the prisoners the way it wanted.... From that time on the provisions were very minimal. [For instance,] as a Christmas present, we got a single apple."[40]

Inspectors visiting the three main Missouri camps holding Germans—Clark, Crowder, and Leonard Wood—received numerous complaints by the POWs about these changes in diet. "They are complaining because of a reduction in the amounts of bread and meat which are supplied," wrote a visitor to Fort Leonard Wood. Another inspector at Camp Clark noted similar fuss about the cutbacks implemented there and pointed out to the prisoners that the order had come from Washington and the camp commander was powerless to do anything to remedy the situation.[41] Prisoners at Camp Crowder griped about the replacement of certain menu items with other less popular dishes. "The objection seemed to be more to certain substitutions (such as substituting 175 lbs. of beans for 500 lbs. of ham) than to shortages of food," noted a Swiss inspector in March 1945.[42]

Historian Arnold Krammer said the problem went beyond a mere absence of the prisoners' favorite dishes. "Depending on the availability of local produce at various camps as well as the length of time until they were repatriated, most prisoners experienced a loss of weight as well as morale," wrote Krammer. "On the average, the men lost about 10 to 12 pounds, although most today concede that it was 'lazy fat' which they had put on during their captivity."[43]

Eventually, because Italian POWs also were affected by these cutbacks in rations, the newly re-established Italian embassy expressed its "grave concern" to the U.S. State Department in October 1945. However, by this time, repatriation seemed so close at hand that the reduced diet was just another annoyance to endure, and the prisoners' focus was almost exclusively on when they would return home.

Delays in Departure

Prisoners naturally spent a great deal of time thinking about when they would go back home, but as the end of the war approached, the tension increased for German POWs as the fate of their country became a ceaseless preoccupation. Although authorities feared mass escapes and suicide attempts among the Germans—especially among those still loyal to Hitler—when the actual announcement came of Germany's capitulation, no such mass distress occurred. Other than a few of the most ardent Nazis, most prisoners were glad for the end of the fighting, though nearly all POWs refrained from any displays of emotion. "There was little talk about it out of continued fear of retribution from the Nazis, but you could see it in people's eyes," said Hermann Half, a Crowder POW.[44] The most exuberant were the strongly anti-Nazi prisoners at Chesterfield, who used their POW newspaper to talk about what the end of the war meant for them and their country. The June 1, 1945, issue of the *Chesterfield-Herold* described what happened when news of Germany's surrender on May 8, 1945, reached the camp:

> This day passed for very few of us without a prayer of thankfulness. No more shooting! Peace finally has arrived for our loved ones at home, Victory is on the side of the liberators! At noon everyone gathered for a church service. In the evening the celebration lasted until deep into the night. Later…the Americans were astonished to hear that we had been celebrating for three days. We answered them in full truth: the Allies are treating us better than the Nazis. The Allies freed our comrades, our fathers, our pastors, and our teachers from the concentration camps.[45]

Speculation and rumor abounded as to what would happen next, and any number of wild possibilities were debated. Few prisoners ever guessed, however, that they would remain in the United States as long as an additional year, and for many prisoners, it would be many months even beyond that before they returned home.

With a departure from the POW camps a much more realistic possibility, some prisoners sought a way to stay in the States. The requests were driven by the widespread destruction in Germany, an economy in shambles, Russian control over certain parts of the country, missing family members, a genuine fondness for the United States, and an appreciation of the opportunities in America. U.S. government policy was clear, however: mandatory repatriation to Europe for all prisoners of war. "Many of them asked us if there wasn't some way they could stay in the country after the war was over," said George Hellwig, whose family operated the farm on which the Chesterfield camp was located.[46] Guard Al Griego said his German friends from the Louisiana camp also wanted to stay after the war instead of going back to Germany. Friends Hans and Rudy had tears in their eyes when they found out they had to leave, Griego recalled, and they asked Griego to go back to Germany with them. "They really hated to see me stay," said Griego, "Of course, I couldn't have gone with them."[47]

Because of the still-chaotic scene dominating Europe, the United States was hesitant to ship large numbers of POWs directly back into an unsettled Germany in late fall 1945, and instead it announced a schedule whereby the remaining 326,000 POWs in the States would be returned over a period of months:

December 1945	60,000
January 1946	70,000
February 1946	70,000
March 1946	83,000
April 1946	43,000

Despite this announcement by the War Department, other parties saw more important issues than a prompt return to Europe for the POWs. Agricultural interests demanded that they be held back, that POW labor was necessary to fill the still-significant shortage of farm workers in many parts of the United States. As the calendar turned to 1946, many German POWs remained in the States, and in the early months of that year, the repatriation of some 14,000 POWs was postponed at the request of the secretary of agriculture so they could be used on essential farm work during the spring months, primarily in the western states working in the sugar-beet fields. This news naturally brought great disappointment to the German POWs who had expected to be leaving the United States.[48] "Hitler told us that we would be going through the United States," muttered one POW. "But that bastard didn't tell us it would be with a beet hoe in our hand."[49]

To compound their frustrations, those held back to work in the United States for the additional months were the cooperative prisoners—those who participated in the POW labor program during their years in America and had not caused any great trouble for their captors. The government decided that it made sense to first ship back 50,000 "useless" prisoners, which meant the non-cooperative Nazis, along with officers and noncommissioned officers not required to work and the physically disabled. The POWs left behind grew increasingly bitter about the process, and the American public was understandably outraged as well. "Genuine Nazis are being rewarded for their convictions with a speedy reunion with their families," howled one letter writer to *The New York Times*, "whereas German prisoners who cooperate by relieving the labor shortage are kept from their families for an indeterminate period of time."[50]

Those still in the States tried to make the best of it, and Kurt Reimer, a Camp Clark POW transferred to Colorado to work in the sugar-beet fields, used the old "dear uncle" trick, feigning kinship to write to his "Uncle" Bill, William McDonald, his former supervisor at the Nevada camp. "It's already eight weeks ago since I left Clark for Camp Carson," wrote Reimer in November 1945. "In the meantime I've been…six weeks in a side camp and doing…hard work in the sugar-beet fields. It wasn't easy to pull and top those beets, especially if you have never done it before."

Reimer described the anxiety and eagerness to return home that gripped the POWs, who still believed repatriation was close at hand. How wrong they were. "I'm well so far and waiting for a final discharge as P.W.," wrote Reimer. "Nobody knows what's going on, but I suppose it won't last any long[er]."[51]

Ultimately, the months passed for Reimer and the other POWs, and as the work was completed, the prisoners were funneled from the labor camps by train to the major camps in each service command and from there to the port of embarkation at Camp Shanks, New York. The final group of prisoners to leave the United States boarded the *Texarkana* on July 22, 1946. Historian Arnold Krammer recalled the scene:

> Through the entire morning, the 1,388 German officers and enlisted men trudged up the gangplank to begin their final voyage home. The last to leave American soil—a 22-year-old former electrician from Heidelberg—ultimately made seven "last trips" up the ramp at the request of insistent newsmen: three in continuous motion for the newsreel cameras and four with stops at fixed points to satisfy the still photographers.
>
> The lines were finally cast off at 3:00 PM and…as the Germans lined the rails of the departing ship to take one last look at the receding shoreline of New York, "waving an indifferent farewell," a significant chapter in American history came to a close.
>
> As the last shipload of German prisoners pulled away from shore, Colonel Harry W. Maas, commanding officer of Camp Shanks, turned to a news reporter and sighed, "Thank God, that is over!"[52]

Leaving America

Even when the United States began returning the working prisoners to Europe, things grew worse for many of them. Though they were leaving the United States and bound for Europe, in many cases, they still were not going home. "Recently the prisoners were reported to have heard a short wave broadcast in which it was stated that 400,000 prisoners of war would be transferred from the United States to France as 'slave laborers' to assist in the rebuilding of that country," said one Fort Leonard Wood visitor, who noted that these reports were also appearing in German-language newspapers received at the camp. "[The camp commander] stated that these two factors had been very depressing to the morale of the prisoners. He stated that the prisoners were all anxious to get home and that the prospect of a new term of imprisonment in a different country might touch off a series of determined and well planned efforts to escape prior to their departure."[53]

The reports were true. In secret, the United States agreed to take part in a joint Allied plan to transfer 1.3 million prisoners of war to Britain, France, and five other smaller countries beginning in September 1945.[54] These nations had substantial damage to their infrastructure and economies, and though they needed the POW laborers, this action was motivated in no small part by a desire to avenge the suffering caused by the Nazis. Of course, this news was devastating for the prisoners, who expected to be returned home, not rerouted to yet another camp for an indefinite time. "This was nothing more than modern slave trading," fumed Alfred Klein in a 1977 letter. "We all deeply resented such treatment, and I am even today of the opinion that the U.S. foolishly nullified its long effort to instill in us the precious seeds of democracy."[55]

Letters from other prisoners back to the States relate their despair at this turn of events. In June 1946, former Fort Leonard Wood POW Edmund Koga wrote to his former boss in the warehouse, O. J. "Andy" Anderson, "I arrived here fine and in good health," mustering the best news he could think of from a British labor camp. "The way back home has gone off course, however, and fate has carried me elsewhere. I don't feel like a human being any more behind these wire fences. When will this end?"[56]

Even worse were the ghastly conditions that prevailed in many French camps. Another of Anderson's former workers, Paul Schanze, wrote and described how he suffered after being handed over to the French in May 1946. "Back in May [1946] we arrived in France, in the harbor of Le Havre. We had bad luck there, and were handed over to the French, so I had to go to work in a French coal mine," wrote Schanze in February 1947. "It was difficult work and we were 500 meters below ground. In October I got very sick and went into the hospital. I was down to 102 pounds."[57]

Though the United States did indeed transfer its prisoners over to its European allies, the government did not wash its hands of the issue. When the International Red Cross revealed the starvation conditions in the French camps in September 1945, General Dwight D. Eisenhower, commander of all Allied forces in Europe, completely halted transfers until better treatment was guaranteed and could be verified by regular inspections of the French camps. Additionally, the United States pressed for fair and humane treatment of POWs held by all European governments, setting the standard when the American military government in Germany hired former POWs at prevailing civilian wages to perform a broad range of work at the same time it moved to extricate itself completely from POW labor program. Beginning in the spring of 1946, the United States applied pressure to the other countries still using German POWs to implement a standard set of choices for the men in their captivity: immediate repatriation or employment as voluntary civilian workers. France needed special encouragement, as historian Arnold Krammer noted—France still maintained more than 440,000 German prisoners as late as April 1947, "and one can only speculate on the date of ultimate return if it were not for American intercession."[58]

Bowing to U.S. insistence, the French offered its German prisoners the same options given them elsewhere: return to Germany or stay as paid workers. Most chose to be repatriated immediately, but nearly 10,000 remained voluntarily to work well into mid-1948.[59]

Return Home

Through fate or circumstance, some prisoners were luckier and returned home more quickly than those ensnared in the European labor camps. Because of his selection to attend the special re-education school at Fort Eustis, Virginia, Crowder POW Hermann Half was certified to hold a position in the postwar German government. This also allowed him direct repatriation to Germany, and Half bypassed the French and British internment camps that snagged most of the other German POWs for another year. The thinking was that Half and the others similar to him would be far more useful in the creation of a democratic German government than they would hoeing sugar beets in Colorado or digging coal in a French mine.

Half's early return to Germany as a result of his attendance at this school ultimately caused him some problems. When the other POWs who had been waylaid in the European work camps started coming home, people in Germany began asking questions. They wondered why Half had returned as quickly as he did. "One guy, who had been in the Afrika Korps, came back a year after I did," said Half. "People asked him why I was home so much sooner. He told them that I had been a traitor, an informer." This man repeated the rumor so often that other German veterans, particularly men from the Afrika Korps, began to grow hostile toward Half. Half finally had to take the man to court, suing to stop him from lying about what had happened in the United States. The situation became so volatile, Half feared for his safety. On one occasion, a man at a dance threatened to hit him over the head with a wine bottle. The lawsuit provided Half with the opportunity to clear his name, and he said people realized he was wronged. "They all came to me to apologize," said Half of the men of the Afrika Korps who lived in his town. "Every one of them."[60]

Regardless of the specific details of when and how the former prisoners actually came back, the men returning to their German homes usually experienced common emotions. What they felt was a tormenting mix of feelings—joy at seeing their families; sorrow over the dead, missing, ill, or maimed; and shock over the destruction and the effects of the war on the people closest to them. "It is nice to come home and see one's folks but to find them in such a pitiable condition that you hardly recognize them gives one an awful shock," wrote Heinz Zimmermann to Emil Moehner, his supervisor at the Jefferson Barracks motor pool.[61]

Another POW who worked at the Jefferson Barracks motor pool, Paul Rahn, told Moehner how, despite his own terrible losses, he had resolved to go on. "Fate has been very hard on me because I lost my wife who lost her life at the hands of the Russians. Only my little six-year-old daughter, my father-in-law and my mother-in-law survived," wrote Rahn. "I have found a home with my sister and will try to find some work and also a place to live for my dependents. It will always be a bitter memory to me because I have lost everything. But I am still willing to begin my life again with my loved ones from the very beginning and I am certain that things will get better in the future."[62]

Karl-Heinz Richter left Camp Crowder in May 1946, traveling by train to New York. Two weeks later he arrived in England, where he was held in a Nottingham labor camp until January 1948. After repatriation, he headed to Berlin to be with his mother. She was living with relatives there after fleeing the family's home in Poland following the death of her husband. Richter did not learn of his father's passing until two years after it happened. "What I saw there [in Berlin] was a city that still three years after the war was utterly destroyed. People were still hungry," wrote Richter. "The very noticeable impact on me was the look on the faces of my comrades who had been POWs in Russia and the young women who had had to endure the abuse of the Russian soldiers."[63]

Of course, with the economy in shambles and much of Germany's infrastructure destroyed, there was little work to be found. Inflation was rampant, and Wolfgang Hampel saw its effects at first hand. The former Fort Leonard Wood POW brought home $400 he had saved by working every chance possible during his eighteen-month internment there. But, by the time Hampel got back to Germany after a stop at a British POW camp, he found that the devalued currency was worth, at most, about 80 deutsche marks, or $20.[64]

Many German prisoners faced near-poverty conditions. "Everybody of my family is ok and they are proud to have their father alright back from U.S.A.," wrote Louis Sack to his former supervisor at Camp Crowder. "I've had a very good time in U.S.A. and I think ever back [on it]. The rations of eating, drinking and smoking have been enough in America, but in Germany are all things very small."[65]

Ultimately, the former German POWs struggled day to day in the postwar years, as did all people in countries ravaged by the war. Captain Burton Marston, an American at Camp Weingarten, wrote to former POW Vincenzo Mancuso and expressed his feelings about what the end of the fighting meant to him and most other soldiers:

> I am glad my war experience is over. It was not an unpleasant experience but I certainly would not care to go through it again and I sincerely hope that none of us ever have to again. I realized that in many respects my experience was more fortunate that others, especially from those who are either lying now under the sod, are wounded or were on the other side of the barbed wire, of any army.
>
> The after-effects of the war are in some respects more serious than the war itself and we are trying to realize the enormity of the task that confronts each of the war-torn countries.[66]

In time, things improved, and life eventually returned to normal. A democratic government sprang up in West Germany. YMCA inspector Karl Gustav Almquist, in his report from Camp Crowder in September 1945, believed this was facilitated by the cooperation between prisoners and authorities and the satisfactory conditions at Crowder, with its zoo, *biergartens*, fountains, and bandstand. "What has been done here will create good will in Europe," said Almquist simply.[67]

The Germans who had been in America eased back into civilian life. And like the Italians, a few former prisoners did return to the United States. Although no firm numbers exist of how many former POWs immigrated to the United States in the years after the war, evidence exists that it is no small number. One former POW, John Schroer, who moved to Los

Angeles, estimated in his informal research that perhaps five thousand returned to the United States seeking citizenship.[68]

Holiday in Amerika

Although the number of German and Italian POWs who returned to the United States seeking citizenship was relatively small, a great many more returned to visit in the decades after the war. They came both to see the places of their imprisonment and to rekindle friendships with those they met during their time in the States.

A number of POW reunions took place starting in the mid-1970s, as the former prisoners reached retirement age and sought to use their free time and money to revisit the places of their youth. A group of former Fort Leonard Wood POWs met in Missouri in 1993 in commemoration of the fiftieth anniversary of their time at the post, and many figured it would be their last trip to the United States. They marveled at how the post had changed, and for the handful of POWs who returned to the laundry, their former place of employment, Building 2353 was the only place on the entire post that they recognized. "They're still using some of the same machinery," observed former POW Lothar Nickel. Another, Kurt Rogge, recognized the pants presser he had operated. "I could do 114 pairs a day," he said.[69]

Many other POWs have made individual trips to the United States. Like the Fort Leonard Wood prisoners, Camp Clark POW Herman Graefe also saw a familiar sight during a return visit to the Nevada, Missouri, facility in the 1980s. Though the post, still used as a National Guard training area, received an extensive renovation in the mid-1960s, many of the buildings date from the time of the POW camp. On a tour of the installation, Graefe recognized the latrines at once and vouched that the improvements must have skipped over those particular buildings. "They are just as I remembered," he said with a laugh.[70]

Rolf Wunderlich maintained contact over many years with some of the people he had met during his work in the Bootheel at the Marston branch camp, paving the way for a long-delayed reunion. "In the 1970s, I had the opportunity to travel with my wife in the U.S.A. and to show her the area of the camp," said Wunderlich, who has made numerous trips back to southeastern Missouri. "Even though we don't have any relatives in the States, we feel very much at home there."[71]

Karl-Heinz Richter is another former prisoner who returned many times to Missouri, where he was held at Camp Crowder. "I wanted to visit places I had been before, and Camp Crowder was one of them," said

Richter, who retired from the Berlin police force. "Even if I was a POW in the U.S.A., it was a place I learned to love." In preparation for his trip, Richter went to the U.S. Army Headquarters in Berlin to get information about Camp Crowder. They told him that the camp had been mostly dismantled but that there was still some National Guard activity at the site, and he would be welcome to go back. In 1980, Richter wrote to the 203d Engineering Battalion in Joplin and told them he was coming for a visit in April. The guard unit rolled out the red carpet for Richter, with a VIP tour and meetings with local officials. Even the local TV station showed up to interview him. "When we arrived I was given a three-man escort and full tour of the headquarters in Joplin before coming to Neosho," said Richter. "The "Burgermeister [mayor] of Neosho and his staff greeted us."

Neosho's chief of police, George Kelly, was there, too, and the two became fast friends following that first meeting. Richter returned to Neosho every two years after that, and Kelly and his wife traveled to Berlin as well. In the alternating years, Richter toured other parts of the United States, growing particularly fond of Naples, Florida, and beginning in the 1990s, traveled there every year.[72]

POW Walter Meier returned to central Missouri in 1977 to visit farmer Oliver Marshall, for whom he had worked some thirty years before. "In six weeks, I guess we got to be pretty good friends," said Marshall, "and we'll probably keep in touch until we die."[73] The two wrote back and forth faithfully, exchanging a couple letters each year. The return trip to central Missouri was a natural step. "There was never an invitation," agreed the pair. "This was just something that was always going to happen."[74]

The Hellwig brothers also hosted visits from former prisoners at Chesterfield, including a German who came in 1988. Though the structures from the camp were no longer standing, the men walked the grounds of the former camp and remembered a time when the Germans were prisoners working in the Gumbo fields with "PW" emblazoned on their work clothes.[75]

These POWs who returned to the place of their captivity represent the 420,000 men who came to the United States during World War II. Though the American government had virtually no experience in handling that great number of men within the United States, the program was by and large a success. There were some rough spots in the early days, to be sure, but through trial and error, the process gradually began to run smoothly. The men who lived in the American camps were humanely treated, and the experience was usually far more pleasant than they had expected, thanks to the U.S. government's insistence on observing the Geneva Convention and its guidelines for the treatment of POWs.

Many POWs look back on their time in America with fondness. The days of working for American farmers, playing soccer, or performing in the camp theater groups were a tolerable way to pass the time, and eventually many POWs gained a respect and appreciation for the American way of life and for the democratic ideals that govern the country. The Americans, too, who encountered the POWs—whether as guards, civilian employees, or residents living nearby—gained a new appreciation for these enemies who came to live among them. Once fearful of the faceless Nazi horde, most Americans who interacted with the prisoners came to see them as individuals, young men far from home with families and feelings not unlike their own. Through these relationships forged in a farm field or on a workboat, many connections were formed that spanned the ocean and the years. Though the letters may have stopped, and the exact names are forgotten, the memories remain of the people who inhabited that unique part of history when the German and Italian POWs came to Missouri.

That time always remained a fond memory for Al Griego, who died in 1998. "Quite often I lie in bed while trying to go to sleep and think about the [prisoners]," said Griego, a guard for three years at several Missouri camps. "I enjoyed the Germans very much."[76]

George Kelly, former Neosho police chief and close friend of former Crowder POW Karl-Heinz Richter, sent a letter to this author in November 2001. "Just a line to let you know that Karl-Heinz Richter passed away on October 10, 2001," wrote Kelly. "He had just arrived in Naples, Florida for his annual visit." Richter called at 11 A.M. to let Kelly know he was there and to ask if Kelly was making plans to visit him in Naples. That afternoon Richter died on the Florida sand, a place he loved. "He was a fine friend and I shall miss him," wrote Kelly simply.[77]

The ranks of former POWs lessen every day, and the reunions and visits occur only infrequently. Soon there will be none left at all. Though these old soldiers are "fading away," in the words of General Douglas MacArthur, the significance of their time as prisoners of war in the United States remains.

Notes

Chapter One

1. Marilyn Grant, interview by author, September 3, 2002.

2. Karl-Heinz Richter, *Recollections of Life as a POW*, 1998.

3. From the Stanley Drury Collection, a collection of material pertaining to the POW camp at Weingarten, Missouri. This collection includes newspaper clippings, personal correspondence, military documents, notes, photographs, and other items compiled over many years by Ste. Genevieve historian Stanley Drury. Held at the time of this writing by Professor Max Okenfuss, Department of History, Washington University in St. Louis.

4. Judith Gansberg, *Stalag, U.S.A.: The Remarkable Story of German POWs in America* (New York: Crowell, 1977), 2.

5. Ibid., 5. In July 1916, the New Jersey Black Tom munitions plant blew up, resulting in a $22 million loss. German saboteurs were believed responsible for that as well as for the destruction six months later of the Kingsland, New Jersey, munitions plant.

6. Ibid., 4.

7. Edward Pluth, "The Administration and Operation of German Prisoner of War Camps in the United States during World War II" (Ph.D. thesis, Ball State University, 1970), 82.

8. Harold Drake, interview by author, January 29, 2003.

9. Pluth, "Prisoner of War Camps," 88.

10. Drake, interview.

11. Louis E. Keefer, *Italian Prisoners of War in America, 1942–1946: Captives or Allies?* (New York: Praeger, 1992), 40.

12. Drake, interview.

13. Ibid.

14. Keefer, *Italian Prisoners*, 40.

15. Gene Waibel, interview by author, October 15, 2001.

16. Keefer, *Italian Prisoners*, 49. Keefer excerpts several sections of Ferraresi's diary throughout his book.

17. Helmut Hörner, *A German Odyssey: The Journal of a German Prisoner of War*, trans. and ed. Allan Kent Powell (Golden, Colo.: Fulcrum, 1991), 269–71.

18. Laurel Sterkel, "They Came as Enemies of Our Country—Some Left as Our Friends" (research paper, Southeast Missouri State University, 1983), 8. Stanley Drury Collection.

19. Fritz Ensslin, "A German Soldier Tells What It Is Like to Visit Ft. Leonard Wood in 1943 as a POW," *Essayons*, June 27, 1991, 3; also distributed as a museum handout by the U.S. Army Engineer Museum at Fort Leonard Wood, called *The Fallen Foe*. Hereafter *Fallen Foe*.

20. Gansberg, *Stalag, U.S.A.*, 24.

21. Arnold Krammer, *Nazi Prisoners of War in America* (New York: Stein and Day, 1979), 37–38.

22. Rufus Jarman, "Italians in Prison Camp Learn Self-Government," *St. Louis Post-Dispatch*, June 11, 1943.

23. Gansberg, *Stalag, U.S.A.*, 49.

24. Lt. George Paddock, "Administration of the Weingarten PW Camp," [1943?], 4. Paddock wrote this document as an overview of the operations at the Weingarten POW camp, where he was stationed. Stanley Drury Collection. The Civilian Conservation Corps (CCC) was a 1930s work program designed to employ idle young men during the Great Depression.

25. Ibid, 4.

26. Krammer, *Nazi Prisoners*, 47.

27. Report to Mr. Weingaertner, Swiss Legation, from Johannes Oertel,

M/Sgt. and POW spokesman of Camp Clinton, July 12, 1944, Stephen M. Farrand Collection, Hoover Institution. As quoted in Krammer, *Nazi Prisoners*, 6.

28. Keefer, *Italian Prisoners*, 52.

29. Krammer, *Nazi Prisoners*, 49.

30. Ibid.

31. Rufus Jarman to Terry Culver, [September 1983?]. Jarman was a reporter for the *St. Louis Post-Dispatch* during World War II and wrote pieces on the POW camps at Weingarten and Fort Leonard Wood.

32. Edmee Viscardi, interview by author, February 26, 2002.

33. Sterkel, "They Came as Enemies," 7.

34. Dr. Ben Spiro, Swiss Legation, inspection report, Camp Clark, March 1, 1944, Office of the Provost Marshal General (hereafter PMGO), Record Group (hereafter RG) 389, National Archives.

35. Otto Deutschmann, interviews by author, October 5, 2001, and August 15, 2002.

36. Gansberg, *Stalag, U.S.A.*, 23.

37. Krammer, *Nazi Prisoners*, 51.

38. Keefer, *Italian Prisoners*, 48.

39. Gansberg, *Stalag, U.S.A.*, 29.

40. P. E. Kretzmann, "The Lutheran Commission for Prisoners of War," *The Lutheran Witness*, December 1943, 421.

41. Gansberg, *Stalag, U.S.A.*, 30.

42. Keefer, *Italian Prisoners*, 55.

43. Paddock, "Administration of Weingarten," 2.

44. Hermann Half, interview by Terry Culver, audiotape, 1983.

45. Inspection report, Camp Weingarten, December 29, 1943, PMGO, RG 389, National Archives.

46. "Minutes of Conference of Chaplains and Pastors Working in Prisoner of War Camps," January 21, 1944, Item 23261, Lawrence B. Meyer Collection, Concordia Historical Institute.

47. Inspection report, Camp Weingarten, September 30, 1943, PMGO, RG 389, National Archives.

48. Inspection report, Camp Weingarten, April 20–22, 1944, March 12,1945, PMGO, RG 389, National Archives.

49. The church body changed its name to the Lutheran Church–Missouri Synod in 1947.

50. Steven V. Dahms, "World War II Prisoners of War and the Missouri Synod," *Concordia Historical Institute Quarterly* 68, no. 3 (fall 1995); "Thoroughly American," *Lutheran Witness* 116, no. 5 (May 1997): 14.

51. Paul L. Dannenfeldt, "Report on POW Work," Box 1, File 5, Item 6, III.IX.01, Supplement IV of Armed Services Commission, Concordia Historical Institute, St. Louis; Dannenfeldt, "Work of Our Planning Council," Item 26156, Lutheran Commision for Prisoners of War; "Letter to Chaplains and Civilian Pastors at Work in Prisoner of War Camps," June 15, 1944, Lawrence B. Meyer Collection, Concordia Historical Institute.

52. Rev. Charles J. Meyer to Military Ordinariate John O'Hara, September 21, 1943, COHA 9/35, University of Notre Dame Archives.

53. Pluth, "Prisoner of War Camps," 203.

54. Robert Billinger, Jr., *Hitler's Soldiers in the Sunshine State: German POWs in Florida* (Gainesville: University Press of Florida, 2000), 119.

55. "Anger at Nazi Atrocities Is Rising but U.S. Treats Prisoners Fairly," *Newsweek*, May 7, 1945, 58.

56. Krammer, *Nazi Prisoners*, 16–17.

57. Keefer, *Italian Prisoners*, 33.

58. Billinger, *Hitler's Soldiers*, 119.

59. Billinger, *Hitler's Soldiers*, 137; Pluth, "Prisoner of War Camps," 285; "The

Report of the House Committee on Military Affairs on Prisoners of War," June 1, 1945, Union Calendar no. 297. Report no. 728 is in the second reel of the four-reel microfilm of PMGO, Prisoner of War Division, "Prisoner of War Operations."

60. Maurice Pate, "Prepared Statement on Relief Supplies for American Prisoners of War in Europe," Committee on Military Affairs, House Report 728, 79th Cong., 1st sess., 1945, 15. See also Pluth, "Prisoner of War Camps," 286.

61. Betty Valle Gegg, "Those Stationed There Reminisce," *Ste. Genevieve Herald*, January 31, 1990.

62. Inspection report, Camp Weingarten, December 29, 1943.

63. Gansberg, *Stalag, U.S.A.*, 17.

64. The only camps in the United States to hold Japanese prisoners of war were Camp Clarinda, Iowa, and Camp McCoy, Wisconsin. Patrick Miller, "Camp Clarinda: A POW Camp in Southwest Iowa" (master's thesis, Bowling Green State University, 1993).

Chapter Two

1. Sterkel, "They Came as Enemies," 11.

2. "Enemies at Large," *American Magazine*, April 1944, 97.

3. "Farmers Here May Get Help of Camp Clark's Prisoners," *Springfield (Missouri) News-Leader*, August 15, 1943.

4. Pluth, "Prisoner of War Camps," 156; Gansberg, *Stalag, U.S.A.*, 44.

5. Vernon Davis, interview by author, July 26, 2002.

6. George G. Lewis and John Mewha, *History of Prisoner of War Utilization by the United States Army, 1776–1945*, Department of the Army pamphlet 20-213 (Washington, D.C.: GPO, 1955), 77.

7. Gansberg, *Stalag, U.S.A.*, 33–34.

8. Maj. Gen. Allen Gullion to Brig. Gen. B. M. Bryan, memorandum, September 14, 1943, following inspection visits to Camp Breckenridge, Kentucky, and Camp Weingarten, Missouri, PMGO, RG 389, National Archives.

9. Paddock, "Administration of Weingarten," 3–4.

10. Gullion to Bryan.

11. Inspection reports, Orrick, Missouri, July 15, 1943, and Camp Crowder, November 24–25, 1943, PMGO, RG 389, National Archives.

12. Inspection report, Fort Leonard Wood, August 26–27, 1943, PMGO, RG 389, National Archives.

13. Gullion to Bryan; "Crash Kills Camp Clark Prisoners," *Nevada (Missouri) Weekly Herald*, August 9, 1945.

14. Inspection report, Fort Leonard Wood, September 14, 1943, PMGO, RG 389, National Archives.

15. Gullion to Bryan.

16. Stanley Borgstom, e-mail to author, August 12, 2002.

17. Vincenzo Mancuso to Stanley Drury, January 31, 1985, Stanley Drury Collection; Patty Gamma, "POW Comes 'Home'—Life Good at Camp Weingarten Says Former Italian Prisoner," *Ste. Genevieve Herald*, July 4, 1984; Bill Berry, interview by author, July 18, 2002; "Prisoners of War Arrive Monday; 100 Italians Will Work for Corn Company, To Live at NYA Center," *Fulton (Missouri) Daily Sun-Gazette,* July 16, 1945, p. 1.

18. Lewis and Mewha, *Prisoner of War Utilization*, 180.

19. Krammer, *Nazi Prisoners*, 192.

20. "Editor Says Nazis Kill Captives Here," *The New York Times*, February 25, 1944.

21. Gansberg, *Stalag, U.S.A.*, 48.

22. The SS, or *Schutzstaffel* (literally, Guard Squadron), was the party police of the

National Socialist (Nazi) party. Its
power was strengthened through formation of the *Waffen-SS* (militarized SS)
and was the principal instrument of
Hitler in the destruction of European
Jewry. In 1946, the SS was identified as
a criminal organization by the
Nuremberg War Crimes Tribunal.

23. Harry Levins, "Germans Once Held
Here Get Salute at Fort Leonard
Wood," *St. Louis Post-Dispatch*,
September 29, 1993.

24. Krammer, *Nazi Prisoners*, 170.

25. Wilma Trummel Parnell with Robert
Taber, *The Killing of Corporal Kunze*
(Secaucus, N.J: Lyle Stuart, 1981).

26. Gansberg, *Stalag, U.S.A.*, 46. Named
for Horst Wessel, a political martyr, the
"Horst Wessel Lied" was the official
Nazi anthem and perhaps the most
famous Nazi song of the war.

27. Gansberg, *Stalag, U.S.A.*, 61–62.

28. Untitled preamble, *Chesterfield-Herold*,
April 1, 1945, reel 3, vol. 10, no. 57,
Library of Congress. Translation by the
author.

29. Krammer, *Nazi Prisoners*, 303–4; end-
notes, "Memorandum on Reorientation
of German Prisoners of War," Secret,
n.d., 4, Farrand Collection, Hoover
Institution.

30. Cumins E. Speakman, "Re-education
of German Prisoners of War in the
United States during World War II"
(master's thesis, University of Virginia,
1948), 25.

31. Krammer, *Nazi Prisoners*, 204; PMGO,
Special Projects Division, "Re-
Education of Enemy Prisoner of War,"
unpublished mss, November 1945;
TAB 12; "Distribution Statistics: *Der
Ruf*," TAB 16, both from File 4-4.1,
BA 1, Office of the Chief of Military
History.

32. Krammer, *Nazi Prisoners*, 208; PMGO,
"Reactions to *Büchereihe Neue Welt*,"
from "Reeducation of Enemy Prisoners

of War—Projects II and III"
(Washington, D.C.: Office of the Chief
of Military History, Department of the
Army, March 1, 1946).

33. Krammer, *Nazi Prisoners*, 210–11;
PMGO, "Office of the Provost Marshal
General: World War II, a Brief History"
(Washington, D.C.: Office of the Chief
of Military History, Department of the
Army, January 15, 1946): 581.

34. Fran Liberatore, "In War and Peace:
German POW Visits Mid-Missouri,"
Boonville (Missouri) Daily News, June
17–18, 1977, p. 1.

35. War Department memoranda nos.
30–45, "Prisoner of War Rations,"
March 7, 1945, Army Service Forces
Circular 150, section 2, part 2, Records
of Headquarters, Army Service Forces,
Modern Military Branch, National
Archives.

36. Ibid.

37. Rev. William Gabler, interview by Terry
Culver, audiotape, 1983.

38. Giuseppe Zanti, interview by author,
July 30, 2002.

Chapter Three

1. Jarman to Culver.

2. Richard C. Overton, *Burlington Route:
A History of the Burlington Lines* (New
York: Knopf, 1965), 477.

3. "Weingarten Camp Folds Up," *The
Lead Belt (Missouri) News*, July 5, 1946.

4. Pauline Laws McKamey, "Prisoner of
War Camp in the Ozarks," *Ozarks
Mountaineer*, January-February 1989,
54.

5. Inspection report, Camp Weingarten,
February 20, 1944, PMGO, RG 389,
National Archives; "Weingarten Folds
Up."

6. "Enemy Alien Camp to Be Located at
Weingarten, Mo.," *St. Louis Globe-
Democrat*, July 15, 1942.

7. "St. Louis Firm Starts on $1,500,000

Camp," *St. Louis Globe-Democrat*, August 15, 1942.

8. "Enemy Alien Camp."

9. "Suit to Be Filed for Alien Camp Acreage," *St. Louis Globe-Democrat*, July 16, 1942.

10. Peggy Bess and Mary McKinstry, "P.O.W. Camp—In the Foothills of the Ozarks Lies Weingarten," *Daily Jefferson County (Missouri) Democrat-Rocket*, April 28, 1982.

11. "Pioneers Being Evicted to Build Alien Camp," *St. Louis Globe-Democrat*, July 19, 1942.

12. "Pioneers Being Evicted."

13. Bess and McKinstry, "P.O.W. Camp."

14. "Weingarten Camp Folds Up."

15. *Farmington News*, August 14, 1942; Stanley Drury notes, part of the Drury Collection.

16. Peggy Bess, "Missouri Town Gets Taste of WWII," *Daily Jefferson County Democrat-Rocket*, April 30, 1982.

17. Bruce Starnes, interview by author, June 26, 2002.

18. Quinton Bianco, personal diary, 9. Bianco kept a detailed diary covering his daily activities throughout his wartime service. Part of the Weingarten Collection housed in the Southeast Missouri State University Cultural Archives.

19. Gegg, "Those Stationed There Reminisce."

20. Mary Lou Correnti, interview by author, November 1, 2001.

21. Bianco diary, 9.

22. Gullion to Bryan.

23. "Weingarten Camp Folds Up."

24. Bianco diary, 25.

25. Stanley Drury notes; also, announcements in the *Ste. Genevieve Herald* on May 15, May 22, and June 3, 1943, mention these events.

26. "Weingarten Camp Folds Up."

27. Bianco diary, 10.

28. Keefer, *Italian Prisoners*, 47.

29. Sterkel, "They Came as Enemies," 5.

30. Mary McKinstry, "Weingarten United a Blend of Cultures," *Daily Jefferson County Democrat-Rocket*, April 29, 1982.

31. Keefer, *Italian Prisoners*, 45.

32. Ibid., 46.

33. "Visit to Weingarten PW Camp," *Farmington Press*, June 25, 1943.

34. Bianco diary, 23.

35. Keefer, *Italian Prisoners*, 54.

36. Inspection report, Camp Weingarten, December 29, 1943, PMGO, RG 389, National Archives.

37. Bianco diary, 12.

38. Inspection report, Camp Weingarten, February 20, 1944, PMGO, RG 389, National Archives.

39. Sterkel, "They Came as Enemies," 2.

40. Inspection report, Camp Weingarten, December 29, 1943; Keefer, *Italian Prisoners*, 50.

41. Keefer, *Italian Prisoners*, 139.

42. Inspection report, Camp Weingarten, December 29, 1943.

43. Ibid.

44. Keefer, *Italian Prisoners*, 4.

45. McKamey, "Prisoner of War Camp," 54.

46. McKinstry, "Weingarten United a Blend."

47. Ibid.

48. Ibid; also, Teresa Drury, interview by author, June 10, 2002.

49. Drury, interview.

50. Keefer, *Italian Prisoners*, 153.

51. McKinstry, "Weingarten United a Blend."

52. Drury, interview.

53. Derek Mallett, "'They Were Just People Like We Were': World War II German and Italian Prisoners of War in

Missouri" (master's thesis, Truman State University, 1997), 57.

54. Ibid.

55. Ibid., 58–59.

56. Edmee Viscardi, interview by author, February 26, 2002.

57. Inspection report, Camp Weingarten, December 29, 1943.

58. McKamey, "Prisoner of War Camp," 54.

59. "Clerk at War Camp Held in Bribery Case," *St. Louis Globe-Democrat*, November 28, 1943.

60. Bianco diary, 9.

61. "Weingarten Camp Folds Up."

62. "Weingarten Camp," *Ste. Genevieve Herald*, April 7, 1945.

63. "Weingarten Camp," *Ste. Genevieve Herald*, April 14,1945.

64. "Weingarten Camp," *Ste. Genevieve Herald*, April 7, 1945.

65. Bianco diary, 17.

66. "Weingarten Camp Folds Up."

67. *The Weingartener* (camp newspaper for American servicemen), June 14, 1945.

68. Ibid.

69. "Weingarten Camp," *Ste. Genevieve Herald*, June 23, 1945.

70. Bianco diary, 25.

71. Bianco diary, 27.

72. McKinstry, "Weingarten United a Blend."

73. Ibid.

74. Bianco diary, 23.

75. Drury notes; Mallett, "They Were Just People," 49.

76. Cleva Laws, interview by author, August 9, 2001.

77. Norma Jacob, interview by author, July 19, 2002.

78. Sterkel, "They Came as Enemies," 9.

79. Newton Margulies, "Proper Treatment of War Prisoners," *Vital Speeches*, May 14, 1945, 479.

80. Bianco diary, 18.

81. Teresa Drury, interview, videotape, included as part of *Italian Prisoners of War in Ste. Genevieve County*, a presentation by Eric Sonnicksen, produced by Ste. Genevieve Public Television, October 17, 2001.

82. Bess and McKinstry, "P.O.W. Camp."

83. "Italian Prisoner at Camp Found Slain," *St. Louis Globe-Democrat*, February 12, 1944; inspection report, Camp Weingarten. September 13, 1945, PMGO, RG 389, National Archives.

84. Keefer, *Italian Prisoners*, 139.

85. "Weingarten Camp Folds Up."

86. "Axis Prisoners Work to Avert Flood at Ste. Genevieve, Mo.," *St. Louis Star-Times*, May 17, 1943.

87. "Flood Threat Is Over Here," Perry County (Missouri) Republican, May 11, 1944; "Italian Prisoners Helped Build Perry County Levees," *St. Louis Post-Dispatch*, May 14, 1944.

88. Paddock, "Administration of Weingarten," 5.

89. Bess, "Missouri Town."

90. Paddock, "Administration of Weingarten," 5–6.

91. Laws, interview.

92. Keefer, *Italian Prisoners*, 61.

93. Paddock, "Administration of Weingarten," 6.

94. Gegg, "Those Stationed There Reminisce."

95. Bianco diary, 15–16.

96. The labor report for December 7, 1943, shows Italian POWs engaged in many types of work.

97. Bill Barnes, interview by author, September 29, 2001.

98. "AFL Group Objects to Using Prisoners of War in Industry," *St. Louis Post-Dispatch*, February 2, 1944.

99. McKinstry, "Weingarten United a Blend."

100. Drury notes.

101. Inspection reports, Camp Weingarten, September 30, 1943; April 20–22, 1944; January 20, 1945; March 12, 1945; August 23, 1945.

102. Ibid.

103. Ibid.

104. Msgr. John P. Cody to Rev. Amleto Cicognani, apostolic delegate to the United States, August 21, 1943, Weingarten file, St. Louis Archdiocesan Archives.

105. Cody to Col. H. H. Glidden, May 12, 1943, Weingarten file, St. Louis Archdiocesan Archives.

106. Cody to William R. Arnold, Chief of Chaplains, U.S. Army. August 12, 1943, Weingarten file, St. Louis Archdiocesan Archives.

107. Cody to Cicognani, August 21, 1943.

108. Inspection report, Camp Weingarten. January 20, 1945.

109. "Weingarten Camp Folds Up."

110. Michele Ruta, camp spokesman, to Cody, September 8, 1945, Weingarten file, St. Louis Archdiocesan Archives.

111. Paddock, "Administration of Weingarten," 7.

112. Bianco diary, 19.

113. Ibid., 26.

114. Special Projects report, Seventh Service Command, March 12, 1945, PMGO, RG 389, National Archives.

115. Antonio De Vecchi, "Chindendo" (Closing the Parenthesis) in *La Luce*, trans. Mary Pontrelli, December 1945. Pontrelli's husband was Lt. Lawrence Pontrelli, chief interpreter at Camp Weingarten for Col. H. H. Glidden.

116. *Ste. Genevieve Herald*, October 20, 1943.

117. Inspection report, Camp Weingarten, April 20–22, 1944.

118. Ibid.

119. Bianco diary, 26.

120. Sterkel, "They Came as Enemies," 6.

121. Bianco diary, 11.

122. Col. H. H. Glidden to Archbishop John Glennon, October 6, 1943, Weingarten file, St. Louis Archdiocesan Archives.

123. Paul Gieringer, "The Shoes Were Shined for President Truman: Axis POWs in Missouri 1942–1946" (master's thesis, Central Missouri State University, 1992), 12–13; Mrs. Ernest Anderson to Eleanor Roosevelt, PMGO, Subject Correspondence File, Box 1430, RG 389, National Archives.

124. Inspection report, Camp Weingarten. September 13, 1945.

125. "Camp Weingarten," *Ste. Genevieve Herald*, April 14, 1945.

126. Inspection report, Camp Weingarten, January 20, 1945.

127. Eugene Phillips, interview by author, August 22, 2001.

128. Francis Schwartz, "Weingarten's POW Camp" (n.p., n.d). Stanley Drury Collection.

129. Sterkel, "They Came as Enemies," 7.

130. Bess, "Missouri Town."

131. Betty Valle Gegg, "Camp Weingarten: The End of an Era of Change," *Ste. Genevieve Herald*, February 7, 1990.

132. Schwartz, "Weingarten's POW Camp."

133. Sterkel, "They Came as Enemies," 9.

134. Mary Lou Correnti, interview by author, November 1, 2001.

135. Keefer, *Italian Prisoners*, 138.

136. Marge Schramm, interviews by author, July 30, 2002, and September 28, 2001.

137. Paddock, "Administration of Weingarten," 2.

138. Bianco diary, 19.

139. Mallett, "They Were Just People," 62.

140. Keefer, *Italian Prisoners*, 95.

141. Josephine Signorino, interview by author, June 21, 2002.

142. Inspection report, Camp Weingarten,

August 23, 1945.

143. Guiseppe Grondona to Ernest Wagner, August 26, 1944, personal collection of Karen Price Myers.

144. Inspection report, Camp Weingarten, January 20, 1945.

145. Pluth, "Prisoner of War Camps," 223–25.

146. Inspection report, Camp Weingarten, April 20–22, 1944.

147. Cody to Rev. Gerold Kaiser, July 19, 1943, Weingarten file, St. Louis Archdiocesan Archives.

148. Edward Gaffney to Cody, August 5, 1943, Weingarten file, St. Louis Archdiocesan Archives.

149. Cody, report on Weingarten, n.d., Weingarten file, St. Louis Archdiocesan Archives.

150. Cody to Cicognani.

151. Alessandro Tarasca to Cody, August 21, 1943, Weingarten file, St. Louis Archdiocesan Archives.

152. Cody to Kaiser.

153. Cody to Cicognani, July 13, 1944, Weingarten file, St. Louis Archdiocesan Archives.

154. Bianco diary, 11.

155. Inspection report, Camp Weingarten, August 23, 1945.

156. "Weingarten Camp Folds Up," which said Colonel H. H. Glidden commanded exceptionally well until July 1945, when he was transferred to Fort Knox, Kentucky.

157. Keefer, *Italian Prisoners*, 47.

158. Sterkel, "They Came as Enemies," 11–12.

159. Gegg, "Those Stationed There Reminisce."

160. "Weingarten, Mo., War Prisoner Camp to Close," *St. Louis Globe-Democrat*, September 15, 1945.

161. "Weingarten Camp Folds Up."

162. "Prisoner of War Camp for Vets Hospital Urged," *St. Louis Globe-Democrat*, January 22, 1946.

163. "City Offered Barracks to House 700 Families," *St. Louis Globe-Democrat*, February 26, 1946.

164. Ibid.

165. Norma Jacob, interview by author, August 22, 2002.

166. Gieringer, "The Shoes Were Shined," 38; Peggy Bess, "County Has Its Own Weingarten Memories," *Daily Jefferson County (Missouri) Democrat-Rocket*, May 11, 1982.

167. Wayman Starnes, interview by author, July 17, 2002.

168. John L. Downes, unpublished recollection, September 28, 2002; Downes, interview by author, March 8, 2002.

169. Bess and McKinstry, "P.O.W. Camp"; Schwartz, "Weingarten's POW Camp."

170. Bess and McKinstry, "P.O.W. Camp."

171. Ibid.

Chapter Four

1. Inspection report, Camp Clark, January 20–21, 1943, PMGO, RG 389, National Archives; Jerome Geisel, "POW Camp: State Legacy," *Columbia Missourian*, April 20, 1975.

2. Geisel, "POW Camp"; Betty Sterett, "Camp Clark Has Long Colorful Past," *The Nevada (Missouri) Daily Mail and Evening Post*, August 22, 1968.

3. Giuseppe Zanti, interview by author, trans. by Pete Puleo, Sr., July 31, 2002.

4. George Breen, interview by author, September 16, 2002.

5. Geisel, "POW Camp."

6. Sterett, "Clark Has Colorful Past."

7. Betty Sterett, *Scenes from the Past (of Nevada, Missouri)*, comp. and ed. Donna Logan (Boulder, Colo.: DGL InfoWrite,1985), 3–4.

8. Sterett, "Clark Has Colorful Past."

9. Ibid.

10. Gieringer, "The Shoes Were Shined," 10.

11. E. H. Busiek to Col. John J. O'Brien, Construction Division, Real Estate Branch, and to Col. Walter J. Reed, Building and Grounds Division, Army Air Corps, both January 31, 1942, Collection C1043, Folder 116-117, Marion T. Bennett Papers, Western Historical Manuscript Collection, Columbia, Missouri.

12. Busiek to Congressman Phil Bennett, February 24, 1942, Collection C1043, Folder 117, Marion T. Bennett Papers, Western Historical Manuscript Collection, Columbia, Missouri.

13. Busiek to Bennett, March 11, 1941, Collection C1043, Folder 117, Marion T. Bennett Papers, Western Historical Manuscript Collection, Columbia, Missouri. Even though Busiek's letter is dated March 1941, in all likelihood it was written in March 1942. Provost Marshal General Allen Gullion was not appointed to that role until July 1941, and the effort by Nevada residents to lobby the government for a big project at Camp Clark did not begin in earnest until spring 1942, after the U.S. entry into World War II.

14. Ibid.

15. "$2,500,000 for Alien Internment Camp at Camp Clark," *Nevada (Missouri) Daily Mail and Evening Post*, May 5, 1942.

16. Sterett, "Clark Has Colorful Past."

17. "$2,500,000 for Internment Camp."

18. Sterett, *Scenes from the Past*, 85.

19. Busiek to Bennett, September 20, 1943, Collection C1043, Folder 117, Marion T. Bennett Papers, Western Historical Manuscript Collection, Columbia, Missouri.

20. Ibid.

21. Sterett, "Clark Has Colorful Past."

22. "A History of Camp Clark" (n.p., n.d.), Vernon County Historical Society, Nevada, Missouri.

23. "Farmers Here May Get Help," A10.

24. Victor Jacobs, interview by author, September 16, 2002.

25. Ken Postlethwaite to Patrick Brophy, January 4, 1993. Vernon County Historical Society.

26. Ben Weir, Jr., interview by author, September 18, 2002.

27. Ted Schafers, interview by author, October 10, 2001.

28. Paul Dygard, interview by author, October 12, 2001.

29. "Cottey Dance November 6," *Camp Clark Sentinel*, October 1944.

30. Ibid.

31. Joanne Thomas Saathoff, unpublished essay, "A Time of War" (n.p., n.d.)

32. Richard Niles, interview by author, October 29, 2002.

33. Schafers, interview, October 10, 2001.

34. Pluth, "Prisoner of War Camps," 112.

35. Schafers, interview, October 10, 2001.

36. Sterett, "Clark Has Colorful Past."

37. Pluth, "Prisoner of War Camps," 174.

38. Don Stukesbary, interview by author, August 17, 2001.

39. "The Sentinel Speaks," *Camp Clark Sentinel*, September 1944.

40. Inspection report, Camp Clark, February 18, 1943, PMGO, RG 389, National Archives.

41. Sterett, "Camp Clark Has Long Colorful Past."

42. Inspection reports, Camp Clark, April 3–5, 1943; September 14–15, 1943; January 20, 1944, PMGO, RG 389, National Archives.

43. Richard Niles, e-mail to author, September 25, 2001.

44. Inspection report, Camp Clark, February 18, 1943.

45. Inspection report, Camp Clark, April 3–5, 1943.

46. Inspection report, Camp Clark, January 20, 1944.

47. Inspection report, Camp Clark. April 3–5, 1943.

48. Inspection reports, Camp Clark, January 20–21, 1943; September 13–14, 1943.

49. Inspection report, Camp Clark, January 20, 1944.

50. Gary L. Johnson, "Former German POW Visits Camp Clark," August 8, 1990. Camp Clark Historical File, Vernon County Historical Society.

51. Inspection report, Camp Clark, February 18, 1943.

52. Ibid.

53. Inspection report, Camp Clark, January 20–21, 1943.

54. Inspection report, Camp Clark, April 3–5, 1943.

55. Ibid.

56. Lt. Col. Richard R. Morrison to PMGO Aliens Division, February 12, 1943. PMGO, RG 389, National Archives.

57. Arthur E. Pratt to PMGO Aliens Division Service/Supply, February 19, 1943, PMGO, RG 389, National Archives.

58. Inspection report, Camp Clark, March 1, 1944, PMGO, RG 389, National Archives; Sterett, "Clark Has Colorful Past."

59. Inspection report, Camp Clark, October 12–15, 1943, PMGO, RG 389, National Archives.

60. Inspection report, Camp Clark, February 18, 1943.

61. Inspection report, Camp Clark, October 12–15, 1943.

62. Zanti, interview.

63. Inspection report, Camp Clark, February 18, 1943.

64. Inspection report, Camp Clark, February 18, 1943.

65. Ibid.

66. Inspection report, Camp Clark, March 1, 1944 .

67. Inspection report, Camp Clark, April 3–5, 1943.

68. "Rail Unions Angry, Harrison Asserts," *The New York Times*, October 15, 1943; Krammer, *Nazi Prisoners*, 104.

69. "Rail Unions Refuse to Have War Captives for Fellow Workers as Army Arranged," *The New York Times*, October 15, 1943, p. 9; Krammer, *Nazi Prisoners*, 104.

70. Inspection reports, Swiss Legation, January 20–21, 1943; February 18, 1943.

71. Inspection report, Camp Clark, April 3–5, 1943.

72. Ibid.

73. Inspection report, Camp Clark, March 1, 1944.

74. Geisel, "POW Camp"; Sterett, "Clark Has Colorful Past."

75. Ibid.

76. Col. I. B. Summers, Director of Prisoner of War Division, Office of the Provost Marshal General, to Special War Problems Division, Department of State, August 16, 1943, RG 59, National Archives; Keefer, *Italian Prisoners*, 140.

77. The Nevada City Library contains the records of the Hays and Milster Funeral Homes. These records indicate eight POWs died during internment at Camp Clark.

78. Inspection reports, Camp Clark, January 20–21, 1943; February 18, 1943.

79. "Enclosure C to Report on Camp Clark Internment Camp, Nevada, Missouri, Prepared by the Representative of the Department of State Who Visited This Camp on July 14–15, 1943, Accompanying the Representative of the Legation of Switzerland, Mr. R. W.

Roth, in Charge of the Italian Interests," July 14–15, 1943, PMGO, RG 389, National Archives.

80. Ibid.

81. George Breen, interview by author, November 11, 2002.

82. "Enclosure C."

83. Inspection report, Camp Clark, July 14–15, 1943.

84. Ibid.

85. Mallett, "They Were Just People," 81.

86. Inspection report, Camp Clark, September 14–15, 1943.

87. George Breen, interview by author, September 16, 2002.

88. Inspection report, Camp Clark, January 20, 1944.

89. "100 Italian Prisoners Given Camp Freedom," *St. Louis Globe-Democrat*, January 21, 1944.

90. Mallett, "They Were Just People," 43; inspection reports, Camp Clark, February 18 1943; January 20, 1944; May 8–9, 1945, PMGO, RG 389, National Archives.

91. Huell Warren, "The Way It Was," *Nevada (Missouri) Daily Mail and Evening Post*, June 22, 1997; Mallett, "They Were Just People," 68.

92. Inspection report, Camp Clark, July 14–15, 1943.

93. Sterett, "Clark Has Colorful Past." Some Nevada residents, including former camp guard George Breen, remember there being only one escape. They believe these are two versions of the same story. A brief history and summary of the camp's operation with an article called "Disposal of Camp Clark" carried in the *Nevada (Missouri) Daily Mail and Evening Post* in June 1997 states that there was only one escape in May 1943 and that the men were recaptured at Diamond, Missouri.

94. Mallett, "They Were Just People," 50; inspection reports, Camp Clark,

January 20–21, 1943; February 18, 1943; April 3–5 1943; October 12–15, 1943.

95. "Farmers Here May Get Help," A10.

96. Michael Coleman, archivist of Archdiocese of Kansas City–St. Joseph, e-mail to author, August 31, 2002; inspection report, Camp Clark, July 14–15, 1943.

97. Sterett, "Clark Has Colorful Past."

98. Gieringer, "The Shoes Were Shined," 10.

99. Sterett, "Clark Has Colorful Past." If this was the case, this action ran at odds with the Geneva Convention, which generally permitted interned military personnel to continue their customary military courtesies and traditions. However, it is possible that Clark authorities banned the Nazi salute and the display of National Socialist imagery, particularly among the group of hardcore Nazis who inhabited Camp Clark.

It could also be the case that the writer of this piece, written some twenty years after the camp's closure, had the time frame incorrect for the implementation of this rule, because following the collapse of the Third Reich in April 1945 the War Department did work to remove all traces of National Socialism from camps.

100. Geisel, "POW Camp."

101. Sterett, "Clark Has Colorful Past."

102. Ted Schafers, "Camp Clark Anniversary," *Camp Clark Sentinel* 4, no. 11 (August 1945).

103. Schafers, interview, October 10, 2001.

104. Niles, interview.

105. Niles, e-mail.

106. Schafers, interview, October 10, 2001. The SA, *Sturmabteilung* (storm troopers), was the military arm of the National Socialist German Worker's Party (NSDAP). The SS, *Schutzstaffel*

(guard squadron), was the NSDAP party police. The Gestapo was the secret police organization in Germany during Hitler's rule.

107. Inspection report, Camp Clark, December 7–8, 1944, PMGO, RG 389, National Archives.

108. Inspection report, Camp Clark, March 8, 1945, PMGO, RG 389, National Archives.

109. Ibid.

110. Ibid.

111. Inspection report, Camp Clark, December 7–8, 1944.

112. Ibid.

113. Ibid.

114. Ibid.

115. Inspection report, Camp Clark, May 8–9, 1945.

116. Ibid.

117. Ibid.

118. Ted Schafers, interview by author, September 24, 2002.

119. Ibid.

120. Inspection report, Camp Clark, December   7–8, 1944.

121. Inspection report, Camp Clark, May 8–9, 1945.

122. Ibid.

123. Schafers, interview, September 24, 2002.

124. Inspection report, Camp Clark, May 8–9, 1945.

125. Schafers, interview, September 24, 2002.

126. Johnson, "Former POW Visits Clark."

127. Inspection report, Camp Clark, May 8–9, 1945.

128. Ibid.

129. Ibid.

130. Schafers, "Camp Clark Anniversary."

131. Inspection reports, Camp Clark, December 7–8, 1944; May 8–9, 1945.

132. Inspection report, Camp Clark, March

133. Ibid.

134. Inspection report, Camp Clark, May 8–9, 1945.

135. Inspection report, Camp Clark, March 3–4, 1945.

136. John Hammond Moore, *The Faustball Tunnel: German POWs in America and Their Great Escape* (New York: Random House, 1978).

137. Eugene E. Barnett, "German War Prisoners and the YMCA," *St. Louis Globe-Democrat*, June 3, 1945.

138. Howard Swain, "The YMCA and the Loving Cup Incident," letter to the editor, PMGO, RG 389, National Archives.

139. Schafers, interview, September 24, 2002.

140. Maj. Paul Neuland, "Report to PMGO POW Special Projects Division on Camp Clark," May 16, 1945, PMGO RG 389, National Archives.

141. Ibid.

142. Schafers, interview, September 24, 2002.

143. Inspection report, Camp Clark, December 7–8, 1944.

144. Inspection report, Camp Clark, May 8–9, 1945.

145. Ibid.

146. George and Norma Breen, interview.

Chapter Five

1. Clair V. Mann, *The Story of Rolla* (Rolla, Mo.: Rolla Bicentennial Commission, 1976), 40. Also, Rolla Chamber of Commerce Web site, http://www.rollanet.org/~commerce/history.html.

2. "New Army Training Area to Be Established in Central Missouri," *St. Louis Post-Dispatch*, November 24, 1940.

3. Ibid.

4. John F. Bradbury, Jr., "Phelps County during World War II," Newsletter of the Phelps County (Missouri) Historical Society, April 1995, p. 4.

5. Fred W. Herman, "Fort Leonard Wood, Missouri," *The Military Engineer* 33, no. 188 (1941): 110; Larry Roberts, "The Engineer Replacement Training Center, Fort Leonard Wood, Missouri," in *Builders and Fighters: U.S. Army Engineers in World War II*, ed. Barry W. Fowle (Fort Belvoir, Va.: Office of History, United States Army Corps of Engineers, 1992), 78–84; "The Construction of Fort Leonard Wood" fact sheet, History Office, U.S. Army Engineer Center, Fort Leonard Wood, Missouri; Steven D. Smith and James A. Ziegler, eds., *A Historic Context for the African American Military Experience*, Department of Defense, Legacy Resource Management Program (Champaign, Ill.: U.S. Army Construction Engineering Research Laboratories, 1998).

6. "Missouri Presbyterian," October 1942, Item 8221, Box 12 111.132, Lutheran Church–Missouri Synod (hereafter LC–MS) Western District History, Concordia Historical Institute.

7. Bradbury, "Phelps County," 4–5.

8. Biography of Maj. Gen. Leonard Wood, http://www.wood.army.mil/MGLeonardwood.htm

9. Larry Roberts, Fort Leonard Wood post historian, e-mail to author, September 10, 2002.

10. "Historical Data, Prisoner of War Camp, Fort Leonard Wood" (n.d., n.p.). Fort Leonard Wood Historical File, 1–4.

11. Inspection reports, Fort Leonard Wood (hereafter FLW), November 14, 1943; January 29, 1944, PMGO, RG 389, National Archives.

12. Arlie Carter, interview by author, September 3, 2002.

13. Inspection report, FLW, May 24, 1944, PMGO, RG 389, National Archives.

14. Inspection report, FLW, August 26–27, 1943, PMGO, RG 389, National Archives.

15. Ibid.

16. Ensslin, *Fallen Foe*, 9.

17. Jarman to Culver.

18. Inspection report, FLW, August 26–27, 1943.

19. Inspection report, FLW, August 19, 1944, PMGO, RG 389, National Archives.

20. Inspection report, FLW, May 24, 1944.

21. Ibid.

22. Inspection report, FLW, August 26–27, 1943.

23. Carter, interview.

24. In May 1944, the total personnel count was allocated like this:

Unit	Officers	Enlisted
Headquarters Detachment	22	86
363d Military Police	2	120
364th Military Police	3	153
365th Military Police	2	139
Medical Detachment	0	8
Total	29	506

Source: Inspection report, FLW, August 26–27, 1943.

25. Jack C. Vineyard, "Surviving the First 18-Year-Old Draft," unpublished memoir, November 2002.

26. Francesco Brasile to Swiss Legation, January 30, 1943, PMGO, RG 389, National Archives.

27. Brig. Gen. B. M. Bryan to State Department, February 19, 1943, PMGO, RG 389, National Archives.

28. "Historical Data."

29. Prisoner of War Circular no. 1 was published September 24, 1943. Somewhat hampering the POW labor program was the fact that the PMGO did not publish Prisoner of War Circular no. 7,

which governed labor policies and payment and maintenance of prisoner accounts, until November 9, 1943.

30. 1st Lt. Daniel G. Deale, Post Chaplain, Camp Chaffee, Arkansas, to Commanding Officer, FLW, Missouri, February 16, 1943, PMGO, RG 389, National Archives.

31. Brig. Gen. B. M. Bryan to War Department, memorandum, February 28, 1943, PMGO, RG 389, National Archives.

32. Ensslin, *Fallen Foe.*

33. Inspection report, FLW, October 14–16, 1943, PMGO, RG 389, National Archives.

34. Ibid.

35. Inspection report, FLW, August 19, 1944, PMGO, RG 389, National Archives.

36. Inspection report, FLW, December 6, 1944, PMGO, RG 389, National Archives.

37. Ibid.; inspection report, FLW, October 14–16, 1943.

38. Ensslin, *Fallen Foe*, 9.

39. Ibid., 13.

40. Inspection report, FLW, May 24, 1944.

41. Ensslin, *Fallen Foe*, 13.

42. Inspection reports, FLW, November 14, 1943; January 29, 1944.

43. Howard Hong, "Report on Visit to Prisoner of War Camp," inspection report, FLW, October 14–16, 1943, PMGO, RG 389, National Archives, 67.

44. Franz Engelmann, letter to author, January 5, 2003.

45. Inspection reports, FLW, November 14, 1943; January 29, 1944.

46. Inspection report, FLW, May 24, 1944.

47. Ensslin, *Fallen Foe*, 13.

48. Inspection report, FLW, August 19, 1944.

49. Ibid.

50. Hong, "Report," 77.

51. Inspection report, FLW, May 15, 1945, PMGO, RG 389, National Archives.

52. Chaplain Joseph Parent to John O'Hara, July 7, 1943, COHA 9/35, University of Notre Dame Archives.

53. Inspection report, FLW, November 14, 1943.

54. Msgr. Cody to Rev. John Godfrey, Ascension Parish, Chesterfield, Missouri, May 2, 1944, RG x A 41.b, St. Louis Archdiocesan Archives.

55. Jarman to Culver.

56. "Historical Data."

57. Inspection report, FLW, May 15, 1945.

58. Inspection report, FLW, December 6, 1944.

59. Inspection report, FLW, March 6–7, 1945, PMGO, RG 389, National Archives.

60. Inspection report, FLW, May 15, 1945.

61. "Historical Data."

62. Inspection report, FLW, October 14–16, 1943.

63. Ensslin, *Fallen Foe.*

64. "Historical Data."

65. "Outline of Talk for Guides Riding in Busses," July 1944, PMGO, RG 389, National Archives.

66. Ensslin, *Fallen Foe.*

67. "Outline of Talk."

68. Jim Rahmy, interview by author, October 26, 2001.

69. "Outline of Talk."

70. "Historical Data."

71. Engelmann, letter.

72. "Historical Data"; inspection report, FLW, December 6, 1944.

73. Inspection reports, FLW, August 26–27, 1943; May 6–7, 1944, PMGO, RG 389, National Archives; transcript of a call between Gen. Clemens, HQ, Seventh Service Command, Army Service Forces in Omaha, Nebraska,

73. and Col. Andrew Duvall, FLW, May 5, 1944, Fort Leonard Wood Historical File.

74. Inspection report, FLW, January 29, 1944.

75. Inspection report, FLW, August 26–27, 1943.

76. Pluth, "Prisoner of War Camps," 154.

77. John "Toot" Smith, interview by author, August 9, 2001.

78. "Allied Enemies," *Columbia Daily Tribune*, October 3, 1993.

79. Krammer, *Nazi Prisoners*, 150.

80. Geoffrey C. Burt, Suzanna Doggett, and Richard Edging, *German POW Stonework at Fort Leonard Wood, Missouri* (Fort Leonard Wood, Mo.: Directorate of Public Works, 1998), sec. A-4.

81. Earline Kuthe, interview by author, October 3, 2001.

82. Paul Schanze, letter to O. J. Anderson, February 6, 1947, personal collection of Earline Kuthe.

83. Traci Bauer, "Prisoners No More," *Springfield (Missouri) News-Leader*, September 29, 1993, p. 3B.

84. Engelmann, letter.

85. Brig. Gen. B. M. Bryan to FLW commander, memorandum, April 7, 1943, PMGO, RG 389, National Archives.

86. Gieringer, "The Shoes Were Shined," 30. Gieringer cites the Records of the PMGO, Enemy Prisoner of War Information Bureau, reporting Branch, Subject File, 1942–46, Box 2478, RG 389, Modern Military Branch, National Archives.

87. Krammer, *Nazi Prisoners*, 38–39; Brig. Gen. B. M. Bryan, "Prisoners of War," Conference of Service Commands, FLW, July 1944, Farrand Collection, Hoover Institution, 14–15.

88. "Outline of Talk."

89. Ensslin, *Fallen Foe*, 11.

90. Pluth, "Prisoner of War Camps," 2.

91. Mallett, "They Were Just People," 47.

92. Krammer, *Nazi Prisoners*, 6.

93. James A. Choate, transcript of interview, June 19, 2002. Missouri Ex-POWs Oral History Project Records, 2000– (C3975), a.c. 116, Western Historical Manuscript Collection, Columbia, Missouri.

94. Inspection report, FLW, August 26–27, 1943.

95. Inspection report, FLW, May 15, 1945.

96. John Morgan, interview by author, September 7, 2002.

97. Pluth, "Prisoner of War Camps," 167.

98. Inspection report, FLW, May 24, 1944; "Escaped Germans Captured at Falcon," *Lebanon (Missouri) Daily News*, April 7, 1944; Gieringer, "The Shoes Were Shined," 32.

99. Inspection report, FLW, May 24, 1944; Bradbury, "Phelps County"; "German Prisoners Captured at Rolla," *Rolla (Missouri) Herald*, May 11, 1944.

100. Tim Roberts, "POWs Spend Duration of War in Missouri," *Bearfacts*, February 1999.

101. Cody to Godfrey.

102. Inspection report, FLW, August 26–27, 1943.

103. Bauer, "Prisoners No More." In this article, Bauer incorrectly implies the POW was stabbed by the American military police, interpreting Kuehmoser's remarks to mean the United States took violent action against Nazis in the camps. See another version of Kuehmoser's remarks at the FLW POW reunion for a more accurate interpretation: Harry Levins, "Germans Once Held Here Get Salute at Fort Leonard Wood," *St. Louis Post-Dispatch*, September 29, 1993.

104. Inspection report, FLW, May 6–7, 1945.

105. Inspection report, FLW, November 14, 1943.

106. "Historical Data." This punishment by the American government of German POWs convicted of crimes under U.S. law was the source of some ongoing conflict between the United States and the postwar German government. In fact, President Truman's decision in July 1945, several months after the end of the war in Europe, to allow the execution of fourteen German POWs convicted of murdering fellow prisoners led to a major international outcry. During the war, the U.S. government had not dared to carry out such executions for fear of certain retribution against American soldiers in German hands.

107. Inspection report, FLW, January 29, 1944.

108. Inspection report, FLW, May 24, 1944.

109. Inspection report, FLW, May 6–7, 1945.

110. Inspection report, FLW, January 29, 1944.

111. Inspection report, FLW, May 24, 1944.

112. Inspection report, FLW, August 19, 1944.

113. Inspection report, FLW, May 6–7, 1945.

114. Inspection report, FLW, May 24, 1944.

115. Capt. Walter Rapp to Director of Special Projects Division, memorandum, May 11, 1945, PMGO, RG 389, National Archives.

116. Capt. Walter Rapp, field service report, FLW to the Special Projects Division, April 26–27, 1945, PMGO, RG 389 National Archives.

117. Gansberg, *Stalag, U.S.A.*, 95–96.

118. Lt. Perry Georgiady to Special Projects Division, memorandum, March 22, 1945, PMGO, RG 389, National Archives.

119. Stuart A. Queen, acting librarian at Washington University, to Maj. Edward Davison, Special Projects Division, January 26, 1945, PMGO, Fort Leonard Wood Historical File.

120. Georgiady to Special Projects Division.

121. Inspection report, FLW, March 6–7, 1945; "Historical Data."

122. Inspection report, FLW, May 6–7, 1945.

123. Inspection report, FLW, September 14–15, 1945, PMGO, RG 389, National Archives.

124. Rapp, field service report.

125. Inspection report, FLW, May 6–7, 1945.

126. Inspection report, FLW, January 29, 1944.

127. Inspection report, FLW, May 24, 1944.

128. Hara-kiri was an act of ritual suicide practiced by high-ranking members of the Japanese military to avoid capture, execution, or disgrace.

129. Capt. Walter Rapp to Brig. Gen. B. M. Bryan, April 27, 1945, Fort Leonard Wood Historical File, Engineer Museum, Fort Leonard Wood, Missouri.

130. Rev. William Gabler, interview by Terry Culver, audiotape, 1983.

131. Ensslin, *Fallen Foe*, 15.

132. General Orders no. 22, "Discontinuance of Activity," May 20, 1946, Fort Leonard Wood Historical File, Engineer Museum, Fort Leonard Wood, Missouri.

133. Inspection report, FLW, May 6–7, 1945.

Chapter Six

1. Hermann Half, interview by Terry Culver, audiotape, August 1983.

2. Inspection report, Camp Crowder, October 7, 1944, PMGO, RG 389, National Archives.

3. Kay Hively, preface to *Red, Hot and Dusty: Tales of Camp Crowder* (Cassville, Mo.: Litho Printers, 1983).

4. Mary Louis Davis, *This Is a Tale of Camp Crowder* (Neosho, Mo.: Crowder College, 1994). Pamphlet distributed by the Crowder College

Museum/Camp Crowder Collection.

5. James Herrin, "Camp Crowder—The Beginning," in *Camp Crowder Memories* (St. Louis: Author, 1995), 14.

6. Pauline Freund, "The Freund Family and Their Struggle with Camp Crowder," in *Camp Crowder Memories*, 159.

7. Charles Lowrey, "Facts from the Past," in *Camp Crowder Memories*, 11.

8. "Neosho Finds 30-Million Army Camp a Headache as Well as a Boon," *St. Louis Globe-Democrat*, December 1, 1941.

9. Les Bond, "Everyone's Camp Crowder Memories Aren't Necessarily Warm Ones," in *Camp Crowder Memories*, 141.

10. Freund, "Freund Family," 159.

11. Bond, "Everyone's Crowder Memories," 141.

12. Hively, *Red, Hot and Dusty*, 3.

13. Ibid., 4.

14. Ibid.

15. Ibid.

16. Ibid.

17. Ibid., 5.

18. "Neosho Camp a Headache."

19. Hively, *Red, Hot and Dusty*, 5.

20. Herrin, quoted in Davis, "This Is a Tale."

21. Hively, *Red, Hot and Dusty*, 6.

22. Ibid.

23. Ibid., 63.

24. Ibid., 62.

25. "Neosho, Mo., Rents Rise 11.4 Pct in Five Months," *St. Louis Globe-Democrat*, May 8, 1942.

26. Arnold Gebhardt and Otto Scheins, "Survey of Neosho, Missouri," Item 8221, Box 12, 111.132. LC–MS Western District, Concordia Historical Institute.

27. Hively, *Red, Hot and Dusty*, 27.

28. Herrin, quoted in Davis, "This Is a Tale."

29. Hively, *Red, Hot and Dusty*, 28.

30. "Report on Inadequate Financing of Neosho Missionary," Item 8322, Box 12, 111.132. LC–MS Western District History, Concordia Historical Institute.

31. Davis, "This Is a Tale."

32. Hively, *Red, Hot and Dusty*, 37.

33. Ibid., 16.

34. "Bus Loads of Girls Coming to Big Dance," *Camp Crowder Message*, April 11, 1946, p.1.

35. Hively, *Red, Hot and Dusty*, 87; "Welcome to Camp Crowder," Camp Crowder Collection, Crowder College Museum. Pamphlet given to all incoming GIs.

36. Davis, "This Is a Tale."

37. "$85,000 for Recreation at Neosho Welcomed," *St. Louis Globe-Democrat*, April 26, 1942.

38. "Neosho Camp a Headache."

39. Davis, "This Is a Tale."

40. Hively, *Red, Hot and Dusty*, 29–30.

41. "Burgess Meredith at Crowder," *Camp Crowder Message*, March 12, 1942, p. 6.

42. Hively, *Red, Hot and Dusty*, 31.

43. Ibid., 26.

44. Ibid., 22–23.

45. Ibid., 27.

46. Ibid., 23.

47. Ibid., 78–79.

48. "Strawberries in Season," *Camp Crowder Message*, May 31, 1945.

49. Ibid.

50. Lewis and Mewha, *Prisoner of War Utilization*, 110.

51. Hively, *Red, Hot and Dusty*, 54–55.

52. Inspection reports, Camp Crowder, October 20, 1943; November 24–25, 1943, PMGO, RG 389, National Archives.

53. Inspection reports, Camp Crowder, October 20, 1943; November 12, 1943, PMGO, RG 389, National

Archives.

54. Inspection report, Camp Crowder, November 12, 1943.

55. Inspection report, Camp Crowder, October 20, 1943.

56. Ibid.

57. Karl-Heinz Richter, unpublished personal recollection, 1998.

58. Ibid.

59. Half, interview, August 1983.

60. Inspection report, Camp Crowder, November 24–25, 1943.

61. Inspection report, Camp Crowder, December 28, 1943, PMGO, RG 389, National Archives.

62. Inspection reports, Camp Crowder, November 24–25, 1943; October 7, 1944.

63. Postal Censor's confidential report, "Camp Praise by German POWs in Camp Crowder, Missouri," November 18, 1941, PMGO, RG 389, National Archives.

64. Richter, recollection.

65. Inspection report, Camp Crowder, December 28, 1943.

66. Inspection report, Camp Crowder, August 17, 1944, PMGO, RG 389, National Archives.

67. Richter, recollection; George Kelly, letter to the author, September 17, 2002.

68. Inspection report, Camp Crowder, November 12, 1943.

69. Postal Censor, "Camp Praise."

70. Richter, recollection.

71. Inspection reports, Camp Crowder, November 24–25, 1943; April 26–27, 1944, PMGO, RG 389, National Archives.

72. Hermann Half, interview by author, June 20, 2002.

73. Inspection reports, Camp Crowder, November 24–25, 1943; December 28, 1943.

74. Richter, recollection.

75. Inspection reports, Camp Crowder, April 26–27, 1944; February 1945, PMGO, RG 389, National Archives.

76. Inspection reports, Camp Crowder, April 26–27, 1944.

77. Cable to Politique Interests, Bern, Switzerland, from "Swissint," December 1, 1943, PMGO, RG 389, National Archives.

78. Inspection report, Camp Crowder, November 24–25, 1943.

79. Ibid.

80. Inspection report, Camp Crowder, November 10, 1944, PMGO, RG 389, National Archives.

81. Inspection reports, Camp Crowder, November 12, 1943; August 17, 1944.

82. Half, interview, June 20, 2002.

83. Inspection report, Camp Crowder, October 7, 1944.

84. Inspection report, Camp Crowder, November 10, 1944.

85. Gansberg, *Stalag, U.S.A.*, 28.

86. Frieda Betts, e-mail to author, October 4, 2001.

87. Inspection report, Camp Crowder, December 28, 1943.

88. Postal Censor, "Camp Praise."

89. Inspection report, Camp Crowder, April 26–27, 1944.

90. Inspection report, Camp Crowder, October 7, 1944.

91. Half, interview, August 1983.

92. Dewey Short to Brig. Gen. Charles Milliken, Commanding General, Fort Crowder, October 26, 1945, Dewey Short file, School of the Ozarks Library.

93. Carson Elliff, letter to author, January 7, 2003.

94. Half, interview, August 1983.

95. Cable to Politique Interests.

96. Inspection reports, Camp Crowder, November 12, 1943; November 24–25, 1943.

97. Inspection report, Camp Crowder, November 24–25, 1943.

98. "Last PWs Here Shipped Back to German Homes," *Camp Crowder Message*, May 9, 1946.

99. Betty Reid, letter to author, August 25, 2001.

100. Richter, recollection.

101. James Osborn, interviews by author, October 10, 2001; October 14, 2002.

102. Verla Mooth, "Memories of Christmas, 1944," *Good Old Days Magazine*, February 2001, 58–59.

103. Inspection report, Camp Crowder, December 28, 1943.

104. Inspection report, Camp Crowder, April 26–27, 1944.

105. Inspection report, Camp Crowder. March 22, 1945, PMGO, RG 389, National Archives.

106. Inspection report, Camp Crowder, May 7–8, 1945, PMGO, RG 389, National Archives.

107. Inspection report, Camp Crowder, November 24–25, 1943.

108. Inspection reports, Camp Crowder. August 17, 1944; October 7, 1944.

109. Inspection report, Camp Crowder, November 10, 1944.

110. Inspection report, Camp Crowder, April 26–27,1944.

111. Ibid.

112. Ibid.

113. Half, interview, August 1983.

114. Inspection report, Camp Crowder, April 26–27, 1944.

115. Ibid.

116. Herman Martinelli, interview by author, October 1, 2001.

117. Inspection report, Camp Crowder, November 10, 1944.

118. Inspection report, Camp Crowder, April 26–27, 1944.

119. Inspection reports, Camp Crowder, August 17, 1944.

120. Inspection report, Camp Crowder, April 26–27, 1944.

121. Ibid.

122. Inspection report, Camp Crowder, August 17, 1944.

123. Inspection report, Camp Crowder, November 10, 1944.

124. Mallett, "They Were Just People," 68–69.

125. Col. Daniel Byrd, Security and Intelligence Division, to Headquarters, Eighth Service Command, memorandum, April 12, 1944, PMGO, RG 389, National Archives; Gieringer, "The Shoes Were Shined," 30, citing from the records of the PMGO, Enemy Prisoner of War Information Bureau reporting branch, Subject File, 1942–1946, Box 2478, RG 389, Modern Military Branch, National Archives.

126. Maj. Howard W. Smith, Jr., Prisoner of War Division, to Commanding General, Seventh Service Command, memorandum, December 12, 1944, PMGO, RG 389, National Archives.

127. Gieringer, "The Shoes Were Shined," 29, citing from the Records of the PMGO, Enemy Prisoner of War Information Bureau reporting branch, Subject File, 1942–1946, Box 2478, RG 389, Modern Military Branch, National Archives.

128. Smith to Commanding General.

129. Inspection report, Camp Crowder, November 24–25, 1943.

130. Capt. Walter H. Rapp to Director, POW Special Projects Division, memorandum, April 27–28, 1945, "Field Services Report on Visit to POW Camp, Camp Crowder, Missouri," PMGO, RG 389, National Archives.

131. Ibid.

132. Ibid.

133. Ibid.

134. Ibid.

135. Ibid.

136. Ibid.

137. Ibid.

138. Ibid.

139. Inspection report, Camp Crowder, March 22, 1945.

140. Rapp to Director, April 27–28, 1945.

141. Postal Censor, "Camp Praise."

142. Ibid.

143. Richter, recollection.

144. Rapp to Director, April 27–28, 1945.

145. Inspection reports, Camp Crowder, September 19–20, 1945; October 18, 1945, PMGO, RG 389, National Archives.

146. "Last PWs Shipped Back."

147. Gebhardt and Scheins, "Survey of Neosho, Missouri."

148. "Camp Crowder Plans Sale of Equipment," *St. Louis Globe-Democrat*, August 30, 1946.

149. "PW Buildings to Go for Housing," *Camp Crowder Message*, May 16, 1946.

150. Jim Tisoto, interview by author, October 10, 2001.

151. "Central College Gets Camp Crowder Building," *St. Louis Globe-Democrat*, November 27, 1947.

152. Herrin, quoted in Davis, "This Is a Tale."

153. "Path Cleared for Senile Institution at Camp Crowder," *St. Louis Globe-Democrat*, August 18, 1949.

154. Hively, "New Life at Camp Crowder These Days," *Neosho (Missouri) Daily News*, July 30, 2001; Hively, *Red, Hot and Dusty*, 89; "Fort Crowder Site Suggested for Hospital," *St. Louis Globe-Democrat*, October 27, 1959.

Chapter Seven

1. Gene Enchelmaier, interview by author, October 29, 2001.

2. Verna Hellwig, interview by author, December 17, 2002.

3. Walter Minning, letter to Terry Culver, March 4, 1985. Translation by author.

4. Inspection Report, Chesterfield Camp Number 2, March 10, 1945, PMGO, RG 389, National Archives.

5. Lewis and Mewha, *History of Prisoner of War Utilization*, 116–18.

6. Ibid., 102.

7. Ibid., 125.

8. "Weingarten Camp," *Ste. Genevieve (Missouri) Herald*, April 7, 1945.

9. "Historical Data."

10. Inspection report, Chesterfield (land), Jefferson Barracks, and Louisiana, Missouri, October 19–23, 1945, PMGO, RG 389, National Archives.

11. Inspection Report, FLW, March 6–7, 1945.

12. Minning, letter.

13. Mallett, "They Were Just People," 52–53.

14. Ibid., 54.

15. Betty Burnett, *St. Louis at War* (St. Louis: Patrice Press, 1987); Terry Dean, "Chesterfield and World War II: POW Camp Recalled as Boost to Area," *West County News*, August 4, 1989; David Fiedler, "Reservists at Risk—Training, Contamination Clean-up Coexist at Weldon Spring," unpublished.

16. William Hellwig, interview by Terry Culver, audiotape, 1983.

17. Beulah Schacht, "Report Finds Nazis Playing Soccer and Hanging Up Their Wash and the Ordnance Plant Is Safe," *St. Louis Globe-Democrat*, n.d.

18. Ibid.

19. Verna Hellwig, interview.

20. Dean, "Chesterfield and World War II."

21. Kim Potter, "How Sweet It Was," *West Countian*, July 26, 1991.

22. "Interesting Happenings in the Ascension Parish" (n.p., n.d.), personal files of Dan Rothwell, Chesterfield,

Missouri; Dick Demko, "Ascension Parish" (Chesterfield, Mo.: Ascension Parish, 1983).

23. "Interesting Happenings."

24. Ibid.

25. Roger Gerth, interview by author, September 29, 2001.

26. Inspection reports, FLW branch camps, October 19–20, 1945; October 23, 1945, PMGO, RG 389, National Archives.

27. Verna Hellwig, interview.

28. Cody to Godfrey, May 2, 1944.

29. Transcript of call between Gen. Clemens, HQ, Seventh Service Command, ASF Omaha, Col. William Hannon, and Lt. Col. Andrew Duvall, May 5, 1944, FLW Historical File, Engineer Museum, Fort Leonard Wood.

30. Lewis and Mewha, *Prisoner of War Utilization*, 128.

31. Ibid., 129.

32. Dean, "Chesterfield and World War II."

33. Rev. Bruemmer to Msgr. Cody, December 26, 1944, St. Louis Archdiocesan Archives.

34. Inspection Report, FLW, May 6–7, 1945.

35. Mallett, "They Were Just People," 88.

36. Bob Leiweke, interview by author, April 4, 2002.

37. Rev. William Gabler, interview by Terry Culver, audiotape, July 10, 1983.

38. Monthly chaplain activity reports, St. Louis Archdiocesan Archives, RG x A 41.b.

39. Rev. Bruemmer to Lt. F. J. Schiavoni, commander of Chesterfield branch camp, May 15, 1945, St. Louis Archdiocesan Archives, RG 1X A4.1b.

40. Rev. Bruemmer to Msgr. Cody, May 20, 1945, St. Louis Archdiocesan Archives, RG 1X A4.1b.

41. Rev. Bruemmer to Msgr. Cody, May 15, 1945, St. Louis Archdiocesan Archives, RG 1X A4.1b.

42. Cody to internal office of the commander, memorandum, May 22, 1945, St. Louis Archdiocesan Archives, RG 1X A4.1b.

43. Bruemmer to Cody, May 20, 1945.

44. William Hellwig, interview.

45. Bruemmer to Cody, May 20, 1945.

46. Minning, letter.

47. Gabler, interview.

48. Lewis and Mewha, *Prisoner of War Utilization*, 150–51.

49. Gabler, interview.

50. Fred Krewer, Jr., interview by author, June 6, 2002.

51. "Two Germans Flee Chesterfield Camp," *St. Louis Globe-Democrat*, October 23, 1945; "Escaped PWs Ask Return to Prison," *St. Louis Globe-Democrat*, November 1, 1945.

52. Henry Hellwig, interview by Terry Culver, audiotape, 1983.

53. Leiweke, interview.

54. Burnett, *St. Louis at War*.

55. Inspection report, Chesterfield Camp Number 1, December 7, 1944, PMGO, RG 389, National Archives.

56. Inspection report, Chesterfield Camp Number 1, March 10, 1945, PMGO, RG 389, National Archives.

57. Otto Deutschmann, interview by author, October 6, 2001.

58. Ruth Cummins, interview by author, November 19, 2001.

59. Ross Wagner, interview by author, December 5, 2002.

60. Nikolaus Pascher to C. R. Wagner, January 7, 1948, personal collection of Ross Wagner.

61. Ed Kusmec, interview by author, October 2, 2001.

62. June Stapleton, interview by author, October 14, 2001.

63. Robert Weiss, interview by author, October 2, 2001.

64. Verna Hellwig, interview.

65. Roice Jones, interview by author, October 13, 2001.

66. Minning, letter to Culver

67. Ibid.

68. Ibid.

69. Tony Fusco, *The Story of Jefferson Barracks National Cemetery* (St. Louis: Fusco, 1967).

70. Doris Kresyman, interview by author, October 19, 2001.

71. Historical file, prisoners of war, Jefferson Barracks Museum, St. Louis, Missouri.

72. "Nazi Prisoners Still Defiant on 3rd Day of Strike," *St. Louis Post-Dispatch*, January 22, 1945.

73. "Nazi Prisoners Continue Their Strike at Barracks," *St. Louis Post-Dispatch*, January 21, 1945.

74. "400 German Prisoners at Barracks Stage Strike," *Naborhood Link News*, January 24, 1945, Historical Data, Fort Leonard Wood Historical File.

75. "Nazis at Barracks End Strike, Taken off Bread and Water Diet," *St. Louis Post-Dispatch*, January 23, 1945.

76. Helmuth Schulz, notation on copy of Army Service Forces orders, September 15, 1945, Weingarten Collection, Cultural Archives, Kent Library, Southeast Missouri State University.

77. Inspection report, Jefferson Barracks, December 7, 1944, PMGO, RG 389, National Archives.

78. Ibid.

79. Harry Levins, "German Soldiers' Graves at Jefferson Barracks," *St. Louis Post-Dispatch*, May 9, 1985.

80. "City Offered Barracks to House 700 Families," *St. Louis Globe-Democrat*, February 26, 1946.

81. Mark Orlando, interview by author,
February 15, 2002.

82. Dell King, interview by author, September 12, 2001.

83. Phil Kratzert, interview by author, October 25, 2001.

84. Inspection report, St. Louis Ordnance Depot, January 22, 1945, PMGO, RG 389, National Archives.

85. Joe Rice, interview by author, October 19, 2001.

86. Kratzert, interview.

87. Cody to O'Hara, April 7, 1944, Weingarten file, St. Louis Archdiocesan Archives.

88. Cody to O'Hara, April 11, 1944, Weingarten file, St. Louis Archdiocesan Archives.

89. Cody to Harry Arthur, manager of the Fox Theatre, May 5, 1944, Weingarten file, St. Louis Archdiocesan Archives.

90. Inspection report, St. Louis Ordnance Depot, January 22, 1945.

91. Cody to Cicognani, July 13, 1944, Weingarten file, St. Louis Archdiocesan Archives.

92. "Italian Prisoners of War Taken to Church on Hill," *St. Louis Post-Dispatch*, July 10, 1944.

Chapter Eight

1. Cody to O'Hara, October 5, 1944; Cody to Rev. S. P. Stocking, pastor at St. Eustachius, Portageville, October 18, 1944, St. Louis Archdiocesan Archives.

2. Benjamin Bird Moore, Mississippi County (Missouri) Historical Society, letter to author, July 24, 2001; Cody to O'Hara, October 5, 1944; "400 War Prisoners to Aid in Cotton Harvest in County," *Charleston (Missouri) Enterprise-Courier*, September 28, 1944; "400 Prisoners of War Here to Pick Cotton," *Charleston (Missouri) Enterprise-Courier*, October 5, 1944.

3. "PW Camp Here Not Responsible for Food Shortage," *Charleston (Missouri)*

Enterprise-Courier, November 2, 1944.

4. Carl Williams, interview by author, December 4, 2002.

5. "War Prisoners to Be Available Here," *Dunklin (Missouri) Democrat*, August 17, 1943.

6. Sue Gill, *Time for Talk*, interviewed and produced by Russ and Rosemary Burcham in conjunction with the Slicer Street Church of Christ, television program (Kennett, Mo., January 2001).

7. Shirley Davis, *Time for Talk*.

8. Pauline Burns, interview by author, January 2, 2003.

9. Cody to Glidden, October 4, 1943; Col. H. H. Glidden to Rev. John J. O'Neill, October 5, 1943, Weingarten file, St. Louis Archdiocesan Archives.

10. Marilyn Grant, interview by author, June 24, 2001.

11. Ibid.

12. Judy Bowman, interview by author, August 15, 2001; e-mail to author, July 26, 2001, December 7, 2002.

13. Ann Clark, interview by author, October 22, 2001.

14. Grant, interview.

15. Mallett, "They Were Just People," 69–70.

16. Ibid., 89–90; Peggy Bess, "Italian's Second US Trip Is His Choice," *Daily Jefferson County (Missouri) Democrat-Rocket*, April 30, 1982.

17. "German Prisoners to Aid in Cotton; Group of Four Hundred Will Work in the County," *The (New Madrid, Missouri) Weekly Record*, October 6, 1944; "Soldiers Guard War Prisoners Chopping Cotton," *St. Louis Globe-Democrat*, March 27, 1945.

18. "Soldiers Guard Prisoners."

19. "Former POW Relates Story," *Sikeston (Missouri) Weekly Standard*, August 8, 1986.

20. Inspection report, Marston Branch Camp–Fort Leonard Wood, March 8,

1945, PMGO, RG 389, National Archives.

21. "Former POW Relates Story."

22. Ibid.

Chapter Nine

1. Keefer, *Italian Prisoners*, 68.

2. Gale Fulghum, "Potatoes by the Carload," personal memoir, September 10, 2002, Jackson County Historical Society, Independence, Missouri.

3. "War Captives to Work," *Kansas City Star*, June 27, 1943.

4. B. F. Larkin, president of the Jackson County Potato Growers Association, to U.S. representative C. Jasper Bell, October 8, 1943, Jasper Bell Collection, Folder 252, C2306-C, Western Historical Manuscript Collection, Columbia, Missouri.

5. Inspection reports, branch camps at Atherton, Missouri, and Orrick, Missouri, July 15, 1943, PMGO, RG 389, National Archives; Fulghum, "Potatoes by the Carload."

6. Frank Adams, interview by author, August 27, 2001.

7. Fulghum, "Potatoes by the Carload."

8. Ibid.; H. S. Mann, president of the Jackson County Potato Growers Association, to Bell, April 11, 1945, Jasper Bell Collection, Folder 252, C2306-C, Western Historical Manuscript Collection, Columbia, Missouri.

9. Adams, interview.

10. Inspection reports, branch camps at Atherton, Missouri, and Orrick, Missouri, July 15, 1943.

11. Ibid.

12. Adams, interview.

13. Inspection reports, branch camps at Atherton, Missouri, and Orrick, Missouri, July 15, 1943.

14. Ibid.

15. Larkin to Bell.

16. Maj. Gen. Allen Gullion, provost marshal general, to C. Jasper Bell, Jasper Bell Collection, Folder 252, C2306-C, Western Historical Manuscript Collection, Columbia, Missouri.

17. "Nazis Arrogance Irks Atherton," *Independence (Missouri) Inter-City News*, May 12, 1961; Fulghum, "Potatoes by the Carload."

18. Sue Gentry, "POWs Helped with Area Potato Harvest in the 1940s," *Independence Examiner*, December 1, 1988.

19. "Nazis Arrogance Irks Atherton"; "Atherton POW Shows Recalled," *Kansas City Star*, December 21, 1972.

20. "Sabotage in Potato Field," *St. Louis Globe-Democrat*, October 27, 1944.

21. Gieringer, "The Shoes Were Shined," 31–32.

22. L. L. Shaw, vice president of the Jackson County Potato Growers Association, to C. Jasper Bell, April 28, 1945, Jasper Bell Collection, Folder 252, C2306-C, Western Historical Manuscript Collection, Columbia, Missouri.

23. Mann to Bell.

24. "PWs Finish Potato Harvest," *St. Louis Globe-Democrat*, July 31, 1945.

25. Alesia Thomas, "German Ex-Prisoner of War Revisits Site of Confinement," *Marshall (Missouri) Democrat-News*, June 17, 1977, p. 1.

26. Harriette Miller and Leon Miller, "World War II Prisoner of War Camp," personal memoir, 1990.

27. Ibid.

28. "German PW's Available to Work," *Kansas City Star*, July 12, 1944.

29. Miller and Miller, "Prisoner of War Camp"; Missouri Department of Natural Resources and the Archaeological Research Center of St. Louis, Section 106 Survey Memo: Phase I Cultural Resource Survey of the Proposed Legacy Park (Lee's Summit, Mo.: August 2000), 10.

30. "600 German Prisoners of War in Clay County," *Liberty (Missouri) Sun Weekly Magazine*, February 1, 1984.

31. Joseph Appelbaum, regional director of the United Gas, Coke, and Chemical Workers Union, to C. Jasper Bell, telegram, April 5, 1945, C. Jasper Bell Collection, Folder F26, C2306-C, Western Historical Manuscript Collection, Columbia, Missouri.

32. Vernon E. Moore to Joseph Appelbaum, April 7, 1945, C. Jasper Bell Collection, Folder F26, C2306-C, Western Historical Manuscript Collection, Columbia, Missouri.

33. "Query on Prisoner Work," *Kansas City Star*, April 8, 1945.

34. Miller and Miller, "Prisoner of War Camp."

35. Shirley Dauzvardis, e-mail to author, July 20, 2001.

36. Jerry Frevert, interview by author, October 28, 2002.

37. *Over Here: The Story of Kansas City and WWII*, Kansas City Public Television, 2000, videotape.

38. Miller and Miller, "Prisoner of War Camp."

39. "Get Kansas City Camp for Use of Local Prisoners," *Nevada (Missouri) Herald*, April 13, 1944.

40. *Over Here.*

41. Vernon Davis, interview by author, July 26, 2002.

42. Dorothy Day, interview by author, July 16, 2002.

43. Michael Coleman, archivist, Kansas City/St. Joseph Archdiocese, email to author, August 31, 2002.

44. *Over Here.*

Chapter Ten

1. Gieringer, "The Shoes Were Shined," 10.

2. "Prisoners of War at SAAF," *Sedalia Democrat*, May 3, 1945; "Historical Data"; inspection report, Sedalia Army Air Field branch, Fort Leonard Wood, May 15, 1945, PMGO, RG 389, National Archives; Whiteman Air Force Base, 509th Bomb Wing Public Affairs Office, "History of George Allison Whiteman," http://www.whiteman.af.mil/history/index.shtml.

3. Jack Webb, "Curiosity and Ambition Combined to Form Missouri Hybrid Seed Co.," *Fulton (Missouri) Daily Sun-Gazette*, April 14, 1949.

4. Lease between Missouri Hybrid Corn Company and Edith Simon, SUNP 3067, records of Missouri Hybrid Corn Company, Box 69770, Western Historical Manuscript Collection, Columbia, Missouri; John Hartman, past grand president, Sigma Phi Epsilon fraternity, e-mail to author, December 12, 2002.

5. "Hybrid Corn Company Has Its Best Year," *Fulton (Missouri) Daily Sun-Gazette*, August 10, 1944, p.1.

6. Marion McGee Guffey, interview by Bill Berry, August 26, 2002.

7. Mancuso to Drury; "Prisoners of War Arrive Monday," *Fulton (Missouri) Daily Sun-Gazette*, July 16, 1945, p. 1; Gamma, "POW Comes 'Home.'"

8. Francis Pike, interview by University of Missouri student, n.d., Haskell Monroe Collection, Western Historical Manuscript Collection. Columbia, Missouri, 3. Haskell Monroe, former chancellor of MU, taught a course on Columbia's history in which students interviewed longtime residents. This activity produced a number of transcribed interviews contained in the Monroe papers.

9. Jimmy Hourigan, interview by Haskell Monroe, April 8, 1996, Haskell Monroe Collection, 18.

10. Loren Reed, interview by Bill Berry, August 25, 2002, audiotape, Boone County Historical Society.

11. Peggy Rhynsburger, interview by University of Missouri student, April 27, 1995, Haskell Monroe Collection, 7–8.

12. Rosemarie Berry, interview by Bob Berry, August 25, 2002.

13. Giuseppe Grondona to Ernest Wagner, September 25, 1945, private collection of Karen Price Myers.

14. Francesco Borelli to Ernest Wagner, December 17, 1944, private collection of Karen Price Myers.

15. Col. H. H. Glidden to Ernest Wagner, February 9, 1945, SUNP 3067, records of Missouri Hybrid Corn Company.

16. Wagner to Glidden, January 31, 1945, SUNP 3067, records of Missouri Hybrid Corn Company.

17. Glidden to Wagner.

18. William S. Hannan to Missouri Hybrid Corn Company, June 6, 1944, SUNP 3067, records of Missouri Hybrid Corn Company.

19. Wagner notes, SUNP 3067, records of Missouri Hybrid Corn Company.

20. F. M. Rootes, secretary, board of education, to Ernest Wagner, April 12, 1945; "Memorandum to Weingarten Commanding Officer," inspection report made by Burton Marston, May 14, 1945, SUNP 3067, records of Missouri Hybrid Corn Company.

21. Contract for prisoner of war labor, June 15, 1945, SUNP 3067, records of Missouri Hybrid Corn Company.

22. Ernest Wagner to Capt. Burton Marston, May 20, 1945, SUNP 3067, records of Missouri Hybrid Corn Company.

23. Marston to Wagner, June 7, 1945, SUNP 3067, records of Missouri Hybrid Corn Company.

24. Wagner to Marston, June 27, 1945,

SUNP 3067, records of Missouri Hybrid Corn Company.

25. Marston to Wagner, July 3, 1945, SUNP 3067, records of Missouri Hybrid Corn Company.

26. "Prisoners of War Arrive Monday," p. 1.

27. Shirley Payne, interview by author, December 12, 2002.

28. Pat Humphries, interview by author, January 24, 2003.

29. Jimmy Crane, interview by Bill Berry, September, 2002.

30. Ernest Wagner to Maj. Frank Kingsland, September 1, 1945, SUNP 3067, records of Missouri Hybrid Corn Company.

31. Nicodemo Callo to Wagner, November 25, 1946, private collection of Karen Price Myers.

32. Carmelo Amadio to Wagner, September 23, 1946, private collection of Karen Price Myers.

33. Anthony Troia to Wagner, January 4, 1946, private collection of Karen Price Myers.

34. Bruno Balocco to Wagner, April 25, 1946, private collection of Karen Price Myers.

35. Gieringer, "The Shoes Were Shined," 20.

36. James Schultz, interview by author, October 10, 2002.

37. Fran Liberatore, "In War and Peace: German POW Visits Mid-Missouri," *Boonville (Missouri) Daily News*, June 17–18, 1977, p. 1.

38. Ibid.

39. John Bradbury, "From Knobview to Rosati," Phelps County (Missouri) Historical Society Newsletter 11, April 1997.

40. Cody to O'Hara, August 16, 1944, Weingarten file, St. Louis Archdiocesan Archives.

41. Leo Cardetti, "Rosati Since 1935," Phelps County (Missouri) Historical Society Newsletter 11, April 1997.

42. Leo Cardetti, interview by author, September 17, 2002.

43. Cardetti, "Rosati Since 1935."

44. Msgr. Cody to Col. H. H. Glidden, October 14, 1943, Weingarten file, St. Louis Archdiocesan Archives.

45. Fredrick J. Dobney, *River Engineers on the Middle Mississippi* (Washington, D.C.: GPO, 1976), 107–9.

46. Orville Clifton, interview by author, July 22, 2002.

47. George Johnson, interview by author, July 15, 2002.

48. Morris Pearle, interview by author, July 15, 2002.

49. Clifton, interview.

50. Merlin Walther, letter to author, April 13, 2003.

Chapter Eleven

1. "War Prisoners to Start Sorting Relief Shoes," *Hannibal (Missouri) Courier-Post*, September 8, 1944.

2. "Recreation Program Has Great Success; Sponsored by Schools and City of Hannibal, with Hundreds Using Facilities," *Hannibal (Missouri) Courier-Post*, August 10, 1944.

3. "War Prisoners to Start Sorting"; "War Prisoners Start Work on Refugee Shoes Soon; Will Use Clemens Field," *Hannibal (Missouri) Courier-Post*, September 9, 1944.

4. Don Smith, interview by author, October 12, 2001.

5. Andy Sisk, interview by author, October 8, 2001; Smith, interview.

6. "Prisoners Won't Attend Games," *Hannibal (Missouri) Courier-Post*, October 12, 1944; Mallett, "They Were Just People," 52.

7. J. Hurley Hagood and Roberta Hurley, *The Story of Hannibal: A Bi-Centennial History, 1976* (Hannibal, Mo.: Standard Printing Co., 1976), 209.

8. "German War Prisoner Dies in Local

Camp," *Hannibal (Missouri) Courier-Post*, September 29, 1944; "War Prisoner's Remains to Iowa," *Hannibal (Missouri) Courier-Post*, September 30, 1944.

9. "War Prisoners Taken Back to Clarinda, Ia.," *Hannibal (Missouri) Courier-Post*, November 14, 1944.

10. *Louisiana (Missouri) Press-Journal*, July 6, 1943, August 10, 1943; inspection report, Chesterfield (land), Jefferson Barracks, and Louisiana, Missouri, October 19–23, 1945, PMGO, RG 389, National Archives; George Luther, interview by author, October 1, 2001.

11. *Louisiana (Missouri) Press-Journal*, December 21, 1943, April 11, 1944; Mallett, "They Were Just People," 61; Luther, interview.

12. Mallett, "They Were Just People," 61–62.

13. Lucille Carroll Keith, e-mail to author, August 15, 2001.

14. Mallett, "They Were Just People," 61–62.

15. *Louisiana (Missouri) Press-Journal*, April 25, 1944.

16. Engelmann, letter.

17. George Minnehans, interview by Terry Culver, audiotape, 1983.

18. "Historical Data"; Ellsworth Bass and Ellen Bass, interview by Terry Culver, audiotape, June 29, 1983.

19. Mallett, "They Were Just People," 52.

20. Rev. August Reyling to O'Hara, July 14, 1945,(RG X A4.1b, St. Louis Archdiocesan Archives.

21. Engelmann, letter.

22. C. D. Hicks to Col. Harry Vaughan, April 24, 1945, Harry S Truman Library, Independence, Missouri.

23. Lt. Col. B. W. Davenport to Vaughan, memorandum, May 2, 1945, Harry S Truman Library, Independence, Missouri.

24. Engelmann, letter.

25. Ibid.

26. *The Growth of a City: Springfield, Capital of the Great Ozark Empire* (Springfield, Mo.: Springfield Chamber of Commerce, 1942).

27. John Rutherford, "O'Reilly General Hospital," *Show Me Route 66 Magazine*, spring 2002; Rutherford, "Springfield's Hospital 'with a Soul': O'Reilly Army Hospital," *Fifty Plus Magazine* 1, no. 11 (February 2002).

28. Rutherford, "Hospital with a Soul."

29. "O'Reilly Gets Gang of PW's," *Springfield (Missouri) Leader and Press*, March 1, 1944.

30. Ibid.

31. Tina Gold, interview by author, July 22, 2002.

32. Ibid.

33. Mike O'Brien, "World War II POWs Found the Ozarks Hospitable," *Springfield (Missouri) News-Leader*, February 17, 2002.

34. Rutherford, "O'Reilly General Hospital"; Rutherford, "Hospital with a Soul."

Chapter Twelve

1. Martin Tollefson, "Enemy Prisoners of War," *Iowa Law Review* 32 (November 1946): 51–77.

2. Keefer, *Italian Prisoners*, 55.

3. "Italian Prisoners in Missouri Accept War Declaration Soberly," *St. Louis Globe-Democrat*, October 14, 1943.

4. Ibid.

5. James H. Keeley, chief of the Special Problems Division, Department of State, to assistant secretary of state, informal note to "Mr. Long," September 9, 1943, RG 59, National Archives.

6. Pietro Badoglio, quoted in Lewis and Mewha, *Prisoner of War Utilization*, 180.

7. J. A. Ulio, quoted in Keefer, *Italian Prisoners*, 75.

8. Keefer, *Italian Prisoners*, 77.

9. "Italian Prisoners in Missouri."

10. Keefer, *Italian Prisoners*, 83.

11. Ibid., 79.

12. Ibid., 80.

13. Ibid.

14. Ibid., 78.

15. Inspection Report, Camp Weingarten, August 23, 1945.

16. John Hammond Moore, "Italian POW in America: War Is Not Always Hell," *Prologue* 1976, 144.

17. Keefer, *Italian Prisoners*, 76.

18. Ibid., 100.

19. Ibid., 85.

20. Ibid.

21. Pete Puleo, Sr., "Italian Service Units: My Personal Experience with the Italian Service Units during WWII," unpublished memoir, 2001.

22. Keefer, *Italian Prisoners*, 98.

23. Ibid., 98.

24. Mario Pertici, "Italian POWs Were Welcome!" unpublished memoir, n.p., n.d.

25. Keefer, *Italian Prisoners*, 173.

26. Ibid., 130.

27. K. P. Aldritch, acting postmaster general, to secretary of state, July 27, 1943, Box 2230, RG 59, National Archives.

28. Inspection report, Camp Weingarten, September 5–6, 1944, PMGO, RG 389, National Archives.

29. Keefer, *Italian Prisoners*, 84.

30. Brig. Gen. John Eager, Report to the Office of War Information, August 23, 1945, RG 389, Box 1467, National Archives; Keefer, *Italian Prisoners*, 158.

31. Felice Ghersi to Elmer Grant, November 18, 1945, private collection of Marilyn Grant.

32. Giovanna di Micela to Ernest Wagner, December 1946, private collection of Karen Price Myers.

33. Giacoma (first name unknown) to Ernest Wagner, February 26, 1947, private collection of Karen Price Myers.

34. Rosario Lostumbo to Ernest Wagner, January 10, 1947, private collection of Karen Price Myers.

35. Giovanna di Micela to Ernest Wagner, April 15, 1948, private collection of Karen Price Myers.

36. Keefer, *Italian Prisoners*, 173.

37. Zanti, interview.

38. Keefer, *Italian Prisoners*, 171.

39. Engelmann, letter.

40. Ibid.

41. Inspection reports, FLW, May 6–7, 1945; Camp Clark, May 8–9, 1945.

42. Inspection report, Camp Crowder, March 22, 1945.

43. Krammer, *Nazi Prisoners*, 241.

44. Half, interview.

45. Mallett, "They Were Just People," 87.

46. Dean, "Chesterfield and World War II."

47. Mallet, "They Were Just People," 89.

48. Lewis and Mewha, *History of Prisoner of War Utilization*, 126.

49. Gieringer, "The Shoes Were Shined," 21.

50. "Return of Rabid Nazis Opposed," *The New York Times*, May 31, 1945, p.14.

51. Kurt Reimer to William McDonald, Camp Clark file, Bushwhacker Museum/Vernon County Historical Society, Nevada, Missouri.

52. Krammer, *Nazi Prisoners*, 255; Gieringer, "The Shoes Were Shined," 39; "Last of the Supermen," *Newsweek*, August 5, 1946.

53. Inspection report, FLW, September 14–15, 1945.

54. In addition to Britain and France, the other five countries were Belgium, Greece, Holland, Luxembourg, and Yugoslavia.

55. Krammer, *Nazi Prisoners*, 243.

56. Edmund Koga to O. J. Anderson, June 16, 1946, private collection of Earline Kuthe. Translation by author.

57. Paul Schanze to O. J. Anderson, February 5, 1947, private collection of Earline Kuthe. Translation by author.

58. Krammer, *Nazi Prisoners*, 249.

59. Ibid., 250.

60. Half, interview.

61. Heinz Zimmermann to Emil Moehner, July 1, 1947, Jefferson Barracks Museum.

62. Paul Rahn to Emil Moehner, May 24, 1947, Jefferson Barracks Museum.

63. Richter, recollection.

64. Lane Beauchamp, "German Visitors Return to a Former POW Camp," *Kansas City Star*, September 29, 1993.

65. Louis Sack to Mr. Eutsler and family, July 1, 1946, Camp Crowder Collection, Crowder College.

66. Burton Marston to Vincenzo Mancuso, n.d., Stanley Drury Collection.

67. Inspection report, Camp Crowder, September 19–20, 1945.

68. Krammer, *Nazi Prisoners*, 266.

69. Harry Levins, "Germans Once Held Here Get Salute at Fort Leonard Wood," *St. Louis Post-Dispatch*, September 29, 1993.

70. Johnson, "Former POW Visits Clark."

71. Rolf Wunderlich, letter to author, September 9, 2002.

72. Richter, recollection.

73. Liberatore, "In War and Peace."

74. Thomas, "German Ex-Prisoner of War," 1.

75. Dean, "Chesterfield and World War II."

76. Mallett, "They Were Just People," 54.

77. George Kelly, letter to author, November 3, 2001.

Books

Billinger, Robert D., Jr. *Hitler's Soldiers in the Sunshine State: German POWs in Florida*. Gainesville: University Press of Florida, 2000.

Bosworth, Allan R. *America's Concentration Camps*. New York: Norton, 1967.

Burnett, Betty. *St. Louis at War*. St. Louis: Patrice Press, 1987.

Burt, Geoffrey C., Suzanna Doggett, and Richard Edging. *German POW Stonework at Fort Leonard Wood, Missouri*. Fort Leonard Wood, Mo.: Directorate of Public Works, 1998.

Carlson, Lewis H. *We Were Each Other's Prisoners: An Oral History of World War II American and German Prisoners of War*. New York: Basic Books, 1997.

Costelle, Daniel. *Les Prisonniers*. Paris: Flammarion, 1975.

Davis, Mary Louis. *This Is a Tale of Camp Crowder*. Neosho, Mo.: Crowder College, 1994.

Dobney, Fredrick J. *River Engineers on the Middle Mississippi*. Washington, D.C.: GPO, 1976.

Gansberg, Judith M. *Stalag, U.S.A.: The Remarkable Story of German POWs in America*. New York: Crowell, 1977.

Hagood, J. Hurley, and Roberta Hurley. *The Story of Hannibal: A Bi-Centennial History, 1776*. Hannibal, Mo.: Standard Printing Company, 1976.

Hively, Kay. *Red, Hot and Dusty: Tales of Camp Crowder*. Cassville, Mo.: Litho Printers, 1983.

Hörner, Helmut. *A German Odyssey: The Journal of a German Prisoner of War*. Translated and edited by Allan Kent Powell. Golden, Colo: Fulcrum Publishing, 1991.

Keefer, Louis E. *Italian Prisoners of War in America, 1942–1946: Captives or Allies?* New York: Praeger, 1992.

Krammer, Arnold. *Nazi Prisoners of War in America*. New York: Stein and Day, 1979.

Larsen, Lawrence H., and Nancy J. Hulston. *Pendergast!* Columbia: University of Missouri Press, 1997.

Lewis, George G., and John Mewha. *History of Prisoner of War Utilization by the United States Army, 1776–1945*. Department of the Army pamphlet 20-213. Washington, D.C.: GPO, 1955.

Mann, Clair V. *The Story of Rolla*. Rolla, Mo.: Rolla Bicentennial Commission, 1976.

Moore, John Hammond. *The Faustball Tunnel: German POWs in America and Their Great Escape*. New York: Random House, 1978.

Overton, Richard C. *Burlington Route: A History of the Burlington Lines*. New York: Knopf, 1965.

Parnell, Wilma Trummel, with Robert Taber. *The Killing of Corporal Kunze*. Secaucus, N.J.: Lyle Stuart, 1981.

Reddig, William H. *Tom's Town: Kansas City and the Pendergast Legend*. New York: Lippincott, 1947.

Roberts, Larry. "The Engineer Replacement Training Center, Fort Leonard Wood, Missouri." In *Builders and Fighters: U.S. Army Engineers in World War II*, edited by Barry W. Fowle. Fort Belvoir, Va.: Office of History, United States Army Corps of Engineers, 1992.

Robin, Ron. *The Barbed-Wire College: Reeducating German POWs in the U.S. during World War II*. Princeton, N.J.: Princeton University Press, 1995.

Smith, Steven D. *A Historic Context Statement for a World War II Period Black Officers' Club: Building 2101, Fort Leonard Wood, Missouri*. Champaign, Ill.: U.S. Army Construction Engineering Research Laboratories, 1998.

Smith, Steven D., and James A. Ziegler, eds. *A Historic Context for the African American Military Experience.* Department of Defense, Legacy Resource Management Program. Champaign, Ill.: U.S. Army Construction Engineering Research Laboratories, 1998.

Smith, William Jay. *Army Brat: A Memoir.* New York: Persea Books, 1980.

Springfield, Missouri, Chamber of Commerce. *The Growth of a City: Springfield, Capital of the Great Ozark Empire.* Springfield, Mo.: Springfield Chamber of Commerce, 1942.

Sterett, Betty. *Scenes from the Past (of Nevada, Missouri).* Compiled and edited by Donna Logan. Boulder, Colo.: DGL InfoWrite, 1985.

Thompson, Glenn. *Prisoners on the Plains.* Phelps County, Nebr.: Phelps County Historical Society, 1993.

Periodicals

"Anger at Nazi Atrocities Is Rising but U.S. Treats Prisoners Fairly." *Newsweek*, May 7, 1945, 58.

Bradbury, John, Jr. "From Knobview to Rosati." Newsletter of the Phelps County (Missouri) Historical Society. New Series Number 11, April 1997.

____. "Phelps County during World War II." Newsletter of the Phelps County (Missouri) Historical Society, April 1995, p. 4.

Cardetti, Leo. "Rosati Since 1935." Newsletter of the Phelps County (Missouri) Historical Society. New Series Number 11, April 1997.

Dahms, Steven V. "Thoroughly American." *The Lutheran Witness* 116, no. 5 (May 1997).

____. "World War II Prisoners of War and the Missouri Synod." *Concordia Historical Institute Quarterly* 68, no. 3 (fall 1995).

"Enemies at Large." *American Magazine*, April 1944, 97.

Ensslin, Fritz. "A German Soldier Tells What It Is Like to Visit Ft. Leonard Wood in 1943 as a POW." *Essayons*, June 27, 1991, 47; also distributed as a museum handout by the U.S. Army Engineer Museum at Fort Leonard Wood, called *The Fallen Foe.*

Herman, Fred W. "Fort Leonard Wood, Missouri." *The Military Engineer* 33, no. 188 (1941).

Kretzmann, P. E. "The Lutheran Commission for Prisoners of War." *The Lutheran Witness*, December 1943.

"Last of the Supermen." *Newsweek*, August 5, 1946.

Margulies, Newton L. "Proper Treatment of War Prisoners." *Vital Speeches*, May 15, 1945, 477–80.

McKamey, Pauline Laws. "Prisoner of War Camp in the Ozarks." *Ozarks Mountaineer*, January-February 1989.

Moore, John Hammond. "Italian POWs in America: War Is Not Always Hell." *Prologue*, fall 1976, 144.

Mooth, Verla. "Memories of Christmas, 1944." *Good Old Days Magazine*, February 2001, 58–59.

Powers, James H. "What to Do with German Prisoners." *Atlantic Monthly*, November 1944.

Roberts, Tim. "POWs Spend Duration of War in Missouri." *Bearfacts*, February 1999.

Rutherford, John. "O'Reilly General Hospital." *Show Me Route 66 Magazine*, spring 2002.

____. "Springfield's Hospital 'with a Soul': O'Reilly Army Hospital." *Fifty Plus Magazine* 1, no. 11 (February 2002).

"600 German Prisoners of War in Clay County." *Liberty (Missouri) Sun Weekly Magazine*, February 1, 1984.

Thomas, Jim. "The Gasconade Boatyard." Gasconade County (Missouri)

Historical Society Newsletter 10, no. 4 (winter 1997).

Miscellaneous Sources

Agee, Stafford A. "Addendum to Camp Clark History," February 2, 2000. Camp Clark Historical File. Bushwhacker Museum, Nevada, Mo.

Arndt, Karl John Richard. *Index to the Library of Congress Collection of German Prisoners of War Camp Papers Published in the United States of North America from 1943 to 1946.* Worcester, Mass.: Pabst Foundation of Wisconsin, 1965.

Dannenfeldt, Paul L. "Report on POW Work." Box 1, File 5, Item 6, III.IX.01, Supplement IV of Armed Services Commission. Concordia Historical Institute, St. Louis.

___. "Work of Our Planning Council." Item 26156 of Lutheran Commission for Prisoners of War. Lawrence B. Meyer Collection. Concordia Historical Institute, St. Louis.

Gebhardt, Arnold, and Otto Scheins. "Survey of Neosho, Missouri." Item 8221, Box 12, 111.132 of Lutheran Church–Missouri Synod Western District History. Concordia Historical Institute, St. Louis.

Johnson, Gary L. "Former German POW Visits Camp Clark." August 8, 1990. Press release, Camp Clark Historical File. Vernon County (Missouri) Historical Society.

"Letter to Chaplains and Civilian Pastors at Work in Prisoner of War Camps." June 15, 1944. Item 23191 of Lawrence B. Meyer Collection. Concordia Historical Institute, St. Louis.

Missouri Department of Natural Resources and the Archaeological Research Center of St. Louis, Inc. "Section 106 Survey Memo: Phase I Cultural Resource Survey of the Proposed Legacy Park, City of Lee's Summit, Jackson County, MO." August 2000.

"Minutes of Conference of Chaplains and Pastors Working in Prisoner of War Camps." January 21, 1944. Item 23261 of Lawrence B. Meyer Collection. Concordia Historical Institute, St. Louis.

Paddock, George. "Administration of a POW Internment Camp." N.p., n.d. Part of the Stanley Drury Collection.

"Report on Inadequate Financing of Neosho Missionary." Item 8322, Box 12, 111.132 of Lutheran Church–Missouri Synod Western District History. Concordia Historical Institute, St. Louis.

Swain, Howard. "The YMCA and the Loving Cup Incident." Letter to the editor from the Records of the PMGO. Record Group 389. National Archives.

Webb, Jack. "Curiosity and Ambition Combined to Form Missouri Hybrid Seed Co." *Fulton (Missouri) Daily Sun-Gazette*, April 14, 1949.

Unpublished Sources

Fulghum, Gale. "Potatoes by the Carload." Personal memoir, September 10, 2002. Jackson County Historical Society, Independence, Mo.

Mallet, Derek. "'They Were Just People Like We Were': World War II German and Italian Prisoners of War in Missouri." Master's thesis, Truman State University, 1997.

Gieringer, Paul. "The Shoes Were Shined for President Truman: Axis POW's in Missouri 1942–1946." Master's thesis, Central Missouri State University, 1992.

Miller, Patrick. "Camp Clarinda: A POW Camp in Southwest Iowa." Master's thesis, Bowling Green State University, 1993.

Pluth, Edward. "The Administration and Operation of German Prisoner of War Camps in the United States during World War II." Ph.D. thesis, Ball State

University, 1970.

Sterkel, Laurel. "They Came as Enemies of Our Country—Some Left as Our Friends." Research paper, Southeast Missouri State University, 1983. Stanley Drury Collection.

Archival Sources

Camp Clark File. Vernon County (Missouri) Historical Society.

Camp Crowder Collection. Crowder College, Neosho, Mo.

Camp Crowder photo file. Missouri State Archives, Secretary of State's Office, Jefferson City, Mo.

Fort Leonard Wood Historical File, Prisoner of War Camp. Fort Leonard Wood, Mo.

Lawrence B. Meyer Collection. Concordia Historical Institute, St. Louis, Mo.

Lutheran Church–Missouri Synod Western District History. Concordia Historical Institute, St. Louis, Mo.

POW Camp Historical File. Jefferson Barracks Museum, St. Louis, Mo.

Records of the Department of State, Special War Problems Division, Record Group 59. National Archives, College Park, Md.

Records of the Provost Marshal General's Office, Prisoner of War Division, 1941–46, Record Group 389. National Archives, College Park, Md.

Report of work at Chesterfield and Louisiana, Mo. Archdiocesan Archives, Archdiocese of St. Louis.

Report of work at Camp Weingarten. Archdiocesan Archives, Archdiocese of St. Louis.

The Stanley Drury Collection: A History of Camp Weingarten, 1942–1946. A collection of material compiled over the years by Ste. Genevieve historian Stanley Drury. Held by Professor Max Okenfuss, Department of History, Washington University, St. Louis.

Newspapers

All the papers listed below are in Missouri, with the exception of *The New York Times.*

Boonville Daily News

Charleston Enterprise-Courier

Columbia Daily Tribune

Columbia Missourian

Daily Jefferson County Democrat-Rocket

Dunklin Democrat

Farmington News

Farmington Press

Festus-Jefferson County Democrat-Rocket

Fulton Daily Sun-Gazette

Hannibal Courier-Post

Independence Examiner

Independence Inter-City News

Kansas City Star

Lead Belt News

Lebanon Daily News

Marshall Democrat-News

Naborhood Link News

Nevada Daily Mail and Evening Post

Nevada Weekly Herald

(New Madrid) Weekly Record

New York Times

Perry County Republican

Rolla Herald

Sedalia Democrat

Sikeston Weekly Standard

Springfield Leader and Press

Springfield News-Leader

St. Louis Globe-Democrat

St. Louis Post-Dispatch

St. Louis Star-Times

Ste. Genevieve Herald

West (St. Louis) Countian

West (St. Louis) County News

Camp Newspapers

Camp Clark Sentinel

Camp Crowder Message

Chesterfield-Herold (POW)

L'Attesa (POW)

La Luce (POW)

Weingartener

Videorecordings

Italian Prisoners of War in Ste. Genevieve County. By Eric Sonnicksen. Ste. Genevieve Public Television, October 17, 2001. Videotape.

Over Here: The Story of Kansas City and WWII. Kansas City Public Television, 2000. Videotape.

Time for Talk. Produced by Russ and Rosemary Burcham in conjunction with the Slicer Street Church of Christ, Kennett, Mo., January 2001. Videotape.

About the Author

David Fiedler is a writer living in Fenton, Missouri. His articles on Missouri, its people, and its history have appeared in publications such as *Missouri Life* and *The Missouri Conservationist*. Fiedler earned degrees in German and political science from Washington University and was a captain in the U.S. Army Reserve.

Notes

Notes

Notes

Notes

Notes